T0292979

Hands-On Prescriptive Analytics
Optimizing Your Decision Making with Python

Walter R. Paczkowski

Hands-On Prescriptive Analytics

by Walter R. Paczkowski

Published by O'Reilly Media, Inc., 1005 Gravenstein Highway North, Sebastopol, CA 95472.

O'Reilly books may be purchased for educational, business, or sales promotional use. Online editions are also available for most titles (*http://oreilly.com*). For more information, contact our corporate/institutional sales department: 800-998-9938 or *corporate@oreilly.com*.

Acquisitions Editor: Michelle Smith	**Indexer:** Ellen Troutman-Zaig
Development Editor: Sara Hunter	**Interior Designer:** David Futato
Production Editor: Jonathon Owen	**Cover Designer:** Susan Thompson
Copyeditor: Tove Innis	**Illustrator:** Kate Dullea
Proofreader: Dwight Ramsey	

October 2024:   First Edition

Revision History for the First Edition

2024-10-16:   First Release

See *http://oreilly.com/catalog/errata.csp?isbn=9781098153175* for release details.

978-1-098-15317-5

[LSI]

Table of Contents

Part II.   Essential Background Material

Part III.   Non-Stochastic Prescriptive Analytic Methods

Preface

I have one overarching theme I painstakingly developed over the years for all my books: data consists of information obfuscated by noise. Data per se are not information; they are the repository for information. This is obvious, almost trivial, to data scientists, but it is profound to business decision-makers. They equate data with the information they need for their decisions.

Information, to be useful for decision making, must be extracted from data. My books, including this one, are concerned with extracting information from data. The topics I covered include business analytics, which incorporates Descriptive Analytics such as data visualization, preprocessing, and transformations; Predictive Analytics, which includes model building, mostly for forecasting; simulation analytics, especially for complex systems; and survey analytics.

Although my theme has been consistent, I felt something was missing. I kept looking back at my consulting, remembering I was always told by my clients that they appreciated the menu of choice options I gave them, but they did not have time to wade through them, even if it was just two or three options. They had many issues to handle; their time was precious. They simply wanted to be told what was the best option on the menu.

My inability to recommend reflected my training. As a classical economist, I was repeatedly told that economists must take a positive approach to analysis, not a normative one involving value judgments. We can only discuss the result of a decision, not what should be done. We do this for scientific research. Business decision-makers, however, are not concerned about scientific analysis, but about practical matters, such as entering a new market, reducing prices, or investing in a new technology. They want to be told the "should."

I was good at Descriptive and Predictive Analytics, but I was missing Prescriptive Analytics. The former two tell decision-makers what did happen, is happening, or will happen under different conditions. These are positive statements constituting two analytical stages leading to a menu based on information extracted from data.

The missing piece tells them what to choose from the menu. This involves normative statements and is more involved. It constitutes Prescriptive Analytics, a third stage for extracting information from data for data-driven decision making that addresses the question: *Which action should a decision-maker select from the menu?*

The Book's Topic

This book is concerned with *Prescriptive Analytics*. Although concerned with what should be done, it remains consistent with the overarching theme I followed and adhered to in my other works.

The Book's Audience

This book is intended for people involved in demand measurement and forecasting; predictive modeling; pricing analytics including elasticity estimation; customer satisfaction assessment; market and advertisement research; new product development and research; capital investment decisions; and any place where these analyses are input into major decisions at the operational, tactical, and strategic levels.

This book will provide background for Prescriptive Analytics by explaining the intuition underlying analytic concepts; developing the necessary mathematical and statistical analytic principles; demonstrating concepts using Python in JupyterLab notebooks; and illustrating analytical concepts with use-cases.

It is also suitable for another audience: students in colleges and universities offering courses and certifications in business data analytics, data sciences, and market research. It could be used as a major or supplemental textbook.

Although I emphasize business applications, public policy audiences are not overlooked. Decision-makers in the public domain must also use Prescriptive Analytics as the basis for their decisions. The concepts I will discuss apply to them as well.

What You Will Learn—and How to Apply It

By the end of this book, you will understand the distinction between Descriptive, Predictive, and Prescriptive Analytics; how Predictive Analytics produces a menu of decision options; how Prescriptive Analytics narrows the menu of options; and Prescriptive Analytics methods, especially two broad classes: non-stochastic and stochastic.

The Book's Structure

I divided this book into four parts:

Part I, "Introduction and Background"
Part II, "Essential Background Material"
Part III, "Non-Stochastic Prescriptive Analytic Methods"
Part IV, "Stochastic Prescriptive Analytic Methods"

Part I sets the stage for all that will follow. Part II contains two chapters on essential material on Python and probabilities needed for the rest of this book. Part III covers non-stochastic methods for Prescriptive Analytics: Mathematical Programming and Decision Trees. The former is prominent in the Prescriptive Analytics literature, and the latter is a key tool in the Operations Research literature. Part IV introduces stochastic Prescriptive Analytics. The major one is simulations. It is also concerned with two critical parts of a decision menu: the menu options and the probability distribution for the paths leading to the expected value calculations. Finally, an implicit assumption is examined: sequential decisions.

Conventions Used in This Book

The following typographical conventions are used in this book:

Italic
    Indicates new terms, URLs, email addresses, filenames, and file extensions.

`Constant width`
    Used for program listings, as well as within paragraphs to refer to program elements such as variable or function names, databases, data types, environment variables, statements, and keywords.

`Constant width italic`
    Shows text that should be replaced with user-supplied values or by values determined by context.

 This element signifies a tip or suggestion.

This element signifies a general note.

 This element indicates a warning or caution.

O'Reilly Online Learning

 For more than 40 years, *O'Reilly Media* has provided technology and business training, knowledge, and insight to help companies succeed.

Our unique network of experts and innovators share their knowledge and expertise through books, articles, and our online learning platform. O'Reilly's online learning platform gives you on-demand access to live training courses, in-depth learning paths, interactive coding environments, and a vast collection of text and video from O'Reilly and 200+ other publishers. For more information, visit *https://oreilly.com*.

How to Contact Us

Please address comments and questions concerning this book to the publisher:

O'Reilly Media, Inc.
1005 Gravenstein Highway North
Sebastopol, CA 95472
800-889-8969 (in the United States or Canada)
707-827-7019 (international or local)
707-829-0104 (fax)
support@oreilly.com
https://oreilly.com/about/contact.html

We have a web page for this book, where we list errata, examples, and any additional information. You can access this page at *https://oreil.ly/hopa*.

For news and information about our books and courses, visit *https://oreilly.com*.

Find us on LinkedIn: *https://linkedin.com/company/oreilly-media*.

Watch us on YouTube: *https://youtube.com/oreillymedia*.

Acknowledgments

As with all my previous books, I noted the support and encouragement I received from my wonderful wife, Gail, and my two daughters, Kristin and Melissa. And each time, I seemed to express my gratitude using the same words, the same emotions. But how else can I say how thankful I am to have them support me the way they do? Gail always encouraged me to sit down and write, and many times even wondered how I could actually do it. My daughters provided a sense of pride in what I wrote, something that every father appreciates so much. They provided me with support and encouragement for this book as for the others. I owe them a lot, both then and now. I have two wonderful grandsons who are still not old enough to contribute to this book or fully grasp the concept of their grandfather writing a book. I can just hope that when they are older, they will look at this one and say "Yup, grandpa was a busy writer."

I have to give a special thanks to the editor at O'Reilly, Michelle Smith, who approached me about writing this book, was patient while I crafted a proposal, and who helped guide me through the O'Reilly publishing process. I owe Jonathon Owen, my production editor, a special thanks for his tireless efforts to put my manuscript into the O'Reilly format and make this book so professional looking. And Sara Hunter, my content development editor, who worked very closely with me on this project. Sara not only kept me on a schedule, but she also encouraged me and gave me valuable feedback on my content. Michelle, Sara—thank you both for all your help.

Introduction and Background

In this book's first part, I set the stage for all that will follow. This includes introducing the three main forms of Business Analytics, the central problem with solely using Predictive Analytics and the role and importance of Prescriptive Analytics in a business decision environment. I pay special attention to the role of uncertainty in decision making and uncertainty's probabilistic nature. Because of this probabilistic feature, I include a probability primer in Part II.

Finally, I will provide an overview of the major Prescriptive Analytics methods commonly used by practitioners and the ones I will focus on. To add structure to what I will discuss and make it easier for you to follow the methods, I will regroup them into two broad classes, Non-stochastic and Stochastic, that form Parts III and IV of the book, respectively.

There are two introductory chapters in this part:

- Chapter 1, "An Analytical Framework"
- Chapter 2, "Prescriptive Methods: Overview"

An Analytical Framework

All books—any written document, in fact—must start somewhere. The authors of many technical books I have read immediately present the technicalities of their subject. They provide neither background on their subject's evolution nor motivation for reading their book. I will not start this way. Instead, I will give you my perspective on why Prescriptive Analytics exists and developed, as well as why it is important for data science and business itself. It exists to help decision-makers make decisions.

I will also present a framework for Prescriptive Analytics, since many analytical methodologies are inapplicable for all decision problems. There is no one-size-fits-all. There are different levels of decision problems with some methodologies applicable to one level, but not another. I will later refer to these levels as *scale-views*.

My main theme is that decision-makers at all scale-views must make decisions that have effects in the future, whether the future is literally tomorrow, next week, next year, or the next decade. They are made under *uncertainty* simply because no one knows what will happen tomorrow.

The decision-makers ask their *data science team* (DST) for information to help them make these decisions. The information comes from *Descriptive Analytics* and *Predictive Analytics* in the form of a *decision menu* of options. Unfortunately, there is almost no guidance as to which menu option is best. This adds another layer of uncertainty: *What is the best choice from the menu? Prescriptive Analytics* narrows the menu and contributes to reducing overall uncertainty.

The menu concept is important, but, unfortunately ignored by discussions about Prescriptive Analytics. It is assumed only one option is given to a decision-maker who then decides *Yes* or *No*. In the real world, however, multiple options are the rule, not the exception. The menu must be considered for analytics to be useful for decision making.

I will address these leading questions in this chapter:

1. What is a general framework for decision making?
2. What is the *Analytics Evolution* from *Descriptive Analytics* to *Predictive Analytics* to *Prescriptive Analytics* for decision making under uncertainty?
3. What is uncertainty, what is its role in decision making, and how can it be reduced?
4. What is a decision menu?
5. What is the role of probabilities in uncertainty reduction and decision making?
6. What is the importance and role of Prescriptive Analytics in decision making?

A Decision-Making Framework

We often talk about a business decision-maker and his or her problems and requirements as a hypothetical representative person with only one function: to make decisions. At an abstract level, postulating such a person and identifying their problems, decision complexities, and how they make, or should make, a rational decision is a good way to build a decision-making framework. After all, this is how scientific principles governing any behavior are advanced.

Economics is a good example. Its theoretical foundation is the representative consumer and the representative (i.e., perfectly competitive) firm, neither of which exists in the real world. Yet economic theory is powerful for helping us understand and solve many real-world problems.

Using a simple, abstract, representative decision-maker, however, to cover all decision situations is impractical because they operate in different environments. This is especially true in a large enterprise when viewed as a *complex system*. I will often refer to a business complex system as an *enterprise* or simply as a business; I will use the two terms interchangeably. The abstract decision-maker falls short when practical real-world decisions must be made because not only are their environments complex systems, but their problems are also complex and multifaceted.

A complex system is a set of interactive and interrelated parts, or subsystems, that, when operating perfectly, flawlessly, and uninhibited, not only produce a result (e.g., output, profit, Net Present Value, shareholder value) but also something more than its constituent parts. Something emerges that is not evident from its parts alone. This is, appropriately, called *emergence*. See Paczkowski (2023, Chapter 2) for a discussion of complex systems and their properties, especially emergence.

An automobile is a good example of a complex system. It has many subsystems that are complex in their own right. The engine, transmission, fuel, electrical, and electronics subsystems all work in unison to produce motion; they also produce comfort, safety, and reliability, among other features, all of which emerge because the subsystems interact. An enterprise, whether small or large, but especially a large one, is a comparable complex system with subsystems such as manufacturing, R&D, marketing, finance, legal, IT, and data science (sometimes called *business research*). This also includes business units, referred to as *sub-business units* (SBU), which are themselves complex systems.

What emerges from these interactions are profit, shareholder value, market share and dominance, and brand recognition, to mention a few results. A problem in any one subsystem, however, could not only negatively impact that subsystem, but also others in the entire enterprise. A wrong decision about price could negatively affect manufacturing, human resources, finance, and legal, not to forget shareholder value and market share. These are multifaceted effects of a decision.

Where you are in the enterprise matters for how you view it and your decisions. I refer to this perspective as the *scale-view*. Scale-views range from broad to narrow. A broad scale-view takes in the entire enterprise, so a manager with this view sees, and is responsible for, everything in the enterprise. But this does not mean every single detail. That is micro-managing, which is impractical and inefficient.

At this scale-view, the enterprise's complexity is obscured, almost hidden. Someone at this level is fully aware that the enterprise is large and complex, but the complexity seen and dealt with is minimal. They do not directly interact with the different parts, but instead interact with the heads of those parts. Those with a broad scale-view include the CEO and the *C-level* team.

The *C-level* team consists of all the "Chiefs" in the business: Chief Marketing Officer, Chief Technology Officer, and so forth.

Line managers are focused on the production line and its daily operations. Their scale-view is narrow. Consequently, more detail is evident. These must be handled daily, which involves working, cooperating, and interacting with other, but certainly not all, parts of the enterprise to complete planned and required daily production. The full complexity of the enterprise is evident.

There is a multitude of scale-views in any business enterprise. The larger it is, the more scale-views that are possible. I define three to make discussions manageable:

- Operational
- Tactical
- Strategic

Decision-makers at the *operational scale-view* level include the line managers I just mentioned. They are responsible for daily production, job assignments, personnel, order taking and processing, data management and maintenance, record keeping (i.e., accounting), and order fulfillment. These all involve coordination with other departments.

Decision-makers at the tactical scale-view level also interact with specific groups but have a narrow focus. As the name suggests, they are concerned with the development and implementation of tactical moves focused on market activities. These are summarized by the *Four Ps of Marketing*, also referred to as the *Marketing Mix*: Product, Price, Placement, and Promotion. See McCarthy and Perreault (1987) for a discussion of the Marketing Mix.

As a pricing example, managers at this level are concerned with the effect a price change has on sales, what a competitor's price move may do to sales, how to promote a price offer or change, and so on. Advertising, customer relationship management (CRM), legal affairs, and R&D are other examples.

Those at this scale-view are concerned with neither daily operations nor the entire enterprise; their concerns are between these extremes. Decisions at the tactical scale-view level impact these extremes, but are distinct enough to be treated separately.

Finally, decision-makers at the strategic scale-view level orchestrate the whole enterprise. They see the big picture and, in fact, define that picture and its evolution. Planning is an important part of their responsibilities, so five-year plans with enterprise-wide target *key performance measures* (KPM) are defined by them.

 KPMs include, but are not limited to, sales, revenue, contribution, contribution margin, return on assets (ROA), return on investment (ROI), return on equity (ROE), and net present value (NPV).

Many of these KPMs, incidentally, are not independent of each other. The *DuPont Analysis*, sometimes also called *ratio analysis*, relates the KPMs logically and mathematically. Its main feature is the decomposition ROE. I depict just a small set of related concepts in Figure 1-1. See Bodie et al. (2022, p. 445) and Brigham and Ehrhardt (2002, p. 92) for further comments and the latter for a more detailed chart.

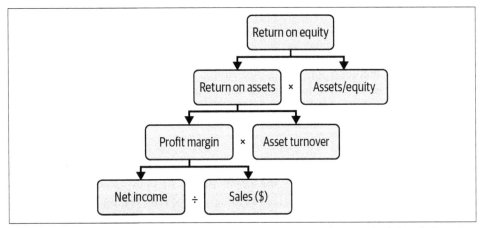

Figure 1-1. An abbreviated DuPont Analysis Chart. See Brigham and Ehrhardt (2002) for a more detailed chart.

Ratio Analysis Definitions

Some definitions for ratio analysis and KPMs are:

- $Net\ Income = Pre-tax\ Income\ After\ Taxes.$
- $Equity = Shareholders'\ Equity\ Outstanding.$
- $ROA = \frac{Net\ Income}{Average\ Total\ Assets}.$
- $ROE = \frac{Net\ Income}{Average\ Total\ Equity\ Outstanding}.$
- $Asset\ Turnover = \frac{Net\ Sales\ Revenue}{Average\ Total\ Assets}.$

See Bodie et al. (2022), Brigham and Ehrhardt (2002), and Ross et al. (2006) for details.

Paczkowski (2023) discusses the business operational, tactical, and strategic perspectives in a complex business system and how analytics is relevant at each level.

The Analytics Evolution

The term "Prescriptive Analytics" may be new to you. You may be aware of, or have used or been exposed to, the word "analytics" from your training in undergraduate and business school courses. It was used in your quantitative courses—statistics, econometrics (for an economics major), and market research (for a business major)—where you learned about two branches of classical statistics: descriptive and inferential:

Descriptive statistics
Consists of methods for saying something about (i.e., describing) a sample or batch of data. There is only one sample and the goal is to understand its main features: central location (e.g., the mean), spread (e.g., the variance), and frequency of occurrence of key values.

Inferential statistics
Consists of methods for assessing the reliability of conclusions about a population based on a sample from the population. You infer something about the population from the sample. This includes hypothesis testing as well as curve fitting, typically *Ordinary Least Squares* (OLS) at the introductory level.

If you were taught OLS, you were told how it is used to make predictions of something, say, sales as a function of the price. You may have been shown how to test different price points to determine their impact on sales. Elasticities were part of those lessons, especially if you were in economics.

This is the typical structure of quantitative courses, and it is your primary and perhaps only training in quantitative methods. After that, you applied and enhanced them on-the-job.

If you continued your quantitative studies beyond an introductory course to econometrics and machine learning (a sub-field of artificial intelligence [AI]), to become a *data scientist* with a business focus, you learned details in these two areas. But you stayed within their confines and applied them to a host of business problems. In the business community, which is my focus, these are collectively known as *data science*. The organization of data scientists is the DST. You are either the recipient of the results of the DST or a member of that team.

As the recipient, your job is to interpret quantitative results using your understanding of statistics and then make or recommend a business decision. You cannot escape knowing something about statistical methods to ask intelligent and probing questions, but this is as far as you can go. You are a business decision-maker who uses quantitative results. You do not know, and you cannot be expected to know, the intricacies of Data Science, specifically its language of data science. This suggests a communication problem between you and the data scientists; there is a language difference.

As a data scientist, however, your job is to apply the best methods to business data to provide the decision-makers, regardless of their scale-view, with the best results for a business problem. The business problem is defined by them and you provide information on its solution. You do not make decisions based on the solution; you merely provide the input for those decisions. See Figure 1-2 for the role of the data scientist.

To complicate matters, you do not know and fully understand the language of the business managers at all the scale-view levels, so you may not provide the correct information they need and in the format they need. Your specialty is data science, not business. There is, therefore, another communication problem because of different languages. Just as the managers do not fully understand you, you do not fully understand them.

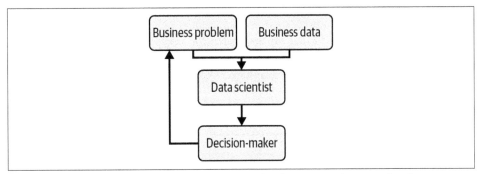

Figure 1-2. The data scientist provides input to the decision-maker. But the decision-maker, in turn, tells the data scientist about the business problem to work on, hence the arrow from the Decision-maker block to the Business problem block.

The term *data science* is relatively new, having evolved from just statistics per se to include and encompass econometric methods, long used in economics, and machine learning, which is also relatively new. From my personal perspective, having been in the quantitative areas of business my entire professional life (almost five decades!), I have seen and been part of the transition from just statistics and econometrics, long my dual focus and passions, to the newer umbrella term of Data Science which emerged in the early part of the 21st century. When this combination-discipline emerged, it immediately splintered into two sub-subjects: *Descriptive Analytics* and *Predictive Analytics*.

The Data Science Split

The split into two sub-subjects should not be surprising because almost all disciplines eventually split into parts. Statistics is an example. There was only one form of statistics when it became a practical discipline in the early 20th century. It was based on experimental procedures and probability principles. The principles were frequency-based, meaning you used a counting function (e.g., a combinatorial function) to count the number of occurrences of an event and the total number of all possible events. The ratio of the two is the probability of the event. Counts are frequencies, hence the frequency-based approach to probabilities, and statistics in general, since statistical theory is probability-based. I will review basic probabilities in Chapter 4 because they are important in Prescriptive Analytics.

A different approach to probabilities, a *Bayesian* approach, has been studied since the late 18th to early 19th centuries. See Wikipedia (2023a). Because of computational issues, however, it was not until the later 20th century and early 21st century with the development of computer software and hardware that its use became practical. Now, at the end of the first quarter of the 21st century, it dominates statistical analysis. The frequency-based approach persists, as it should, since not all problems require a Bayesian approach. Nonetheless, statistics is now bifurcated into classical frequency-based statistics and Bayesian-based statistics. I illustrate this division in Figure 1-3. See McGrayne (2012) for an interesting perspective of Bayesian analysis. Also, see Paczkowski (2022b) for the use of Bayesian methods for survey analysis and Gelman et al. (2013) for a technical discussion of Bayesian methods.

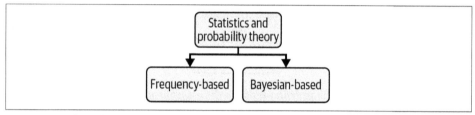

Figure 1-3. The split of statistics and probability theory into frequency-based and Bayesian-based segments.

Data science went through a similar split into Descriptive Analytics and Predictive Analytics. The former is based on classical statistical descriptive methods and the latter on classical statistical and econometric predictive methods. The predictive methods, however, also use machine learning approaches which extend the base for making predictions.

The Information Glue

Data science, regardless of which aspect, has one overarching charge: to provide information. Information, however, is contained or hidden inside data. Data are not information. My central paradigm is:

$$Data = Information + Noise.$$

Information inside data must be extracted to be actionable, insightful, and useful for decisions. Extracting information is easy, almost trivial, for small data sets. In the extreme, this is just a batch of numbers typical of an introductory statistics course. For instance, a simple scan of such a batch might reveal a central tendency (aka the mean) and if the data have a wide or narrow spread (aka the variance). Also, a simple hand sketch of a distribution of the batch might reveal a pattern such as its skewness. This was the gist of the approach to data analysis in Tukey (1977): *Exploratory Data Analysis* (EDA). Not only is this information easily extracted, but it is also probably the only meaningful extractable information.

Tukey's stem-and-leaf plot, a standard in most elementary statistics textbooks such as Weiss (2005) and Triola (2022), is a good example of a hand sketch. It is useful for small data sets to identify and understand patterns, but is less useful for large ones. See Weiss (2005, p. 68) for a comment about this. Its focus is the "pen & pencil" creation of a simple data display. This simple data visualization tool was developed when personal computers were just being introduced (i.e., in the early 1970s). Large mainframe computers were the dominant technology, but were largely inaccessible.

Statistical and data visualization software were also mostly non-existent. The software product SAS, for example, now recognized as the premier statistical software package, was developed in the late-1960s to mid-1970s. Modern technology and software, not to forget modern and ubiquitous personal computers, especially laptop computers, changed the need for Tukey's "pen & pencil" approach to data analysis. This, nonetheless, is the basis for modern statistical and data visualization software such as the S language, developed at Bell Labs in the 1970s, and its variants, especially R and many others, as well as its connection to many statistical techniques. Analysis methods, however, have gone beyond it. See Wikipedia (2023e) for the connection of R to EDA.

 SAS was originally called the "Statistical Analysis System." See Wikipedia (2023l).

The approach in Tukey (1977) is powerful for small data sets. What is small? There is no answer except that they are manageable. This is not the case, however, with larger data sets, so-called *Big Data*, which are composed of millions of records and probably as many variables or *features*. Big Data, more the norm than the exception in modern enterprises, complicates data analysis. For a discussion of Big Data and its many definitions, see Paczkowski (2018, Part IV) and Paczkowski (2020, Chapter 1).

 My contention is that data science is a discipline for extracting information from Big Data.

Data science, from its outset, split into two parts similar to statistical analysis and probability theory. But the split was pragmatic—it matched business information requirements.[1] Business decision-makers require two forms of information from their data:

- What did happen or is currently happening?
- What will happen?

The first is a monitoring or tracking function to keep managers aware of developments, internal and external to the business, regardless of scale-view. The second is a predicting and planning function that varies in focus and content depending on a manager's scale-view. *Descriptive Analytics* arose to satisfy the first, and *Predictive Analytics* the second.

Business managers and decision-makers are not interested in scientific investigations, except, of course, if this is in the business's best interest (e.g., for new product development) or if this is the focus of its mission statement. The distinguishing feature of both branches is their design to provide *rich information*, not *Poor Information*. I illustrate this split in Figure 1-4 with a focus on Rich Information.

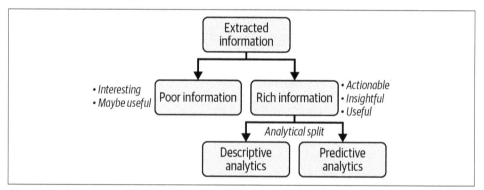

Figure 1-4. The split of data science to provide business decision-makers with rich information. Two analytical areas were developed, Descriptive Analytics and Predictive Analytics, to support this.

 Rich information is insightful, useful, and most importantly, actionable. Poor information may be just interesting at best. Poor information, simple means and proportions without any substantial business action insight, is not part of my paradigm, *Data = Information + Noise.*

---

1 I am not ignoring public policy requirements. My focus is strictly business.

How the Analytics Fit Together

Although Descriptive and Predictive Analytics are two separate approaches for extracting rich information, they are, nonetheless, complements. Your first task in any statistical analysis, well-understood from basic statistics, is to "look" at your data. This is a legacy of Tukey (1977) as well as Mosteller and Tukey (1977). The statistical analysis could include predictions and forecasts. These are different, yet related, with forecasts as a subset of predictions. Predicting is concerned with what will happen under given or assumed conditions. Forecasting is similarly concerned except it is time oriented. Predicting per se is in time or space; forecasting is strictly time. See Paczkowski (2022a, Chapter 6) and especially Paczkowski (2023) for further discussions and examples.

It is best-practice in statistical analysis to do descriptive or exploratory data analysis before formal hypothesis testing and/or modeling; this is a well-defined *research sequence* which I depict in Figure 1-5. In the business domain, however, the focus is on practical operational, tactical, and strategic activities.

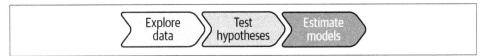

Figure 1-5. The sequence of steps in any quantitative research process.

Managers at each scale-view have different information requirements. Operational managers need real-time, detailed information at the lowest level of the business. For example, a production manager with a team of robots producing products in a job-shop set-up, needs information on raw materials, the status and health of each robot, and the workflow through the entire production process (e.g., bottlenecks that impact downstream production). Tactical managers need information on current market conditions and competitor activities such as promotions, price points, and new product offerings. Strategic managers in the *C-level* suite need information on the business's financial health (e.g., stock prices), personnel developments and training, economic conditions (e.g., pending recession, interest rate changes), and legal/regulatory developments (e.g., lawsuits).

In each case, the focus is on telling managers and decision-makers what happened and what is currently happening in the business and its markets (i.e., its environment). Managers at all scale-views need to know and understand the current position of the business and developing trends that could lead to growth opportunities in the best, or severe problems in the worst, of circumstances.

Descriptive information is provided in *dashboards* constructed to give managers at each level access to what they need for a greater understanding of conditions and trends in real time and in interactive ways with drill-down functionality. See Paczkowski (2023, Chapters 1 and 11). This provisioning of information is grouped under the umbrella term *Descriptive Analytics*. This is sometimes referred to as *Business Intelligence*.

Regardless of how well Descriptive Analytics provides information, decision-makers at all three levels make decisions with implications for the future performance, even viability, of the business. These are future implications and ramifications (*I&R*). The future could be tomorrow, next week, next year, next decade, or any unknown time frame. Unfortunately, since they are in the future, there is no way to know the final *I&R*. Decisions are made today under a cloud of uncertainty which imposes a cost on the business. This is not an accounting cost, but an opportunity cost of a wrong decision. This cost could be reduced, but not eliminated, by having the best information today when the decision is made. This is the rich information. See Paczkowski (2022a) and Paczkowski (2023) for further discussions.

Rich Information comes from the "best" predictions or forecasts of the *I&R* of a decision made today. The modeling and analysis leading to the best predictions are grouped under the umbrella term *Predictive Analytics*. This is sometimes referred to as *Business Analytics*.

There is a process flow for these analytics which I depict in Figure 1-6. The boundaries I show are fuzzy, so you should not interpret them as definitive. The Descriptive Analytics phase is based on historical and current (i.e., real-time) data which are inputs to dashboards. The dashboards are provided to decision-makers at all three scale-views, so there are multiple dashboards. They assess the dashboards and identify an issue which is sent to another relevant manager, who may issue a study directive. This is the beginning of the Predictive Analytics phase. That relevant manager, incidentally, could interpret the dashboard directly and issue a study directive.

What is a study directive? It is, fundamentally, a request to the DST for rich information in the form of a statistical, econometric, or machine learning study leading to a prediction. See Paczkowski (2023) for the predictive models that could be used in this phase.

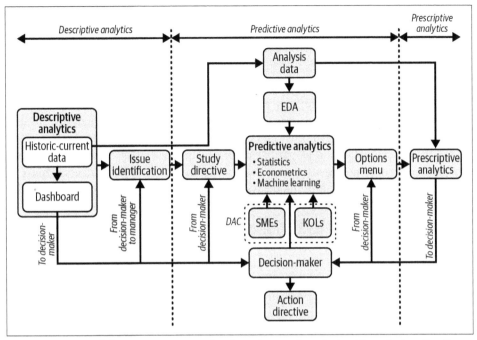

Figure 1-6. A workflow incorporating the three forms of analytics: Descriptive, Predictive, and Prescriptive.

Historic and current data form the base for an analysis data set that is studied, perhaps using enhanced EDA methods (now referred to as *data visualization*), and then used in formal analytical methods. Those methods, usually handled by the DST, also use input from the decision-maker (in the form of requirements for KPMs or business constraints) as well as *subject matter experts* (SME) and *key opinion leaders* (KOL). The former could be internal people who, because of their experience and expertise, know the business operations and markets. The KOLs could be external people who, for example, regularly publish papers, reports, and large-scale studies on the industry and its markets.

The predictive studies result in a menu (which could have a single item, a singleton menu) of several options. The menu is input to *Prescriptive Analytics*.

Descriptive Analytics

As I have noted, Descriptive Analytics is concerned with what did happen in the business, which includes its markets and overall environment such as legal and regulatory, and what is currently happening in these areas.

A blog article at the *Harvard Business School Online*'s Business Insights website describes Descriptive Analytics as "the process of using current and historical data to identify trends and relationships. It's sometimes called the simplest form of data analysis because it describes trends and relationships but doesn't dig deeper." See Cote (2021). I agree with the first part of this description, but not the second. It is not the simplest form of data analysis, although it could be.

At the operational scale-view, Descriptive Analytics may focus on production planning, daily absence and tardiness reporting, supply chain slowdowns, inventory management reporting, and so on. In a robotic manufacturing system, the "health" of a robot is important to monitor. One "sick" robot, requiring unexpected maintenance or replacement, could jeopardize all production activities. So real-time robotic health monitoring and reporting is vital. In addition, fulfillment processes must be constantly monitored for shipping delays such as packaging slowdowns (perhaps due to a lack of packaging materials such as boxes, wrappings, and stuffings).

The main tool for Descriptive Analytics in our modern, technology-driven and software-dominant era, is the dashboard I introduced earlier. At a high level, a business dashboard is a graphical reporting system, perhaps with interactive and drill-down capabilities. See Wikipedia (2023c) for a discussion. At a minimum, it is just a display of a KPM. The measure of performance could be a specific number, a number relative to a target, or a number relative to a trend, not to overlook the trend itself. The specific KPM, and therefore the dashboard, will vary by the three scale-views. The CEO and the *C-level* team, for instance, would be interested in revenue, net earnings, ROI, stock prices, and the like, all at the enterprise level. A tactical manager would be interested in, as examples, advertising *gross rating points* (GRP) overall and by advertising medium, sales by customer segments, and so on. At the operational level, they would include the items I listed previously.

Dashboards for real-time data tracking are important for systems producing a steady stream of data. The robotic health tracking and monitoring I described earlier is an example. Robots operate in real time, meaning they operate continuously, do not slow down or take lunch breaks, do not strike, and operate 24/7/365. You only need shifts of human operators to monitor them, and probably very few of them since computer systems and AI can do that monitoring. See Sun et al. (2022) for an example.

Dashboard interactivity is an important feature of Descriptive Analytics. A dashboard could be static, merely reporting on current conditions as measured by the KPMs. This is useful, but limited because the major factors determining the KPM's value or trend are hidden, and not revealed by the dashboard reports. An interactive dashboard is more useful and insightful regardless of scale-view. The interactivity could take two forms:

- Drill-downs
- Queries

Drill-down interactivity allows you to select a KPM and see a report, or series of reports, of the factors comprising it. In modern terminology, there is a link to another report which you can choose to see or not. The detail is hidden on the higher-level report where the summary KPM is reported. Linking allows you to see as much information as you want when you want it, thus avoiding information overload.

Query interactivity provides a further capability to literally ask the dashboard questions about the KPMs. For example: "Which marketing region has the highest net income average annual growth rate for the past five years?" Sans this capability, you have to contact the IT department, ask them the question, and then wait until they assign someone to fulfill the request and provide the answer. This requires time. As a result, the purpose of the question may be forgotten or the answer's usefulness may have passed. Of course, the requesting manager's level has to be factored into the speed of the response; the CEO will not wait very long—or forget!

Interactivity is costly. First, the end user (i.e., a line manager or CEO) has to be trained to use the querying capability. This requires time and a budget since training is neither immediate nor free. The line manager may be able to spare time for training, but a CEO and members of the *C-level* team may have difficulty allocating time. Second, the querying capability is expensive to develop, implement, and maintain. An IT team has to be created and dedicated to it. Again, this requires a budget. Perhaps an AI system will someday automatically create dashboards to any configuration and manager scale-view.

Predictive Analytics

An important piece of rich information, missing from Descriptive Analytics, is the answer to the question: "What will happen under different conditions?" These could be a KPM's trend, such as sales, or an action, such as a price change. The answer is important because no business operates in a static situation, devoid of time or consequences. Remember, all decisions take place in time. Monitoring, as in Descriptive Analytics, also takes place in time, but that time is basically "now." Even trend tracking—the "what did happen" part of Descriptive Analytics—is a "now" situation: what has been happening until now. Decisions, however, are forward-looking, not now-looking.

There are situations in which time is subtle, but still there. For instance, it is common in new product development to conduct a discrete choice study to assess which product design would sell best. Each design has different attributes or features such as size, shape, weight, and price. The assessment involves creating prototypes, including potential price points, that could be designed and offered. Sets of these, called *choice sets*, are created based on experimental design principles, with each set containing several prototypes. These are sequentially presented to consumers who are asked which one they would buy (or none of them). The demand for each product is estimated from the collected data. That demand is the most likely demand, the proportion of the market that would buy the product if it is offered as configured and priced. It is not an actual demand at the time of the study because the product is not yet available, and may never be available. This is why prototypes are used. Most importantly, the time frame for the demand is not specified: is it next month, next quarter, or next year? The study only estimates a proportion of the market, a market share. When that share will be attained is unclear, but at some point in time, it will be attained. So time is still a factor.

As a result of the time dimension, a forecast, a special case of a prediction, is needed. A prediction per se is information that offsets something missing in our knowledge or data. For a discrete choice study, the demand is a prediction. A forecast is a proper subset and, thus, a special case of a prediction: it is strictly in time. A *proper subset* of a set A is defined as a set, B, such that all elements of B are strictly contained in A and at least one member of A is not in B. See Wolfram Mathworld (2024). All forecasts are predictions, but not all predictions are forecasts. The level of sales for each month for the next five years is a forecast. I show the relationship between prediction and forecast in Figure 1-7.

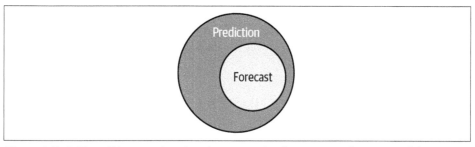

Figure 1-7. A Venn Diagram showing the connection between predictions and forecasts. Note that forecasts are a proper subset of predictions.

There are many ways to predict the outcome of a decision, and even non-decision, if just trends are needed. The applicable methods and their level of detail depend on the scale-view of the users. Someone with an operational scale-view will need a simple linear time trend forecast for ordering raw materials for the next day's production run. A manager with a tactical scale-view, say for pricing, will need a multiple regression model for elasticity estimation and sales prediction at different price points. The model should include competitor price points and customer demographics as details. A manager with a strategic scale-view will need a multi-equation econometric model or a time series model for market or financial predictions. See Paczkowski (2018) for elasticity estimation and Paczkowski (2023) for predictive models by scale-views.

Forms of Predictive Analytics

Predictive Analytics is the use and application of methods in the three formal areas that I mentioned several times: statistics, econometrics, and machine learning. Predictive Analytics is a family of methods, each family member providing a different set of tools, although there is a commonality that draws from classical statistics. I illustrate the family tree in Figure 1-8. See Paczkowski (2023) for an extensive discussion of Predictive Analytics.

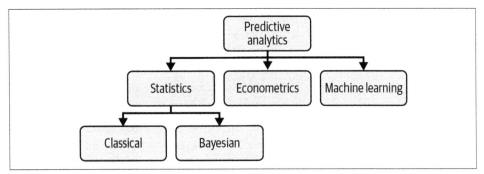

Figure 1-8. The family tree for Predictive Analytics.

Menu of prediction options

A major misconception, an oversight perhaps, of the Predictive Analytics block of Figure 1-6 is that one prediction results. This is the one used in an *Action Directive*, the order from the decision-maker to an *Action Processor* who implements the directive. For example, a product manager may observe, via Descriptive Analytics, that sales are either below target or are steadily declining because of the competitive structure of the industry or the nature of the product. If it is known that the product is price elastic based on an econometric model, then this immediately suggests a price decrease to stimulate sales and increase revenue. This is Predictive Analytics. The product manager issues an Action Directive to the Chief Pricing Officer (CPO), the Action Processor, to reduce price, say 1%. The expected sales and revenue growth are the prediction implications of an econometric model. This is a standard textbook description. Only one prediction results so a decision is either Go or No-Go. See Paczkowski (2023 Chapter 2) for a detailed discussion of this series of steps in a business system context. See Paczkowski (2018) for the relationship between price elasticity, sales stimulation, and revenue changes.

In reality, more than one action is possible. The product manager could consider a 2% or 3% price reduction in addition to the 1% based on the number of actions that can be tested at the same time along with their interactions. For example, a tactical pricing predictive model could test an own-price change, a competitor's price change, and a different attribute setting for a product. Each change results in a different prediction. The result is a *decision menu* that is developed of predictions of possible courses of action. But only one option from the menu can be selected. Which one?

Decision Menu Analogy

A decision menu is exactly the same as a restaurant menu. The former has options, each defined by one or more KPMs. The latter also has options, each defined by price, ingredients, and perhaps nutritional content (e.g., calories). The KPMs are attributes of the decision menu options just the way price and ingredients are attributes of a restaurant menu. In each case, an option is selected based on the attributes to maximize something: satisfaction, utility, profit, market share, shareholder value, to mention a few.

The discrete choice framework I outlined earlier is an example of a menu's development. The prototype will have different attributes (e.g., physical features such as size and shape), and functionalities (e.g., buttons and switches), not to overlook price points. Suppose there are three features, each at two levels such as high and low, and two price points, also high and low. These could be arranged to create $2^4 = 16$ prototypes which constitute a menu. The business decision-maker (e.g., a product manager with a tactical scale-view) must select one product from the menu to produce and market. The level of predicted demand is the deciding factor—but not always. The cost of producing each product must be considered for net contribution. Selecting from the menu becomes complicated.

An *experimental design* helps to sort out the combinations of the changes and their results, but a list of results, that is, a menu, will still result. This menu is presented to the decision-maker, as I depict in Figure 1-6. The length of the menu might vary directly with the scale-views: a singleton menu for an operational scale-view; a multi-item menu for a tactical and strategic scale-view. The relevant manager must still select. The question remains: *Which menu option should be selected?*

As a final example, imagine a large, multi-SBU telecommunications enterprise. Five-year plans are set, well, every five years, but they are updated annually to reflect and incorporate market, economic, and technology changes. These are at the enterprise level, so the responsible managers have a strategic scale-view. The predictive models are extremely complex requiring multiple inputs, each with different settings. Although experimental design principles can be used to create the input combinations, usually the strategic planning management team just specifies a combination. I will refer to this as a *Most Likely View*. Multiple *Most Likely Views* are frequently created, not just one, thus negating the notion of "Most Likely." These are labeled ML_1, ML_2,..., ML_n. This set is the menu given to the CEO who has to choose one for the enterprise's plan. The question is still: *Which menu option should be selected?*

The menu concept is succinctly stated as: "Decision making involves making a choice from a list of possibilities" (Zdanowicz [2015]).

Another point about a menu from Predictive Analytics is that each option has a cost. The adage "There's no such thing as a free lunch" holds here as everywhere else. The costs are constraints on which option can be selected. It is easy to select from a menu for potential projects, for example, in which they are ranked by their NPV: select the project with the highest NPV. But there are costs associated with each project, such as the investment cost. This constraint may result in the project with the highest NPV not being selected simply because it is too expensive. The decision-maker, confronted not only with the menu but also the costs of each menu option, has to weigh all aspects of each project. The answers to the questions—"What should I do?" "Which one do I select?"—are more complicated. Prescriptive Analytics addresses these complications. I further explore this in "Prescriptive Analytics as a Separate Discipline" on page 32.

Creation of the menus

A menu does not just appear. Each item on it is a stand-alone project whose specification and description are created by different organizations and key stakeholders. They all have a vested interest in seeing their project selected and funded. They are a project's champion.

Politics is involved at this stage of menu creation, but nonetheless, there is still a general flow of inputs in a bottom-up process to create the menu. I illustrate this bottom-up flow in Figure 1-9. You can see that I divide projects (i.e., the menu options) into two categories:

- Natural projects
- What-if projects

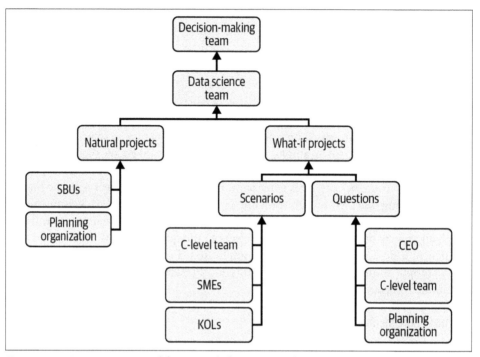

Figure 1-9. An organizational framework for creating the menus presented to the decision-makers.

Natural Projects

Natural Projects arise from general business planning at the SBU level or from overall business planning, such as a five-year plan. They are natural in the sense they must be considered to expand the business, remain competitive, keep abreast of technological development, streamline operations (i.e., be more efficient), and so forth. This does not mean they are self-evident or trivially defined or identified. A lot of planning goes into building a *business case* for each one. The business case is the menu option given to the decision-maker. See Paczkowski (2020) for a discussion of the role of business cases for new product development.

I provide a high-level view of the *Business Case Process* (BCP) leading to a decision menu item in Figure 1-10. This view is only for illustrative purposes since every business has its own process. I conjecture, without empirical evidence, that there are as many BCPs as there are businesses.

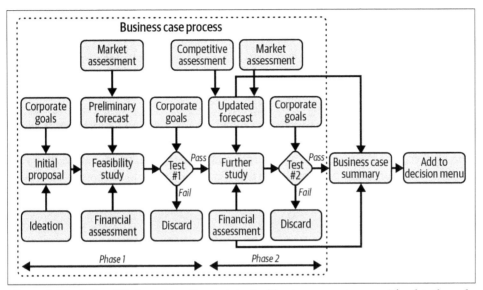

Figure 1-10. A simplified version of a prototypical business case process. The details and structure will, of course, vary widely by business.

I divide the BCP into two phases. Phase I is the initial ideation/proposal phase in which a project is proposed. The inputs are the results of ideation exercises (e.g., brainstorming, text analytics, focus groups) and corporate goals. At the operational scale-view level, this could be a rearrangement of job shop production flows to more efficiently produce a product (i.e., reduce costs). At the tactical scale-view level, it could be a new marketing campaign to increase market awareness. At the strategic scale-view level, it could be a major investment in a new office or manufacturing facility. Regardless of the level, a feasibility study is conducted to determine if the proposal has any merit. A preliminary financial analysis is done to gauge its financial viability, especially with respect to the corporate goals. The feasibility study may also include a preliminary forecast of relevant KPMs. And a market assessment, perhaps based on focus groups, will determine its market viability. At the end of this stream of activities, the proposal is assessed for its viability, and if it passes the assessment, it is then passed on to Phase II; otherwise, the proposal is discarded, although it could be reconsidered at some future time. The viability test is a comparison to corporate goals and mandates from the *C-level team.*

In Phase II, the same basic activities are repeated, but with more detail and focus. At the end of this phase, another viability test is done, although this is more stringent. If the proposal passes this test, it is then added to the decision menu. That new menu option is a summary of the findings from the BCP, primarily the financial analysis and forecasts. Both are dependent on predictive models so this is the tie to Predictive

Analytics. In fact, the BCP is the tie to both Descriptive Analytics and Predictive Analytics because both are used to develop the menu options.

I further summarize in Figure 1-11, again for illustrative purposes only, what the decision menu would look like with input from the BCP. In this example, only three projects are proposed, although, obviously, many more could be included. The analysis at the decision-maker level (e.g., the CEO, an SBU president, a member of the *C-level team*, or a line manager) is aided by the DST and a *decision advisory council* (DAC). I will discuss the DAC in "Decision-Makers' Options" on page 33. The DST will use the methods I will describe in the later chapters to assess the menu options based on the summary data (e.g., financial data and forecasts) and make a recommendation for what the decision-maker should do. This is the Prescriptive Analytics phase of the analysis stream.

> The whole work flow—from the BCP to the analysis of the decision menu—involves the three analytical phases: Descriptive Analytics, Predictive Analytics, and Prescriptive Analytics. The decision menu summarizes and captures all three.

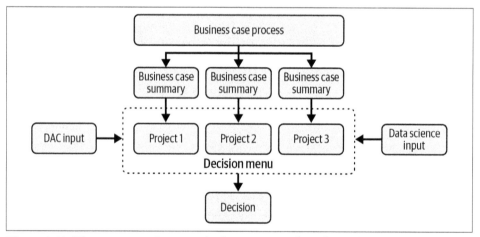

Figure 1-11. The connection between the business case flow chart, the decision menu, the data science team, and the DAC.

What-if projects

What-if projects are a special set of questions asked by a myriad of people for different reasons than these projects defined in a business case, at least initially. As questions, they will, or should, have answers. These could turn into business case projects if the questions and answers are compelling and urgent enough to warrant this.

What-if inputs have two sources:

- Scenarios
- Questions

Scenarios are stories about the future, so they are inventions of the mind. Stories about what? Only those aspects of the world with implications to be planned for now at best, or begin to just ponder and wonder about now at worst. These obviously have to be futuristic since planning for the past is nonsensical and the present is, well, immediately gone as it turns into the past. I will discuss scenarios in Chapter 9.

Scenarios could be developed at the SBU level or by a central planning organization. The latter is responsible for developing and managing all strategic scale-view plans, such as a five-year plan. At a tactical level, the same function might be in a departmental organization, such as the marketing or engineering departments. At the operational level, it might be in the human resources, logistics, or engineering departments. The actual organizational location is immaterial; the function is the same: to plan. Consequently, members of the planning organization are responsible for developing projects for the decision menu.

The planning organization does not develop the scenarios without input. This could come from the *C-level team* itself, but most likely from SMEs and/or KOLs. Both have valuable insight into creating the scenario stories.

The questions are *what-if questions* that could be, and usually are, asked every day by all levels of management. But only a few have a sense of urgency or major business implications. For example, a pricing manager could have anecdotal evidence that a major competitor will cut their price by 10%. Two logical questions the manager could ask are:

- What will be the effect of the 10% price cut on our sales if we do not respond?
- What will be the effect on our sales if we also cut our prices 10%? Or 11%?

These are three menu options: no response, 10% response, and 11% response. What should the pricing manager do?

I will discuss what-if questions and analysis in Chapter 9.

Inventing the Future

"It's easier to invent the future than to predict it."

—Alan Kay

Examples of decision menus

Let me describe three vignettes of decision menus for the three scale-views since the menu concept is so important.

Vignette 1: Operational scale-view. A line manager with an operational scale-view has to assign production jobs to different machine stations, one job per machine, each morning before the production crews arrive. The assignment has to minimize the total cost of producing the products. Suppose there are three jobs and three machines. The DST estimates the expected cost for each job for each machine. I show these in Table 1-1. The menu is the job-machine combinations. What is the best job-machine combination to minimize total cost?

Table 1-1. The predicted production costs per job on three different machines.

Job	Machine 1	Machine 2	Machine 3
A	$4	$6	$11
B	$5	$8	$16
C	$9	$13	$21

Vignette 2: Tactical scale-view. An advertising manager wants to place ads in one or more media. Each outlet reaches a predicted number of potential customers. *Reach* is defined as communicating with, touching, or making a customer aware of your products and services. The more customers you can reach, the higher the probability of making a sale. Unfortunately, media are not free; there is a cost of placing ads.

For each media outlet, the total expected customer reach, the cost of reaching those customers, the cost in man-hours of designing a reach program, and the cost of a sales contact also in man-hours are known. For each cost constraint, the total budget is known from the business plan. These data are in Table 1-2. The objective is to maximize the total customer reach subject to the three cost constraints. The outlets are the menu. Which media outlet(s) should she use?

Table 1-2. The predicted costs and reach for six tactical media outlets. The reach, dollar cost, and person-hours are the menu option attributes.

	TV	Trade magazine	Newspaper	Radio	Popular magazine	Promotional campaign	Total resources
Reachable customers	1,000,000	200,000	300,000	400,000	450,000	450,000	
Cost ($)	500,000	150,000	300,000	250,000	250,000	100,000	1,800,000
Designers (person-hours)	700	250	200	200	300	400	1,500
Salespeople (person-hours)	200	100	100	100	100	1,000	1,200

Vignette 3: Strategic scale-view. A CEO must decide which of five capital projects to choose. The menu consists of the five projects. The objective is to choose two to maximize the NPV. For this problem, assume that the DST predicted the NPV for each project along with the amount that has to be invested in each. I display this data in Table 1-3. Assume that the total amount to invest is $25 million. The decision-maker must select the projects that yield the highest NPV, but whose total investment does not exceed the amount of financial capital available. The projects are the menu. Which one(s) are selected?

Table 1-3. *The predicted NPV and investment costs for five strategic projects. The NPV and Investments are the attributes for the menu options.*

	Project 1	Project 2	Project 3	Project 4	Project 5
NPV	2.0	2.8	2.6	1.8	2.4
Investment	8.0	14.0	12.0	6.0	10.0

There are many more examples that can be developed, but these three should provide sufficient examples. Incidentally, I will analyze these three in Chapter 5.

Uncertainty: Multiple Sources and Problems

Uncertainty is introduced into the menu analysis because of a prediction's time dimension (i.e., a forecast). Our inability to perfectly know the future is the reason; anything could happen tomorrow that we could not and cannot expect beforehand. The further out we predict, the greater the uncertainty because more unknown "things" can happen, good or bad. This holds, no matter how good the predictive analytics.

Uncertainty hangs over every decision regardless of the scale-view. It is like a cloud over the head of the decision-maker, ready to bring bad events, but also good ones.

 This is similar to the perpetual storm cloud over the head of Al Capp's Li'l Abner character *Joe Btfsplk*.[2]

There is an additional uncertainty to consider: the menu selection. In the simplest case, there is only one option, a singleton, presented to a decision-maker. This is the *Most Likely View* taken literally. The decision is binary: to act or not on that singleton

2 See the Wikipedia article on Li'l Abner (*https://en.wikipedia.org/wiki/Li%27l_Abner*). Last accessed April 10, 2023.

option. So the uncertainty is what I just described: *What will happen tomorrow*? The decision could produce a result exactly the way predicted, fall short of prediction, or exceed it. If it meets or exceeds prediction, then it was the correct one; otherwise, it was wrong. It is that simple. But, a wrong decision could be devastating for the enterprise, resulting in not just lost market share, but also lost jobs and people's livelihoods and well-being. It is of paramount importance to remember lives are behind each decision. Unfortunately, the decision-maker will not know the result until a future time. And this is for just one decision option!

Quote on Chances

"Well, gentlemen, we all have to take a chance. Especially if one is all you have."

—Captain Kirk in the *Star Trek* episode "Tomorrow Is Yesterday"

When a menu of multiple options is involved, uncertainty is increased. Which one to choose? The selection of one from a multi-item menu increases uncertainty and also angst over the decision since there are now multiple decisions.

Sometimes, decision-makers will request a non-singleton menu believing it will give them a better chance of finding the "right" one. This is the basis for multiple *Most Likely Views*. Some of these might be immediately eliminated because their predicted result is clearly negative or just outright inferior. A price change, for example, that reduces sales and revenue, two KPMs, is an obvious option to eliminate. Unfortunately, others cannot be so simply eliminated because the KPMs may be numerous and/or contradictory. I will provide examples of menus in Chapter 5 and show you how to select one to optimize a criterion function (i.e., a KPM).

So what does the decision-maker do? This is where Prescriptive Analytics becomes important.

Uncertainty Versus Risk

I should comment on an interpretation of uncertainty since this concept is so germane to decision making. Most people define uncertainty as not knowing the future. This is insufficient because uncertainty could have different causes.

Paczkowski (2023) describes two forms of uncertainty: *aleatoric* and *epistemic*. The former involves random events you have no control over. And you cannot eliminate them. Maybe you can reduce them by knowing more and having a wider and deeper knowledge-base (i.e., more Rich Information), but ultimately aleatoric uncertainty cannot be eliminated.

Epistemic uncertainty is "strictly information-based and is inversely related to the amount of information we have." See Paczkowski (2023, Chapter 1). This form can be eliminated by knowing more, but the "more" has to be rich, not poor, information. Poor information is insufficient by definition. It only skims the surface of what is hidden inside data and cannot, therefore, provide the needed depth and breadth for complex decisions. Epistemic uncertainty is why many decision-makers, primarily at the tactical and especially at the strategic scale-view levels, ask for multiple *Most Likely Views*. These are their only source of information. However, the reduction of epistemic uncertainty is costly.

Another perspective regarding uncertainty takes a purely probabilistic approach. This is due to Knight (1921) who distinguished between risk and uncertainty based on our knowledge of an event's probability distribution. He claimed we face a situation of risk if we know the probability distribution of an event, and a situation of uncertainty otherwise. This distinction is still used today in much of the formal analysis of, say, financial markets. Using the aleatoric and epistemic definitions, when the amount of rich information is very high so that epistemic uncertainty is eliminated and only aleatoric uncertainty remains, then we are in a Knightian uncertainty situation. See Paczkowski (2023, Chapter 1 and Figure 1.3).

The Menu Cost of Uncertainty

Another cost due to uncertainty cannot be ignored: a menu cost. The larger the menu presented to a decision-maker, the longer it will take for that person to make a decision. And time is money. This time will rise exponentially because each added menu option contributes not only its time factor, but also adds a factor to the other options already on the menu. Those other options have to be reconsidered in light of new information from the new menu item. I depict this time dynamic in Figure 1-12.

The data scientist using Prescriptive Analytic methods can narrow the menu, but this is now a cost imposed on the data scientist. This is their time and resources that have to be committed to narrowing the menu. From an enterprise perspective, there is a trade-off.

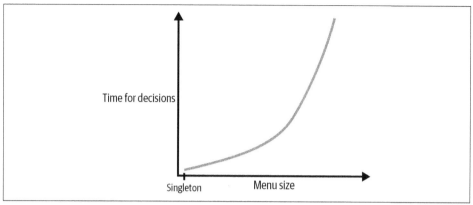

Figure 1-12. The effect of the menu size on the time for a decision.

Probabilities and Uncertainty

Probability distributions are involved in decision making by the nature of random-ness. There are two ways to view probabilities: frequency-based and subjectively-based. The former is grounded in experiments that can be repeated an infinite number of times (at least theoretically), while the latter is grounded in our beliefs which in turn are based on our knowledge, understanding, and rich information. Subjective probabilities are the foundation for the Bayesian approach to probability theory and statistics I mentioned previously.

Frequency-based probabilities are the first, and perhaps last, introduction most people have to probability theory. This is partly due to their almost intuitive nature: they are simple ratios based on counts of something happening to the count of everything that could happen. The statement "everything that could happen" is qualified to be all events of the same ilk. The former is the count of the members in, or the size of, an *event space* and the latter is the count of the members in, or the size of, a *sample space*. The sample space is the space you use to sample an event. You can immediately deduce several probability rules from these ratios, such as a probability must lie between zero and one and the probabilities of all events in the sample space must sum to 1.0.

A coin toss is a simple example usually used in an introductory statistics or probabil-ity course. The toss is a *trial* in an *experiment*. The event may be getting a heads-up on a toss of a fair coin; the sample space is heads and tails. For one toss, the count of the members in the event space is 1 while the count for the sample space is 2. So the probability is 0.5. Most people know this from experiences outside the classroom so they immediately accept the result.

This simple example is then extended to multiple tosses of a fair die; tosses of a pair of dice; draws from a deck of cards; draws from a sack containing different colored marbles; and so on. For the coin toss, a computer program can be written to generate a very large, but less than infinite, number of tosses. The results will verify the 0.5 probability. See Paczkowski (2023) for an example. Also see "Example 1: Coin Toss" on page 229 for an example.

Subjective probabilities are different. There are no trials and no experiments because the probabilities are formulated in our heads with no objective basis. Yet we know and accept them just as readily as the frequency-based ones because we hear them every day. For instance, you always hear statements such as: "There is a 40% chance of rain tomorrow." Depending on the magnitude of the probability, you know what action you should take; your decision to carry an umbrella tomorrow is based on this probability. But tomorrow will be a unique event in history. It cannot be experimentally repeated an infinite number of times in an experiment to determine whether or not it will rain tomorrow. That 40% probability is strictly subjective.

It is probably safe to say that all business decisions involving risk and uncertainty are based on subjective probabilities. The collection of probabilities for any decision situation is a probability distribution. The distribution, however formulated, could then be assigned to the Predictive Analytics menu to assist the decision-makers in their selection. I will review the main features of probability theory in Chapter 4 and discuss the use of subjective probabilities in decision making in Chapter 6.

Whatever subjective probability distribution is assigned to the decision menu will not be the final one. As new rich information becomes available, either through more research or outside sources regarding market changes or competitive actions, the subjective probability distribution must be updated. The updating is via *Bayes' Theorem*. This uses the previous subjective assessment of the probability of the event, appropriately called the *prior probability*, and adjusts it for the likelihood of the new information. The updated probability is called a *posterior probability*. I develop Bayes' Theorem in "Bayes' Theorem: Derivation" on page 126.

While powerful and intuitively appealing, Bayesian probabilities do become complicated to use. Nonetheless, they are the ones needed for decision making. There is an extremely large literature on Bayesian probabilities and analysis. I will summarize the main points in Chapter 10.

Subjective probabilities allow decision-makers to include their beliefs (i.e., gut-feel, intuition, suspicion) into their decision. This adds a new, but often overlooked, dimension to decision making. You can interpret the word "belief" in a narrow sense —a vague idea or conception of what you think is true—or in a broader sense of your idea of the world and your position in that world. The latter is called a *self-locating belief* because you locate yourself in the world: where do you fit or belong? For a business, managers at all scale-levels have a belief about the markets they operate in, so the markets are their world. Their beliefs may be that the markets are highly competitive, dynamic, and technologically oriented. Their self-locating beliefs may be that they are the dominant firm in the industry, or they are technology leaders always at the forefront of new ideas and innovations.

Both forms of belief, subjective and self-locating, work in tandem to influence the decisions made at each scale-view level. This means that decisions are not always based on quantitative measures or analytics, but instead are based on biases about the world and the business. This is a philosophical approach to decision making that is beyond the scope of this book. I will take a strict quantitative, almost mechanical approach to decision making. The quantitative explication of my beliefs of the world are captured in Bayesian probabilities. See Lin (2023).

For more on self-locating beliefs from a philosophical perspective, see Egan and Titelbaum (2022). I say more about beliefs in Chapter 10.

Prescriptive Analytics as a Separate Discipline

Descriptive Analytics and Predictive Analytics, which have long been the backbone of business decisions, are not as complex as they may seem. In fact, they are closely related, sharing a common base: statistical analysis. All quantitative areas in popular use (e.g., econometrics and machine learning) are really statistics-based. The statistical concepts are just specialized to a domain. For example, econometrics is the application of statistical theory and techniques to economic problems with their own complications not dealt with by statisticians.

There have always been two steps in a data analysis approach to providing rich information for data-driven decisions. What is new, however, is the third form of analytics that has become more popular in recent years, but which itself is built on tools that have been used by quantitatively oriented practitioners for a long time. These require advanced training, usually at the graduate school level. And even then, they are out of the mainstream of instructional courses at the undergraduate and graduate departments. This is Prescriptive Analytics. It is the third piece of the overall Business Analytics series consisting of:

Descriptive Analytics
> Basic understanding of business position and trends, for the entire business or a segment of it;

Predictive Analytics
> Prediction of where the business, or a segment of it, may be headed either because of fundamental economic and market trends and developments, or likely outcomes of policy decisions; and

Prescriptive Analytics
> What should the business decision-makers decide based on the trends (from Descriptive Analytics) and what is predicted (from Predictive Analytics).

This is a *Tripartite Analytics Paradigm* with Prescriptive Analytics as the component that narrows the decision menu from Predictive Analytics and enables a decision. I depict the flow in Figure 1-13.

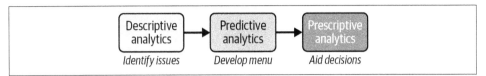

Figure 1-13. The connection among the three forms of analytics as a single flow of analysis leading to a decision. I comment on this flow in "The Analytics Flow" on page 37.

Decision-Makers' Options

To understand the role of Prescriptive Analytics in this *Tripartite Analytics Paradigm*, it is important to understand what the middle piece, Predictive Analytics, contributes to decision making.

When prediction analysis is taught, and the way it appears in most textbooks, only one predictive model is trained on a training data set. But more importantly, the trained model, as taught, produces only one prediction! If the recommended methodological approach is followed, that prediction is tested using a testing data set with a battery of prediction statistics. If the prediction fails the tests, then the data scientists go back to the model development stage and build a new one, perhaps from the beginning if the test results are very poor, or modify the model and test again. When the model "passes" the tests, a prediction is deemed credible. That prediction is then passed to a decision-maker. I illustrate this in Figure 1-14. See Paczkowski (2022a) for details about training and testing data sets as well as prediction statistics.

In this view, data are used at the Descriptive Analytics stage of the *Tripartite Analytics Paradigm* to just produce understanding: understanding of the current business situation and environment as well as trends leading up until "now." The data basically come from or represent three sources: the business itself, the economy, and the business's markets. Most people immediately focus on the business when they think of Descriptive Analytics because they view this as just informing decision-makers about where the business stands. To some extent, this is correct, but it depends on the scale-view of the decision-maker. A line manager with a very narrow scale-view focuses on operations, so business measures (operational ones) would be a primary concern. A CEO has a very wide scale-view: the entire enterprise, so only business data does not provide a good enough picture of the business. The economy and the markets must also be considered.

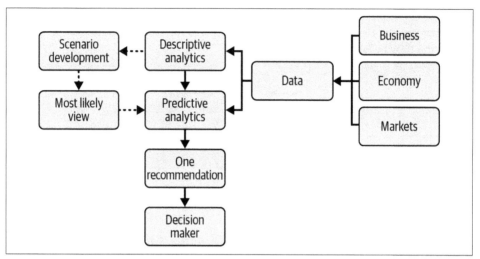

Figure 1-14. A highly simplified framework for a decision recommendation system. Only one prediction comes out of the Predictive Analytics block, so there is only one action to recommend.

The data not only feed Descriptive Analytics, but also the Predictive Analytics. After all, predictions do require data. The amount and type of data may very well differ from what is used in Descriptive Analytics, but the general sources are the same.

The important point to note about this scenario is that only one prediction, one recommendation, is given to the decision-maker. That person has to then decide to use the prediction or not: it is a "Yes" or "No" decision. The data scientist has no further input or role to play. Unfortunately, real decision problems are not that simple or trivial. This is not to say that what the decision-maker does is simple or trivial; a decision is still hard and challenging. But there is, in this case, only one option to decide on. Real problems, as I have argued, often involve a non-singleton menu. The menu changes the complexity of the decision.

I illustrate a more complex view of prediction in Figure 1-15. The beginning of the *Tripartite Analytics Paradigm* is the same: data from three sources (depending on scale-view) feeding the Descriptive Analytics and Predictive Analytics phases. The difference is that Descriptive Analytics now feeds the development of scenarios because Descriptive Analytics should, and does, spur thoughts about what could happen. The exact scenarios depend on the scale-view, but they are developed, nonetheless. These are the *Most Likely Views*. They are then used as inputs for the Predictive Analytics. In essence, they are conditions, or *hyperparameters*, for the prediction models. A hyperparameter is a parameter that is not set by or determined by data, but is instead set by the analyst before a model is trained. As an example, the growth rate of the market could be a hyperparameter. See Paczkowski (2023) for a discussion of hyperparameters.

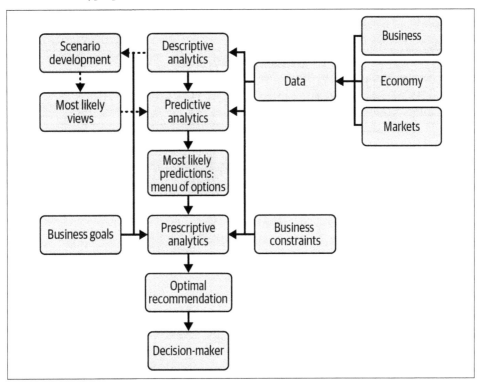

Figure 1-15. An enhanced framework for a decision recommendation system that involves Prescriptive Analytics as a focal point. A menu of prediction options is developed from which one must be recommended to the decision-maker.

The immediate implication of these *Most Likely* scenarios is that multiple *Most Likely* predictions result. This, of course, depends on the scale-view of the decision-maker for whom the predictions are made. An operations line manager may have only one as I described earlier: a daily orders prediction, for example. The CEO, on the other hand, would have many *Most Likely* predictions, especially when she is in the process of developing a business plan, say a five-year plan, or a major strategic move such as a merger or acquisition. The requirements are just different.

This is where Prescriptive Analytics enters the *Tripartite Analytics Paradigm*. Decision-makers will make a final decision regarding a scenario to use as an Action Directive. But they typically ask for recommendations, which are qualitative judgments and opinions, about the best one, or seek advice from SMEs, KOLs, key financial stakeholders and investors, legal counsel, and others regarding the best one to choose. By qualitative, I mean stated in words without any or little numeric qualification. These people form a DAC. Whether such a cabinet exists in reality or not is immaterial since these advisers are available, nonetheless. The decision-makers never decide without qualitative input from the DAC. I illustrate a possible DAC framework in Figure 1-16.

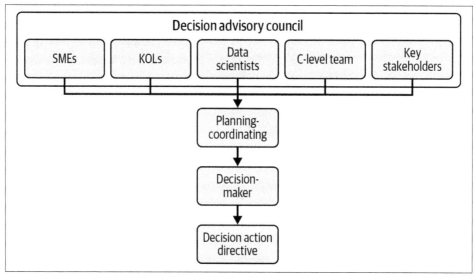

Figure 1-16. A decision advisory council framework. The DAC does not actually have to exist, but the functions will be accessed, nonetheless.

Prescriptive Analytics should be viewed as one more piece of qualitative advice, but qualitative advice is based on data, so it is quantitatively-based qualitative advice about what the decision-maker should do; which *Most Likely* view and prediction, which decision menu option, should be chosen. The extent of the advice depends on the scale-view even at this stage.

The Prescriptive Analytics is based on the set of predictions from the Predictive Analytics phase. It also draws, however, from three other sources of input. The first is the data (business, economy, and markets) relevant for the *Most Likely Views*. This is, perhaps, the first, and often only, one most analysts think about. The goals of the business and any business constraints are two pieces of information that cannot be ignored. They could, in fact, be considered hyperparameters for the Prescriptive Analytics.

Business Goals and Constraints

Businesses often develop mission statements that specify a goal (or several). They could, however, be qualitatively vague. For example, a stated goal could be: "To be the industry's technology leader. Always at the forefront of new ideas." What technology? What is forefront? In some instances, what industry? The business constraints, on the other hand, are often stated in quantitative terms. For example, to have a 10% ROI for the next fiscal year or a compound annual growth rate (CAGR) for sales of 7% for the next five years. The quantitative constraint could also be implied. For instance, to maintain head-count at the previous fiscal year maximum. In either case, these goals and constraints may be important factors to include in the Prescriptive Analytics of the menu options. Not all the menu items may completely meet them so the decision-maker is forced to balance or trade off one for the other. This should be part of the Prescriptive Analytics.

Key Decision Question: What Is the Best Decision?

Once these factors are all accounted for, to the best they can be accounted for, then the Prescriptive Analytics methodologies are applied to the decision menu from the Predictive Analytics. A menu item is then chosen and submitted as a recommendation to the decision-maker. See Figure 1-15 for the complete analytical flow.

The Analytics Flow

The overall analytics flow is depicted in Figure 1-13. It is important to recognize and acknowledge the role of each piece of this flow. Descriptive Analytics identifies issues and problems, hopefully before they become serious problems, via the constant monitoring and reporting of the health of the business and its environment (e.g., the economy and markets). Predictive Analytics produces a prediction or forecast under different conditions or scenarios in the context of these problems. The predictions are used to build a menu of decision options as I will describe in Chapter 9. The menu is input into the Prescriptive Analytics which aids or supports the decision making. Decision making is the selection of one option from the menu.

It is important to understand that Prescriptive Analytics does not have a set of tools for telling the decision-maker what to do. This is a normative issue, not a positive one. Prescriptive Analytics advises the decision-maker by narrowing the options on the menu, and that is all. This is an important function since real-world menus, unlike textbook examples (including this one!), are complex, detailed, and often overwhelming. Nonetheless, the decision-maker will do whatever the decision-maker wants to do, and that is beyond the scope of Prescriptive Analytics or any other science.

I depict a summary of the salient parts of this analytics flow in Figure 1-17. I omitted some details, like the data sources and the role of the DAC, but these should be obvious. This depiction is a streamlined version of Figure 1-6. The important segments of the flow are the development of the *Most Likely Views*, that is, the decision menu, and the Prescriptive Analytics in providing a recommendation. My focus in this book is the last segment of the flow and the fact that it uses the decision menu as an input.

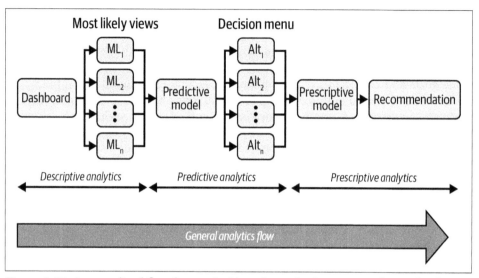

Figure 1-17. A generalized flow from a dashboard to a final recommendation for the decision-maker. The Most Likely Views are $ML_1, ML_2,..., ML_n$. The results or alternatives from the Predictive Model are $Alt_1, Alt_2,..., Alt_n$. The overall flow is from Descriptive Analytics to Predictive Analytics to Prescriptive Analytics.

Prescriptive Analytics and Decision Making

I described three analytical methods—Descriptive, Predictive, and Prescriptive—that have a role in aiding decision-makers at all scale-view levels. But only one—Prescriptive Analytics—has a direct input into decision making. Descriptive Analytics is tangential; it raises questions or issues at best, and provides poor information at worst. Otherwise, it does not directly deal with a decision. Predictive Analytics aids in building the menu, but it does not inform the decision-makers about which option to select. At worst, it can confuse and befuddle a decision-maker by producing too many predictions (i.e., too many menu options). Only Prescriptive Analytics helps the decision-maker by providing a set of tools to either narrow the menu or actually pick one option. You will see many examples of this in Parts III and IV.

The overall implication is that Prescriptive Analytics is really directly focused on assisting in decision making, while the other two analytics are not.

This does not mean the decision-maker is relieved of the burden or responsibility of making a decision; Prescriptive Analytics just directly assists in the decision. There is another assistant: AI. This technology can work in collaboration with a decision-maker to select from a menu by applying the Prescriptive Analytics tools more efficiently and effectively. The decision-maker is not replaced, but supplemented by AI. Of course, there is also the potential for it to collaborate with a data scientist to build the menu and to raise issues. AI, therefore, has the potential to help with decision making at all levels of analytics.

Summary

In this chapter, I introduced a general framework for Prescriptive Analytics within the context of the levels, or scale-views, of decision-makers: operational, tactical, and strategic. A fundamental analytical paradigm, one I use in all my work, was presented as the driving force behind data science: $Data = Information + Noise$. The goal, the reason for the existence of data science, is to extract the Information component. But not any information. It must be rich information. Data science is concerned with this information extraction.

Data science is divided into three interconnected, yet separate, phases: Descriptive Analytics, Predictive Analytics, and Prescriptive Analytics. They form the *Tripartite Analytics Paradigm*, a continuous analytical flow from Descriptive to Prescriptive focused on rich information extraction.

Descriptive Analytics informs decision-makers at any one of the scale-views about what did or is currently happening. Predictive Analytics tells them what will happen, under different conditions, recognizing uncertainty in that prediction. Uncertainty extends to, and is endemic to, the decisions that must be made every day. These two result in a menu of options at each scale-view. Prescriptive Analytics helps or enables the decision-maker to choose (i.e., decide) an option from the menu that is best for the business.

The main concepts from this chapter are:

- Scale-views
- Uncertainty
- Tripartite Analytics Paradigm
- SMEs, KOLs, and DAC
- Decision menu

CHAPTER 2

Prescriptive Methods: Overview

The many Prescriptive Analytics methodologies available for narrowing a decision menu can easily overwhelm and stymie your analytical work. It is helpful, therefore, for you to not only know them, but also to know their pros and cons so you can efficiently and effectively work with them. Fortunately, only a few, I believe, are important. Therefore, the leading questions for this chapter are:

- What are the primary methods mentioned in the Prescriptive Analytics literature?
- How can we categorize the methods?
- Can we create general umbrella categories to aid understanding?
- What are the most important methods?

The umbrella categories are non-stochastic and stochastic methods. They form the structure of Parts III and IV of this book.

Introduction to Prescriptive Analytics Methods

Trying to name, much less summarize, the many Prescriptive Analytics methodologies is a challenge, to say the least. A simple first, but not useful, approach is to group them by classes. There are two major classes:

- Proprietary
- Public domain

Proprietary Methods

Proprietary methods are the intellectual property of consulting firms and the internal data science divisions of major enterprises. In each instance, there is a definite competitive advantage from not disclosing how decisions are made, including the methods used to develop and provide rich information. This is not an issue for governmental agencies that are transparent in this regard because of the *Freedom of Information Act*. See United States Department of Justice (2023).

Consulting firms sell their methods behind a nondisclosure agreement or internally developed software that makes accessing proprietary methods impossible. This is how they make money. They, thus, have a vested interest in keeping their methods secret. They will advertise just enough on their website, or develop sales pitches and presentations with just enough content to describe what they do and are capable of doing, but no more, to entice new clients. They will also provide success stories (i.e., very short descriptions at best), sometimes called *use-cases*, along with testimonials, but still without providing much, if any, detail on their approach. They walk a tightrope between announcing and demonstrating their competency to get clients, on the one hand, and revealing too much to aid their competitors, on the other hand. After all, they have to protect their intellectual property. Incidentally, a potential client could replicate their methodology in-house given enough information, thus bypassing the consultants and acting like a competitor. This is another reason to protect the intellectual property.

Enterprises do not have to worry about selling their methods, but they do have to be concerned about a competitor learning what they do, duplicating it, and then shadowing them to develop counter tactics and strategies. So they also keep their analytical methods secret and protect their intellectual property.

Public Domain Methods

Methodologies developed and used in academics are published in professional journals. These are in the public domain so anyone can read and implement them. Intellectual property concerns, except for proper citation, are unimportant.

Unfortunately, full details of a method are often unavailable because of limited print space in professional journals. Just enough is mentioned to outline the method, but not much more. This is not unusual. Regardless of how much is disclosed, it is still more than proprietary methods.

There are two other issues with academic publications: the numerous ways to publish and their sheer volume.

Academics are notoriously under pressure to publish (the "publish or perish" feature of academia), and the best way is via papers rather than books. Books take longer to write.

There are many ways for academics to publish papers. There are:

- Traditional journals (usually with a top-tier, very prestigious group, and a lower tier)
- Online, peer-reviewed and non-peer reviewed
- Books
- Book chapters
- Working papers and technical reports that are never formally published
- Blogs

Fortunately, search engines such as *Google Scholar* make it easier to search for and retrieve many of these. The volume, however, remains.

Summary of Prescriptive Analytics Methods

Lepeniotia et al. (2020) is the best summary of public domain Prescriptive Analytics methods used in a wide range of contexts. Not only did they summarize the incidence of use of methods to highlight which are the most popularly used, but they also categorized them into groups and showed how their use overlaps. This latter point is important because methods, regardless of their analytical types, can be combined to handle complex problems to obtain more robust and pragmatic solutions (i.e., Richer Information). The very nature of complex problems suggests one approach may be insufficient. For example, *mathematical programming*, which I will discuss in Chapter 5, could be used to find an optimal combination of products to produce to maximize profits or ROI. The inputs to produce them, however, are subject to random variations (e.g., supply chain disruptions), so a *simulation* is needed to supplement the mathematical programming solutions to produce a *steady state solution*, basically a long-run average. So the two, mathematical programming and simulation, are a powerful combination. The contribution of Lepeniotia et al. (2020) is, therefore, not only summarizing and categorizing Prescriptive Analytics methods, but also showing their overlap.

My experience has been that many "home-grown" methodologies are really simplistic standard ones cleverly rebranded as unique and state-of-the-art. So the universe of proprietary methods may be identical to those cited by Lepeniotia et al. (2020).

Methods Reviewed in the Literature

Lepeniotia et al. (2020) categorized methods into six groups or families:

- Probabilistic modeling
- Machine learning/data mining
- Mathematical programming
- Evolutionary computations
- Simulations
- Logic-based methods

I show the frequency counts for each group in Figure 2-1. Notice that mathematical programming is the most dominant. I will give a brief synopsis of each method in the following sections.

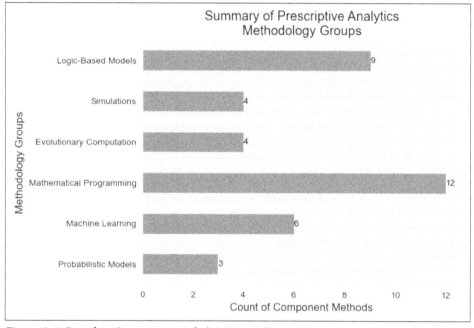

Figure 2-1. Based on Lepeniotia et al. (2020, p. 61).

Probabilistic models

This is a family of data-driven models to quantify uncertainty by calculating the likelihood of events occurring. They implement key probability concepts to handle specialized problems such as customer analytics, inventory analytics, competitive analytics, and so forth. The methods in the family rely on *Markov Decision Processes* (MDP) as a common element.

An inventory management problem at the operational scale-view level is an example of a *Markov Decision Problem*. Inventories are run down or depleted on a random basis during normal operations because of random customer demand. The operational manager must replenish the inventory by placing an order with the supply chain, but this order has a risk. The manager could order too much, which is costly, or too little, which is also costly. The costs reflect the unknown states of the inventory when the materials arrive: they could be too much or too little. If too much, then the surplus must be stored somewhere, perhaps in a temporary facility, or allowed to perish. If it is too little, then a new order must be placed, which reproduces the original inventory problem.

This simple, but enhanced, description of an inventory management problem has several key concepts:

Initial state of a system
  Initial inventory level which is the state

Transition to a future state
  Inventory restocking or further depletion

Probability of transition to a new state
  Unexpected customer demand

Reward (or penalty)
  Cost of too much or too little inventory

The transition from one state to the next is governed by the random event of customer demand. So it is the transition probabilities that matter.

More generally, the collection of all possible states is called the *state space*, the transitions are compiled in a *transition matrix*, and their associated probabilities are in a *transition probability matrix*. The reward or penalty is a function called the *reward function* or *value function*. These four elements define an MDP, summarized as a four-tuple: $M(S,A,T,R)$ with:

S
  Set of all possible states, including the initial one

A
  Set of actions

T
  Matrix of transition probabilities

R
  Reward function

This is based on a *Markov Process*, sometimes referred to as a *memoryless process*. This process develops over time as you move from one state to another, but the movements only depend on the current state, not any states before that one. All earlier states are irrelevant, hence the memoryless designation.

The implication is that a prediction of the probability of a future event depends only on the current state of the system. Of course, that state changes from period to period, but, nonetheless, earlier ones are irrelevant.

A classic example of a Markov Process is a random walk. You can interpret a walk as a series of transitions. These are $+1$ and -1 along a number line. The initial state is an arbitrary number on the line and subsequent states are other numbers on the line. The transition probabilities are assumed to be the same for the two states: 0.50. So the transitions from the current state are to the next one ($+1$) with probability 0.50, or to the previous one (-1) with probability 0.50. Any earlier state is irrelevant for that transition (i.e., the next walk).

More formally, the Markov Process probabilities are defined as

$$Pr(S_{t+1} = s \mid S_0 = s_0, S_1 = s_1, ..., S_t = s_t) = Pr(S_{t+1} = s \mid S_t = s_t)$$

where the subscripts designate successive time periods from the initial state, 0, to the current state, t.

For a decision problem, such as an inventory problem, there are not only the transitions and their probabilities but also the rewards for a correct decision and penalties for an incorrect one. For inventories, these are satisfied/dissatisfied customers, profits/losses, excess inventory carrying costs (including insurance and inventory policing or monitoring costs), and so on. To solve this MDP, you must specify all these elements; that is, all the elements in the four-tuple. For large systems, the storage and computational burdens are onerous to say the least, even with modern computer, data management, and software technologies. See, for example, Das et al. (1999) and Zhang et al. (2023).

Probabilities are a complex and contentious topic with a large technical and philosophical literature. I highlight a few results in Chapter 4.

Machine learning and data mining

Machine learning is a large and complex group of methods for handling diverse data types and analysis problems. These are grouped into two subcategories depending on the presence of a target variable: *Supervised Learning* and *Unsupervised Learning*.

A target variable guides or supervises how the unknown parameters of a model are determined. The model is said to learn the values of the parameters from the data under the supervision of the target. Hence, these are supervised learning methods.

If there is no target, then there cannot be a model per se. The purpose of a model is to explain the target: no target means nothing to explain. Instead, an algorithm is used to group the variables, but nothing (i.e., no target) supervises the groupings. The algorithm uses rules to create the groupings. Hence, these are unsupervised learning methods.

Prime examples of supervised learning methods are the regression family members. Prime examples of unsupervised learning methods are cluster analysis and classification methods such as *Support Vector Machines* (SVM) for continuous and discrete data. See Paczkowski (2022a) for a detailed discussion of supervised and unsupervised learning methods in Business Analytics.

 A target variable in machine learning is a dependent variable in statistics and econometrics. The variables used to explain the target are *factors* in machine learning, and *independent variables* in statistics and econometrics. Also, models are trained as the way to obtain the factors' unknown parameters in machine learning, while they are estimated in statistics and econometrics.

These methods are a subset of *Artificial Intelligence* (AI). Models are trained to make decisions, perhaps faster and with more precision than humans. This is a rapidly growing area, one I expect will become more dominant in the Prescriptive Analytics space as the overall AI area develops beyond what it is today.

Data mining is the search for patterns, relationships, and trends in very large data sets (i.e., Big Data). Its methods are the same as those in machine learning. I prefer to view the label "data mining" as older nomenclature, now replaced by "machine learning."

Aside from the potential for AI, machine learning and data mining cannot be effectively used for Prescriptive Analytics because they require data—lots of data—to train and test models. It is a cardinal rule in modeling that the training data should never be used to test a trained model because the model already knows the data. If you reuse the training data, you would just be checking that the model did learn well, but not that it is useful for predicting. A separate data set, the testing data, is used for that purpose. Both data sets (training and testing) come from one *master data set*; the master data set is simply split into two parts. I illustrate the split in Figure 2-2.

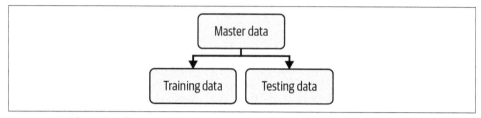

Figure 2-2. The split of a master data set into two disjointed subsets: training and testing.

Aside from this, you should not use the training and testing data to select from a decision menu because it already contains insight from the data. This further limits the usefulness of machine learning and data mining. The insight is from Predictive Analytics which are machine learning methods that feed Prescriptive Analytics. Prescriptive Analytics, a family of methods for selecting projects from a menu to satisfy criteria, are not data intensive. You will see many examples of this throughout this book.

For more on machine learning see Alpaydin (2014), Muller and Guido (2017), and Raschka and Mirjalili (2017). For data mining, see Hand et al. (2001). For data mining and machine learning, see Witten et al. (2011). See Paczkowski (2022a) and Paczkowski (2023) for issues and procedures for splitting the master data set and Predictive Analytics.

Mathematical programming

This is by far the most used category of Prescriptive Analytics methods. It is actually a family, and like all families, it starts somewhere and has descendants that form a family tree which I display in Figure 2-3.

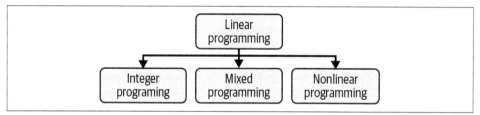

Figure 2-3. The linear programming methods' family tree. The whole class of four methods in mathematical programming.

The members of this family all descend from linear programming which was first developed in the 1930s, but it was computationally intensive and impractical. After all, computer technology was almost nonexistent at that time. It was not until the mid-1940s, however, that it was further developed and made operational using emerging electronic computers. George Dantzig is credited with developing the linear programming method to solve planning problems for the U.S. Air Force. His approach, based on the *simplex method*, which I will describe in Chapter 5, enabled planners to quickly solve their problems.

The word "programming" is a misnomer. It is really a purely mathematical technique for optimizing a function, the *objective function*, subject to a set of constraints. All the variations have this feature. Optimization could be maximization or minimization. Some programs, such as the Python package SciPy, only handle minimization. This is not an issue, however, because multiplying the objective function's coefficients by -1 converts a maximization problem into a minimization problem. The variables for the objective function are *decision variables*, and the constraints are limits and relationships among the decision variables. The decision variables are continuous in basic linear problems. The objective function and constraints are linear because they are easy to handle. Hence, the original mathematical programming family member was linear programming. Its goal is to find values for the decision variables that optimize a linear objective function.

Programming problems often contain numerous decision variables and constraints as well as complex objective functions. The speed and efficiency of the simplex method for finding the values for the decision variables was the breakthrough due to Dantzig. Once he showed how to solve basic linear programming problems, the method was immediately extended to handle integer decision variables. This extension enabled Data Scientists to find optimal combinations of those variables to enable selection from a menu. Further extensions to a mixture of integer and non-integer decision variables, and non-linear objective functions enabled selections from more complex menus.

 Wikipedia notes that "Dantzig's original example was to find the best assignment of 70 people to 70 jobs. The computing power required to test all the permutations to select the best assignment is vast; the number of possible configurations exceeds the number of particles in the observable universe." See Wikipedia (2023h) for some background.

This category of methods is in the *operations research* (OR) domain, a highly mathematical discipline focused on tools for decision making. As noted by Hillier and Lieberman (2010, p. 2):

Operations research involves "research on operations." Thus, operations research is applied to problems that concern how to conduct and coordinate the operations (i.e., the activities) within an organization. The nature of the organization is essentially immaterial, and, in fact, OR has been applied extensively in such diverse areas as manufacturing, transportation, construction, telecommunications, financial planning, health care, the military, and public services, to name just a few. Therefore, the breadth of application is unusually wide.

See Baumol (1965) and Liebhafsky (1968) for economic applications of linear programming. Also see Hadley (1962), Hillier and Lieberman (2010), and Winston (2004) for detailed discussions and examples of linear programming and its variations. It is used in Prescriptive Analytics because, as succinctly stated by Baumol (1965, p. 71): "It has…been somewhat less successful in describing what is than in indicating what…ought to be." The "ought to be" is the key normative description of Prescriptive Analytics. This sentiment has not changed. I will discuss mathematical programming and its offshoots in Chapter 5.

Evolutionary computation

This is a collection of algorithms based on evolutionary biology principles in which solutions evolve through trial and error. It is another subfield of AI and most likely will become more developed as AI itself grows and matures. See Wikipedia (2023d) for some discussions of its development and history.

There are many disciplines with an evolutionary view of how processes develop. For example, there is *evolutionary economics, evolutionary psychology, evolutionary game theory,* and *evolutionary sociology* to mention a few that draw on evolutionary principles. Although the evolution concept has been around for a long time,[1] I do not believe it has developed enough at this point to be a widely accepted methodology for Prescriptive Analytics. Lepeniotia et al. (2020) listed only four applications where it has been used.

Simulations

Simulations are used to analyze complex systems with arrangements and organizations beyond what most people can comprehend. Classic examples are the human body, the human brain, Earth's climate, the economy (especially the global economy), and any ecosystem to mention a few. A business, especially a large, multinational enterprise, is another example.

An analysis of these systems is hampered, if not outright impeded, by their key feature: their parts appear to operate in isolation, but, yet, together they produce output (which, of course, is appropriate for that system). How this happens is the issue. Because of the nature of a system, you cannot directly interfere with it to study its operations firsthand. This is the problem in economics: it is impractical and unethical to experiment with the economy. The parts can be made to work together, however, in a simulation of a simplified and controlled system enabling an analyst to determine, to learn, how it works without having to directly work with it.

---

1 Since the publication of C. Darwin's *On the Origin of Species* in 1859, if not before. See Lennox (2019) and Sloan (2019).

Simulations are not restricted to systems analysis. They are also powerful for solving complicated, if not humanly intractable, mathematical and statistical problems, perhaps producing new solutions to old problems. See, for instance, Hartley (1977) for use of a form of simulation called *Monte Carlo simulation* for dealing with probability distributions. I will discuss this form of simulation in Chapter 7.

A major feature of simulations is the use of probability distributions and pseudo-random numbers for generating stochastic variations. See Paczkowski (2023) for a detailed development of simulations. I will discuss pseudo-random numbers also in Chapter 7.

Simulations are frequently included under the umbrella of OR. I will, consequently, treat simulations as another OR tool.

I believe that simulations, along with other OR methods, offer a powerful combination for Prescriptive Analytics just as simulations and Predictive Analytics offer a powerful duo for predictions. This latter combination is the focus of Paczkowski (2023). My focus in this book is the use of OR tools, including simulations, for Prescriptive Analytics.

Some have argued that we are in the *Age of Simulations*, indicating that they are now the major analytical tool and the "wave of the future." See Paczkowski (2023) for a discussion of this Age and prior Ages.

Logic-based models

These are rule-based methods for connecting hypothesized causes with effects in a logical manner based on specific domain knowledge. I hesitate to call these "models" since they are rule-based or algorithmically-based rather than empirically-based. Lepeniotia et al. (2020) list nine methods under logic-based models, six with the word "rule" in their name. One, *Association Rules*, is popular in marketing and market segmentation because it identifies groupings in large data sets. A classic example is the identification of grocery items typically purchased together on a shopping occasion. A rule might be that when a customer buys milk, they also buy bread and eggs. This is useful to know for designing a grocery store's layout, creating promotions (e.g., buy a quart of milk and get a dozen eggs for half price), and product placement on shelves. See Data Camp (2023) for some discussion about association rules analysis using Python.

Rule-based methods can be viewed as *assignment problems*. For example, assign a product to be marketed along with another product. These are OR problems involving assigning one object to work with or be handled by another such as assigning n workers to operate n machines. I will address this in Chapter 5.

There are criticisms of association rules in general. First, the methodology tends to produce a lot of rules, many of which are meaningless or redundant. The objective of Prescriptive Analytics is to narrow a menu to get one recommendation; association rules and, therefore, logic-based models, in general, do the opposite. Second, they are data intensive just like machine learning and data mining. So this puts them in the same class as machine learning and data mining.

Three Categories of Methods

Another feature of the literature review by Lepeniotia et al. (2020) is the overlap of the six general methodologies.[2] They display their results in a Venn Diagram with the size of the Venn bubbles proportional to the methods' use. Mathematical Programming had the largest bubble reflecting its use in Prescriptive Analytics. The remaining five had significant use, but were nowhere comparable to Mathematical Programming. However, the Simulation class overlapped with three others: Mathematical Programming, Machine Learning, and Logic-Based Models. This is understandable considering that simulations enable you to extend an analysis to include values for key variables that are either stochastic by their nature or hypothesized to be particular values. For the latter, you could hypothesize that a competitor's price point will be one percent higher one year from now even though they have not recently changed their price. I will discuss simulations in Chapter 7 because of this overlap.

Although the categories reviewed by Lepeniotia et al. (2020) are useful and enlightening, I prefer to consider just three, partly because of my own interests which I cannot hide from this discussion. But I also selected these using the number of articles they cited for each, both individual methods and combinations of them. See Figure 2-4. These form the cornerstone of what I will focus on in this book:

- Mathematical programming
- Simulations
- Decision trees

---

2 Lepeniotia et al. (2020) included a seventh—statistical analysis—but this is for predictions. In fact, their overlap analysis showed that two Prescriptive Analytics methods are also used in prediction. I am only concerned with their prescriptive use.

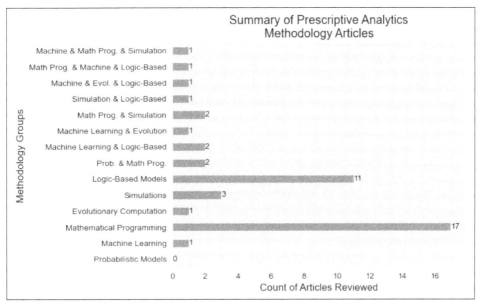

Figure 2-4. Based on Lepeniotia et al. (2020, p. 63).

There is a strong probability context for these which leads to the umbrella categories I introduce later. Since nothing is known for sure, so there is uncertainty about everything, a probability distribution is associated with all decisions. Hence, methods that focus on probability distributions are very important. The probability distributions of an event reflect its variation due to unknown causes. Unknown causes of something, anything, is the very definition of uncertainty. If you know the causes of an event so you can perfectly predict its outcome, then there is only one possible outcome. This is certainty, not uncertainty.

Any outcome is possible with uncertainty due to unknown factors. Of course, you could always bound the outcomes (e.g., sales would fall into the range of 1,000 to 1,200 units per month) and have a high confidence in that range, but that still does not allow you to say with 100% accuracy what the exact number will be (e.g., exactly 1,000 units sold per month). I will introduce a probability distribution in Chapter 8 useful for bounding outcomes while reflecting a single most likely outcome between the bounds. This is the *triangular distribution.*

Ignoring bounds, you could specify a probability distribution for the outcomes, the variance of which is the level of uncertainty. A low-variance distribution expresses or represents more certainty, but not perfect certainty, while one with a high variance expresses the opposite. Perfect certainty is represented by a degenerate distribution: its mass or density is concentrated at one point. Refer to Figure 2-5 for several illustrative distributions.

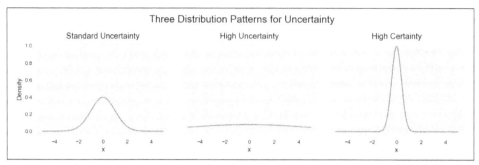

Figure 2-5. Three illustrative distributions reflecting different levels or amounts of uncertainty. The High Certainty distribution approaches a degenerate one, which would be a case of certainty.

Mathematical programming

Mathematical programming is the most popular method in Prescriptive Analytics because its sole purpose is the optimization of a function subject to constraints on its inputs (i.e., the decision variables). The original formulation used a linear function with linear constraints (as well as non-negativity constraints on the inputs), but its formulation has expanded. Methods now exist, for example, to handle discrete, non-divisible inputs measured by integers and mixtures of perfectly divisible and non-divisible inputs. With its focus on optimization, mathematical programming methods have been a mainstay of Prescriptive Analytics which is concerned with the optimal choice (i.e., decision) from a decision menu. The method and application seem to be perfectly matched. Also, as you can see in Figure 2-4, Mathematical Programming is definitely the most used, either alone or in combination with others. I will discuss Mathematical Programming in Chapter 5. But more importantly, I will focus on *integer programming* in "Integer Programming" on page 162 because of my menu paradigm. The integers could be binary (0, 1) for each option with the constraint that the sum of the integers across all menu options must be 1 as a special case and less than or equal to some integer (e.g., 2) as a general case. The constraint of 1 means "select only one"; 2 means "select exactly 2."

Simulation

Simulations are a very powerful, but often overlooked or downplayed tool for analyzing complicated problems, especially those for complex systems. In many instances, such as for mathematical and statistical problems, the problem may be intractable for our current level of mathematical knowledge and prevent us from finding a solution. A simulation is the only way it can be solved. Monte Carlo methods are simulation methods developed to handle this class of problems. In this case, the simulations are *stochastic simulations* because they rely on probability distributions. See Paczkowski (2023) for a detailed introduction to stochastic simulations.

Simulations are also used for problems dealing with large complex processes involving dynamic flows of objects around a system of interconnected and interrelated parts. The flow through these interrelated parts is a *process* with methodologies used in the process. A process is a series of steps or actions performed in a somewhat sequential manner to achieve an end result. For example, we can talk about a manufacturing process consisting of a series of production steps:

1. Collect raw materials
2. Preprocess the raw materials, perhaps through a transformation such as melting, cutting to size, or trimming damaged components
3. Combine each prepared raw material with others
4. Produce the final product
5. Inspect the final product for flaws (e.g., no blemishes) and tolerance specification satisfaction

Of course, this production process must be combined with handling and shipping processes to deliver the final product to a customer as well as an invoicing process to get paid.

For another process example, a large enterprise may have, and most likely does have, a forecasting process for predicting overall sales and earnings for the enterprise. As a process, it also has a series of sequential, logical steps:

1. Collect data
2. Preprocess the data
3. Specify a model
4. Train the model
5. Generate and evaluate a forecast
6. Communicate the forecast throughout the enterprise

A methodology is a specific approach to doing something in the context of a process such as manufacturing. Each process step relies on a methodology to complete it. For manufacturing, the step of checking the final product to determine if it is within tolerable limits relies on statistical methodologies such as random sampling without replacement, mean calculations, and hypothesis testing. Each is a separate methodology. For forecasting, data preprocessing involves data visualization, data transformation, and statistical checks for, say, data normality. The forecast generation would use, perhaps, a linear econometric time series model with lagged dependent and independent variables (i.e., an Autoregressive Distributed Lag model; see Paczkowski [2023] for this model specification). Each is an example of a methodology. There are clearly many methodologies that could be applied at each point in a process. I will use the terms process and system interchangeably.

These flows of a process form a network, another topic in OR. Hand-offs from one business unit to another, say during a business planning cycle, is an example. There may be a stochastic element involved with the hand-off processes (e.g., one department could be late in completing its part of the plan, thus delaying all the downstream departments), but this is not the focus of a simulation. The focus is on understanding the flows through the network. In a large enterprise, they can obviously be very intricate, and confusing, to say the least. Simulations of this type are referred to as *system dynamic simulations*. See Paczkowski (2023) and Forrester (1968).

The interesting feature of simulations is that they can be used in conjunction with other Prescriptive Analytical methods as well as, of course, standing on their own. I prefer to view them as an adjunct to the others, especially mathematical programming. The real strength of simulations is that they allow you to introduce a stochastic element into your analysis, even if the underlying Prescriptive Analytic methodology is not stochastic. This is important because in many applications, unknown and unknowable factors suddenly "make an appearance" in a process a decision-maker has to deal with. These are random factors. A simulation that includes or accounts for these random factors can help them prepare for all possibilities or outcomes of their decisions.

Finally, there are problems that require data to solve them, but data do not exist. This situation can be handled by *synthesizing* the data. Synthesizing is a form of simulation. The synthesized data can then be used with, say, what-if analysis or machine learning methods to solve the problem. I will discuss data synthesizing in Chapter 9.

Decision trees

There is a methodology missing from the descriptions I provided earlier: *decision trees*. This is in the broader class of *Decision Analytics* in OR.

Decision trees are a powerful visual tool for understanding the logical path from one part of a complex decision to another. The path is displayed as a tree diagram with a starting point, say the time when a decision is made, and tree-like branches emanating from it in directions based on the decision. The starting point is called the *root* and the branches are, well, *branches*. Each branch terminates in a *node* or *leaf*. The terminating nodes form the decision menu.

Any of the paths down a tree from the root to a leaf defines a rule. The rule is the logic to arrive at a leaf. This means that decision trees are in the class of Logic-based models.

The strength of a decision tree is not so much the visualization, although this is a benefit for identifying a rule, but the inclusion of the probability of following each branch of the tree. The probabilities are based on beliefs and take the form of *Bayesian Probabilities*. These are used as weights to calculate the weighted or *expected value* of a KPM at each point in the development of a tree. It is the resulting set of expected values that helps a decision-maker select from a menu.

I will discuss decision trees in Chapter 6.

Umbrella Classes: Non-Stochastic and Stochastic

Because of random factors, I prefer to divide the Prescriptive Analytics methods into two broad categories: non-stochastic and stochastic.

The first consists of Mathematical Programming and Decision Tree methods. The second consists of probabilistically-based methods. Simulations tie them together. I will, nonetheless, for expository purposes, initially treat them as separate. But then I will combine them because, in reality, they are combined to solve a problem.

Definition of Non-Stochastic and Stochastic Methods

If I am going to divide Prescriptive Analytic methodologies into non-stochastic and stochastic parts, I should define what these are to avoid confusion.

A non-stochastic method used in a process does not directly incorporate randomness. Randomness, however, is inherent in your data since all data are fundamentally random. Recall that

$$Data = Information + Noise$$

where $Noise$ is random variation due to unknown and unknowable causes. You may be able to speculate about it, but ultimately you reach a point where you cannot speculate anymore; that is the $Noise$.

The methods I include in this category do not rely on data randomness such as $Noise$. Examples of non-stochastic methodologies I will discuss are in the class of Mathematical Programming and Decision Trees which yield a set of decision rules. I have found these to be the most useful non-stochastic categories of Prescriptive Analytical methodologies. I will discuss mathematical programming methods in Chapter 5 and decision trees in Chapter 6.

A stochastic method explicitly acknowledges and uses random variations. A classic example is Monte Carlo simulation. This involves generating numerous random draws from a probability distribution. The result of each draw is used in a calculation. The entire collection of calculated values is analyzed, perhaps with other statistical methods, to eventually solve the problem at best or shed more light on it for further work at a minimum. The randomness due to the draws is over and beyond any in the data per se. For example, I do not consider OLS to be a stochastic method for curve fitting since the formulas for calculating the intercept and slopes are deterministic. You could apply a Monte Carlo simulation to the formulas, however, in which case the combined approach—curve fitting and Monte Carlo—is stochastic. I will provide an example of this combination in Chapter 8.

Examples Based on Scale-Views

The approach you use depends on the scale-view of the decision-maker in a process. The operational scale-view involves day-to-day decisions, many of which are routine and similar, if not identical, to those made the day before or the week before. In short, there is little variation in problems in operational processes and how they are handled. Machines do randomly fail, supply chain disruptions randomly occur, and random employee events such as illnesses, slow-downs, and strikes occur, but these are self-contained within the operation problem itself and are not uncommon or unknown to the operational manager; they have daily experience with them. For these, non-stochastic methods, such as in the Mathematical Programming class, are appropriate. In fact, many of the examples of mathematical programming are operational in nature: machine scheduling, delivery scheduling, sales force allocation, and so forth. This is not to say that stochastic elements do not play a role in these applications; they do. However, it is safe to say that the primary focus is on allocation and selection from a menu.

The tactical scale-view is at a level midway between operational and strategic, with features of both. This scale-view is concerned with an external environment which includes its customers (current and potential), market dynamics due to its competitors, and, to a lesser degree, legal and regulatory actions by government agencies. There are stochastic situations and unknowns to deal with that are not normal, day-to-day actions. Planning and execution are dominant at this level: planning a new advertising campaign or promotion; planning a price level change (which includes the new price point and how to communicate that change to customers); the introduction of a new product or product line; and so on. Everything could be adversely impacted by random conditions in the market. For example, a major competitor could suddenly, unexpectedly offer a new, superior product. Stochastic Prescriptive Analytic methods are more appropriate for this scale-view level.

Finally, the strategic scale-view is a wider, more encompassing view of the business. This is the view of the various *C-level* managers for their particular domains. Examples are the Chief Operating Officer (COO or President), Chief Marketing Officer (CMO), the Chief Pricing Officer (CPO), and the Chief Research Officer (CRO) responsible for R&D. The CEO is certainly at this level making decisions about enterprise structure such as mergers and acquisitions, divestitures, organization, legal, and personnel (i.e., head-count). A combination of non-stochastic and stochastic methods is appropriate for these problems. At this level, and sometimes at the tactical level, multiple plans are developed, what I previously referred to as *Most Likely Views* (i.e., a menu), and the decision-makers must choose one of them. Integer programming is useful for this, but not necessarily with a stochastic component. I will discuss integer programming in "Integer Programming" on page 162.

There are further implications of a scale-views perspective. There are not just three, but a continuum of scale-views because every manager has some input and some degree of responsibility for operations, tactics, and strategy. This results in a spectrum of decision dimensions and types.

Decision dimensions are *unidimensional* or *multidimensional*. A unidimensional decision has only one implication. For example, I will later discuss job assignments (see Chapter 5) where the only implication is which employee will work where at any moment. A multidimensional decision has multiple *I&Rs* that are far-reaching with big impacts. A decision to merge with another company is an example because of the implications on personnel, shareholder value, company goals, key stakeholders (e.g., the supply chain constituents), customers, regulators, and so forth. All these must be considered, hence the multidimensions. *Decision types* are routine or highly specialized as I already discussed. I illustrate these aspects of scale-views in Figure 2-6. Although there is a scale-views continuum, I will only mention the three —operational, tactical, and strategic—in most of this book.

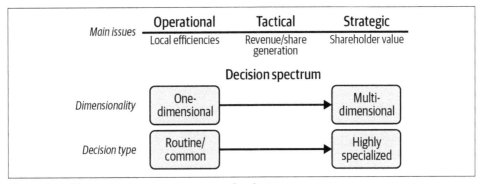

Figure 2-6. *The scale-views continuum and a decision spectrum.*

The Role of Operations Research

A major feature of Prescriptive Analytics that I stress is the use of and reliance on OR methods to optimize the selection from the decision menu. A leading OR textbook (Hillier and Lieberman (2010, p. 3)) states very emphatically:

> OR frequently attempts to search for a best solution (referred to as an optimal solution) for the model that represents the problem under consideration....Rather than

simply improving the status quo, the goal is to identify a best possible course of action. Although it must be interpreted carefully in terms of the practical needs of management, this "search for optimality" is an important theme in OR.

This "search for optimality" involves finding the best menu item consistent with the enterprise's goals and objectives.

A perusal of the contents of this textbook, and others such as Winston (2004), shows the scope of topics such as:

- Game theory
- Decision analysis
- Queueing theory
- Inventory analysis
- Markov decision processes

These suggest a decision orientation for OR. This orientation is important for Prescriptive Analytics. In fact, I propose that OR and Prescriptive Analytics are the same and I will approach the latter this way. Regarding the above five-point list, I will at least mention some of them in this book, but detailed coverage of them is best handled by an OR textbook such as the ones I referenced.

Summary

A main result of this chapter is the description of a set of methodologies, and their relationships, used in Prescriptive Analytics. I narrowed this list to a few which I categorized as non-stochastic and stochastic. They have their roots in the highly mathematical field called Operations Research. The two categories form the structure of this book.

The main concepts from this chapter are:

- Non-stochastic
- Stochastic
- Operations Research

PART II

Essential Background Material

This part of the book contains material needed for the rest of this book: Python essentials and probability essentials.

I include these because the material in both is used throughout this book and because they form the backbone of much done in Prescriptive Analytics. In fact, they are heavily used in all three analytics: Descriptive, Predictive, and Prescriptive. So you should have a good background in both. You can skip this part if you already know and understand how to use Python and are comfortable with basic probability theory.

Since the subtitle for this book is "Optimizing Your Decisions with Python,"" I will review the key features of Python in a Python primer. This book emphasizes practicality, not theory, so hands-on Python applications will be provided. I will only skim the surface of Python; anything in more detail and depth would require its own book, which would probably be encyclopedic. Consequently, you should not feel lost if you are not conversant in the basics of the Python programming language and infrastructure. Everything will be developed in a JupyterLab notebook.

As I mentioned, I review basic probability concepts in this part. A major probability theorem, Bayes' Theorem, is developed and illustrated. The concept of a prior probability is introduced to reflect or capture a subjective view of the chance of something happening. This is important because the probabilities used in Prescriptive Analytics are subjective.

There are two primer chapters in this part:

- Chapter 3, "Python Essentials"
- Chapter 4, "Probability Essentials"

CHAPTER 3
Python Essentials

I focus on applications in this book. These are restricted to the business domain reflecting my background, but the ideas and concepts can be applied equally well to the public domain. So you should broadly interpret the word "application."

Regardless of the domain, software is needed for applications since computers are used everywhere in our modern technology-driven world and are run by software. To do any credible analytical work as a data scientist, you not only need software capable of doing it, but you also need an understanding of how to use it.

My software of choice is Python. I will discuss the reasons for this in "Python Structure: Overview" on page 64. Then, I will review the Python language in the remainder of this chapter. The leading questions for this chapter are:

1. Why use Python for data science?
2. What are Python's advantages?
3. What are packages?
4. How do you use packages in Python?
5. What is Best Practices?
6. What are data containers in Python?
7. What are the main data types and containers in Python?
8. How do you process data in Python?
9. What are some key Python functions and their use in data science?
10. How can you create your own Python functions?
11. What is the most efficient way to access and use Python for data science?

Since I use Python in this book, this chapter will provide you with some basic material to get you started. Many of the Python tools discussed here will be illustrated throughout this book. I will provide references in this chapter for more details on the Python language if you want to learn more.

Python Structure: Overview

I use Python for six reasons. These are equally important without one superseding the others, so there is no order to my list. Python:

- Has a worldwide community of supporters
- Has a large and rich array of support packages that extend its capabilities
- Is easy to learn and use
- Runs on many operating system platforms
- Is programmable
- Is free

Worldwide Community

Many data scientists have adopted Python since its creation by Guido van Rossum in the late 1980s and its subsequent introduction in 1991. A worldwide community of users has evolved which contributes to its development and expansion. The Python release is 3.12.3 as of May 27, 2024. They not only add to the language, but also provide support and training for anyone with problems. This is extremely important because you always have someone, or a group, to turn to for help. And they all are willing to help. You are not alone. Stack Overflow, for example, has a section for Python where users and developers ask questions. As of April 2023, there were 2,198,855 questions posted and addressed.[1] I personally know how beneficial this is because I use it extensively in my own work.

Extensive Array of Packages

All modern software is built on a package model. A *package* is a collection of programs with a common theme and focus that extends the capabilities and functionalities of the main program. For example, there could be one for data visualization, regression modeling, data management, and so on. Each package, regardless of the software or language, is self-contained meaning that everything you need is part of it.

---

1 As of May 27, 2024. Stack Overflow (*https://stackoverflow.co/*) is a website platform where users and developers can help each other by exchanging their expertise. There is a Python page on Stack Overflow (*https://stackoverflow.com/questions/tagged/python*).

This includes links to the main software for anything needed to expand the package's functionality.

Python relies on packages. It has an extensive and growing set in general programming, data management, statistical analysis, machine learning, and many other areas. Some are intimately connected so that you can seamlessly pass your data from one package to another without worrying about your underlying data.

Packages in Python are called *packages* or *libraries*. I prefer "package." Subcomponents of a package, individual programs comprising a package, are *modules*, although I sometimes refer to them as "subpackages." Subpackages provide their own functionalities.

Easy to Use

Python was originally designed for ease-of-use with a syntax close to a human language syntax. This is embodied in what has become known as *The Zen of Python*, originally listed by Tim Peters (see Peters [2023]):

> Beautiful is better than ugly.
> Explicit is better than implicit.
> Simple is better than complex.
> Complex is better than complicated.
> Flat is better than nested.
> Sparse is better than dense.
> Readability counts.
> Special cases aren't special enough to break the rules.
> Although practicality beats purity.
> Errors should never pass silently.
> Unless explicitly silenced.
> In the face of ambiguity, refuse the temptation to guess.
> There should be one—and preferably only one—obvious way to do it.
> Although that way may not be obvious at first unless you're Dutch.
> Now is better than never.
> Although never is often better than "right" now.
> If the implementation is hard to explain, it's a bad idea.
> If the implementation is easy to explain, it may be a good idea.
> Namespaces are one honking great idea—let's do more of those!

Operating Systems

Python runs on the three most popular platforms: Linux, Mac, and Windows. This is important because everything you write or develop is portable across them.

A Programming Language

Python is a programming language. A Python program is called a *script*. This can be kept in a text file editable with any text editor such as Notepad or Notepad++ (my preferred editor) on a Windows computer, or TextEdit or Atom on a Mac.

The file extension for a script file is *.py*, although any text-identifying extension, such as *.txt*, can be used. However, *.py* is conventional, plus it signifies to Python that the file is a Python script with Python commands and is to be treated as such. The *.py* extension is also read as a Python program by the Windows operating system which will automatically call Python. In fact, Windows does this automatically for a large number of built-in extensions plus the ones you specify. For example, it will automatically open a text editor when it sees *.txt*.

You need to know the minimal basics of computer languages to effectively use Python for your projects, just as you need to know the basics of any spoken language such as English, French, Chinese, and so forth. Python's advantage over other computer languages is that its basic structure is simple to master which means you can almost immediately begin using it. It has, of course, many deep nuances and complexities as does any language, computer or spoken, that make it a rich and powerful language.

As a programming language, Python has all the logic found in any programming language such as C#, C++, Java, Fortran, and so on. This includes *for* and *while* loops; *if* statements for logical, conditional testing; and function definitions. There is also an extensive input-output system, although you will most likely use a package, pandas, to handle data import and export because its data management functionality is more flexible, intuitive, and extensive. I will discuss pandas later.

Python's programmability actually has a side benefit missing from other languages: it has a definite "Pythonista" way of programming. A major one, seemingly trivial, is indentation. There are operations that all programming languages implement, such as *for* and *if* statements to perform certain operations. The implementations, of course, differ. Some use brackets, parentheses, or braces to delineate the components of one of these operating statements from others, one at the beginning of a block of programming statements (i.e., *code*) and another at the end. This can be confusing, but, more importantly, it can be cumbersome because you will inevitably omit one of the delimiters (usually an ending one) causing an error. You then have to spend your time tracking down that error. In Python, indentations are used to form blocks of code making it clear which statements go with which operation. The standard indentation is four spaces. Many, if not all, of the programming environments for Python, called *integrated development environments* (IDE), will automatically indent these four spaces for you as a standard. The IDE I use and will use for this book is *JupyterLab*. I will comment on this environment later.

It Is Free

Finally, Python is free. This is often used as a strong "selling point" because so many other software products are licensed, meaning you pay for them. Some are inexpensive, but many are quite expensive which is a definite hindrance to their use. For the power, support, and usability of Python, the value is definitely there.

Python Basics

When you speak or write in another language, such as French, German, or Chinese, you have to translate your thoughts and your words into that language. You can, obviously, do your own translations by mastering the language, and you can do them very well the more fluent you become. You may also use someone else, a translator, to do it for you. There are even programs that will do the translations, such as Google Translate, DeepL, Alexa Translations, and Microsoft Translator to mention just a few. See McFarland (2024) for a review of AI translators.

Just as we need a language to communicate with other people, so you also need a language to communicate with your computer. And this communication with a computer also requires a translation. In this case, the translation is from a high-level human language, regardless if it is English, French, German, or Chinese, into *machine language*. For our purpose, there are two levels of computer languages: low and high.

A high-level language is what we read and write. Sometimes, I have to admit, it may be a bit arcane. This is the case for C#, C++, Java, and Fortran to name a few. Nonetheless, you can look at something written in one of them and understand it (maybe). Python is a high-level language that is actually easy for humans to read and write, which is a major advantage over other high-level languages.

A low-level language is what the computer understands, and is largely unintelligible to you and me. There are several gradations to low-level languages, but the lowest is machine language itself. This is what the heart of a computer really understands and what it uses to think (i.e., do computations). All computers know this language.

What is machine language? The answer is complicated, but fundamentally it is a language comprised solely of 0s and 1s: it is a *binary language*. Everything a computer does is based on a series of 0 and 1 values, the particular arrangement of which has meaning to the computer. And, very importantly, with the correct interpretation, has meaning to us through our high-level language, whatever that may be. There may be some intermediate translations of high-level to machine-level language, but that is not important for you at this stage.

The translation is done by a *compiler* or an *interpreter*. Compilers translate an entire human-readable program before execution and produce an *executable program* indicated by the *.exe* file extension. The translation is done once and the executable can be repeatedly used by you for different problems (with the appropriate inputs, of course). Examples are C++, Java, and Fortran. Interpreters, on the other hand, translate and execute human-readable programs one line at a time. They are, thus, interactive; compilers are not. Python is an *interpreted language* which means it will execute commands immediately. I illustrate the translation process in Figure 3-1.

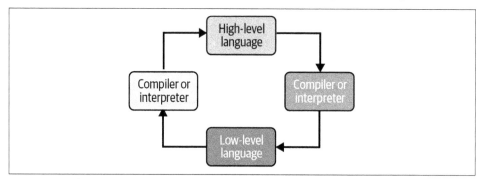

Figure 3-1. The translation from a high-level human-understandable language (e.g., English) to a low-level computer language (i.e., machine language).

An interpreter operates by accepting a script (a Python script in our case) and then performs three operations. It:

1. Checks for errors in the script code (validation function)
2. Compiles or translates the submitted code into an intermediate language for the compute (translation function)
3. Runs that intermediate language (execution function)

I depict this workflow in Figure 3-2 which is modeled after Hunt (2020).

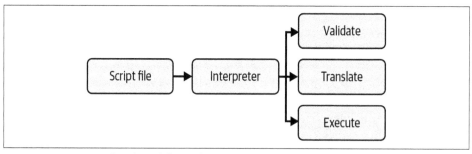

Figure 3-2. A generalized workflow of a computer interpreter.

Normally, an interpreter is used interactively via a *Read-Execute-Print-Loop* (REPL) strategy. This involves reading a human-based command, one command at a time, either from a text file (with the extension *.py* for Python) or from a terminal; executing each command as it is read; printing or displaying results; and then looping back to read the next command. This looping involves operating on one command at a time, which may seem cumbersome and inefficient, but the program code is optimized to quickly process the input lines (which are called *records*). In fact, except for very long and complicated programs, you will never notice delays in processing a script using an interpretative language.

The Python interpreter uses this REPL setup. Consequently, in addition to performing very complex operations, it can also perform simple, almost trivial ones. For example, you can use the Python interpreter to do simple arithmetic, although this is an abuse of its power and functionality. I show an example of this in Figure 3-3 using the basic built-in math operations I list in Table 3-1. The built-in operators are automatically loaded when you start a Python installation so you do not do anything more than start Python. The Python math package has more math operations which I illustrate throughout this book.

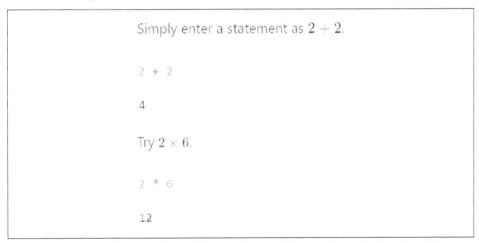

Figure 3-3. How Python can be used for simple calculations. But using Python this way is overkill. The shaded areas are code cells where you enter commands (e.g., 2 + 2). The result (e.g., 4) is displayed in a cell immediately below.

Table 3-1. The math operations built into Python. More are available from the math package.

Operation	Operator	Example	Result
Addition	+	2 + 2	4
Subtraction	−	5 − 3	2
Multiplication	*	3 * 6	18
Division	/	8/4	2
Modulo (Remainder)	%	9%2	1
Division Quotient	//	9//2	4
Quotient & Remainder	divmod(number, divisor)	divmod(9, 2)	(4, 1)
Power	* *	2 * * 3	8
Power	pow(number, power)	pow(2, 3)	8
Absolute Value	abs(number)	abs(- 5)	5

The operators in Table 3-1 are really functions although you may not think of them that way. A *function* takes *arguments* and returns a result. The +, −, and several others may not seem like functions because you are used to using them in your everyday calculations, but they are functions, nonetheless. The operators divmod, pow, and abs may appear more like functions because they have arguments. I will discuss functions later. For now, all functions return something.

There are several ways to add, subtract, multiply, and divide in Python. For example, you could use $x +$ = 2 rather than $x = x + 2$. In the first example, x is implicitly returned, while it is explicitly returned in the second. Similarly, you could use $x −$ = 2, $x *$ = 2, $x/$ = 2, and $x * *$ = 2. These functions are sometimes more efficient and easier to understand. See Table 3-3.

A *scalar* is returned for operator functions like +. A scalar is a single number such as 2 or 3.14159. It could be an integer, such as 2, or a floating point number such as 2.0 or 3.14159. Real numbers are represented as floating point numbers (or *floats*) in Python. The decimal is said to "float" because these numbers can be written in scientific notation. Floats are distinctive in that they have a fractional part to the right of the decimal point, while integers do not so there is no decimal. If the Python interpreter detects a decimal, it treats the number as a float; otherwise, it treats it as an integer.

You can have the Python interpreter reassign or *cast* integers to floats and floats to integers. To cast a float to an integer, use the int function; to cast an integer to a float, use the *float* function. I show two examples in Figure 3-4. Notice that 3.14159 is returned as 3 without a decimal part while 2 is returned as 2.0. I will tell you later how to check the data types.

```
1  ##
2  ## Convert 3.14159 to be an integer
3  ##
4  int( 3.14159 )
5

   3
1  ##
2  ## Convert 2, an integer, to a float
3  ##
4  float( 2 )
5

   2.0
```

Figure 3-4. It is easy to convert integers to floats and vice-versa. This illustrates how you can do these two conversions.

You will occasionally receive what you will perceive to be numeric data, but the data are surrounded by quotation marks (single or double). For example, "3.14159." The Python interpreter interprets this as a character string, even though it looks like a number. This happens because of the quotation marks. Strings are handled differently than numbers in Python (and most languages). So you cannot do numerical operations on them because they are not numbers.

All character strings (e.g., "3.14159", "Moe", "Larry", "Curly") are surrounded by quotation marks, either single or double. The quotation marks must match at the beginning and end.

You can cast this string into a float using the `float` function. So `float( "3.14159" )` returns 3.14159. Similarly, you can cast "2" to an integer using `int( "2" )`. However, if you try `int( "2.0" )` you will get an error message. Instead, use `int( float( "2.0" ) )`.

You may also want to do the reverse. For example, cast 3.14159 as a string with `str( 3.14159 )`.

The functions `float`, `int`, and `str` are called *built-in functions*. They are part of Python, which means they are automatically available to you when you start Python.

Naming Conventions

There are several recommended naming conventions that Python users and developers follow, more or less:

- Use lowercase
- Use descriptive names rather than x or y
  - An exception: i and j in looping constructs. This is a holdover from legacy programming languages such as Fortran.
- Separate words by underscores for readability
  - For a name such as "user name," the space is treated as a separator, so Python thinks there are two things "user" and "name." Use "user_name" instead.

Using Camel Case Names

I frequently use *camelCase* with the words run together and the first letter of each word capitalized, except for the first word. Some people capitalize all the words. I recommend you use the *camelCase* for enhanced readability. See Wikipedia (2023b).

 Be aware that Python is case-sensitive. This means that "statistics," "Statistics," "STATISTICS," etc., are all different to the Python interpreter. So watch the case!

See Hunt (2020, p. 28), from which this is based, for more discussion about naming conventions

Python Data Structures

The simple functions I listed in Table 3-1 return scalars, except for divmod. A scalar is the simplest data object, while the returned object for divmod is a more complex one. Python has several complex objects, some of which are *containers*,[2] you need to be aware of. These containers are:[3]

---

2 Hunt (2020, Chapter 31) uses this term. It is an appropriate descriptor.

3 I list three containers. There is a fourth: sets. I rarely use this form.

- Tuples
- Lists
- Dictionaries

I will describe these in the following subsections.

Tuples

A *tuple* is an ordered collection of objects or elements (terms I use interchangeably), such as numbers or strings, each separated by a comma and the entire collection surrounded or delimited by parentheses. The Python interpreter interprets a collection as a tuple once it sees the opening and closing parentheses around the collection, so these are important. The object returned by *divmod* in Table 3-1 is a tuple, sometimes called a *two-tuple* because it has two elements, with the (fixed) order of quotient and remainder from a division: (4, 1) in Table 3-1.

If you want a collection to be interpreted as a tuple, be sure to use opening and closing parentheses.

A tuple could contain other structures such as another tuple, a list, or a dictionary. So you could have a three-tuple such as (*4, 1, ("cat", "dog"))* which has three elements: 4, 1 and a two-tuple.

The location of an object in a tuple is given by that object's index. Python is a zero-based indexing language meaning that locations, such as in a tuple, begin with location 0, followed by location 1, etc. You can interpret the index number as the distance or *offset* from the first element of the tuple. So the first object is at index 0 since it is offset zero elements from the beginning; the second is offset by one from the beginning so its index is 1; and so forth.

You access an element using its location inside square brackets. For the divmod example in Table 3-1, if you name the tuple x so that $x = (4,1)$, then you access the "4" using x[0] and the "1" using x[1]. The values in the square brackets are said to *point to* the element's location in the tuple. So x[1] points to the element in location 1 which is in the second position; it is offset by one spot from the beginning. This is confusing at times because of the zero-based positioning Python uses and errors are always possible. Unfortunately, many languages use a zero-based system, so it is very common.

Remember that indexing starts with 0 since Python is zero-based. The index indicates the offset from the first element.

You can access several consecutive elements using the notation *start:end* where *start* is the place you want to begin and *end* is *up to but not including* where you want to end. This *end* is, therefore, tricky and another source of confusion—and errors. The last element you want is actually one place *before* the position specified by *end*; the element in the *end* position is *not* returned. So if $x = (4,1,5,2)$, a four-tuple, then x[1:3] returns the two-tuple (1, 5) even though the "3" points to the "2". See Figure 3-5 for an example.

```
1  ##
2  ## Define a 4-element tuple
3  ##
4  tup = ( 4, 1, 5, 2 )
5  tup
6

   (4, 1, 5, 2)

1  ##
2  ## Slice out the elements 1 to 2 from x: note how this is specified
3  ##
4  tup[ 1:3 ]
5

   (1, 5)
```

Figure 3-5. How to extract a slice of elements from a tuple. Notice that the returned values are in a tuple with only two elements. The slicing indicator includes the first, or start, element but only goes up to and does not include the end element.

[1:3] is a *slice* starting at the 2nd element (i.e., the first offset from the beginning) up to (*but not including*) the 3rd element. If either index is missing, then that indicates the start or end of the tuple, respectively. Remember that the end value listed in a slice is one place more than where you actually want to stop.

Once a tuple is created, it cannot be changed by altering the elements; you cannot reorder them, add a new one, or delete one. You may be tempted to say that a tuple is useless because of this immutability, but this is actually a strength. You will frequently depend on a tuple simply because you do not want the elements to change.

A tuple is fixed or *immutable*.

Lists

A list is a mutable container that can hold any type of element, including another list. Unlike a tuple, you can add, delete, and modify its elements. Also, unlike a tuple, the order of the objects is unimportant. You can access a list's elements the same way as for a tuple. I show examples in Figure 3-6. You will see many applications of lists in this book.

```
1  ##
2  ## Create a list
3  ##
4  lst = [ 'Moe', 'Larry', 'Curly' ]
5  lst
6

   ['Moe', 'Larry', 'Curly']

1  ##
2  ## Access the element in the third position
3  ##
4  lst[ 2 ]
5

   'Curly'

1  ##
2  ## Slice out the first two elements
3  ##
4  lst[ 0:2 ]
5

   ['Moe', 'Larry']
```

Figure 3-6. How to create, access, and extract a slice of elements from a list.

 As for a tuple, [1:3] indicates a slice of a list starting at the 2nd element up to (but not including) the 3rd element. If either is missing, then that indicates the start or end of the list, respectively.

There are several ways to create a list:

- Simply place the list items inside square brackets, each item separated by a comma. For example, you create a list as lst = [1, 2, 3]. The square brackets tell the Python interpreter this collection is a list.

- Use a `for` loop to populate a list using an `append` method. This, unfortunately, can be inefficient if the `for` loop becomes large. The program could also become difficult to read and interpret. I will describe `for` loops later.

- Use a *list comprehension*, in many instances the best and most recommended way to create a list. A list comprehension has the basic list structure of square brackets. However, a comma-separated list of objects is not inside the brackets. Instead, you write a series of programming statements that the interpreter executes in a manner like a `for` loop (which I have yet to describe). The statements are in order:

    `[expression for item in iterable if condition == True]`.

The expression could be any Python command or operation. This could be as simple as the `print` function or as complex as a math calculation. The *iterable* is a Python object that allows you to iterate over something. For example, you can iterate over a range of values from 0 up to *but not including* 10 (the "not including" is important) using a single function: `range( 10 )`. This function might be written as `list( range( 10 ) )` for the list of values [0, 1, 2, 3, 4, 5, 6, 7, 8, 9] where the keyword `list` instructs the interpreter to create a list. More complex iterables are available. Notice that this list has 10 elements: 0 - 9.

The *condition* statement uses a double equal sign for "equal to." The reason is that a single equal sign is interpreted as "assign," which is a different operation. Finally, *True* is a keyword if the condition is true. The opposite is *False*. Note the capitalizations.

I provide an example list comprehension in Figure 3-7. I will illustrate list comprehensions in Chapter 4 when I create fictitious data. You will also see me use it throughout this book.

```
1  ##
2  ## Create list comprehension and print the list
3  ##
4  lst = [ x + 1 for x in range( 4 ) ]  ## range produces 0, 1, 2, 3
5  print( lst )
6

   [1, 2, 3, 4]
```

Figure 3-7. How to create a list using a list comprehension. The `range` function iteratively produces the values 0, 1, 2, 3 and puts them in the variable x. Notice that 4 is excluded. The expression x + 1 adds 1 to x. The resulting list is then printed.

The range function is very powerful and useful. Its basic structure is

```
range( start, stop, step )
```

where "start" is an optional integer specifying where to begin (the default is 0); "stop" is a required integer number specifying where to stop (BUT the actual stopping point is one before this value; the stopping value is NOT included or returned); and "step" is an optional integer specifying the increments (the default is 1). So range(10) starts at 0, stops at 9, and increments by 1.

If you want a collection to be interpreted as a list, be sure to use opening and closing square brackets regardless of how you create it.

Dictionaries

A dictionary (or dict) is a container with *key:value* pairs as associations. A *key* is a unique label or identifier for the values which do not have to be unique. In this respect, a Python dictionary is like a vocabulary dictionary where a word is unique and has a definition (perhaps several in a list) associated with it.

A Python dictionary is like a Python list in that the objects, the *key:value* pairs, are not in any order. A dictionary is also mutable so you can add, delete, and modify its objects.

You create a dictionary by specifying the *key:value* pairs in curly brackets. So you create the dictionary X_{dict} as X_{dict} = { 'X1' : 10, 'X2' : 3, 'X3' : [1, 2, 3] }. Notice that the last object is a list. You can also create a new dictionary using a dictionary comprehension similar to a list comprehension. I will illustrate dictionary comprehensions in later chapters.

If you want a collection to be interpreted as a dictionary, be sure to use opening and closing curly brackets. Also, to avoid an error, the *key:value* pairs must be separated by a colon with the key on the left and the value on the right.

Finally, you can access the values in a dictionary using the associated key. This is done using either the square bracket, which you saw for tuples and lists, or a special function: get( ). I show several examples in Figure 3-8.

```
1  ##
2  ## Create a dictionary
3  ##
4  X = { 'X1': 10, 'X2': 3, 'X3':[ 1, 2, 3 ] }
5  X
6
```

{'X1': 10, 'X2': 3, 'X3': [1, 2, 3]}

```
1  ##
2  ## Access the second element of the dictionary
3  ##
4  X[ 'X2' ]
5
```

3

```
1  ##
2  ## Access the list in the dictionary
3  ##
4  X[ 'X3' ]
5
```

[1, 2, 3]

```
1  ##
2  ## Access the second element (position 1) in the list container in the dictionary
3  ##
4  X[ 'X3' ][ 2 ]
5
```

3

```
1  ##
2  ## Access the third element using the get function
3  ##
4  X.get( 'X3' )
5
```

[1, 2, 3]

Figure 3-8. How to create, access, and extract a slice of elements from a dictionary.

Iterables

A major feature of Python is the *iterables*. An iterable, which I introduced previously, is an object that you can iterate or loop over. The looping is built into its structure. Tuples, lists, dictionaries, and the range function are iterables.

Basic Python Operators

Python has an array of fundamental operators similar to those you might know from other software, such as spreadsheets. Two classes are arithmetic and comparison. I list several of the former in Table 3-1 and the latter in Table 3-2. There is also a series of shortcut operators that are more efficient to use, and provide more readable code, than their not-so-short counterparts. I show these in Table 3-3. See Hunt (2020) for more discussion.

Table 3-2. The standard comparison operators in Python. Notice that equality uses a double-equal sign. A double sign is used because a single equals sign represents assignment.

Comparison	Operator	Example
Equality	==	$x == y$
Inequality (not equal)	!=	$x != y$
Greater than	>	$x > y$
Less than	<	$x < y$
Greater than or equal to	>=	$x >= y$
Less than or equal to	<=	$x <= y$

Table 3-3. Shortcut operators for routine calculations. For example, it is very common to write x = x + 1 as part of a for loop, but using x += 1 is more efficient. This expression means: add 1 to x and the set x equal to the sum.

Operation	Operator	Example	Equivalence
Increment by value	+=	$x += 2$	$x = x + 2$
Decrement by value	-=	$x -= 2$	$x = x - 2$
Multiply by a value	*=	$x *= 2$	$x = x * 2$
Divide by a value	/=	$x /= 2$	$x = x / 2$
Integer divide by a value	//=	$x //= 2$	$x = x // 2$
Modulus	\%=	$x \%= 2$	$x = x \% 2$
Exponentiate	**=	$x **= 3$	$x = x ** 3$

Introduction to Built-In Functions

Python is rich with built-in functions. A function takes an argument(s), processes it (them) following the instructions (i.e., the Python code) defined in the body of the function, and returns a result. The arguments are indicated by position or name in a list after the function name, with the list enclosed in parentheses.

A slew of built-in functions[4] is made available to you when you start a Python session; you do not have to import them. Out of all the available functions, there are four that I have found particularly useful and that you will see me use throughout this book:

- `enumerate`
- `round`
- `print`
- `range`

---

4 See the Python documentation (*https://docs.python.org/3/library/functions.html*) for a list with links.

Remember, if you use the range function, be sure to not capitalize, or it will produce an error.

enumerate

The enumerate function operates on iterables such as a list or a tuple and returns its elements and their location in the iterable. The returned object is a two-tuple with the element's location as the first element and the element itself as the second. For instance, if lst = ["Moe", "Larry", "Curly"], then enumerate returns the tuples (0, "Moe"), (1, "Larry"), (2, "Curly"). This is used in a for loop, which I will discuss later. See Figure 3-9 for an example.

```
1  ##
2  ## Use of enumerate
3  ##
4  lst = [ "Moe", "Larry", "Curly" ]
5  for x in enumerate( lst ):
6      print( x )
7

(0. 'Moe')
(1. 'Larry')
(2. 'Curly')
```

Figure 3-9. An example of the enumerate function.

round

The round function simply rounds a float to however many decimal places you want. For example, if you use the math package to display π, you would see 3.141592653589793. Obviously, all the decimal values are unnecessary; two is sufficient. You can use round(math.pi, 2) to get this. In general, the integer following the comma is the number of decimal places displayed. The general call is round(*num ber*, decimals = None). If the number of decimals is omitted (the default is *None*), then the number input is rounded to the nearest integer. You can see an application in Figure 3-11.

print

The print function does exactly what its name says: it prints. Specifically, it prints to your monitor. This will probably be the most used function in your Python toolkit. You can see from some of my examples that I use it extensively. The function is very flexible beyond what my examples show. In my examples, I just print a number, or some text, or, as in Figure 3-9, a series of tuples.

You could print clarifying text along with whatever else you want to print. For example, you could have Python code to calculate the square of a number, say 5, and then print it with a message to clarify the result (obviously 25). You do this by passing to the print function a string preceded by the letter *f*, a single or double quote, the message, then the calculation result enclosed in curly brackets, and ending with a matching single or double quote. The *f* indicates to the interpreter that what follows is a formatted string literal or *f-string*. Any expression enclosed in curly brackets will be evaluated if needed and displayed. I show examples in Figures 3-10 and 3-11.

```
1  ##
2  ## Simple print statement
3  ##    Three variations
4  ##
5  n = 5
6  x = n**2
7  print( f'Variation 1: 5 squared equals {x}' )
8  print( f'Variation 2: {n} squared equals {x}' )
9  print( f'Variation 3: {n} squared equals {n**2}' )
10

   Variation 1: 5 squared equals 25
   Variation 2: 5 squared equals 25
   Variation 3: 5 squared equals 25
```

*Figure 3-10. An example of the print function. I show three variations that are worth studying. The last is most efficient because you do not have to previously define "x = n * * 2"; hence, you have shorter code.*

There are times when you want to format a result, perhaps display a float with only two decimal places. You can do this by modifying the object inside the curly brackets to include a colon followed by a formatting code. I provide some examples in Figure 3-11.

```
1  ##
2  ## Formatting print statement
3  ##    Three variations
4  ##
5  print( f'Variation 1: Pi without formatting: {math.pi}' )
6  print( f'Variation 2: Pi with rounding: {round( math.pi, 2 )}' )
7  print( f'Variation 3: Pi with formatting: {math.pi:0.2f}\
8  alternative way to print' )
9

   Variation 1: Pi without formatting: 3.141592653589793
   Variation 2: Pi with rounding: 3.14
   Variation 3: Pi with formatting: 3.14 alternative way to print
```

Figure 3-11. Another example of the print function with formatting. I show three variations that are worth studying. One of them uses the round function with 2 decimal places. The math package is used to get π.

range

The `range` function is an iterable, which means you can iterate over its contents in a `for` loop, a `while` loop, or in a list comprehension as I often do. It creates a series of integers starting at some value, ending at some value, and incrementing by steps you specify. The general call is `range( start, end, step)`. The default for the increment *step* is 1; a zero raises an error. If *start* is omitted, it defaults to 0. I show an example of the `range` function in Figure 3-20. I provide some examples in Figure 3-12.

```
1  ##
2  ## Example range specifications
3  ##
4  print( f'list( range( 5 ) ): {list( range( 5 ) )}' )
5  print( f'list( range( 0 ) ): {list( range( 0 ) )}' )
6  print( f'list( range( 0, 5 ) ): {list( range( 0, 5 ) )}' )
7  print( f'list( range( 1, 5 ) ): {list( range( 1, 5 ) )}' )
8  print( f'list( range( 1, 5, 2 ) ): {list( range( 1, 5, 2 ) )}' )
9

   list( range( 5 ) ): [0, 1, 2, 3, 4]
   list( range( 0 ) ): []
   list( range( 0, 5 ) ): [0, 1, 2, 3, 4]
   list( range( 1, 5 ) ): [1, 2, 3, 4]
   list( range( 1, 5, 2 ) ): [1, 3]
```

Figure 3-12. Some examples of a `range` specification. The `list` function converts the returned range to a list. Otherwise, just an iterable is returned. Notice the example in line 5: it returns an empty list.

Introduction to User-Defined Functions

There will be times when you will want to create your own *user-defined function* to repeatedly reuse programming steps. If you have a set of user-defined functions, you should place them up-front in your JupyterLab notebook so they are easily found. I consider this to be Best Practice for all your data science work. You can also put them into a text file with a *.py* extension and then input that file, also up-front in your JupyterLab notebook. This, unfortunately, begs a question: "How do you create your own functions?"

Creating a function is not difficult. You use the Python command def, which tells the interpreter that the code following it is for a function. Follow this with a function name, an argument list (enclosed in parentheses) if required, and an ending colon. The colon is important because it tells the interpreter that the following lines are the function. The Python statements comprising the function are indented (4 spaces) for readability. Usually, a return statement is included (typically, but not always) as the last line (also typically, but not always) because a function is meant to return something. You could omit a return statement if you merely have your function print a result. You can see the use of this statement in the examples later.

 Be sure to indent the first line after the function definition. Otherwise, the Python interpreter will display an error message.

The argument list contains those variables used by the function, if needed. There are two types: *positional arguments* and *named arguments*.

 Any variable defined inside a user-defined function is said to be *local* to that function. This means it is not related to a similarly named variable elsewhere in your program. So you could have a variable named X in your program and one named X in your function. One will not affect the other. Your function, incidentally, could access a variable in your program that is not in your function. Such a variable is called a *global* variable.

Positional arguments

The function recognizes positional arguments by their position in the list. They must appear in the argument list in that order. Once you define them in your function definition, they are then mandatory in that order. For example, if the argument list is ($X1$, $X2$, $X3$), then the subsequent function code will expect these three variables and expect the value for $X1$ to be in the first position, $X2$ in the second, and $X3$ in the third. If you put the values in the wrong positions, then you will simply get a wrong answer. Position counts. If you omit one of them, you will get an error message. I show an example of positional arguments in Figure 3-13.

```
1   ##
2   ## Define a function
3   ##    Suppose X1 = 2, X2 = 3, X3 = 4
4   ##
5   def exmpl( X1, X2, X3 ):
6       z = X1 * X2 + X3
7       return( z )
8   print( f'Correct answer: {exmpl( 2, 3, 4 )}' )
9   print( f'Incorrect answer: {exmpl( 2, 4, 3)}' )   ## Wrong positions for X2 and X3
10  print( f'Error: {exmpl( 2, 3 )}' )   ## X3 is omitted
11


    Correct answer: 10
    Incorrect answer: 11
    ------------------------------------------------------------------
    TypeError                              Traceback (most recent call last)
    Cell In[9], line 10
        8 print( f'Correct answer: {exmpl( 2, 3, 4 )}' )
        9 print( f'Incorrect answer: {exmpl( 2, 4, 3)}' )   ## Wrong positions for X2 and X3
    ---> 10 print( f'Error: {exmpl( 2, 3 )}' )

    TypeError: exmpl() missing 1 required positional argument: 'X3'
```

Figure 3-13. An example of what happens when the values for variables are in the wrong positions for positional arguments or one is omitted. Notice how the error is highlighted for debugging.

 Remember, position counts for positional arguments.

Named arguments

Named arguments have names for the values passed to the function. These must correspond to those used in the function. You cannot name an argument X and then use $X1$ in the function; an error will result saying that $X1$ is undefined. Unlike positional arguments, the order of named arguments does not matter; only the names matter. I show an example in Figure 3-14.

You could provide default values for some or all of your named arguments. If you provide a default, but then supply a value in the function call, that value will override the default. Otherwise, the default is used. A frequently used default is the Python data type *None*. This is an odd data type because it is not a missing value (i.e., *NaN*, which stands for "not a number") or zero; it is just nothing. You will see examples of its use throughout this book.

```
1   ##
2   ## Define a function with named arguments
3   ##
4   a = 2
5   b = 3
6   c = 4
7   ##
8   def exmpl( X1 = a, X2 = b, X3 = c ):
9       z = X1 * X2 + X3
10      return( z )
11  print( f'Correct answer: {exmpl( X1 = a, X2 = b, X3 = c )}' )
12  print( f'Correct answer: {exmpl( X3 = c, X2 = b, X1 = a )}' )
13

    Correct answer: 10
    Correct answer: 10
```

Figure 3-14. An example of what happens when the arguments are named. Notice that the second print *statement has two arguments in different positions, yet the answer is the same.*

 There is a restriction on the use of positional and named arguments: you can use a mix of both but you cannot put positional arguments after a named argument. Positional arguments come first since position matters. Also, positional arguments cannot have defaults, while named arguments can.

 There is a subtle distinction programmers and developers make between a *parameter* and an *argument* to a function. A parameter is the variable inside the parentheses of the function definition. So for the function list written as (X1 = 3.14), the "X1" is a parameter. An argument is the value associated with the parameter and is what is used inside the function whenever the interpreter sees "X1." For my example, the 3.14 is the argument. Most times, I ignore this fine distinction and use the word "argument."

Conditional Statements: if-else

The *if-else* conditional statement is a very powerful programming tool in general, one found in every language, statistical and otherwise. This very frequently used statement, or set of statements, allows you to test conditions and then proceed one way or another depending on the test result. Although all software has conditional statements, the implementations differ, but not by much. The logic, however, is the same regardless of the implementation.

The structure of the conditional in Python is:

```
if condition:
    statement(s)
elif condition:
    statement(s)
else:
    statement(s)
```

 Be sure to watch your colons and indents. Notice the lower case `if`, `elif`, and `else` keywords. Remember, Python is case sensitive.

The "condition" is a statement that evaluates to either *True* or *False*. Such a statement is called a *Boolean* and has only one of these two values. In all programming languages, a *True* statement is represented as 1 and a *False* as 0, so the condition actually results in a binary. You can use any of the conditional operators in Table 3-2 for the conditional test.

The statements following the `if` line are executed if the condition is True; otherwise, they are skipped. The `elif` is an "else if" follow-up or second condition; you can have as many as you need, and you can certainly not use it. The `else` is a terminal or default; if all else fails, these statements are executed. You could have several `elif` statements; it all depends on your problem.

I show a general flowchart for the conditional statements with only one condition in Figure 3-16, Panel (a) and an example with one `elif` in Figure 3-15. The flowchart of this example is in Figure 3-16, Panel (b).

```
1   ##
2   ## Example of a conditional
3   ##
4   n = 2
5   x = 5
6   ##
7   if x > n:
8       print( f'x > {n}' )
9   elif x < n:
10      print( f'x < {n}' )
11  else:
12      print( f'x = {n}' )
13

    x > 2
```

Figure 3-15. An example of a simple conditional set of statements. They are checking the value of x to determine if it is 2 or not. I show the flowchart for Figure 3-15 in Figure 3-16, Panel (b).

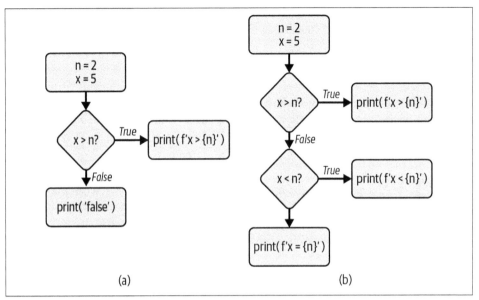

Figure 3-16. Two flowcharts for conditional statements. Panel (a) is a simple example: just one conditional test. Panel (b) is the flowchart for Figure 3-15.

Python Looping Constructs

Python has two constructs to iteratively loop through Python statements and, on each iteration, perform a series of operations. These are +*for*+ *loops* and +*while*+ *loops*.

These are standard in all computer software programs, so their functionality is the same regardless of software. Their implementation, however, will differ.

for loops

Many problems require you to repeatedly, i.e., iteratively, process or execute the same statements. For example, you can process or loop through a list such as [1, 2, 3] and print each element in the list. The simplest, almost brute-force way to do this is to repeat the `print` function three times. That is doable for this small list, but impractical and inefficient for a list of, say, 1,000 elements. A `for` loop is more practical and efficient for handling this.

The structure of a `for` loop is

```
for i in iterable:
    statement(s)
```

Be sure to include the colon and indents. Also, notice the lowercase for keyword. Remember, Python is case sensitive.

The first line of the looping code has several key parts. The keyword for at the beginning of the looping command line alerts the Python interpreter that this is the beginning of a for loop. The symbol "i" is a looping counter variable that automatically increments by 1 for each loop through the statements.

You are not restricted to using i for the loop counter. You can use any symbol or variable name you want. The i is a conventional holdover from legacy Fortran programming.

The *iterable* is a Python object that allows you to iterate over it. The most used iterable is range. The colon at the end of the first line signifies the end of this loop command line. The *statements* on the next line is indented, typically four spaces, and consists of any valid Python statement. The number of statements depends on what you want to do. The indentation is important because this is how the Python interpreter knows the statements are part of the looping. The looping is done by reading the first element of the iterable and placing it in the loop counter, i. So for the previous example, you could use the code I show in Figure 3-17. You could include conditional statements if needed, as in Figure 3-18.

```
1  ##
2  ## For-loop structure
3  ##
4  lst = [ 1, 2, 3 ]
5  for i in range( 3 ):
6      print( lst[ i ] )
7

   1
   2
   3
```

Figure 3-17. A simple for loop. The iterable is range. The counter is set to the first value of the iterable, which begins with 0. That counter is then used to access each element of the list which is defined before the for loop.

```
1  ##
2  ## For-loop structure with conditional
3  ##
4  lst = [ 1, 2, 3 ]
5  for i in range( 3 ):
6      if i >= 2:
7          print( lst[ i ] )
8

   3
```

Figure 3-18. A simple *for* loop with a conditional statement. The conditional tests if the counter is greater than or equal to 2. If True, then the `print` statement is executed. Otherwise, the next loop is processed unless there are no more steps in the loop.

A common programming operation is to populate, or append objects to, a list. For example, for the list I used in the previous example, I just had three integers: 1, 2, and 3. A list like this is obviously easy to create "by hand." Suppose, however, you want a list of 10 elements with each element the square of the first 10 integers. So you want [1, 4, 9, ..., 100]. Since there are only 10 elements, again, this is not difficult to create by hand, but you do have to square each integer which becomes tedious. A `for` loop can be used as in Figure 3-19.

```
1  ##
2  ## For-loop with squares
3  ##
4  lst = [ ]
5  for i in range( 1, 11 ):
6      lst.append( i**2 )
7  print( lst )
8

   [1, 4, 9, 16, 25, 36, 49, 64, 81, 100]
```

Figure 3-19. How to populate a list. The *append* method is used to add (i.e., append) an object to the end of the list. An empty list is created before the *for* loop. See Figure 3-20 for a more efficient way to get the same result.

For this example, three lines of code (ignoring the print statement) were used. An even easier, more efficient, and more readable way to accomplish the same end result is to use a list comprehension. I illustrate how to do this in Figure 3-20. Notice that only one line of code (ignoring the print statement) is used. I will show other examples of list comprehensions throughout this book.

```
1  ##
2  ## Use a list comprehension
3  ##
4  lst = [ i**2 for i in range( 1, 11 ) ]
5  print( lst )
6

   [1, 4, 9, 16, 25, 36, 49, 64, 81, 100]
```

Figure 3-20. An example of a list comprehension to replace the more verbose code in Figure 3-19.

Try to use a list comprehension whenever possible rather than a for loop. Your Python code will be greatly improved.

while loops

while loops are similar to for loops because they allow you to repetitively loop through a series of Python code statements. They are different because this looping mechanism will continue until a condition is satisfied. A for loop also has a condition, but that is just a fixed number of iterations, dictated, perhaps, by the range function.

The structure of a while loop is:

```
while test-condition:
    statement(s)
```

The looping will continue as long as the test condition is true.

You can easily get into an infinite loop if the test condition is never satisfied. The only way to get out of such a loop is to kill your program—or your computer. I do not recommend while loops because of the infinite looping possibility.

Python Packages

Python's suite of packages cover all the major programming, data management, and scientific tools you will need for any data science problem. This also includes packages for handling text and date-time data. Some are standard with Python, meaning they are built-in and automatically available for you at any time. Others were written and maintained by the community of users I mentioned earlier. You have to install these contributed packages on your local computer and then import them into a

Python script before you can use them. I will show you how to install and import packages in the following sections.

There are several Python packages you will use regardless of the type of analytical work you do. They transcend the analysis. I group these into three categories:

1. Data management

2. Data visualization

3. Statistical analysis and modeling

Data Management

The data management group consists of two packages: NumPy and pandas.

NumPy

NumPy is a powerful package for the management and manipulation of arrays of data. At the simplest level, an *array* is a *vector* or *matrix*. A vector is a special case of a matrix. A matrix is defined by its size measured by its number of rows and columns. A matrix $\mathbf{X}$ with n rows and p columns has size $n \times p$. The number of rows always comes first in the size designation. A matrix is two-dimensional. I use bold-faced uppercase letters, such as $\mathbf{X}$, for vectors and matrices.

A vector, as a special case, has n rows and 1 column and is usually referred to as a column vector. Its size is $n \times 1$. A vector is one-dimensional.

A matrix with p columns has p column vectors. If $\mathbf{X}_i$ is a column vector, then $\mathbf{X} = \begin{bmatrix} \mathbf{X}_1, \mathbf{X}_2, ..., \mathbf{X}_p \end{bmatrix}$.

A vector is created using a list as an argument to the NumPy function `array`. The full command might look like $np.array(\begin{bmatrix} 1,2,3 \end{bmatrix})$ where np is a conventional alias for NumPy. I will explain aliases in "Importing Packages" on page 101.

There are data requiring more than two dimensions. They are handled by a generalization of a matrix: an array. While a matrix is two-dimensional, an array is m-dimensional. If $m = 2$, you can imagine your data displayed as a rectangle. If $m = 3$, then a cube. An array with $m \geq 3$ is sometimes referred to as a *tensor*. The size of an array is the total number of cells. The number of dimensions and the size are *attributes* of an array which are retrieved from a NumPy array using `ndim` and `size`, respectively. I show an example NumPy array in Figure 3-21.

```
 1   ##
 2   ## Create an array
 3   ##
 4   arr = np.array(
 5       [
 6           [
 7               [ 1, 2, 3 ],
 8               [ 4, 5, 6 ]
 9           ],
10           [
11               [ 7, 8, 9 ],
12               [ 10, 11, 12 ]
13           ],
14           [
15               [ 13, 14, 15 ],
16               [ 16, 17, 18 ]
17
18           ]
19       ])
20   arr
21
```

```
array([[[ 1,  2,  3],
        [ 4,  5,  6]],

       [[ 7,  8,  9],
        [10, 11, 12]],

       [[13, 14, 15],
        [16, 17, 18]]])
```

```
 1   print( f'Dimensions: {arr.ndim}\nSize: {arr.size}' )
 2
```

```
Dimensions: 3
Size: 18
```

Figure 3-21. An example of a NumPy array. It is 3-dimensional. Each dimension is a 2 × 3 matrix. I separated the three dimensions when I created the array so you can see the components.

Regardless of its size, any array must be managed; that is:

- Sorted
- Transposed
- Reshaped
- Sliced into smaller arrays
- Concatenated into a larger array

NumPy can do all of these and more. Refer to the NumPy documentation (*https://www.numpy.org*) for extensive documentation.

pandas

pandas is built on NumPy which makes NumPy a base package. pandas extends NumPy's functionality giving you increased flexibility. It has a more intuitive approach and syntax to handle your data since NumPy itself is, at times, complicated to use. If you need to quickly become productive in analytics, then pandas is your go-to package.

Not only does pandas improve the functionality of NumPy, but it also extends and improves the functionality for many of the built-in Python packages, the main one being datetime. This package has rich date and time functionalities and a date/time *mini-language* for parsing and writing date/time strings. This functionality, however, has problems. pandas was built to "correct" them and to be more compatible with what a data scientist needs to handle and deal with. In fact, pandas was created to improve how *panel data*, a combination of time series and cross-sectional data, are handled. The name pandas is derived from the words *panel data set*. Since its inception, it has morphed into a general data management package, so handling panel data is just a small part of what it now does. It will handle any type of data: time series, cross-sectional, panel, and text.

In addition to improving how you deal with dates and times, pandas makes it easier for you to import data of any format: CSV, Excel, JSON, SAS, Stata, and even the Clipboard to mention a few. The most popular format is *comma-separated values* (CSV). Almost all, if not all, software packages, statistical and otherwise, read and write a CSV-formated data file because this is just a plain text file you can look at with any text editor. The pandas `read_csv` import function has an extensive array of arguments allowing you to handle almost any issue you might encounter, such as:

- Identifying missing data
- Ignoring variables you do not want to import (i.e., skip over rather than import)
- Renaming columns
- Parsing dates and times when you import

pandas does not stop with data management. The goal of its developers seems to be to make it an all-encompassing data analytic tool. It has built-in data visualization methods and some statistical functionality such as descriptive statistics, cross-tabulations, and correlation methods. Many Python packages read and write pandas data sets called *Series* for a single variable and *DataFrames* for multiple variables (what NumPy calls an *array*).

Note the capitalization for Series and DataFrame.

You are not restricted to just importing a formatted data set, say in CSV format. You could create a DataFrame as needed for your analysis. One way, the one I try to use whenever possible, is to create a dictionary and then pass it to pandas. I show how to do this in Figure 3-22. In this example, I use lists in the dictionary so you can see the versatility of the different data containers.

```
1  ##
2  ## Create a DataFrame from a dictionary
3  ##
4  data = { 'X':[ 1, 5, 9, 3 ],
5           'Y':[ 5, 6, 7, 8 ],
6           'Z':[ 'a', 'b', 'c', 'd' ] }
7  df = pd.DataFrame( data )
8  df
9

      X  Y  Z

   0  1  5  a

   1  5  6  b

   2  9  7  c

   3  3  8  d
```

Figure 3-22. An example of how to create a DataFrame using a dictionary. The dictionary is named data and has three keys that will be the variables with one list that will be the "values" for the key:value pairs. The prefix pd is an alias for pandas that I explain in "Importing Packages" on page 101.

I will describe different pandas methods and tools throughout this book so you will be exposed to much of what pandas can do. See the book by McKinney (2018), the original developer of pandas, for a very extensive coverage of pandas.

Data Visualization

I mentioned in the previous subsection that pandas includes data visualization capabilities. The standard statistical graphs are available:

- Line plot (the default)
- Vertical bar plots
- Horizontal bar plots

- Histogram
- Boxplot
- Kernel Density Estimation (KDE) plot
- Area plot
- Pie plot
- Scatter plot

The scatter plot option is available only for a DataFrame; all the others could be used with a DataFrame or a Series. I show an example in Figure 3-23 using the data from Figure 3-22 to illustrate how to plot some data using pandas.

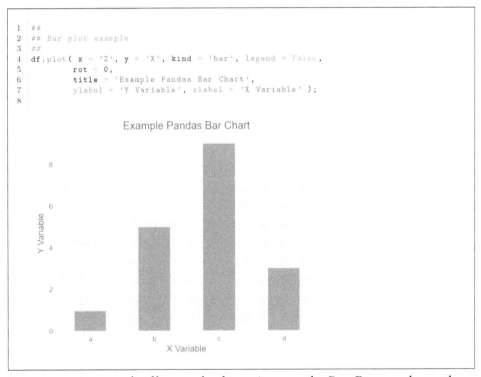

```
1  ##
2  ## Bar plot example
3  ##
4  df.plot( x = 'Z', y = 'X', kind = 'bar', legend = False,
5          rot = 0,
6          title = 'Example Pandas Bar Chart',
7          ylabel = 'Y Variable', xlabel = 'X Variable' );
8
```

Figure 3-23. An example of how to plot data using a pandas DataFrame and a pandas plot method. In this example, I plot a bar chart of a variable in the DataFrame from Figure 3-22. Notice how I suppressed the legend and added titles. I also rotated the x-axis labels, which otherwise would be rotated 90, using rot = 0.

The pandas plotting functions are based on Matplotlib, which is a very powerful data visualization Python package. Matplotlib gives you the ability to:

- Create any data display you want
- Access any graph element to tailor it to your needs
- Add annotations to help clarify and enhance your visuals

Unfortunately, Matplotlib's extensive functionality and flexibility is a hindrance to its wider use. In many respects, this is the same problem shared by NumPy and other Python packages, such as datetime I mentioned above. This is why the pandas developers incorporated a data visualization component in pandas using a simplified syntax.

There are a number of data visualization packages in the Python infrastructure you could use. seaborn, for example, also uses Matplotlib as a base but tries to provide more flexibility and versatility than pandas. A very convenient feature of seaborn is its use of pandas DataFrames. This means there is a seamless connection between pandas for data management and seaborn for data visualization; you do not have to do anything special to your data to visualize it with seaborn.

I will use seaborn as well as pandas in this book so you will see some of their data visualization functionalities.

 I recommend you use seaborn if you need more sophistication for your data visualization.

Statistical Analysis and Modeling

There are three main packages I will focus on for statistical, econometric, and machine learning functions for Prescriptive Analytics, each with a number of specialty sub-packages. These are:

- statsmodels
- scikit-learn
- SciPy

I did not order these by importance or usefulness for Prescriptive Analytics. However, in the general area of Business Analytics, of which Prescriptive Analytics is a subset, each one provides functionality in the three domains I have been listing: statistics, econometrics, and machine learning. I show a mapping of the packages and domains in Figure 3-24.

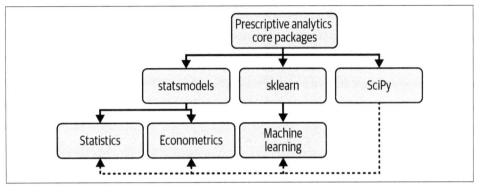

Figure 3-24. A mapping of the core Prescriptive Analytics packages to the three analytic domains I mention in the text. The dotted arrows from SciPy indicate that this package's functionality can be used with the three domains.

There are other specialty packages that I will use in this book. I will introduce them as needed. These three are the core. I will provide a brief overview of each in the following subsections.

statsmodels

This package allows you to estimate a number of statistical and econometric models such as:

- Classical linear regression models
- Generalized Linear Models:
  — Gaussian
  — Inverse Gaussian
  — Binomial
  — Poisson
  — Negative Binomial
  — Gamma
- Discrete and count models:
  — Logit
  — Probit
  — Multinomial Logit
  — Ordered Models
  — Poisson
  — Negative Binomial

— Multivariate Models

- Time Series models, both univariate and multivariate as well as forecasting

and a wealth of other function classes. In addition, it has the capability to provide a number of descriptive statistics and some elementary statistical graphs.

scikit-learn

scikit-learn is also commonly known by an alternate name: sklearn. The fact that there are two acceptable names for the same package creates confusion; there is just one package, but two names.

Of the two names for this package, sklearn is the most used. So you are best off using this one when referring to this package.

You might be wondering what this package does since *statsmodels* handles almost all the standard and commonly accepted statistical and econometric methods. What is missing from *statsmodels* is all the methods in the machine learning domain. This is where sklearn focuses.

Machine learning methods are generally divided into two groups I introduced in Chapter 2: supervised learning methods and unsupervised learning methods.

Statistics and econometrics refer to the procedures for obtaining numeric values for unknown parameters as *estimation*. In machine learning, it is referred to as *learning*, which is a broader concept. So in statistics and econometrics, parameters are estimated, while in machine learning the method learns the parameter values from data or the structure of the data.

In supervised learning, there is a model in the traditional form of a dependent variable (on the left-hand side) and a set of independent variables on the right-hand side. A simple linear regression model is written as

$$Y_i = \beta_0 + \beta_1 \times X_i + \epsilon_i$$

where Y_i is the ith observation, $i = 1,2,...,n$, on a dependent variable; X_i is the ith observation on an independent variable; and ϵ_i is a random disturbance term on that observation. The two terms, β_0 and β_1, are the unknown population parameters to estimate.

In machine learning, the dependent variable is called a *target* and the independent variables are *features*. The objective is to learn the unknown parameters of a model's features using, or under the supervision of, the target variable.

In unsupervised learning, there is no target, just a set of features. This implies that there is no model such as the previous equation. Instead, finding or identifying the structure of the data is the objective. This structure may include groupings, *clusters* of the features, or segmentation so that a new observation on the features could be classified into one of the segments. The former is called *cluster analysis* and the second is called *classification analysis*.

sklearn provides a large, extensive library of methods for supervised and unsupervised learning. In fact, it is probably the premier package in the machine learning domain.

See Paczkowski (2022a), for an extensive discussion of machine learning methods in business analytics. Also see Alpaydin (2014), Deisenroth et al. (2020), Muller and Guido (2017), Raschka and Mirjalili (2017) (who focus on sklearn), and Witten et al. (2011) for more on the methods of machine learning.

SciPy

The last package is probably the most versatile for overall scientific analysis in Python. This is, in fact, the basis of the name: *scientific Python*. Its forte is a comprehensive suite of algorithms for:

- Optimization
- Integration
- Interpolation
- Eigenvalue problems
- Algebraic equations
- Differential equations
- Statistics

and much more.[5] Because SciPy has general, powerful functions for optimization, its usefulness cuts across the three quantitative domains I have been listing: statistics, econometrics, and machine learning. You will see a number of uses of it in this book.

---

5 See the SciPy website (*https://www.scipy.org*), from which I drew this list.

Working with Python Packages

In order to use the Python packages I have summarized, and many more, you have to complete two steps:

1. Install the packages on your local computer
2. Import them into a Python session

You should have to do the first only once, but the second will need to be done each time you begin a new analysis session on your local computer.

I will first describe two general steps for installing packages on your local computer. The first uses a package platform that manages a Python installation. I recommend Anaconda. The second uses a specialty installation function, the main ones being pip and conda. I will describe how to import packages into a Python session in "Importing Packages" on page 101.

Using Anaconda

You can manually install Python and all the packages you will need for any analysis you do using the method I will describe in "Updating Python Packages" on page 101. But I do not recommend this. It is not only very inefficient, but error prone—you could easily miss a package or grab an outdated version. Anaconda provides you with all you need to begin using Python and its core packages, plus more. It also gives you access to several statistical and machine learning platforms you will find useful and powerful for any analysis you will do. For instance, I will use *JupyterLab* in this book; Anaconda gives you access to it. Finally, Anaconda gives you the ability to install specialty packages as well as update all installed packages when new versions become available, including Python itself, and new versions are always released.

You will, of course, have to install Anaconda on your local computer (*https://www.anaconda.org*). and select the version appropriate for your computer. There are versions for Linux, macOS, and Windows. Simply select the appropriate version, download it, and execute the downloaded version. The software is free. After you install Anaconda, Python and a plethora of packages are automatically installed on your local computer.

Once Anaconda is installed and you open it, you will see a navigation panel appropriately called the Anaconda Navigator. There is a series of large icons for a number of analytic applications. Each icon displays the application's name and version number (if appropriate), a brief description of the application, and a button to either install or launch that application once it is installed. To use a particular application for the first time, you install it by clicking the Install button on the icon. Once installed, the button label changes to Launch. To launch the application, you will, of course, just click this button.

Updating Python Packages

Package developers update their packages, some on a regular basis. This includes Python itself. It is to your benefit to ensure you have the latest version of your key packages so you are using the latest methods, have packages with corrected errors or bugs, and are more efficient in terms of processing. You can update all your packages through the Anaconda Navigator by clicking on the Environment tab on the left panel. You will see a list of the installed packages. You can then choose which to update using the drop-down menu as indicated.

You can also update packages using either pip or conda. pip is the *Package Installer for Python*, a general-purpose application for managing Python packages. conda is the Anaconda version. See Anaconda (2024) for a good explanation of the differences between conda and pip.Typically, when you find a non-standard package that Anaconda does not maintain, you can go to that package's website and most likely find the pip install commands specific to it. Just copy the command to your clipboard, and then paste and execute it on your local computer at the command line. For instance, if you are using Anaconda, go to the Anaconda Prompt in the Anaconda directory listing, open the prompt window, and paste the copied command.

Installing Packages

How do you find new packages? You can use the *Python Package Index* (PyPI) (*https://pypi.org*). This is a comprehensive index of packages. Almost all developers post their package here so you should be able to find any package. Once you find a package through PyPI, you can install it very easily by copying the install command you find at PyPI and pasting it into the Anaconda Prompt window.

 Do not confuse PyPI and PyPy. The latter is an alternative implementation of Python. See Stackoverflow (2024) for a comparison.

Importing Packages

There are two classes of Python packages: built-in and user-contributed.

The built-in packages are part of the Python infrastructure and are automatically loaded when you first initiate Python for an analysis session. The user-contributed packages, however, have to be loaded, or *imported*, by you before you can use them.

There are two ways to import a package. The first is to simply use the import command followed by the name of the package. This assumes, of course, that the package is installed on your local computer. I illustrate package importing in Figure 3-25. In this example, I import three packages: pandas, NumPy, and math. The last package contains many math functions the standard Python implementation either does not have or extends those it does have.

```
1  ##
2  ## Basic package import
3  ##
4  import pandas as pd
5  import numpy as np
6  import math
7
```

Figure 3-25. The basic method for importing a user-contributed Python package. Notice the alias after the as statement.

 I recommend always importing the math package.

Notice that pandas and NumPy each have two statements after the name of the package. The as is a Python keyword that tells the interpreter the next word is to be treated as an *alias* for the full package name. This alias is very useful. The math package does not typically have an alias by convention.

Recall that each package contains a number of functions; they are containers of functions. When you call a particular function, the Python interpreter has to know where to find it; it basically does not know where it lives. Consequently, the interpreter will return an error message telling you it cannot find the function (it is undefined) and then stop processing all subsequent statements. To fix this problem, you call each function you want to use by the name of the package it resides in and the function name. You connect or *chain* the package name and the function name into one string using a dot between the two names. For instance, pandas has a function to import CSV data called `read_csv` (notice the underscore). You tell the interpreter to use this function by entering `Pandas.read_csv` in a JupyterLab code cell. Unfortunately, some package names are long (e.g., Matplotlib) which can become tedious (and error-prone) to type. Hence the alias. The conventional alias for pandas is `pd`, so you would use `pd.read_csv`.

There are a number of conventional aliases, but of course, you can always define your own. I list a number of conventional ones in Table 3-4. Notice that math does not have one although I have seen *ma* used.

Table 3-4. Typical package import commands and associated aliases. Notice that a few packages do not have a conventional alias; you can assign one if you wish.

Package	Alias	Example
pandas	pd	import pandas as pd
NumPy	np	import numpy as np
seaborn	sns	import seaborn as sns
Matplotlib Pyplot	plt	import matplotlib.pyplot as plt
statsmodels	sm	import statsmodels.api as sm
statsmodels Formula	smf	import statsmodels.formula.api as smf
sklearn	sk	import sklearn as sk
SciPy stats	stats	import scipy.stats as stats
random		import random
Regular Expressions		import re
SciPy		import scipy
math		import math
itertools		import itertools

I strongly recommend that you place your package import statements in one code cell at the very top of your project notebook. All import statements should go into this one cell as Best Practice. The reason is simple: they are all together in one location so you do not have to search for them throughout your notebook. In addition, I strongly recommend that you categorize your import statements to make it even easier to locate a particular statement if you need to check it. Some possible categories are:

- Data management
- Data visualization
- Modeling
- Specialty

I show an example in Figure 3-26.

```
 1  ##
 2  ## ===> Data Management <===
 3  ##
 4  import pandas as pd
 5  import numpy as np
 6  ##
 7  ## ===> Data Visualization <===
 8  ##
 9  import matplotlib.pyplot as plt
10  import seaborn as sns
11  plt.style.use( "ggplot" )  ## set plotting style; could also use sns.set()
12  ##
13  ## ===> Modeling <===
14  ##
15  import statsmodels.api as sm
16  import statsmodels.formula.api as smf
17  import scipy
18  ##
19  ## ===> Specialty <===
20  ##
21  import random
22  import math
23  import itertools
24
```

Figure 3-26. A recommended Best Practice package import layout. You can also set some needed parameters as I show for the data visualization.

You can also import standard packages you use all the time, as well as formats and your own functions, by placing these in a script file (i.e., a plain text file) with the extension *.py*. You import this file using a JupyterLab *magic* command. There are many magic commands that are really macros or short programs for specialized JupyterLab operations. One magic command is %run which imports and runs a script file. For example, I have a short script file, *setup.py*, in a directory called *c:/scriptlib/*; this is the path to the file. I can import the contents of *setup.py* as I show in Figure 3-27.

```
 1  ##
 2  ## ===> Load a script file with run magic <===
 3  ##
 4  %run c:/scriptlib/setup.py
 5
```

Figure 3-27. How to import a script file using the %run magic command.

 I encourage you to place routine package, format, and function import commands in a script file and then import that file with the %run magic command. This will ensure consistency in your work.

Go-To References

There are a number of very good books available to help you build your knowledge of Python and how to use it in data science. A few are:

- Chongchitnan (2023): See the Appendix for a Python tutorial
- Hunt (2019) and Hunt (2020)
- McKinney (2018): The go-to book for pandas
- Sedgewick et al. (2016)
- VanderPlas (2017): A comprehensive handbook

Summary

This is the first of three primers on material at the core of this book. This primer is a tutorial on the Python language, the one most used (and in demand) for data science in general, and Prescriptive Analytics in particular. I provided a short background on Python, including the benefits of using it. I covered the language's structure and made recommendations on its optimal use in data science.

The main concepts from this chapter are:

- The benefits of Python versus other languages
- The key elements of the programming language
- Instruction on installing, importing, and managing packages
- The use and structure of an interactive development tool: JupyterLab
- Advice on structuring JupyterLab notebooks for efficient data science work

CHAPTER 4

Probability Essentials

I provide a high-level background on probability theory and its use in Prescriptive Analytics in this chapter. The reason for this chapter is twofold. First, decision-makers deal with uncertainties every day: they make decisions under a cloud of uncertainty as I noted in Chapter 1. There are no definitive statements, conclusions, or answers to the complex issues they must decide. Each decision involves a simple "Go/No Go" order such as:

- Reduce price or not
- Perform preemptive maintenance on a manufacturing robot today or wait until it fails
- Introduce a new product or not
- Remain at the current head count or reduce (increase) it
- Sell part of the business or not
- Make the decision today or wait until next year

This is a small listing, not meant to be exhaustive. It is, nonetheless, sufficient to show what decision-makers confront. And for each decision, anything could result. So they try their best to get the most Rich Information to help them make the right choice to maximize their chance for success. In some instances, however, they may be so overwhelmed by the complexity of the decision that they may even feel they would do as well tossing a (fair) coin and letting the "chips fall as they may." This, of course, immediately introduces probabilities into decision making. So the second reason for this chapter is that uncertainties are expressed in probabilistic terms.

Unfortunately, many decisions are not as simple as my examples. Those are deceiving. Consider the first one: reducing a price. This appears simple enough. But three questions are begged:

- How much should the price be reduced?
- When will you reduce the price?
- What will happen if the price is not reduced?

There may be several candidate price points constituting a decision menu. For each price on the menu, there is a probability of success measured by a KPM such as incremental net revenue earned, the increment being over the trend net revenue without a price change (i.e., status quo). What is that probability? It is important to know this because that probability, actually a *probability distribution* for each price on the menu, will inform the decision-maker about what should be done, which is what Prescriptive Analytics strives to do.

I will explore in this chapter some of the foundational topics of probability theory useful for Prescriptive Analytics. This is not meant to be a comprehensive treatment, let alone a treatise, on probability theory. For comprehensive treatments, see Keynes (1921), Feller (1950), Feller (1971), and Hajek (2019). These are highly technical. For an application-oriented book, but yet with theoretical developments, see Ross (2014).

The leading questions for this chapter are:

- What is the role of probabilities in everyday affairs?
- What is the meaning and interpretation of probabilities?
- What are the fundamental probability concepts?
- What are the key probability distributions and their implementation in Python?

The World Is Ruled by Probabilities

There are two ways to view everyday events in the so-called real world: they are either *stochastic* or *non-stochastic*. The word stochastic means *randomly determined* or *selected from a probability distribution*. You can view "stochastic" as a synonym for "random" although stochasticity and randomness are distinct concepts. I will use them, however, as synonyms. See Wikipedia (2023m) for some comments.

If stochastic means random, then non-stochastic means non-random or *deterministic*. The extreme implication is that whatever happens is predetermined by a powerful, omnipotent force which we have no control over. This brings up the entire topic of *Free Will*. There is, of course, a very deep and extensive philosophical literature on this, a literature too deep for our discussion and beyond the scope of this book.

Nonetheless, the idea that events are either random or deterministic has profound importance for Prescriptive Analytics. In fact, it has profound importance for Predictive Analytics which feeds into Prescriptive Analytics because each relies on not knowing what will happen because of a decision. If everything is deterministic (i.e., non-stochastic), then you do not even have to make a decision; the event will happen regardless of what you do. Even your very choice is determined. See Pink (2004).

Hawking on Chances

"I have noticed that even those who assert that everything is predestined and that we can change nothing about it still look both ways before they cross the street."

—Stephen Hawking, *Black Holes and Baby Universes and Other Essays*

Aside from philosophical discussions, most people, and this includes business managers with great responsibilities, will (correctly) contend that everything is not determined, but random. They base this on their everyday experience. The weather on a particular day (rain, cloudy, or sunny; mild or blustery; cold or warm); the traffic pattern on the way to work; train or bus delays; an encounter in an elevator with a potential new client or your boss: these all occur with neither rhyme nor reason. Even in our personal lives, chance occurrences change us, sometimes for the good, other times not so good; sometimes in a small way, other times in a big way; sometimes temporarily, other times permanently. In all cases, the events are unforeseen, unexpected, unpredictable—just random.

The outcome of a decision (e.g., go to work, go to dinner, sleep-in late) could be anything. Some events are more likely to occur than others because all the "anythings" are distributed in some fashion. They are drawn from a *probability distribution*. In a business context, the incremental change in net revenue from a price reduction is a draw from a probability distribution; a merger decision could be jeopardized by an unexpected intervention by the Department of Justice (DOJ) for antitrust violations, the intervention being a draw from a binary (to intervene or not) distribution; a competitor introduces a superior new product one month after you introduce your new product, the degree of superiority and timing being independent draws from two separate distributions.

My position is that all events, more specifically the outcomes of decisions, are all stochastic, the results of draws from probability distributions. But more importantly, these random draws are in every part of our lives and, thus, rule our lives. This means the menu presented to a decision-maker should have a probability assigned to each option, but what actually occurs after the decision is made is anyone's guess. I will revisit the probabilities for menu options in Chapter 6 when I discuss decision trees and decision analysis.

What Are Probabilities?

An obvious question is: "What is a probability?" This is not easy to answer.

Russell on Probabilities

"Probability is the most important concept in modern science, especially as nobody has the slightest notion what it means."

—Bertrand Russell, 1929 lecture, cited in Hajek (2019)

Almost everyone believes they have an intuitive, almost sixth sense of probabilities, most likely developed in early grade school when they were first tossing a coin or a die.[1]

Consider a coin toss. Most school-age children understand there is a 50% chance of getting a heads-up on a toss. This may happen by tossing a coin as a game in a school playground or by a K-12 math teacher demonstrating percentages in a math lesson. Regardless of where or how this lesson is learned, young children do grasp the concept. After that, they treat it as "intuitively obvious." Consequently, they believe they know exactly what is a probability.

Unfortunately, defining probabilities has vexed mathematicians and philosophers for two thousand years. Yet this is a concept we have to deal with, it cannot be avoided, because, as noted by Hajek (2019, p. 2):

> Probability is virtually ubiquitous. It plays a role in almost all the sciences. It underpins much of the social sciences…. It finds its way, moreover, into much of philosophy….Since probability theory is central to decision theory and game theory, it has ramifications for ethics and political philosophy….Thus, problems in the foundations of probability bear at least indirectly, and sometimes directly, upon central scientific, social scientific, and philosophical concerns. The interpretation of probability is one of the most important foundational problems.

Part of the problem defining probabilities is its use as a synonym for chance.[2] And, of course, defining "chance" is philosophically challenging. I cannot go into the details of this issue any more than I can delve into the issues surrounding the definition of probability; there is not enough room in this book plus I would exceed my scope. For issues on interpreting chance, see Eagle (2021).

---

1 The word "dice" is plural and the word "die" is singular for a cube with dots, called "pips," on each side. The cube is used in games.

2 When I ask my students what is a probability, they say it is a chance. When I ask them what is chance, they say it is a probability. A little circular and not helpful.

The concept of probability becomes confusing when you consider the following two statements:

- There is a 50% chance of getting a heads-up on a toss of a fair coin.
- There is a 75% chance of rain tomorrow.

The first is a belief, but one based on the experience of tossing a (fair) coin. Tossing a coin a number of times is an *experiment*, with each toss a *trial* in the experiment. These terms are not introduced to someone until they take a basic statistics course or a course in probability theory if they are a math major in college. Regardless of where or when they are introduced, the notion of repeating the toss is treated as "intuitively obvious," so, once again, they believe they understand the concept of a probability.

If the experiment notion is introduced in a statistics course, most likely the professor will run a number of trials in a simulation of a coin toss and show that the proportion of heads will approach 50%. The proportion will, in fact, become exactly 50% as the number of trials becomes very large. I will show such a simulation in "Example 1: Coin Toss" on page 229. In that simulation, the conditions for the (fair) coin toss are repeated. The 50% for the coin toss is experimentally determined. More importantly, we make decisions all the time based on these probabilities.

The second statement is fundamentally different, yet almost everyone will say they understand it. What is different is the probability, 75% in this case: it does not result from an experiment. The conditions tomorrow will be unique to tomorrow. In fact, because of the inherent randomness of events I discussed previously, no one can say (i.e., predict) exactly what those conditions will be. The 75% is a belief about what will happen; it is not experimentally determined. It is a subjectively based view of what may happen. Yet we intuitively accept these probabilities and make decisions based on them all the time (e.g., carry an umbrella tomorrow).

An Old Joke

A local radio station reported a 60% chance of rain the next day. A listener called and asked the basis for 60%. The station manager said: "I have 10 meteorologists. Six said it will rain."

So what is a probability? The result of an experiment conducted under fixed conditions and repeated a large number of times? Or a belief that something will or will not happen? Mathematicians and philosophers are torn on these questions. Consequently, there are two opposing schools: experimental or frequency-based on the one side, and belief or subjectively-based on the other side.

Fundamental Probability Concepts

I illustrated these two views of probabilities in Figure 1-3. I will follow that paradigm in this section.

Frequency-Based Probabilities

As I have stated, most people's first, and perhaps only, introduction to probabilities is through either a coin or die toss, perhaps in the lower grades in school. Let me focus on the coin toss and define the problem somewhat formally, but remaining within the bounds of what you know. I will change these bounds later.

Suppose you toss a normal coin with two sides: heads and tails. The objective is to see which side is face-up when it lands on a surface. The coin is "fair" if it has the same chance of coming up heads or tails on a single toss; it is not weighted to either side. If it is weighted to one side, say heads, then heads will appear more frequently than tails; it is biased to heads, which is unfair. Anyone betting on heads with such a coin will win more times than not; that person will have an unfair advantage.

We define an *event* as something that happens as a result of the coin toss. It could be a heads-up, denoted by H, or a tails-up, denoted by T. Let me denote by E the set containing the event. This is called the *event space*. For my example, the event is a heads-up when the coin lands on a surface, so $E = \{H\}$ where the curly brackets indicate a set. Read this as "The event space is the set containing a head." The *complement* to this is the set containing another result. Denote the complement as E^C so $E^C = \{T\}$.

There is only one result in set E, so the size of the set is simply one. It will be useful to have a function that counts the number of objects in the event set even though there is only one object in it at the moment. Let me denote this counting function as $n(E)$. For my example, $n(E) = 1$.

When you toss a fair coin, there are two possible results, only one of which will happen: getting heads-up or tails-up. We call the set of all possible results the *sample space* and denote it as S. This is the sample space because an event is drawn, or sampled, from it. Think of S as a population and E as the sample. For the coin toss, $S = \{H, T\}$. The counting function also counts the size of this set, so $n(S) = 2$.

The elementary definition of probabilities is in terms of relative frequencies:

$$Pr(E) = \frac{n(E)}{n(S)}.$$

So for the coin toss with $E = \{H\}$ and $S = \{H, T\}$,

$$Pr(E) = Pr(H) = \frac{n(E)}{n(S)} = \frac{1}{2}$$

Other probability problems can now be handled by this simple counting. For example, what is the probability of drawing a King from a normal deck of 52 shuffled playing cards? The event is drawing a King. Since there are four Kings in a normal deck, $n(K) = 4$ where K is a King. For the sample space, since this is a normal deck, $n(S) = 52$. Therefore,

$$Pr(K) = \frac{n(K)}{n(S)} = \frac{4}{52} = \frac{1}{13}.$$

I can now derive an important result. Clearly, the sample space is composed of the event and its complement, so I can write $S = E + E^C$. This allows me to further write

$$n(S) = n(E) + n\left(E^C\right).$$

Now divide both sides by $n(S)$ so

$$1.0 = \frac{n(E)}{n(S)} + \frac{n\left(E^C\right)}{n(S)}$$
$$= Pr(E) + Pr\left(E^C\right).$$

This is a rule for probabilities: they must sum to 1.0 for a sample space. This always holds and is a fundamental property of probabilities. You can check this with the coin toss example. You have $Pr(H) = \frac{1}{2}$ from before, but also $Pr(T) = \frac{1}{2}$ where $Pr(T)$ is the complement to $Pr(H)$. They sum to 1.0. This is the first rule of probabilities: $\sum_{i=n}^{n} Pr(E_i) = 1.0$.

This all depends on the counting function, $n(\cdot)$, which is a simple count for this problem. For many problems, a more complex counting problem is needed, which is what I will discuss in the next subsection.

Counting Functions

Counting functions are in the class of functions and methods called *combinatorics*. This mathematical area deals with ways to arrange objects, but, more importantly, how to count the number of arrangements.

To understand this, let me first focus on counting, then on arrangements. For counting, I could (inefficiently) simply count as in 1, 2, 3, and so on. This quickly becomes cumbersome for complex problems. For example, consider a trip from Princeton, NJ to the Museum of Natural History in Upper Manhattan, New York City. This involves two legs: going from Princeton to Lower Manhattan and then from Lower Manhattan to Upper Manhattan for the Museum. Suppose there are three ways to travel from Princeton to Lower Manhattan: bus, car, light rail train. Once in Lower Manhattan, there are four ways to travel to Upper Manhattan to the Museum: cross-town bus, subway, taxi, or walk.[3] I show these options in Figure 4-1.

Figure 4-1 is a decision tree, which I will return to in Chapter 6. Trees are fundamental to decision analysis, another important topic in OR. For a menu selection problem, each branch of the tree is a menu option. A probability can be assigned to the branches as I noted previously. I will return to these probabilities in Chapter 6, but ignore them now.

There are three ways into Manhattan, and for each of these there are four ways to get to the Museum. The total number of ways is 12, which equals 3×4. This is not a coincidence. It is an application of the *Fundamental Principle of Counting*.

The Fundamental Principle of Counting

If event E_1 can be done in n_1 ways and event E_2 can be done in n_2 ways, then the total number of ways E_1 and E_2 can be done is $n_1 \times n_2$. This assumes E_1 and E_2 do not affect each other (i.e., one happening has no bearing on the other).

---

3 I assume if I drive into New York City, I will leave my car at a City parking lot because driving in New York is hazardous to my health. So driving my car is not an option for me. The light rail will leave me at Penn Station and the bus will leave me at the Port Authority Bus Terminal, both within blocks of each other.

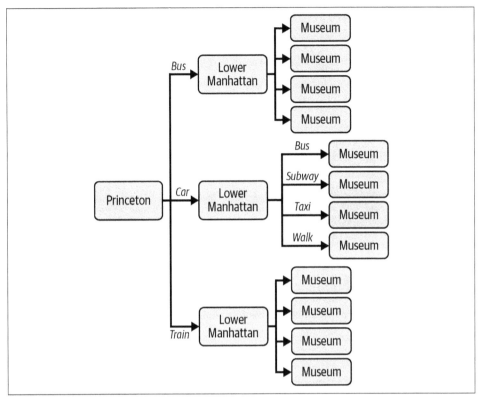

Figure 4-1. A decision tree showing the many ways to travel to a New York City museum

I need to clarify the word "arrangement." Formally, an arrangement is the placing of objects in a line. For example, if you have two objects, a and b, then a possible placement is the two-tuple (a,b). The placement, however, can be in any order; it is just the placement that matters. An arrangement is a placement in which the order of the objects matters for distinguishing one placement from another. For our two objects, the tuples (a,b) and (b,a) are different even though the two objects are in both. When the order matters, we say the objects are *arranged* or *permuted*, and the result is a *permutation* of the objects.

If n is the number of distinct objects, then the number of arrangements using all n objects is $n \times (n-1) \times (n-2) \times \ldots \times 1$. This is called a *factorial*, or *n-factorial*, and is abbreviated as $_nP_n = n!$. $n!$ is sometimes read as "n-factorial" or "n-bang". I show an example of how to calculate a factorial in Python in Figure 4-2. I use the math package which has a function called *factorial* that requires just one argument: the number of the factorial.

```
1   ##
2   ## Calculate 5!
3   ##
4   n = 5
5   fac = math.factorial( n )
6   print( f'{n}! = {fac}' )
7

    5! = 120
```

Figure 4-2. How to calculate a factorial in Python using the math package's function factorial. Notice that n is a positional argument in the function.

Some people define 0! = 1 to avoid dividing by zero. This is not correct. 0! = 1 because it is the number of ways to arrange nothing. See Conway and Guy (1996, p. 65).

If you want to arrange only $r < n$ of the objects, then the factorial is $_nP_r = n \times (n-1) \times (n-2) \times ... \times (n-r+1)$ and is read as "the number of permutations of n objects taking r at a time." This last statement is simplified as:

$$_nP_r = n \times (n-1) \times (n-2) \times ... \times (n-r+1)$$
$$= \frac{n \times (n-1) \times (n-2) \times ... \times (n-r+1) \times (n-r) \times (n-r-1) \times ... \times 1}{(n-r) \times (n-r-1) \times ... \times 1}$$
$$= \frac{n!}{(n-r)!}.$$

This is much easier to use.

As an example, how many ways can you permute (i.e., arrange) all the letters of "dog" to create new words where a "word" does not mean something you would necessarily find in a dictionary? The answer is $_3P_3 = 3! = 3 \times 2 \times 1 = 6$. So you can create six new "words." (Try listing them.) For another example, how many ways can you seat 10 people at a conference table with 4 chairs? This is $_{10}P_4 = \frac{10!}{(10-4)!} = 5,040$. (Obviously, do not try to list them all.) I show you how to calculate these in Figure 4-3. This uses the math package which has a function called perm that has two parameters: n and r, in that order. The second parameter, r, is optional, but the first, n, is required. If you omit r, you will get $n!$. If $r > n$, you will get an error message. If $n < 0$ or $r < 0$, you will get an error message.

```
1  ##
2  ## Number of permutations of the letters of "dog"
3  ##
4  n = 3    ## 3 letters in the word
5  p = math.perm( n  )
6  print( f'Number of permutations: {p}' )
7
```

    Number of permutations: 6

```
1  ##
2  ## Number of permutations of 10 people using 4 seats
3  ##
4  n = 10   ## 10 people
5  r = 4    ## 4 seats
6  p = math.perm( n, r  )
7  print( f'Number of permutations: {p:,}' )
8
```

    Number of permutations: 5.040

Figure 4-3. The math package has a perm function for calculating permutations. Notice that a factorial is just a permutation. Also, I included a comma in the print function's last term to make the output easier to read.

A more complicated counting problem, and one applicable to probability problems, involves the number of unique arrangements. For permutations, order matters for distinguishing one arrangement from another. So (a,b) differs from (b,a). However, for probability problems, order does not matter. In this case, you want to count the number of arrangements without regard to order. These are called *combinations*. A combination is a permutation with duplicate arrangements deleted since the duplicates are redundant: they add nothing to a probability. If you calculate the permutations as $_nP_r$, you will find that $r!$ terms are duplicates and should be deleted. You do this by dividing the number of permutations by $r!$. So the number of combinations of n objects using r at a time is:

$$_nC_r = \frac{_nP_r}{r!}$$

$$= \frac{n!}{(n-r)! \times r!}.$$

For notation, I use $_nC_r$ for combinations to be consistent with the permutation notation. Another acceptable notation is $\binom{n}{r}$.

As an example, suppose the Board of Directors (BOD) wants you, as the data scientist, to interview the members of their *C-level team* to learn how they use data for decisions. There are five Team members: Chief Executive Officer (CEO), Chief Operating Officer (COO), Chief Financial Officer (CFO), Chief Marketing Officer (CMO), and Chief Legal Officer (CLO). Unfortunately, you are restricted to interviewing only two. How many groups (i.e., combinations) of size $r = 2$ can you create from the $n = 5$ officers? You can determine the number of pairs using the combination formula. I show how you implement this in Python in Figure 4-4. I use the math package's comb function which takes the same arguments as the perm function in Figure 4-3.

```
1  ##
2  ## Number of combinations of C-Level Team
3  ##
4  n = 5   ## 5 Officers
5  r = 2   ## 2 to interview
6  p = math.comb( n, r )
7  print( f'Number of combinations: {p}' )
8

   Number of combinations: 10
```

Figure 4-4. The math package has a comb function for calculating the number of combinations.

Independence and Conditional Probability

My discussion has involved one event. What if there are two or more? How does the frequency-based calculation of probabilities change, if at all? Let me consider two, say A and B, and then I can always generalize to n. What is the relationship between the two?

There are only two possibilities: they are either separate events with no interaction or they have some commonality (i.e., they are not separate) with an interaction. An example of the first is getting a 1-dot face-up and a 5-dot face-up on a single toss of a fair die; this is impossible. The two events are *mutually exclusive* or *disjointed*: they both cannot happen at the same time; either one happens *or* the other happens. This is sometimes referred to as a *logical or*. An example of the second possibility is drawing a card at random from a normal deck of 52 shuffled playing cards and that card being King of Hearts: it is a King *and* a Heart at the same time. This is a *logical and*.

Logic Concepts

In logic, especially mathematical logic, there is a *logical and* and a *logical or*. The logical *and* says that both objects must be present; the logical *or* says that one object, the other object, or both must be present. For example: "Buy a box of spaghetti *and* a loaf of bread" means to come home with both. However, "Buy a box of spaghetti *or* a loaf of bread" means to come home with a box of spaghetti, a loaf of bread, or both. The first is a logical *and*, and the second is a logical *or*.

There is nothing in common between two mutually exclusive events. The count of A does not depend on the count of B, and vice versa. You express this as $n(A \& B) = 0$, where the ampersand represents the logical *or*. If you still want to count both events, you have to consider if event A occurs or event B occurs. You then simply count the occurrence of each and add them: $n(A \text{ or } B) = n(A) + n(B)$. Now you determine the probability of A or B occurring as:

Equation 4-1.

$$
\begin{aligned}
Pr(A \text{ or } B) &= \frac{n(A \text{ or } B)}{n(S)} \\
&= \frac{n(A) + n(B)}{n(S)} \\
&= \frac{n(A)}{n(S)} + \frac{n(B)}{n(S)} \\
&= Pr(A) + Pr(B).
\end{aligned}
$$

You now have a second rule of probabilities: $Pr(E_1 \text{ or } E_2) = Pr(E_1) + Pr(E_2)$ if E_1 and E_2 are mutually exclusive.

However, if A and B are not mutually exclusive so if one occurs then the other also occurs, you cannot simply add them because there is an overlap. If you did add the counts, you would double count the overlap and, therefore, overstate the true count. To avoid this, you subtract the overlap. The size of the overlap is $n(A \& B)$. This means the probability of A or B is now:

Equation 4-2.

$$
\begin{aligned}
Pr(A \text{ or } B) &= \frac{n(A \text{ or } B)}{n(S)} \\
&= \frac{n(A) + n(B) - n(A \& B)}{n(S)} \\
&= \frac{n(A)}{n(S)} + \frac{n(B)}{n(S)} - \frac{n(A \& B)}{n(S)} \\
&= Pr(A) + Pr(B) - Pr(A \& B).
\end{aligned}
$$

This is a third rule of probabilities: $Pr(E_1 \text{ or } E_2) = Pr(E_1) + Pr(E_2) - Pr(E_1 \& E_2)$ if E_1 and E_2 are not mutually exclusive.

Notice that Equation 4-2 is a generalization of Equation 4-1 because if $n(A \& B) = 0$, so there is no overlap, then $Pr(A \& B) = 0$.

Now consider a more complex problem. Suppose you conducted a survey of $n = 300$ customers to determine their opinion of a new product concept you want to introduce. You ask them if they like the concept or not. As part of the survey, you also collect data on their gender so you can understand preferences by gender. I show the (fictitious) data in Figure 4-5. The 100 in the *Male-Like* cell is the count of respondents who were *Male* and *Liked* the new product concept. This is an overlap of two events.

 I use the `enumerate` function inside a list comprehension to create my data in Figure 4-5.

```
1   ##
2   ## Generate some data
3   ##
4   gender = sum( [ [ 'Male' ]*j if i == 0 else [ 'Female' ]*j for i, j in enumerate(
                                    [ 150, 150 ] ) ], [] )
5   like = sum( [ [ 'Like' ]*j if i%2 == 0 else [ 'Not Like' ]*j for i, j in
                                    enumerate( [ 100, 50, 95, 55 ] ) ], [] )
6   ##
7   ## Create Dataframe and crosstabs
8   ##
9   data = { 'gender': gender, 'like': like }
10  df = pd.DataFrame( data )
11  display( pd.crosstab( df.gender, df.like, margins = True, margins_name = "Total"
                                    ).style.set_caption( 'Crosstab' ) )
12  display( pd.crosstab( df.gender, df.like, normalize = 'all', margins = True,
                                    margins_name = "Total" ).\
13         style.set_caption( 'Normalized Crosstab' ).format( precision = 3 ) )
14
```

Crosstab

like	Like	Not Like	Total
gender			
Female	95	55	150
Male	100	50	150
Total	195	105	300

Normalized Crosstab

like	Like	Not Like	Total
gender			
Female	0.317	0.183	0.500
Male	0.333	0.167	0.500
Total	0.650	0.350	1.000

Figure 4-5. The cross-tabulations (or crosstabs) for fictitious survey data for a new product concept preference. I show how the fictitious were generated and both the crosstab and its normalized version. The crosstable was created using the pandas `crosstab` *method.*

The top crosstab in Figure 4-5 shows the frequency or count of each combination (i.e., pair) of gender and liking. Since there are two gender groups and two liking groups, there are four cells as shown. The sum of the four cells equals the sample size of $n = 300$. If you divide the cell values by the sample size, you get estimates of the probabilities for each cell. I also show these estimates in Figure 4-5 as the *normalized crosstab*. The 0.333 value in the *Male-Like* cell is the estimate of the probability a person selected at random from the population will be *Male* <u>and</u> *Likes* the new product concept; it is the *joint probability*. Similarly for the other cells. Notice the probabilities sum to 1.0. The row totals are called the *row marginals* which give the estimated probabilities of a person selected at random being male or female—regardless of liking the concept. Similarly, the column totals are the *column marginals* and give the estimated probabilities of liking the concept—regardless of their gender.

The row marginal is the sum of the columns for each row and, so, is the last column of the table. Similarly for the column marginal.

You can now ask an interesting question: "What is the estimated probability of a randomly selected male liking the concept?" Or, to slightly rephrase it: "What is the estimated probability of a randomly selected person liking the concept, given the person is male?" This is a *conditional statement* and the probability is a *conditional probability*. Gender is the condition. We express this conditional probability as $Pr(A \mid B)$ where the vertical line indicates this is a conditional statement and the symbol after that vertical line is the condition. So $Pr(Like \mid Male)$ is the probability of someone liking the new product concept given the person is male.

This type of question is very common, and also very subtle, in real-world applications. You will see examples later. See Pinker (2021) for an extensive discussion and examples of how people overlook these conditionalities in addressing real-world problems.

To answer this conditional question, you have to recognize you are confined to the first row of Figure 4-5 so that the relevant divisor for calculating the estimated probabilities is not the total sample, $n = 300$, but the smaller one for the first row, the marginal total of $n = 150$. The estimated probability is then $Pr(Like \mid Male) = 0.667$. I show how to calculate these conditional probabilities in Figure 4-6.

```
1    ##
2    ## Calculate conditional probabilities
3    ## By gender
4    ##
5    display( pd.crosstab( df.gender, df.like, normalize = 'index', margins = True,\
6            margins_name = "Total" ).\
7            style.set_caption( 'Liking Probabilities Conditioned on Gender' ).\
8            format( precision = 3 ) )
9
```

Liking Probabilities
Conditioned on Gender

gender	like	Like	Not Like
Female	0.633		0.367
Male	0.667		0.333
Total	0.650		0.350

Figure 4-6. How the conditional probabilities can be calculated from the crosstab in Figure 4-5. The condition in this example is gender. The last row labeled "Total" is the column marginal distribution for liking.

If you have a sharp eye, you might notice if you divide the 0.333 in the normalized crosstabs in Figure 4-5 by the row marginal probability for *Males*, which is 0.500, you get 0.667 (with rounding, of course). This is not a coincidence. It will always be the case that

Equation 4-3.

$$Pr(A \mid B) = \frac{n(A \ \& \ B)/n(S)}{n(B)/n(S)}$$
$$= \frac{Pr(A \ \& \ B)}{Pr(B)}.$$

The probability of A occurring given B occurred equals the probability of A and B jointly occurring divided or adjusted by the marginal probability of B occurring alone. The marginal probability adjustment factor is the event to the left of the vertical line in the conditional probability statement on the left-hand side of Equation 4-3. This gives you a fourth rule of probabilities:

$$Pr(E_1 \mid E_2) = \frac{Pr(E_1 \ \& \ E_2)}{Pr(E_2)}$$

I can now reach a very important conclusion. Suppose liking or not liking the new product concept does not depend on the consumer's gender: they are *independent* of gender. The distribution for males is the same as for females; there is only one distribution for liking given by the column marginal distribution (i.e., the last row) in Figure 4-6. This implies that I can write:

$$Pr(Like \mid Male) = \frac{Pr(Male \text{ \& } Like)}{Pr(Male)}$$

$$Pr(Like) = \frac{Pr(Male \text{ \& } Like)}{Pr(Male)}$$

so,

$$Pr(Male \text{ \& } Like) = Pr(Like) \times Pr(Male).$$

 Be careful about mutual exclusivity and independence. If E_1 and E_2 are mutually exclusive, then $Pr(E_1 \text{ \& } E_2) = 0$ and they are not independent. If E_1 and E_2 are independent, then $Pr(E_1 \text{ \& } E_2) = Pr(E_1) \times Pr(E_2)$ and they are not mutually exclusive.

In general, under independence, $Pr(A \text{ \& } B) = Pr(A) \times Pr(B)$: the joint probability can be factored into a product of marginal probabilities. You now have a final rule of probabilities: $Pr(E_1 \text{ \& } E_2) = Pr(E_1) \times Pr(E_2)$ under independence.

Summary of Probability Rules

The five rules of probabilities are:

Rule 1
$$\sum_{i=n}^{n} Pr(E_i) = 1.0.$$

Rule 2
$$Pr(E_1 \text{ or } E_2) = Pr(E_1) + Pr(E_2) \text{ if } E_1 \text{ and } E_2 \text{ are mutually exclusive.}$$

Rule 3
$$Pr(E_1 \text{ or } E_2) = Pr(E_1) + Pr(E_2) - Pr(E_1 \text{ \& } E_2) \text{ if } E_1 \text{ and } E_2 \text{ are not mutually exclusive.}$$

Rule 4
$$Pr(E_1 \mid E_2) = \frac{Pr(E_1 \text{ \& } E_2)}{Pr(E_2)}.$$

Rule 5

$Pr(E_1 \,\&\, E_2) = Pr(E_1) \times Pr(E_2)$ under independence.

Limit Definition of Probabilities

The probabilities in the previous sections all have a common foundation: they are based on frequencies, counts of an event for a defined problem such as tossing a fair die. Those frequencies are normalized by the frequency of all possible events for that problem. This is the classical definition of probability taught in elementary math and statistics courses. A deeper development defines a probability with respect to the number of trials in an experiment. In particular, as the number of trials becomes infinitely large, the ratio of the frequency of the event to the frequency of the sample space converges to a value. That value is the probability. See Clayton (2021) for a discussion.

The complete mathematical theory of probabilities relies on limit theorems. A probability is formally defined as the limit as the count of events goes to infinity. This is, of course, not possible to implement for practical problems, although you can work around this using simulations. I will discuss simulations in Chapter 7. For now, just be aware of the issue. See Clayton (2021) for a discussion of this limiting issue.

Subjective-Based Probabilities: Introduction

In many situations, we quote probabilities, and have an intuitive sense regarding their meaning, that has no logical basis in experiments. For these cases, there are no experiments that can be performed, yet we quote these probabilities all the time. A classic example is the probability of rain I noted in "What Are Probabilities?" on page 110. You cannot perform an experiment where you repeat tomorrow exactly as tomorrow will occur—it has not occurred yet, so we cannot know the conditions let alone repeat tomorrow. You cannot repeat tomorrow any more than you can repeat today, yesterday, or any period. You may like to, but you simply cannot. Hence, there are no frequencies available; tomorrow is a unique event, and you do not know what it will be.

The only way to specify these probabilities is by using your knowledge base to specify a most likely "guess" regarding the probability of an outcome. That knowledge base is actually a part of the frequency-based probabilities because you usually state something about the conditions for the experiment. For example, the coin is "fair." This means the head is as likely as the tail to occur on a toss. This is part of what you know, part of your knowledge base. This is a problem because this likelihood is itself a probability (this is an interpretation of the word likelihood) so you use a probability to calculate a probability—a circular argument. This is, however, usually overlooked. See Clayton (2021) for a discussion of this finer point about frequency-based probabilities.

A non-frequency-based probability, based on your knowledge base, is subjective. What is that knowledge and where does it come from? First, your knowledge is whatever is relevant to a problem. For the probability of rain tomorrow, knowledge of current weather patterns and general meteorological theory are certainly necessary. Knowledge of stock market behavior is obviously useless (to most people). However, to state the probability the stock market will rise tomorrow requires knowledge about the economy, economic theory, financial theory, and past stock market behavior; current weather patterns and meteorological theory are not useful (most times; there are exceptions). The sources of that knowledge are wide and varied. A good, worthwhile descriptor is *experience*. You know things. And it is your knowledge from experience that allows you to formulate and state these subjective probabilities.

Wilde on Experience

"Experience is simply the name we give our mistakes."

—Oscar Wilde

Obviously, your knowledge base must be in place in your mind before, or prior to, you formulating the probabilities since this knowledge is, after all, a base. A probability formed from this prior knowledge is a *prior probability* (or *prior* for short).

Your knowledge-base, however, constantly changes as you learn more, as you gain more experience. So you need a mechanism to update your prior, to incorporate that new knowledge into your probability formulation, and revise your prior. The revised prior is a *posterior probability* (or *posterior* for short). This can become confusing because that posterior will become a new prior to be further updated when newer information becomes available. Thus, a cycle is established as I illustrate in Figure 4-7.

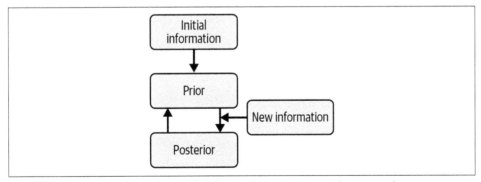

Figure 4-7. The circular flow of probability updating as new information becomes available. The posterior is the updated prior which in turn becomes a new prior. This circular flow continues ad infinitum. This is an example of an infinite loop.

Our formulation of subjective probabilities is based on two factors:

1. A prior probability representing our relevant knowledge before the event occurs
2. A mechanism for updating the prior as new knowledge becomes available

The mechanism is the important theorem called *Bayes' Theorem*. There is a simple derivation of the main result of this theorem, but its use and significance are beyond being simple. Its depth goes beyond just calculating probabilities based on knowledge other than frequencies from experiments. It extends to whole research programs and applications in statistics, econometrics, machine learning, and even marketing, psychology, and philosophy. For statistics, see Kenett et al. (2012), Gelman (2006), and Gelman et al. (2013); for econometric applications, see Zellner (1971); for marketing, see Rossi et al. (2005); for psychology, see Pinker (2021); and for philosophical applications and implications, see Lin (2023). I will discuss Bayes' Theorem and its application to decision making in the context of a decision menu in Chapter 10.

Bayes' Theorem: Derivation

The derivation of Bayes' Theorem relies on the posterior as a conditional statement: the probability conditioned on new information. So you can use the conditional probability statements from "Independence and Conditional Probability" on page 118. First, define A as the event you are interested in and I as information. Then, from Equation 4-3 you have

Equation 4-4.

$$Pr(A \mid I) = \frac{Pr(A \& I)}{Pr(I)}$$

where $Pr(I)$ is the probability of the new information. You can reverse this as

Equation 4-5.

$$Pr(I \mid A) = \frac{Pr(A \& I)}{Pr(A)}.$$

Now solve for $Pr(A \& I)$ in Equation 4-5 and substitute the result into Equation 4-4 to get

Equation 4-6.

$$Pr(A \mid I) = \frac{Pr(I \mid A) \times Pr(A)}{Pr(I)}.$$

This is Bayes' Theorem. It has a long history. See Clayton (2021) for an interesting historical account as well as Pinker (2021) for its use in rational decision making. Finally, see Paczkowski (2022b, Chapter 8) for a derivation similar to what I show here. A more technical derivation is in Lin (2023, Section 2).

The right-hand side of the Bayes' Theorem equation has three parts. The $Pr(A)$ in the numerator is the prior: the probability of A without regard to any knowledge or information, that is, data, beyond what you already know or have. The second term in the numerator, $Pr(I \mid A)$, is the probability of you realizing the information or data about an event given that the event occurred. This is called the *likelihood*. The term in the denominator, $Pr(I)$, is the marginal probability of seeing the information you have over all possible states of the event A. It is a scaling factor to ensure the probabilities sum to 1.0. As noted in Paczkowski (2022b, Chapter 8), this marginal probability is $Pr(I) = Pr(I \& A) + Pr(I \& \neg A)$ where the symbol $\neg$ means "not" or "the complement of." Finally, the term on the left-hand side is the posterior probability.

The entire expression in Equation 4-6 says the prior, initially founded on your existing knowledge base, is updated or revised by the likelihood of seeing your new information or data, the adjustment being normalized by the probability of seeing that information. The posterior becomes the new prior as I illustrated in Figure 4-7. Bayes' Theorem has become a major force in statistical analysis and is at the heart of the analytical split I illustrated in Figure 1-3.

Bayes' Theorem: Python Implementation

To illustrate the application of Equation 4-6 in Python, reconsider the new product problem that led to the crosstab in Figure 4-5. Suppose a male customer is randomly selected, perhaps from a database of existing customers. What is the probability the male customer will like the product concept? The "liking" is the information from the survey. Just for this example, further, suppose 65% of surveyed customers like the concept and 35% do not. Also, suppose of those who like it, 51.3% are male, and of those who do not like it, 47.6% are male. I summarize these numbers in Table 4-1.

Table 4-1. Bayes' Example

Pr(Like) = 0.65	Pr(Male | Like) = 0.513
Pr(Not Like) = 0.35	Pr(Male | Not Like) = 0.476

Using the equation for the conditional probability, then:

$$Pr(Like \mid Male) = \frac{Pr(Like) \times Pr(Male \mid Like)}{Pr(Male)}$$

$$= \frac{0.65 \times 0.513}{0.50}$$

$$= 0.667.$$

I calculated the probability of a Male as $0.65 \times 0.513 + 0.35 \times 0.476 = 0.50$. I implement these calculations in Python in Figure 4-8.

```
1   ##
2   ## Known priors and likelihoods
3   ##
4   prior = [ 0.65, 0.35 ]        ## Order: Male/Female
5   likely = [ 0.513, 0.476 ]     ## Order: Like/Not Like
6   ##
7   ## Marginal probability
8   ##
9   marginal = np.inner( prior, likely )   ## Use inner product of two lists
10  ##
11  ## Posterior probability
12  ##
13  post = ( prior[ 0 ]*likely[ 0 ] )/marginal
14  print( f'Bayes Posterior Probability: {post:0.3f}' )
15

    Bayes Posterior Probability: 0.667
```

Figure 4-8. The implementation of Bayes' Theorem in Python.

I define the two sets of probabilities in Lines 4 and 5. The marginal probability is created in Line 9 using NumPy's inner function, which calculates an inner or *dot product* of two vectors. The posterior probability is calculated in Line 13 using the first value of the prior and the likelihood.

 This example used the inner product (also called the *dot product*) of two lists. The inner product is defined as $A \times B = \sum_{i=1}^{n} a_i b_i$ where A and B are lists (i.e., vectors) of the same length. The NumPy function inner calculates the inner product.

Probability Distributions: Overview

I introduced the concept of probability distribution in the previous section. A distribution summarizes the entire array of probabilities for a class of events. For example, suppose you toss a fair coin three times. The array of possible events are: no heads, one head, two heads, and three heads. As you will see shortly, the corresponding probabilities are $[0.125, 0.375, 0.375, 0.125]$, respectively, which sum to 1.0. This list is a distribution. I show what this looks like in Figure 4-9.

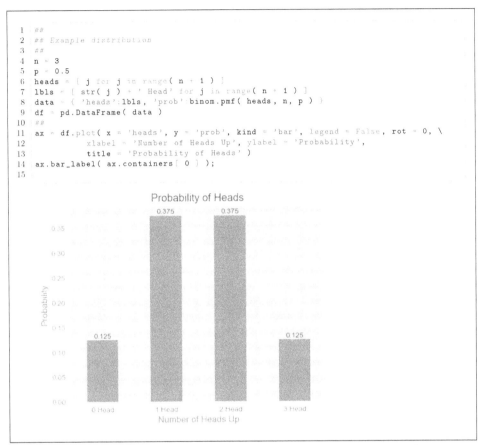

```
1   ##
2   ## Example distribution
3   ##
4   n = 3
5   p = 0.5
6   heads = [ j for j in range( n + 1 ) ]
7   lbls = [ str( j ) + ' Head' for j in range( n + 1 ) ]
8   data = { 'heads':lbls, 'prob':binom.pmf( heads, n, p ) }
9   df = pd.DataFrame( data )
10  ##
11  ax = df.plot( x = 'heads', y = 'prob', kind = 'bar', legend = False, rot = 0, \
12          xlabel = 'Number of Heads Up', ylabel = 'Probability',
13          title = 'Probability of Heads' )
14  ax.bar_label( ax.containers[ 0 ] );
15
```

Figure 4-9. The probability distribution for tossing a fair coin three times. A dictionary defines heads and their corresponding probabilities. I use a list comprehension for the heads labels and the heads list.

Figure 4-9 uses the pandas `plot` method with the "bar" plot kind. The plot is saved in a variable named `ax`, which I could call to annotate the graph. In this case, descriptive labels were added to the X-axis.

Three Basic Probability Distributions: Binomial, Uniform, and Normal

There are three probability distributions that appear often in applied analytics, whether Predictive or Prescriptive: binomial, uniform, and normal.

Binomial distribution

The *binomial distribution* is based on repeated trials of an experiment where the result of a trial is one of two possible outcomes, usually called "success" or "failure." These are unfortunate labels, but, nonetheless, conventional ones. There is really no reason why you have to use them. There are n trials in the experiment, and each is independent of any other. The probability of a success is assumed to be a constant, p, and, so, a failure is a constant, $q = 1 - p$, for a single trial. This strong assumption states that the likelihood is the same regardless of the trial. The probability is sometimes written as $X \sim Bin(n,p)$.

Under these assumptions, the probability the random variable X will have x successes in n trials is given by

$$Pr(X = x) = \frac{n!}{x! \times (n - x)!} \times p^x \times q^{(n - x)}$$
$$=_n C_x \times p^x \times q^{(n - x)}.$$

As an example, suppose the experiment is tossing a fair coin $n = 3$ times. The probability of a heads-up on a single toss is a constant $p = 0.5$. You want to know the probability of a single heads-up in the three tosses: $Pr(X = 1)$ where X is the event of a heads-up. The probability using the previous equation is $Pr(X = 1 \; heads) =_3 C_1 \times 0.5^1 \times 0.5^2 = 0.375$. The entire distribution is

$$_3C_0 \times 0.5^0 \times 0.5^3 = 0.125$$
$$_3C_1 \times 0.5^1 \times 0.5^2 = 0.375$$
$$_3C_2 \times 0.5^2 \times 0.5^1 = 0.375$$
$$_3C_3 \times 0.5^3 \times 0.5^0 = 0.125.$$

This distribution is the *binomial probability mass function (pmf)*. I show a graph of this distribution in Figure 4-9. I use a list comprehension in Line 6 to create a list of heads: [0,1,2,3] for $n = 3$ tosses. Another list comprehension in Line 7 creates the labels. These two lists are put into a dictionary in Line 8 which I use to create a DataFrame in Line 9. The binomial package's probability mass function (*pmf*) is used in the dictionary for the probabilities. I then plotted the DataFrame using the "bar" option.

Uniform distribution

The *uniform distribution* is sometimes the first that statistics students are introduced to because of its simplicity and commonsense appeal. Basically, it provides the probability for a range of values in the closed interval $[a,b]$. Usually the interval is $[0,1]$ and we write $U \sim Unif(0,1)$. This could be rescaled to cover any general interval $[min,max]$ using

$$U_i^{New} = \frac{U_i - U_{Min}}{U_{Max} - U_{Min}} \times \left(U_{Max}^{New} - U_{Min}^{New}\right) + U_{Min}^{New}.$$

This is a linear transformation so that the distributional properties of U are preserved. For example, if $U \sim Unif(0,1)$, then $X \sim Unif(3,6)$ using $U_i^{New} = 3 \times U_i + 3 = 6 \times U + 3 \times (1 - U)$. See Paczkowski (2022a, Chapter 5) for a discussion of linear transformations.

The height or density of the curve for a uniformly distributed random variable, U, in the general interval $[a,b]$, is $\frac{1}{b-a}$. I show an example in Figure 4-10 for the interval $[0,1]$.

```
1  ##
2  ## Plot the Uniform pdf for [0, 1]
3  ##
4  x = np.linspace( 0, 1, 100 )
5  data = { 'x':x, 'density':uniform.pdf( x ) }
6  df = pd.DataFrame( data )
7  df.plot( x = 'x', y = 'density', ylabel = 'Uniform Density', legend = False,
8          title = 'Uniform PDF\nfor the Interval [0, 1]' );
9
```

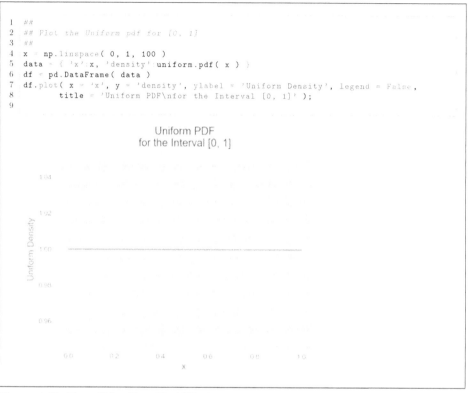

Figure 4-10. The pdf for $U \sim Unif(0,1)$.

Normal distribution

There are many distributions for a wide range of applications. The most used is the *normal distribution*, commonly called the "bell-shaped distribution." You should avoid calling the normal distribution the "bell-shaped distribution"—it is the *normal distribution*. There are many others that are bell-shaped. For example, the Student *t*-distribution.

I illustrate a typical normal distribution in Figure 4-11. All distributions are defined by two parameters: the mean and variance. For the one I show in Figure 4-11, the mean is zero and the variance is 1.0. With these parameter settings, the proper name is the *standardized normal distribution*. For notational purposes, the normal is written as $\mathcal{N}(\mu,\sigma^2)$ where μ is the mean and σ^2 is the variance. For the distribution in Figure 4-11, the notation is $\mathcal{N}(0,1)$. You will see this, and many others throughout this book.

```
1   ##
2   ## The Normal Distribution
3   ##
4   x = np.arange( -4, 4, 0.001 )
5   data = { 'x':x, 'density':norm.pdf( x ) }
6   df = pd.DataFrame( data )
7   df.plot( x = 'x', y = 'density', legend = False, ylabel = 'Density',
8           title = 'Standardized Normal Distribution' );
9
```

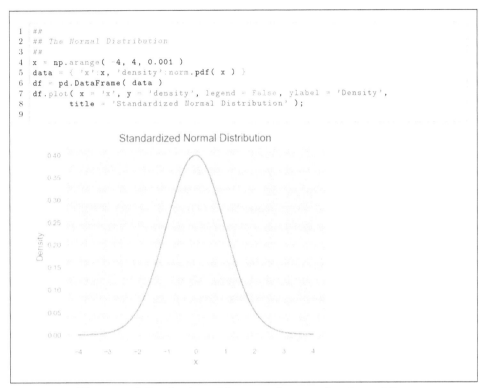

Figure 4-11. The normal distribution with mean of zero and variance 1.0.

Key Distribution Parameters

All distributions are characterized by two parameters: mean and variance.

The *mean* of a random variable X is called the *expected value*, represented by $E(X)$. Its definition depends on the type of random variable: discrete or continuous. If the random variable, X, is discrete, then

$$E(X) = \sum_{-\infty}^{+\infty} x_i p(x)$$

where $p(x) = \Pr(X = x)$, the probability that $X = x$, is the *pmf* with $0 \le p(x) \le 1$ and $\sum p(x) = 1$. So $E(X)$ is just a weighted average.

If X is continuous, then

$$E(X) = \int_{-\infty}^{+\infty} x f(x) dx$$

with $f(x) \geq 0$, $\forall x \in \mathbb{R}$, and $\int_{-\infty}^{+\infty} f(x) = 1$. The function $f(x)$ is the *probability density function (pdf)* of X at x. The *pdf* is NOT the probability of seeing $X = x$.

The *variance* is comparably defined except that squared deviations from the mean are used:

$$V(X) = \sum_{-\infty}^{+\infty} [x_i - E(X)]^2 p(x)$$

and

$$V(X) = \int_{-\infty}^{+\infty} [x_i - E(X)]^2 f(x) dx.$$

I show a function in Figure 4-12 for calculating the expected value for a discrete random variable. I then show an application of this function in Figure 4-13 using a small list of values and associated probabilities.

```
1   def expected_value( values, probs, what = 'mean' ):
2       ##
3       ## Calculations with list comprehensions
4       ##
5       mu = sum( [ values[ i ]*probs[ i ] for i in range( len( values ) ) ] )
6       if what == 'mean':
7           return( mu )
8       else:
9           sigsq = sum( [ ( ( values[ i ] - mu )**2)*probs[ i ] for i in range( len(
                           values ) ) ] )
10          return( sigsq )
11
```

Figure 4-12. A function to calculate the expected value and variance for a discrete random variable. Notice that I used a list comprehension and the enumerate *function to do the calculations.*

```
1   ##
2   ## Calculate expected value and variance
3   ##     Discrete case
4   ##
5   values = [ 4, 6, 8, 10, 12 ]
6   probs = [ .125, .1667, .375, .25, .0833 ]
7   ##
8   ## Mean
9   ##
10  mu = expected_value( values, probs )
11  print( f'Expected Value = {mu:0.3f}' )
12  ##
13  ## Variance
14  ##
15  sigsq = expected_value( values, probs, what = 'var' )
16  print( f'Variance = {sigsq:0.3f}' )
17

    Expected Value = 8.000
    Variance = 5.000
```

Figure 4-13. How to calculate the expected value and variance for a discrete random variable. I use the function in Figure 4-12.

Summary

This is the second of three primers for this book. This one covers probabilities, the backbone of all data science efforts to extract Rich Information from data. The reason for probabilities is simple: all data reflect random variations due to unknown and unknowable causes. This is the Noise in the paradigm: $Data = Information + Noise$.

In this chapter, I reviewed basic probability concepts summarized as fundamental probability laws. I then showed how you can do some probability calculations, derived Bayes' Theorem, discussed prior and posterior probabilities, and showed you how to access probability distributions using Python's random and NumPy packages.

The main concepts from this chapter are:

- The intuitive and formal probability concept
- Five Probability Rules
- Bayes' Theorem: its derivation, interpretation, and importance in data science and Prescriptive Analytics
- Prior and posterior probabilities
- Probability distributions using Python

PART III

Non-Stochastic Prescriptive Analytic Methods

In this book's third part, I will focus on non-stochastic methods for Prescriptive Analytics. My primary focus will be on Mathematical Programming and Decision Trees. The former is prominent in the Prescriptive Analytics literature, and the latter is a key tool in the Operations Research literature. There are two chapters in this part:

- Chapter 5, "Mathematical Programming: Overview"
- Chapter 6, "Decision Tree Analysis: Overview"

Mathematical Programming: Overview

I will introduce several popular and often used non-stochastic mathematical programming methods for Prescriptive Analytics in this chapter. These are:

- Classical linear programming
- Integer programming
- Mixed programming as a hybrid of the first two

The leading questions for this chapter are:

- What is the essence of mathematical programming?
- Why use mathematical programming in Prescriptive Analytics?
- What is linear programming and what is its use in decision making?
- What is integer programming and what is its use in decision making?
- What is mixed programming and what is its use in decision making?
- How is mathematical programming implemented in Python?

Background

Mathematical programming has a long practical history dating to the 1940s. This broad and powerful tool finds the combination of decision variables that optimizes an objective function. This function could be a production function, for example, based on classical economic theory. The decision variables in this case are capital and labor amounts. See Baumol (1965), Henderson and Quandt (1971), Ferguson (1972), and Gould and Lazear (1989) for economic discussions of production functions.

Optimization means either maximization or minimization, depending on the problem. For example, if the problem is to allocate manufacturing robots (the inputs) to the production of output (the objective function), then this is a maximization problem since you want the most output. If, however, the problem is to find the best route to deliver products to customers (the routes are the inputs) as quickly as possible (time is the objective function), then this is a minimization problem since you want the least amount of time possible.

Optimization, however, is not unconstrained; you cannot pick any combination of inputs. There are always constraints. A trivial one, of course, is that all inputs must be non-negative. A negative robot or a negative route are nonsensical, yet they could result just because of the mathematics. To guard against this, non-negativity constraints are placed on the inputs. Non-negativity means greater than or equal to zero, so a zero input is possible. Other constraints, written in terms of the decision variables, depend on the problem.

The term "programming" refers to a plan of action. This is appropriate for Prescriptive Analytics which is concerned with identifying the optimal item from a menu of possible actions.

The term "linear" refers to the objective function and the constraints (but not the non-negativity ones). In both cases, they have to be expressed as linear statements so all the crucial parts of an optimization statement (to repeat, excluding the non-negativity constraints) must be linear. This is a restriction on the framework, but not a severe one since non-linear programming methods have been developed. These handle situations in which the objective function and/or some constraints are non-linear. I will not discuss non-linear programming problems since they are quite complex and beyond the scope of this book. See Avriel (2003), Bazaraa and Shetty (1979), and Hadley (1970) for extensive development of this topic.

Reason for Popularity

The mathematical programming formulation of a problem is very popular in Prescriptive Analytics because of what a decision-maker must do: optimize a KPM.

The Objective Function: Prescriptive Analytics Goal

The KPM constitutes the objective function. Actually, it is an objective function once it is expressed as a linear function of the inputs. The KPM depends on the scale-view of the decision-maker. At the strategic level, it could be ROI or shareholder value. At the tactical level, it could be net product contribution or advertising reach. See Wikipedia (2023j) for an explanation of advertising reach. At the operational scale-view level, it could be production at several manufacturing plants or the time to get products to customers.

Linear Programming

In this section, I will develop the background for linear programming. Specifically, I will define the objective function, linear constraints, and non-negativity constraints in general terms and then describe how a linear programming problem is solved. I will illustrate the method using Python packages and functions. In my opinion, these methods are ideal for non-stochastic operational scale-view problems, so my use-cases will be at this level. The operations manager has fixed factors (jobs and manufacturing units, for example) and the issue is their optimal assignment. Another mathematical programming approach, a variation on linear programming, is better for the tactical and strategic scale-views, as I will show in "Integer Programming" on page 162.

Technical Overview

There are three components to a linear programming formulation:

- A linear objective function
- Linear constraints on the inputs
- Non-negativity constraints on the inputs

A classic example, based on economic theory, but with real-world daily operational significance, is a production function. An economist writes this function using simple functional notation. If Q is the level of output and the inputs are capital (K) and labor (L), then the function is:

$$Q = Q(K,L)$$

It is assumed that increases in K and L increase output, Q, but that the increases in Q diminish as each input is increased. This is the *Law of Diminishing Returns*. Maximization, however, is not without a constraint. Otherwise, the firm is free to produce an infinite amount of output. The constraint is cost-of-input, or total cost, written as

$$C = w \times L + r \times K$$

where C is the total cost of the inputs, w is the real wage per unit of labor, and r is the real rate of return on capital. This total cost function makes sense only if all the terms on the right-hand side are non-negative.

The economic production problem is succinctly expressed as:

$$MAX \ Q = Q(K,L)$$
$$ST:$$
$$C = w \times L + r \times K$$
$$w,r \geq 0$$
$$K,L \geq 0$$

where "ST" is a shorthand notation for "Subject To." This indicates that the expressions following it are the constraints: linear and non-negativity.

Output maximization leads to some key economic results such as the ratio of the marginal products of the inputs equals the ratio of the input prices. It is because of this fundamental economic problem that linear programming became important in economic studies in the early development of linear programming. See Baumol (1965) and Liebhafsky (1968) for discussions of linear programming in the context of economic theory, especially production and firm theories. Also, see Brigham and Ehrhardt (2002, p. 532) for comments about linear programming for capital rationing decisions.

The simplex approach

The first and basic solution of a linear programming problem uses the *simplex* method developed by Dantzig (1951). A simplex is a triangular figure: a triangle in two dimensions and a pyramid or tetrahedron in three. There is also a simplex in zero dimension and one dimension. It is a point in the former case and a line segment in the latter. I show the 1-, 2-, and 3-dimensional simplexes (a line segment, triangle, and tetrahedron, respectively) in Figure 5-1 and I list some possible figures in Table 5-1.

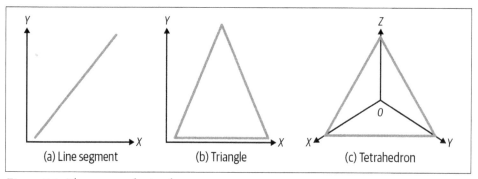

Figure 5-1. Three example simplexes.

The corners of a simplex are called *vertices*. A triangle has three vertices, a triangle-based pyramid has four, and a square-based pyramid has five.

Table 5-1. The dimensional representations of different simplexes. The 4-dimensional simplex is complicated to draw. See Wikipedia (2024a). The table is based on Wikipedia (2024i).

Dimensions of simplex	Figure
0-Dimensional	Point
1-Dimensional	Line Segment
2-Dimensional	Triangle
3-Dimensional	Tetrahedron
4-Dimensional	5-Cell

The simplex method involves iteratively testing the space defined by this figure until a solution is found at a vertex or a corner. I illustrate the method in Figure 5-2. I will provide a detailed example in "Operational scale-view: Example 1" on page 151.

Suppose there is only one linear constraint: $c_1^1 x_1 + c_2^1 x_2 \leq a^1$. This defines a region, called the *Feasible Region*, in the $x_1 - x_2$ plane as I show in Figure 5-2, Panel (a). The region is found by solving this inequality for x_2, which is the vertical axis in the figure. The solution is $x_2 \leq \dfrac{a^1}{c_2^1} - \left(\dfrac{c_1^1}{c_2^1}\right) x_1$. The Feasible Region is defined as a figure with points that go up to, but do not exceed, the line that defines this region.

All the points in the Feasible Region are potential solutions to the problem with this one constraint. They are potential solution points because they all satisfy the linear constraint.

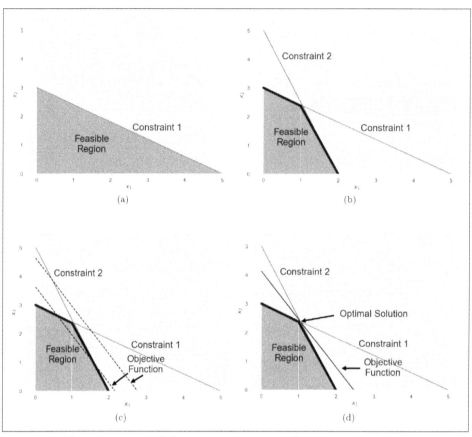

Figure 5-2. The components of a linear programming solution.

Now introduce a second linear constraint, $c_1^2 x_1 + c_2^2 x_2 \le a^2$, which can also be solved for x_2. This further narrows the Feasible Region as I show in Figure 5-2, Panel (b) because, intuitively, more constraints simply reduce the number of potential solutions; that is what constraints do. Clearly, even more linear constraints will further narrow the Feasible Region. Of course, too many could narrow it so much that a solution becomes difficult, if not impossible, to find. Also, some constraints could offset others so that a solution is, again, impossible. In both cases, the problem is *over-constrained*. I will stay with just two for this example.

A linear objective function can now be introduced. Let this be $z = z_1 x_1 + z_2 x_2$, which can also be re-expressed in terms of x_2 for plotting purposes. This is $x_2 = \frac{z}{z_2} - \left(\frac{z_1}{z_2}\right) x_1$. The slope is $-\frac{z_1}{z_2}$, which is a constant. The simplex method works by "moving" this constant-slope objective function in the $x_1 - x_2$ plane, each time checking if all the constraints are satisfied. The objective function cannot be arbitrarily moved by, say, rotation because the slope is constant as $-\frac{z_1}{z_2}$. This means that only parallel shifts are possible. I illustrate two such shifts in Figure 5-2, Panel (c). Notice that the dashed line furthest to the left satisfies the two constraints since part of the dashed line is in the Feasible Region. The one furthest to the right, however, does not satisfy either constraint and so does not give a solution.

The left-most objective function dashed line in Figure 5-2, Panel (c), although it satisfies the constraints, provides an infinite number of solutions: all the points on the dashed line inside the Feasible Region. Obviously, this is useless. However, if you shift it further to the right but not as far as the dashed line in Panel (c), you can find an even better solution, a single one. There is only one parallel shift that satisfies both constraints and that provides one solution: the point where the objective function touches a vertex of the Feasible Region. When an optimal solution exists, it will be at a vertex or one corner of the Feasible Region, and there will be only one (which could be an unbounded solution). See Hadley (1970, pp. 76–77). I illustrate this optimal solution in Figure 5-2, Panel (d).

You can quickly see or determine the optimal solution, of course, for a simple example as the one I show here.

This description of the simplex method is highly simplified. The mathematics behind it is complex and involves advanced mathematical knowledge, primarily matrix algebra, to understand it. An excellent and classic treatment is Hadley (1970). This method works by iteratively examining the objective function for a feasible solution and then moving to another feasible solution if the objective function is improved. So it goes step-by-step from one solution to another as long as the objective function improves. This is actually a very common approach for finding numeric solutions to complex problems: to iteratively home in on the optimal solution.

Digression: The production function

I previously mentioned the economic problem of maximizing output subject to a cost constraint. In economics, the production function is typically displayed as a convex-to-the-origin curve called an *isoquant*. A basic production function is the *fixed-proportions production function* (also called a *Leontief Function*) that shows that one, and only one, ratio of inputs can be used in the production process. If output is to be expanded or contracted, all inputs must be expanded or contracted so that the ratio of inputs is fixed. Adding a small amount of one input will not change the level of output.

Mathematically, this is represented by:

$$Q = min\left(\frac{K}{v}, \frac{L}{u}\right)$$

where "min" means find the minimum of the two arguments and use that as Q. The u and v are technological constants (e.g., $\frac{1}{v} = \frac{Q}{K}$ is the average product of capital and has the units of output per unit of capital; similarly for $\frac{1}{u}$).

Two properties of this function are:

1. If $\frac{L}{u}$ is the smallest, then increasing K will do nothing; and

2. Q can be no higher than the minimum of either the first or second argument.

As an example of this function's use, suppose you have a ditch-digging crew of two men, each with one shovel. So $L = 2$, $K = 2$, and $\frac{K}{L} = 1$. Adding another worker or another shovel will not increase the number of ditches dug. Output is just what the first two workers with their two shovels could produce, not the three workers. Adding another worker, however, with another shovel will increase the number of ditches dug. Note that $\frac{K}{L} = 1$ after the addition of the third worker and the third shovel.

I illustrate this production function in Figure 5-3. The dashed line from the origin is the capital-labor ratio which has a slope of 1.0. The right-angled lines are the isoquants. The one labeled Q_1 is sub-optimal: you can produce more. The one labeled Q_2 is infeasible: it is outside the Feasible Region. The one labeled Q_{OPT} is the optimal amount that just satisfies the cost constraint.

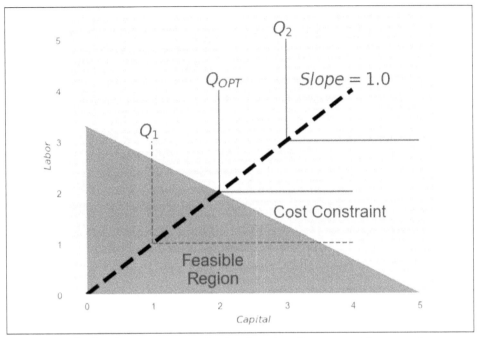

Figure 5-3. The fixed proportions production function. Output must be somewhere on the dashed line from the origin. The optimal production is Q_{OPT}.

Other solution methods

There are several optimization algorithms, called *solvers*, available in SciPy:

- `highs` (the default)
- `highs-ds`
- `highs-ipm`
- `interior-point` (to be deprecated)
- `revised simplex` (to be deprecated)
- `simplex` (to be deprecated)

 Although SciPy has several methods, three are maintained as legacy methods at the time I am writing this book and will be deprecated in future editions of SciPy.

The simplex method is the oldest for finding an optimal solution for a linear function when there are multiple linear constraints. The implementation involves a table or matrix, called a *tableau*. This is updated for each iteration in the algorithm. Unfortunately, this tableau maintenance can become computationally expensive, especially for large problems. A modified version, the *revised simplex method*, provides the same solution as the original simplex method, but is computationally more efficient. See Wikipedia (2023k).

The *interior-point method* was developed in the 1980s, at least in the U.S. See Wikipedia (2023k). This is even more efficient. It finds an optimal solution by reversing the simplex method which searches the boundary of the Feasible Region for a solution. The interior-point method, instead, approaches the solution from the interior points. As a result, it can find solutions in less computational time than the simplex method.

A class of methods called *HiGHS* is based on open-source software for efficiently solving a wide variety of optimization problems. It has been ported to a number of platforms such as C, Python, Julia, Rust, JavaScript, Fortran, and C#. See Wikipedia (2023f).

HiGHS is also a project with a project team responsible for the development and maintenance of this class of solvers.

HiGHS is a class of solvers for linear programming problems. Two specific ones are `highs-ipm`, which uses the `interior-point method` (hence, the *ipm* extension), and `highs-ds`, which uses a *dual-simplex method* (hence, the *ds* extension). Technically, these are *wrappers* for the underlying algorithms developed by the *HiGHS* project. The `highs` method automatically chooses between `highs-ipm` and `highs-ds`, although you can certainly select one of them. The SciPy documentation recommends you use one of the `highs` methods.

HiGHS is an acronym for the original developers. See Hall (2023) for a good overview presentation.

Handling special issues

There are two issues you have to be aware of which must be addressed:

- Inequality constraints
- Maximization of the objective function

First, the constraints in a linear programming problem are usually expressed as inequalities, in the form of "less-than-or-equal" (i.e., $\leq$) or "greater-than-or-equal" (i.e., $\geq$). These may be realistic, but they needlessly complicate computations. Equalities are easier to handle. This is not an issue for linear programming problems, however, since new variables could be added that take up the slack between a "less-than-or-equal" problem and an equality on the one hand, or the surplus between an equality and a "greater-than-or-equal" problem on the other hand. The former is called a *slack variable* and the latter is called a *surplus variable*. Linear programming software automatically handles slack and surplus variables, so there is nothing for you to deal with. The amount of the slack or surplus is indicated in the output.

Second, problems can be either minimization or maximization. For example, a production problem is a maximization because most production facilities want to maximize output. You would be hard-pressed to find any production problems where management wants to minimize the amount produced; minimization is irrational. If they do want to minimize output, then the solution is easy to find: simply stop production. A cost problem, however, is a minimization. In a manner like production, you would be hard-pressed to find any manager who wants to maximize how much it costs to produce something; maximization is irrational.

It is more efficient computationally to have an algorithm that handles only one of these problems, but the output, the optimal solution, can be applied to either case. This is how SciPy handles it. It assumes that all problems are minimizations. So you must convert maximization problems to minimization problems. It turns out that any maximization problem can be converted to a minimization problem simply by multiplying the coefficients of the objective function by -1. You do not multiply the constraints by -1, just the coefficients of the objective function.

I will use the operations research toolkit developed by Google: OR-Tools. This comprehensive toolkit has many powerful optimization functions plus an intuitive syntax for specifying a problem. OR-Tools "is an open-source software suite for optimization, tuned for tackling the world's toughest problems in vehicle routing, flows, integer and linear programming, and constraint programming." See Anaconda (2023). In addition to the syntax, it has several *solver* routines that solve complex mathematical programming problems. The list of solvers includes (based on pypi [2023]):

Constraint programming
> *CP-SAT solver* that uses SAT (i.e., satisfiability) methods and the original *CP solver*, a constraint programming solver.

Linear and mixed-integer programming
> GLOP: a linear optimizer for a linear objective function given a set of linear inequality constraints. This is recommended for linear programming and mixed integer problems.

MPSolver, ModelBuilder
> Wrappers around commercial and other open source solvers such as the mixed integer solvers: CBC, CLP, GLPK, Gurobi, or SCIP. I recommend SCIP, short for "Solving Constraint Integer Programs," for integer programming problems. Refer to Bolusani (2024).

Vehicle routing
> A specialized library for identifying best vehicle routes given constraints.

Graph algorithms
> Code for finding the shortest paths in graphs, min-cost flows, max flows, and linear sum assignments.

You install the OR-Tools on your local computer using the following:

- `pip install ortools`
- `conda install -c conda-forge ortools-python`

Once it is installed, you import the package from the toolkit using the following:

```
\emph{from ortools.linear\_solver import pywraplp}
```

This will provide you with the needed tools in Python. The OR-Tools package is also available for C++, Java, and C#. I recommend, as always, that you put this import command in your Best Practices section at the beginning of your JupyterLab notebook.

Menus and Linear Programming

The menu for a linear programming problem consists of the vertices or corners of the simplex defined by the constraints. In Figure 5-4, which is Figure 5-2, Panel (b), the menu options are the points A, B, and C. The attributes of these options are the decision variables, X_1 and X_2 in this case. Which menu option—A, B, or C—is best? "Best" is defined in the sense of satisfying the two constraints.

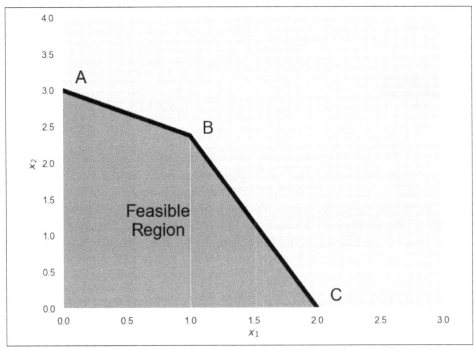

Figure 5-4. A repeat of Figure 5-2, Panel (b), without the constraints but with the menu options—possible solutions—indicated as A, B, and C.

Python Use-Cases

In this section, I will provide examples of the use of linear programming for operational purposes.

Operational scale-view: Example 1

Consider a large, sophisticated, and very well-established family-owned bakery company in midtown Manhattan, New York City, that uses two 3-D printers to produce two different forms of pastries, which I simply call X and Y. The "printing" is just mixing the dough and forming the pastries. These are made in four batches according to the time of day customers enter the bakery:

- Early morning for the morning rush hour
- Mid-morning for a morning snack
- Lunch time
- Mid-afternoon for a mid-day snack

Regardless of the time of day, the pastries are sold at the price points I show in Table 5-2.

Table 5-2. The pastry prices for the linear programming example.

Pastry	Price/Pound
X	$5.00
Y	$3.00

The owner of the bakery, a third-generation owner who recently earned an MBA from a prestigious school, hired a consulting company to build a simple model to forecast daily pastry sales in pounds. The consultant built an *ARIMA* times series model that predicts daily sales for each pastry. See Paczkowski (2023) for a description of *ARIMA* times series modeling in Predictive Analytics. The model accounts for the time of day and day of the week. Suppose for one particular day, the model predicts 4.2 pounds of pastry X will be sold per batch, and 3.1 pounds of Y will be sold at the same times.

Regarding the two 3-D printers, one is slightly older so it takes longer to make a batch of pastries. Suppose the older one needs 15 minutes and the newer one 10 minutes. The time per pastry also varies by printer. The older one needs 3 minutes per pound of X and 5 minutes per pound of Y, while the newer one needs 5 minutes and 2 minutes, respectively. The owner needs to know how many pounds of each pastry to "print" per batch to maximize the net contribution of the two pastries.

The problem set-up is:

$$Maximize\ R = \$5 \times X + \$3 \times Y$$
$$ST$$
$$3 \times X + 5 \times Y \leq 15 \quad Printer\ 1$$
$$5 \times X + 2 \times Y \leq 10 \quad Printer\ 2$$
$$0 \leq X \leq 4.2$$
$$0 \leq Y \leq 3.1$$

The first line is the objective function. This indicates that net contribution, R, which is to be maximized, is composed of the total net sales of X and Y. Each individual contribution is just price times quantity. This assumes the amount produced of each pastry is sold so there are no pastries left for a next-day "day-old" sale.

The second line indicates the beginning of the constraints. The "ST" stands for "Subject To," a common indicator. The two printer conditions reflect the processing time of the two printers and the two inequality conditions reflect the predicted sales from the *ARIMA* model. These are non-negativity constraints since the bakery is unable to produce negative amounts of pastry (that should be obvious) but it needs to produce no more than predicted.

 Notice the connection between Predictive Analytics and Prescriptive Analytics. The connecting point is the sales forecast in this example. I illustrate this in Figure 5-5.

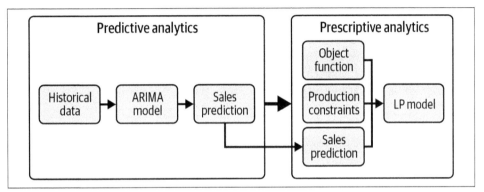

Figure 5-5. The connection between Predictive Analytics and Prescriptive Analytics for the pastry example. The same connection will hold for any problem, with appropriate adjustments, of course.

The problem is usually specified with matrix notation. The constraint conditions are $\mathbf{A_{ub}x} \le \mathbf{b_{ub}}$ where the subscript ub means "upper bound" and the boldface type indicates a matrix or vector. You could have several equality constraints, in which case you have $\mathbf{A_{eq}x} = \mathbf{b_{eq}}$ where the subscript eq means "equality." The $\mathbf{A_{ub}}$ term is the coefficient matrix, the $\mathbf{x}$ term is the vector of decision variables, and the $\mathbf{b_{ub}}$ term is the vector of constraint values. This notation follows that used in the SciPy documentation. For the bakery problem,

$$\mathbf{A_{ub}} = \begin{pmatrix} 3 & 5 \\ 5 & 2 \end{pmatrix}$$

$$\mathbf{x} = \begin{pmatrix} x \\ y \end{pmatrix}$$

$$\mathbf{b_{ub}} = \begin{pmatrix} 15 \\ 10 \end{pmatrix}$$

so that

$$\begin{pmatrix} 3 & 5 \\ 5 & 2 \end{pmatrix} \begin{pmatrix} x \\ y \end{pmatrix} \le \begin{pmatrix} 15 \\ 10 \end{pmatrix}$$

The objective function is $R = \mathbf{c}'\mathbf{x}$ where R is the net revenue (a scalar) and $\mathbf{c}$ is a vector of coefficients for the linear function. For the bakery problem, $\mathbf{c} = \begin{pmatrix} 5 \\ 3 \end{pmatrix}$. The prime indicator on the $\mathbf{c}$ vector indicates the vector is transposed so $\mathbf{c}' = (5\ 3)$.

I will use the Google OR-Tools for this problem. The recommended solvers are GLOP for linear and mixed integer problems and SCIP for pure integer problems. There are five steps for specifying an optimization problem, whether it is a linear, integer, or mixed programming problem. These are:

1. Specify the solver.
2. Specify the decision variables.
3. Specify the constraints.
4. Specify the objective function.
5. Summarize the results.

I show the Python code set-up and results for the bakery problem in Figure 5-6. A graphical display of this problem is in Figure 5-7. You can see from the graph that the results summarized in Figure 5-6 agree with the graphical solution.

```
1   ##
2   ## Linear programming example
3   ## Based on Hadley, p. 9, Eqs. 1-16
4   ##
5   ## ===> Step 1: Specify solver <===
6   ##
7   solver = pywraplp.Solver.CreateSolver( 'GLOP' )
8   ##
9   ## ===> Step 2: Specify decision variables <===
10  ##
11  infinity = solver.infinity()            ## Sets upper bound
12  x = solver.NumVar( 0.0, infinity, 'x' )  ## Use NumVar for numeric variables
13  y = solver.NumVar( 0.0, infinity, 'y' )
14  ##
15  ## ===> Step 3: Specify constraints <===
16  ##
17  solver.Add( 3*x + 5*y <= 15 )
18  solver.Add( 5*x + 2*y <= 10 )
19  ##
20  ## ===> Step 4: Specify objective function <===
21  ##
22  solver.Maximize( 5*x + 3*y )
23  status = solver.Solve()
24  ##
25  ## ===> Step 5: Summarize results <===
26  ##
27  sol = solver.Objective().Value()
28  prod_x = x.solution_value()
29  prod_y = y.solution_value()
30  ##
31  print( f'Optimized Net Contribution:\n\t\${sol:0.0f}' )
32  print( f'Production:\n\tX: {prod_x:0.2f}\n\tY: {prod_y:0.2f}' )
33

    Optimized Net Contribution:
            $12
    Production:
            X: 1.05
            Y: 2.37
```

Figure 5-6. The set-up and resulting solution for the bakery linear programming example. The optimized net contribution is $12 based on producing 1.05 pounds of X and 2.37 pounds of Y.

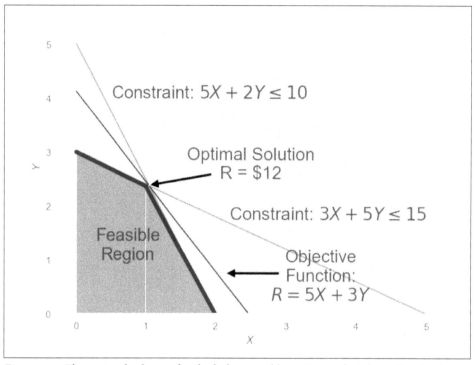

Figure 5-7. The optimal solution for the bakery problem. Notice that the optimal solution is $12 as in Figure 5-6.

I specify the solver as GLOP in Line 7. This is necessary for the remaining key parts of a programming problem: the decision variables, constraints, and objective function, as well as to retrieve the optimized solution. The decision variables are in Lines 12 and 13. Since this problem requires floats as answers, the solver's NumVar method is used. There is an IntVar method for integer answers, but you will see this one later. The NumVar method requires three arguments:

- The minimum value for the decision variable. This is zero in most instances since negative values often do not make physical sense.

- The maximum value for the decision variable. This could be specified as being unbounded unless a specific number is known. In most instances with many decision variables and constraints, you will not know these values, so it is advisable to specify them as unbounded. You can do this using the solver's infinity method as I show in Line 11.

- The last argument is the symbol for the decision variable. The whole method is stored in a variable as I show in Lines 12 and 13.

You can print the number of decision variables as a sanity check using

```
print( f'Number of variables: {solver.NumVariables()}' ).
```

The constraints are added to the solver using the ADD method. This method is an example of the simpler syntax of the OR-Tools: you algebraically specify the constraint. You can see two examples in Lines 17 and 18. You can print the number of constraints using

```
print( f'Number of constraints: {solver.NumConstraints()}' ).
```

The objective function is also algebraically specified as I show in Line 22. For a maximization problem, use the keyword Maximum; use Minimum otherwise. This is an advantage over SciPy which only allows minimization problems.

Table 5-3. The costs per pallet of printing three printing jobs on three different printers.

Job	Printer 1 (P1)	Printer 2 (P2)	Printer 3 (P3)
A	$4	$6	$11
B	$5	$8	$16
C	$9	$13	$21

Once you specify the objective function, you have to run the solver to get the solution. You do this using the solver's *Solve* method as in Line 23. A quirk of OR-Tools is that the solver's return status must be accessed, as I show in Line 23. If the status is 0, then the optimal solution was found.

Finally, you can retrieve and display the solutions as I show in Lines 27 to 32. Sometimes, it is useful to display them only if an optimal value was found. You can do this using code such as:

```
if status == pywraplp.Solver.OPTIMAL:
    print( 'Solution:' )
    print( f'Objective value = solver.Objective().Value()' )
    print( f'x = x.solution_value()' )
    print( f'y = y.solution_value()' )
else:
    print( 'The problem does not have an optimal solution.' )
```

Operational scale-view: Example 2

Now consider a second use-case. However, it will be instructive to view this one slightly differently, although it is, at heart, a linear programming problem. For this example, suppose an operations manager for a cardboard box manufacturing company has large orders for four different types of boxes to be produced in one day. Each order is unique with the client's logo, company name, and address printed on the box. The sizes also differ. Once printed, the boxes are loaded on pallets and shipped to the client. Let the size of each order, that is the number of pallets, be the same for this example. The boxes are produced on large, complex printing presses, but the manufacturer has only four of them. The operations manager has to assign each order to one and only one of these printers. He has a narrow, operational scale-view since he is solely concerned with meeting a production requirement for that day.

The printers, unfortunately, are not all equally efficient so the printing costs per pallet vary depending on the job. I show a cost matrix in Table 5-3. The problem for the manager is the optimal assignment of the jobs, one to a machine, to minimize the total cost of producing the boxes. This is an *assignment problem*. There is a wide variety of problems of this type so, from an operations scale-view perspective, this is a very real problem.

There are five conditions for this problem:

- The number of assignees and tasks are the same (n).
- Each assignee is assigned to only one task.
- Each task is performed by only one assignee.
- There is a cost associated with assignee i, $i = 1,2,...,n$, performing task j, $j = 1,2,...,n$.
- The objective is to make all n assignments to minimize the total cost.

Hillier and Lieberman (2010, p. 334) note that the first three assumptions are restrictive, but not major issues. When the number of assignees and tasks are equal, the assignment problem is a *balanced problem*; it is *unbalanced*, otherwise. An unbalanced problem is easily handled using *dummy assignees* or *dummy tasks* as appropriate. These "dummies" are all zero costs for the assignees or tasks. I will illustrate how to handle this. At first, however, I will assume a balanced assignment problem.

An assignment problem, balanced or unbalanced, is actually a permutation problem. Since there are n assignees, the permutation problem is how to assign each of them to each task. Once an assignee is assigned, there are $n - 1$ left to assign. This continues until the last one is assigned. The total number of possible assignments is $_nP_n = n!$ from Chapter 4. For this printer problem, $_3P_3 = 3! = 6$. I show the calculation in Figure 5-8 using the `math.perm` function from Chapter 4. You can easily list all the arrangements of the three jobs using all three of them or you can use the permutation function from Chapter 4. I show this listing in Figure 5-9.

```
1   ##
2   ## Number of permutations for printer example
3   ##
4   n = 3   ## assignees
5   p = math.perm( n )
6   print( f'Number of permutations: {p}' )
7

    Number of permutations: 6
```

Figure 5-8. The printer permutation calculation using the math.perm function.

```
1   ##
2   ## Permute the following list of words
3   ##
4   lst = [ 'A', 'B', 'C' ]
5   n = 3
6   perm( size = None, select = n, kind = 'list', obj = lst )
7

    The number of permutations of 3 things select 3 at a time is: 6
    The listing is:

        0  1  2

    0   A  B  C

    1   A  C  B

    2   B  A  C

    3   B  C  A

    4   C  A  B

    5   C  B  A
```

Figure 5-9. A listing of the permutations of three jobs assigned to three printers. The column labels correspond to printers P1 – P3 in Table 5-3.

I show a possible function in Figure 5-10 for our balanced assignment problem. The cost matrix is square: it is a 3×3 matrix. This matrix, expressed as a pandas Dataframe, is passed to a function that applies an algorithm to make the optimal assignments. The rows are the assignees and the columns are the tasks. For our problem, the assignees are jobs, but they could be projects, salespeople, locations, and so on.

Do not interpret "task" literally. The columns could be tasks per se, or machines (as in this example), manufacturing locations, clients, and so on. The assignees are objects assigned to a task.

The results of the assignments are indicators of the column and task for each assignee. The result is a two-tuple unpacked into a row indicator (the assignees) and their associated column indicator (the tasks). I add these appropriately to the original cost matrix along with the cost associated with each assignment. The total cost is the sum of these assignment costs.

For the assignments in Figure 5-10, the first job (A) is assigned to printer $P3$, the second (B) to $P2$, and the third (C) to $P1$. The cost of each assignment is indicated in the *Cost* column. The total cost is $28, which is a minimum.

```
1   ##
2   ## Assignment problem with balanced cost matrix
3   ##
4   ## Create dictionary of data: costs, time, distance, etc.
5   ##
6   data = { 'P1':[ 4, 5, 9 ], 'P2':[ 6, 8, 13 ], 'P3':[ 11, 16, 21 ] }
7   cols = list( data.keys() )
8   df = pd.DataFrame( data, index = [ 'A', 'B', 'C' ] )
9   ##
10  ## Do assignments
11  ##
12  row_ind, col_ind = linear_sum_assignment( df )
13  ##
14  ## Display results
15  ##
16  df[ 'Assignment' ] = [ cols[ i ] for i in col_ind ]
17  df[ 'Cost' ] = [ df.iloc[ row_ind[ i ] ][ col_ind[ i ] ] for i in range( len(
                    row_ind ) ) ]
18  display( df )
19  print( f'Minimal Total Cost: \${df.Cost.sum()}' )
20

        P1 P2 P3  Assignment  Cost

    A   4  6  11          P3    11

    B   5  8  16          P2     8

    C   9  13 21          P1     9

    Minimal Total Cost: $28
```

Figure 5-10. The optimal assignment and the minimal cost of three jobs assigned to three printers.

Now consider an unbalanced assignment problem. Suppose instead of three jobs, there are four. But there are still three printers. What are the assignments now? The cost matrix is 4×3 as I show in Table 5-4.

Table 5-4. The costs per pallet of printing four printing jobs on three different printers.

Job	Printer 1 (P1)	Printer 2 (P2)	Printer 3 (P3)
A	$9	$26	$15
B	$13	$27	$6
C	$35	$20	$15
D	$18	$30	$20

The algorithm expects a square matrix, so this current one must be augmented with an additional column to make it square. This additional column is composed of all zero values and is a *dummy task*, or dummy printer for this problem. I show in

Figure 5-11 how this is handled using [0] * 4. This replicates the list, [0], four times to yield [0,0,0,0].

The optimal assignments are produced as before. The "D" job is assigned to the dummy printer which means it is not assigned to any printer. The total minimum cost is $35. Notice that the costs are $7 higher than when there is a square cost matrix. This should be expected because a job is not done. The $7 is an opportunity cost or lost revenue.

```
1  ##
2  ## Assignment problem with unbalanced cost matrix
3  ##
4  ## Create a dictionary of data: costs, time, distance, etc.
5  ##
6  data = { 'P1':[ 9, 13, 35, 18 ], 'P2':[ 26, 27, 20, 30 ], 'P3':[ 15, 6, 15, 20 ],
                                    'P4':[ 0 ]*4 }
7  cols = list( data.keys() )
8  df = pd.DataFrame( data, index = [ 'A', 'B', 'C', 'D' ] )
9  ##
10 ## Do assignments
11 ##
12 row_ind, col_ind = linear_sum_assignment( df )
13 ##
14 ## Display results
15 ##
16 df[ 'Assignment' ] = [ cols[ i ] for i in col_ind ]
17 df[ 'Cost' ] = [ df.iloc[ row_ind[ i ] ][ col_ind[ i ] ] for i in range( len(
                                    row_ind ) ) ]
18 display( df )
19 print( f'Minimal Total Cost: \${df.Cost.sum()}' )
20
```

	P1	P2	P3	P4	Assignment	Cost
A	9	26	15	0	P1	9
B	13	27	6	0	P3	6
C	35	20	15	0	P2	20
D	18	30	20	0	P4	0

Minimal Total Cost: $35

Figure 5-11. The optimal assignment and the minimal cost of four jobs assigned to three printers. A dummy printer is included with zero costs for each job. Values for costs from BrainKart (https://www.brainkart.com/article/Solution-of-assignment-problems-(Hungarian-Method)_39044/).

A variation of the unbalanced problem is to have more tasks than assignees. Suppose for our problem there are five rather than four printers, but there are still four jobs. What is the best assignment of these four jobs to the five printers? I show a different cost matrix in Figure 5-12. This matrix is augmented with a dummy row for a fifth "job." The solution is obtained as before.

```
 1  ##
 2  ## Assignment problem with unbalanced cost matrix
 3  ##
 4  ## Create dictionary of data: costs, time, distance, etc.
 5  ##
 6  data = { 'P1':[ 4, 6, 4, 0 ], 'P2':[ 5, 4, 5, 2 ], 'P3':[ 9, 0, 8, 6 ], 'P4':[
                      4, 4, 5, 1 ], 'P5':[ 5, 3, 1, 2 ]}
 7  cols = list( data.keys() )
 8  df = pd.DataFrame( data, index = [ 'A', 'B', 'C', 'D' ] )
 9  ##
10  ## Concatenate or append a dummy row to the cost matrix
11  ##
12  data = { 'P' + str( i ):0 for i in range( 1, 6 ) }
13  df2 = pd.DataFrame( data, index = [ 'E' ] )
14  df = pd.concat([ df, df2 ], axis = 0, ignore_index = False )
15  ##
16  ## Do assignments
17  ##
18  row_ind, col_ind = linear_sum_assignment( df )
19  ##
20  ## Display results
21  ##
22  df[ 'Assignment' ] = [ cols[ i ] for i in col_ind ]
23  df[ 'Cost' ] = [ df.iloc[ row_ind[ i ] ][ col_ind[ i ] ] for i in range( len(
                      row_ind ) ) ]
24  display( df )
25  print( f'Minimal Total Cost: \${df.Cost.sum()}' )
26
```

	P1	P2	P3	P4	P5	Assignment	Cost
A	4	5	9	4	5	P4	4
B	6	4	0	4	3	P3	0
C	4	5	8	5	1	P5	1
D	0	2	6	1	2	P1	0
E	0	0	0	0	0	P2	0

```
Minimal Total Cost: $5
```

Figure 5-12. The optimal assignment and the minimal cost of four jobs assigned to five printers. A dummy job is included with zero costs for each printer.

Integer Programming

Linear programming is powerful and popularly used in many real-world business problems, primarily operational scale-view ones. Tactical and strategic scale-views are different. They frequently have a menu of *Most Likely Views*. Paczkowski (2023) outlines predictive methods, some of which can easily lead to the development of these menus. For example, the regression family of models can be used to develop menus. In fact, Paczkowski (2023) describes scenarios, which are the Most Likely Views, and thus lays the groundwork for this discussion. The issue for Prescriptive Analytics is which menu option to select or recommend to the decision-maker.

Linear programming per se cannot handle this issue because of the continuous nature of the decision variables. The non-negativity constraints ensure they will never be negative, but they can still have a decimal value. For example, a decision variable x could equal 1.5. In the context of a menu, if x is an option, then what is 1.5? It would make more sense if $x = 1$, implying the option is selected, and $x = 0$, implying otherwise. The x is a binary or a dummy variable in this case. In fact, it is even better if the objective function is the sum of the dummy variables, one dummy for each menu option, such that sum is 1.0. This is the basis of *integer programming* and its use in tactical and strategic scale-view decision problems.

I will review the background for integer programming in the next section and provide several use-cases.

Technical Overview

Integer programming differs from linear programming in two important respects. First, and most obviously, the decision variables are restricted to be *integer numbers* rather than *real numbers*. The integer restrictions are called *integrality restrictions*.An integer is defined as:

- Whole or *natural numbers*, sometimes called *counting numbers*, such as 1,2,3,..., without a decimal component
- The number zero
- The negative of the natural numbers

The mathematical symbol for integers is $\mathbb{Z}$ so that $\mathbb{Z} = \{..., -3, -2, -1, 0, 1, 2, 3...\}$. You might also see this more compactly written as $x \in \mathbb{Z}$ for x as an integer. The natural numbers, represented by $\mathbb{N}$, is the set $\{1,2,3...\}$ which is a subset of $\mathbb{Z}$: $\mathbb{N} \subseteq \mathbb{Z}$. The set of all real numbers is represented by $\mathbb{R}$ and includes any value with a decimal component. The natural and integer numbers are subsets of the real numbers: $\mathbb{N} \subseteq \mathbb{Z} \subseteq \mathbb{R}$. There are actually two others that I do not consider here: *rational* ($\mathbb{Q}$) and *complex* ($\mathbb{C}$) numbers so the whole number system is: $\mathbb{N} \subseteq \mathbb{Z} \subseteq \mathbb{Q} \subseteq \mathbb{R} \subseteq \mathbb{C}$. See Wikipedia (2024g) for a good description of the number system.

This very brief and incomplete description of numbers is important because you have to specify the restrictions correctly for an integer programming problem. If x is a decision variable, then you cannot specify it as $x \geq 0$ for an integer programming problem because x could be any value such as 3.14159. The only acceptable values are negative whole numbers, zero, and positive whole numbers. This is not the case for linear programming.

You might believe this distinction is unimportant because you can round any continuous, real number to its integer part. There are certainly many applications in which this is done, but this is not one of them. Or, you might believe a linear programming problem is simpler to solve so it could be used with, again, rounding. This is not advised because of the Feasible Region carved out by the constraints. Any solution must satisfy this Region. In the case of linear programming, the solution is a vertex or corner of the simplex resulting from the constraints, so the Region is satisfied. In the case of integer programming, it might be in the interior of the Feasible Region. Rounding may result in the solution being outside the Region and, therefore, suboptimal. See Hillier and Lieberman (2010, p. 489) for an example.

The second important distinction between linear and integer programming is the flexibility you have in handling an array of problems with integer programming. For example, the solution could be restricted to be binary, either *Yes* or *No*: introduce a new product; merge with another company; advertise in print media. In this case, the decision variable is specified as:

$$x_i = \begin{cases} 1 \text{ if decision is Yes} \\ 0 \text{ otherwise.} \end{cases}$$

This is a *binary integer programming* problem. Binary variables are used for menu selection. You can now handle different cases:

Case 1
> You can select as many as needed from the menu to meet the objective.

Case 2
> You could have a decision that involves selecting a specific number, m, from a menu. For example, you could manage only two new products with the current resources. Which two? The restriction is $\sum_{i=1}^{n} x_i = m, m < n$ (e.g., $m = 2$).

Case 2a
> You could have an *only one* problem: you will merge with one of your partners—which one? The restriction is $\sum_{i=1}^{n} x_i = 1$. These could be used on any subset of binary restrictions so they are not meant to be used solely for all the decision variables. This is a special case of Case 2 with $m = 1$. This special case occurs quite often.

Case 3
> You could have a *conditional* problem: one or more menu options can only be selected given a decision about other menu options. For example, you would build a warehouse in a region only if you also build a factory in that same region. These are sometimes referred to as *logical conditions*.

See Hillier and Lieberman (2010) for many examples.

This flexibility comes at a cost: computational complexity. Linear programming, although not trivial itself, is simpler to deal with. This is why some analysts prefer to use linear programming to solve an integer problem. But you must avoid this temptation.

Integer Programming Algorithms

Many integer programming algorithms incorporate a linear programming component, but one that relaxes the integer restrictions. In this case, this is called an *LP Relaxation*. The details of this are beyond the scope of this book. See Hillier and Lieberman (2010, p. 488) for a discussion.

Menus and Integer Programming

In an integer programming context, a menu consists of a series of projects, and the decision-maker must select one or more from the menu based on the decision variables. The choice is specified as any of the cases I have noted. The menu will be clear in the following use-cases.

Python Use-Cases

I will present several use-cases in this section using Python to illustrate integer programming. The set-up for each uses the OR-Tools I previously introduced. The set-up is identical to what you saw earlier except the decision variables are all specified to be integers. This will change slightly for the Mixed Integer problem in "Mixed Integer Programming" on page 178.

Tactical scale-view

There are many tactical scale-view problems: pricing, new product development and introduction, advertising, promotion, channel selection, and so on. In fact, the *Four Ps of Marketing* are all tactical scale-view problems. For this use-case, suppose a marketing executive must select a media outlet for advertising the enterprise's products. This example, based on Bradley et al. (1977, p. 305, Exercise 3), has six media outlets:

- TV
- Trade magazine
- Newspaper
- Radio
- Popular magazine
- Promotional campaign

These six outlets constitute the menu.

For each outlet, the total expected customer reach, the cost of reaching those customers, the cost in man-hours of designing a reach program, and the cost of a sales contact (also in man-hours) are known. These are the attributes of the menu options.

For each cost constraint, the total budget is known from the business plan. These data are in Table 5-5. The objective is to maximize total customer reach subject to the three cost constraints.

Table 5-5. The data for the tactical problem of the optimal media to use to reach the most customers.

	TV	Trade magazine	Newspaper	Radio	Popular magazine	Promotional campaign	Total resources
Reachable customers	1,000,000	200,000	300,000	400,000	450,000	450,000	
Cost ($)	500,000	150,000	300,000	250,000	250,000	100,000	1,800,000
Designers (person-hours)	700	250	200	200	300	400	1,500
Salespeople (person-hours)	200	100	100	100	100	1,000	1,200

Customer Reach Definition

Reach is the total number of customers contacted, touched, or informed about a product or strategy through a media outlet. This does not mean they will buy a product; they only become informed. See Paczkowski (2018) for a discussion about reach in the TURF (*totally unduplicated reach and frequency*) methodology for pricing.

Case 1: Select as many as needed. I show the set-up for this problem in Figure 5-13.

```
1   ##
2   ## Tactical integer problem: Marketing reach
3   ## Case 1: Select as many media as needed
4   ##
5   ## ===> Step 1: Specify the solver <===
6   ##
7   solver = pywraplp.Solver.CreateSolver( 'SCIP' )
8   ##
9   ## ===> Step 2: Specify the decision variables <===
10  ##
11  x1 = solver.IntVar( 0.0, 1, 'x1' )
12  x2 = solver.IntVar( 0.0, 1, 'x2' )
13  x3 = solver.IntVar( 0.0, 1, 'x3' )
14  x4 = solver.IntVar( 0.0, 1, 'x4' )
15  x5 = solver.IntVar( 0.0, 1, 'x5' )
16  x6 = solver.IntVar( 0.0, 1, 'x6' )
17  ##
18  ## ===> Step 3: Specify the constraints <===
19  ##
20  solver.Add( 500*x1 + 150*x2 + 300*x3 + 250*x4 + 250*x5 + 100*x6 <= 1800 )
21  solver.Add( 700*x1 + 250*x2 + 200*x3 + 200*x4 + 300*x5 + 400*x6 <= 1500 )
22  solver.Add( 200*x1 + 100*x2 + 100*x3 + 100*x4 + 100*x5 + 1000*x6 <= 1200 )
23  ##
24  ## ===> Step 4: Specify the objective function <===
25  ##
26  solver.Maximize( 1*x1 + 0.2*x2 + 0.3*x3 + 0.4*x4 + 0.45*x5 + 0.45*x6 )
27  status = solver.Solve()   ## Check solution status
28  ##
29  ## ===> Step 5: Summarize the results <===
30  ##
31  data = [
32          [ 1, 0.2, 0.3, 0.4, 0.45, 0.45 ],
33          [ 500, 150, 300, 250, 250, 100 ],
34          [ 700, 250, 200, 200, 300, 400 ],
35          [ 200, 100, 100, 100, 100, 1000 ],
36          [ x1.solution_value(), x2.solution_value(), x3.solution_value(),
37            x4.solution_value(), x5.solution_value(), x6.solution_value() ]
38  ]
39  sol = solver.Objective().Value()
40  cols = [ 'TV', 'Trade', 'Newspaper', 'Radio', 'Popular', 'Promotion' ]
41  idx = [ 'Reach (Millions)', 'Cost', 'Designers', 'Sales', 'Solution' ]
42  df = pd.DataFrame( data, columns = cols, index = idx )
43  display( df )
44  print( f'Maximum Reach: {sol:0.2f} Million Viewers' )
45
```

	TV	Trade	Newspaper	Radio	Popular	Promotion
Reach (Millions)	1.0	0.2	0.3	0.4	0.45	0.45
Cost	500.0	150.0	300.0	250.0	250.00	100.00
Designers	700.0	250.0	200.0	200.0	300.00	400.00
Sales	200.0	100.0	100.0	100.0	100.00	1000.00
Solution	1.0	0.0	1.0	1.0	1.00	0.00

```
Maximum Reach: 2.15 Million Viewers
```

Figure 5-13. An example of an integer programming set-up and output for Case 1 for the customer reach project decision.

For this integer problem, I use the SCIP solver which I specify in Line 7. This is the recommended solver for integer problems. The integer variables are specified in Lines 11 to 16 using the IntVar method for integers. Its arguments are the same as NumVar except the maximum value is 1 for this problem.

I collected all the data from Table 5-5 along with the decision variable values in a NumPy array in Lines 31 to 38. I then used it in Line 42 to create a pandas DataFrame for a nice display of the data and results.

There are four out of six advertising media that will yield the maximum reach: TV, Newspapers, Radio, and Popular Magazines. You can see this in the last line of the displayed DataFrame output. The total reach using these four will be 2.15 million customers.

Case 2: Select a specific number.   The Case 2 set-up is similar to Case 1 set-up. I show this in Figure 5-14.

```
 1  ##
 2  ## Tactical integer problem: Marketing reach
 3  ## Case 2: Select Specific Number: 2
 4  ##
 5  ## ===> Step 1: Specify the solver <===
 6  ##
 7  solver = pywraplp.Solver.CreateSolver( 'SCIP' )
 8  ##
 9  ## ===> Step 2: Specify the decision variables <===
10  ##
11  x1 = solver.IntVar( 0.0, 1, 'x1' )
12  x2 = solver.IntVar( 0.0, 1, 'x2' )
13  x3 = solver.IntVar( 0.0, 1, 'x3' )
14  x4 = solver.IntVar( 0.0, 1, 'x4' )
15  x5 = solver.IntVar( 0.0, 1, 'x5' )
16  x6 = solver.IntVar( 0.0, 1, 'x6' )
17  ##
18  ## ===> Step 3: Specify the constraints <===
19  ##
20  solver.Add( 500*x1 + 150*x2 + 300*x3 + 250*x4 + 250*x5 + 100*x6 <= 1800 )
21  solver.Add( 700*x1 + 250*x2 + 200*x3 + 200*x4 + 300*x5 + 400*x6 <= 1500 )
22  solver.Add( 200*x1 + 100*x2 + 100*x3 + 100*x4 + 100*x5 + 1000*x6 <= 1200 )
23  solver.Add( x1 + x2 + x3 + x4 + x5 + x6 <= 2 )
24  ##
25  ## ===> Step 4: Specify the objective function <===
26  ##
27  solver.Maximize( 1*x1 + 0.2*x2 + 0.3*x3 + 0.4*x4 + 0.45*x5 + 0.45*x6 )
28  status = solver.Solve()   ## Check solution status
29  ##
30  ## ===> Step 5: Summarize the results <===
31  ##
32  data = [
33           [ 1, 0.2, 0.3, 0.4, 0.45, 0.45 ],
34           [ 500, 150, 300, 250, 250, 100 ],
35           [ 700, 250, 200, 200, 300, 400 ],
36           [ 200, 100, 100, 100, 100, 1000 ],
37           [ x1.solution_value(), x2.solution_value(), x3.solution_value(),
38             x4.solution_value(), x5.solution_value(), x6.solution_value() ]
39  ]
40  sol = solver.Objective().Value()
41  cols = [ 'TV', 'Trade', 'Newspaper', 'Radio', 'Popular', 'Promotion' ]
42  idx = [ 'Reach (Millions)', 'Cost', 'Designers', 'Sales', 'Solution' ]
43  df = pd.DataFrame( data, columns = cols, index = idx )
44  display( df )
45  print( f'Maximum Reach: {sol:0.2f} Million Viewers' )
46
```

	TV	Trade	Newspaper	Radio	Popular	Promotion
Reach (Millions)	1.0	0.2	0.3	0.4	0.45	0.45
Cost	500.0	150.0	300.0	250.0	250.00	100.00
Designers	700.0	250.0	200.0	200.0	300.00	400.00
Sales	200.0	100.0	100.0	100.0	100.00	1000.00
Solution	1.0	0.0	0.0	0.0	0.00	1.00

```
Maximum Reach: 1.45 Million Viewers
```

Figure 5-14. An example of an integer programming set-up and output for Case 2 for the customer reach project decision. The target number of media is 2.

The key to this set-up is in Line 23 where the sum of the decision variables, which are binary variables, must be less than or equal to 2. So none, 1, or 2 media can be selected, but not 3, 4, 5, or all 6. The output shows that two media are optimal: TV and promotions with a reach of 1.45 million customers.

Case 2a: Select only one. The special case is selecting only 1. This is probably very common because of resource constraints. I show the set-up and results for this situation in Figure 5-15. For this problem, the one media outlet to select is obvious from Table 5-5, but it is instructive, nonetheless, to see the integer programming set-up because other problems may not be so obvious. The optimal medium is TV, and the total reach is 1 million customers.

```
1   ##
2   ## Tactical integer problem: Marketing reach
3   ## Case 2a: Select only 1
4   ##
5   ## ===> Step 1: Specify the solver <===
6   ##
7   solver = pywraplp.Solver.CreateSolver( 'SCIP' )
8   ##
9   ## ===> Step 2: Specify the decision variables <===
10  ##
11  x1 = solver.IntVar( 0.0, 1, 'x1' )
12  x2 = solver.IntVar( 0.0, 1, 'x2' )
13  x3 = solver.IntVar( 0.0, 1, 'x3' )
14  x4 = solver.IntVar( 0.0, 1, 'x4' )
15  x5 = solver.IntVar( 0.0, 1, 'x5' )
16  x6 = solver.IntVar( 0.0, 1, 'x6' )
17  ##
18  ## ===> Step 3: Specify the constraints <===
19  ##
20  solver.Add( 500*x1 + 150*x2 + 300*x3 + 250*x4 + 250*x5 + 100*x6 <= 1800 )
21  solver.Add( 700*x1 + 250*x2 + 200*x3 + 200*x4 + 300*x5 + 400*x6 <= 1500 )
22  solver.Add( 200*x1 + 100*x2 + 100*x3 + 100*x4 + 100*x5 + 1000*x6 <= 1200 )
23  solver.Add( x1 + x2 + x3 + x4 + x5 + x6 <= 1 )
24  ##
25  ## ===> Step 4: Specify the objective function <===
26  ##
27  solver.Maximize( 1*x1 + 0.2*x2 + 0.3*x3 + 0.4*x4 + 0.45*x5 + 0.45*x6 )
28  status = solver.Solve()   ## Check solution status
29  ##
30  ## ===> Step 5: Summarize the results <===
31  ##
32  data = [
33          [ 1, 0.2, 0.3, 0.4, 0.45, 0.45 ],
34          [ 500, 150, 300, 250, 250, 100 ],
35          [ 700, 250, 200, 200, 300, 400 ],
36          [ 200, 100, 100, 100, 100, 1000 ],
37          [ x1.solution_value(), x2.solution_value(), x3.solution_value(),
38            x4.solution_value(), x5.solution_value(), x6.solution_value() ]
39  ]
40  sol = solver.Objective().Value()
41  cols = [ 'TV', 'Trade', 'Newspaper', 'Radio', 'Popular', 'Promotion' ]
42  idx = [ 'Reach (Millions)', 'Cost', 'Designers', 'Sales', 'Solution' ]
43  df = pd.DataFrame( data, columns = cols, index = idx )
44  display( df )
45  print( f'Maximum Reach: {sol:0.2f} Million Viewers' )
46
```

	TV	Trade	Newspaper	Radio	Popular	Promotion
Reach (Millions)	1.0	0.2	0.3	0.4	0.45	0.45
Cost	500.0	150.0	300.0	250.0	250.00	100.00
Designers	700.0	250.0	200.0	200.0	300.00	400.00
Sales	200.0	100.0	100.0	100.0	100.00	1000.00
Solution	1.0	0.0	0.0	0.0	0.00	0.00

```
Maximum Reach: 1.00 Million Viewers
```

Figure 5-15. An example of an integer programming set-up and output for Case 2a for the customer reach project decision. The target number of media is 1 for this special case.

Case 3: Select based on logical conditions. I will illustrate this case in the next subsection for a strategic scale-view. The menu consists of five projects with option attributes that I will define.

Strategic scale-view

Suppose a decision-maker with a strategic scale-view is considering five long-range projects. There is only a set amount that can be invested, so the question is which project or multiple projects the enterprise should invest in. This is an example of *capital budgeting*.

An investment decision requires a process and a set of decision rules. Four rules are commonly used:

- Payback period (PB)
- Net present value (NPV)
- Profitability Index (PI)
- Internal rate of return *(IRR)*

See Ross et al. (2006) for descriptions of each of these. I will only consider the NPV rule for this example.

Each rule depends on a cash-flow prediction which comes from Predictive Analytics. The predictions are then input into the decision process which is the Prescriptive Analytics. I illustrate a process in Figure 5-16.

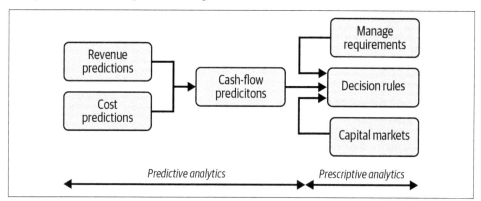

Figure 5-16. A capital budgeting process that combines Predictive and Prescriptive Analytics.

The predictions for revenue and costs are generated by the Chief Financial Organiza-tion[1] in conjunction with the DST. There are many ways to predict these values. See Paczkowski (2023) for a general discussion of different prediction methods. Also see Brigham and Ehrhardt (2002) for financial predictions.

Once the revenue and cost predictions are completed, they are then used in a decision rule along with management criteria (e.g., target KPMs such as shareholder value) and capital market data. The capital markets, for our purposes, are markets where stock prices and rates of return are determined by overall financial market forces. The rates of return are used as discount factors which are required, at a minimum, to justify an investment. The minimum is a standard that could be earned in the capital markets; anything earned on a project that exceeds what could be earned in the market would increase shareholder value. This is, in fact, the IRR rule. See Ross et al. (2006) for a discussion of this rule and others.

The NPV is the present value of an investment project's net cash flows minus the project's initial cash outflow over its expected life. This is a financial measure often used in capital budgeting and investment planning. See Brigham and Ehrhardt (2002, Chapter 4) for present value calculations and how they are used in financial analysis. The NPV is calculated as:

$$NPV = \sum_{t=1}^{n} \frac{CF_t}{(1+k)^t} - ICO$$

where CF_t is the cash flow in period t; k is the required *rate of return* (ROR) determined by the capital market; and ICO is the initial cash outlay for the project. The ICO is the investment amount required for a project. The cash-flow is calculated as the project's operating cash flow less the change in working capital less the capital spending on the project. The operating cash flow is net earnings before taxes plus depreciation less taxes. So a number of projected values are needed to calculate the NPV. This is all Predictive Analytics.

The NPV decision rule is: accept a project if $NPV \geq 0$; reject it otherwise. For one project, which is the usual textbook example, the rule is simple and intuitive. For mutually exclusive projects, you accept the one with the largest NPV. An issue is what to do when there are several projects and you can invest in just a subset. That is, when you have a menu. Normally, an enterprise is constrained by how much it can invest. After all, no enterprise has infinite funds! So what is that optimal menu subset given a funds or capital constraint?

---

1 Also referred to as the CFO, not to be confused with the Chief Financial Officer.

For my problem, assume that the DST predicted the NPV for each project along with the amount that has to be invested in each one. I display this data in Table 5-6 as a menu of projects. Assume the total amount to invest is $25 million. This is the capital constraint.

Table 5-6. The data for the capital investment integer programming problem. The values are all in millions of dollars. This example is based on Hillier and Lieberman (2010, p. 524).

Project menu	Project 1	Project 2	Project 3	Project 4	Project 5
NPV	2.0	2.8	2.6	1.8	2.4
Investment	8.0	14.0	12.0	6.0	10.0

The decision-maker must select those projects that yield the highest NPV but whose total investment does not exceed the amount of financial capital available.

Case 1: Select as many as needed.   I show the set-up for this problem in Figure 5-17.

```
1  ##
2  ## Strategic integer problem -- Strategic Capital Investment Decision
3  ## Case 1: Select several projects
4  ##
5  ## ===> Step 1: Specify the solver <===
6  ##
7  solver = pywraplp.Solver.CreateSolver( 'SCIP' )
8  ##
9  ## ===> Step 2: Specify the decision variables <===
10 ##
11 x1 = solver.IntVar( 0.0, 1, 'x1' )
12 x2 = solver.IntVar( 0.0, 1, 'x2' )
13 x3 = solver.IntVar( 0.0, 1, 'x3' )
14 x4 = solver.IntVar( 0.0, 1, 'x4' )
15 x5 = solver.IntVar( 0.0, 1, 'x5' )
16 ##
17 ## ===> Step 3: Specify the constraints <===
18 ##
19 solver.Add( 8*x1 + 14*x2 + 12*x3 + 6*x4 + 10*x5 <= 25 )
20 ##
21 ## ===> Step 4: Specify the objective function <===
22 ##
23 solver.Maximize( 2*x1 + 2.8*x2 + 2.6*x3 + 1.8*x4 + 2.4*x5 )
24 status = solver.Solve()
25 ##
26 ## ===> Step 5: Summarize the results <===
27 ##
28 data = [
29         [ 2, 2.8, 2.6, 1.8, 2.4 ],
30         [ 8, 14, 12, 6, 10 ],
31         [ x1.solution_value(), x2.solution_value(), x3.solution_value(),
32           x4.solution_value(), x5.solution_value() ]
33 ]
34 sol = solver.Objective().Value()
35 cols = [ 'Project ' + str( i ) for i in range( 1, 6 ) ]
36 idx = [ 'NPV', 'Investment', 'Solution' ]
37 df = pd.DataFrame( data, columns = cols, index = idx )
38 display( df )
39 print( f'Maximum NPV: \${sol:0.1f} Million' )
40
```

	Project 1	Project 2	Project 3	Project 4	Project 5
NPV	2.0	2.8	2.6	1.8	2.4
Investment	8.0	14.0	12.0	6.0	1.0
Solution	1.0	0.0	0.0	1.0	1.0

Maximum NPV: $6.2 Million

Figure 5-17. An example of an integer programming set-up and output for Case 1 for the capital budgeting decision.

The optimal projects are Projects 1, 4, and 5 with a total NPV of $6.2 Million.

Case 2: Select a specific number. Select two projects. The set-up is in Figure 5-18. Projects 2 and 5 are selected with a total NPV of $5.2 million.

```
1   ##
2   ## Strategic integer problem -- Strategic Capital Investment Decision
3   ## Case 2: Select two projects
4   ##
5   ## ===> Step 1: Specify the solver <===
6   ##
7   solver = pywraplp.Solver.CreateSolver( 'SCIP' )
8   ##
9   ## ===> Step 2: Specify the decision variables <===
10  ##
11  x1 = solver.IntVar( 0.0, 1, 'x1' )
12  x2 = solver.IntVar( 0.0, 1, 'x2' )
13  x3 = solver.IntVar( 0.0, 1, 'x3' )
14  x4 = solver.IntVar( 0.0, 1, 'x4' )
15  x5 = solver.IntVar( 0.0, 1, 'x5' )
16  ##
17  ## ===> Step 3: Specify the constraints <===
18  ##
19  solver.Add( 8*x1 + 14*x2 + 12*x3 + 6*x4 + 10*x5 <= 25 )
20  solver.Add( x1 + x2 + x3 + x4 + x5 <= 2 )
21  ##
22  ## ===> Step 4: Specify the objective function <===
23  ##
24  solver.Maximize( 2*x1 + 2.8*x2 + 2.6*x3 + 1.8*x4 + 2.4*x5 )
25  status = solver.Solve()
26  ##
27  ## ===> Step 5: Summarize the results <===
28  ##
29  data = [
30              [ 2, 2.8, 2.6, 1.8, 2.4 ],
31              [ 8, 14, 12, 6, 10 ],
32              [ x1.solution_value(), x2.solution_value(), x3.solution_value(),
33                x4.solution_value(), x5.solution_value() ]
34  ]
35  sol = solver.Objective().Value()
36  cols = [ 'Project ' + str( i ) for i in range( 1, 6 ) ]
37  idx = [ 'NPV', 'Investment', 'Solution' ]
38  df = pd.DataFrame( data, columns = cols, index = idx )
39  display( df )
40  print( f'Maximum NPV: \${sol:0.1f} Million' )
41
```

	Project 1	Project 2	Project 3	Project 4	Project 5
NPV	2.0	2.8	2.6	1.8	2.4
Investment	8.0	14.0	12.0	6.0	1.0
Solution	0.0	1.0	0.0	0.0	1.0

```
Maximum NPV: $5.2 Million
```

Figure 5-18. An example of an integer programming set-up and output for Case 2 for the capital budgeting decision. Two projects are required.

Case 2a: Select only one. The special case is selecting only 1. This is probably very common because of resource constraints. I show the set-up and results for this case in Figure 5-19. The one project to select is obvious from Table 5-6, but it is still instructive to see the integer programming set-up because other problems may not be so trivial.

```
1   ##
2   ## Strategic integer problem -- Strategic Capital Investment Decision
3   ## Case 2a: Select only one project
4   ##
5   ## ===> Step 1: Specify the solver <===
6   ##
7   solver = pywraplp.Solver.CreateSolver( 'SCIP' )
8   ##
9   ## ===> Step 2: Specify the decision variables <===
10  ##
11  x1 = solver.IntVar( 0.0, 1, 'x1' )
12  x2 = solver.IntVar( 0.0, 1, 'x2' )
13  x3 = solver.IntVar( 0.0, 1, 'x3' )
14  x4 = solver.IntVar( 0.0, 1, 'x4' )
15  x5 = solver.IntVar( 0.0, 1, 'x5' )
16  ##
17  ## ===> Step 3: Specify the constraints <===
18  ##
19  solver.Add( 8*x1 + 14*x2 + 12*x3 + 6*x4 + 10*x5 <= 25 )
20  solver.Add( x1 + x2 + x3 + x4 + x5 <= 1 )
21  ##
22  ## ===> Step 4: Specify the objective function <===
23  ##
24  solver.Maximize( 2*x1 + 2.8*x2 + 2.6*x3 + 1.8*x4 + 2.4*x5 )
25  status = solver.Solve()
26  ##
27  ## ===> Step 5: Summarize the results <===
28  ##
29  data = [
30          [ 2, 2.8, 2.6, 1.8, 2.4 ],
31          [ 8, 14, 12, 6, 10 ],
32          [ x1.solution_value(), x2.solution_value(), x3.solution_value(),
33            x4.solution_value(), x5.solution_value() ]
34  ]
35  sol = solver.Objective().Value()
36  cols = [ 'Project ' + str( i ) for i in range( 1, 6 ) ]
37  idx = [ 'NPV', 'Investment', 'Solution' ]
38  df = pd.DataFrame( data, columns = cols, index = idx )
39  display( df )
40  print( f'Maximum NPV: \${sol:0.1f} Million' )
41
```

	Project 1	Project 2	Project 3	Project 4	Project 5
NPV	2.0	2.8	2.6	1.8	2.4
Investment	8.0	14.0	12.0	6.0	1.0
Solution	0.0	1.0	0.0	0.0	0.0

Maximum NPV: $2.8 Million

Figure 5-19. An example of an integer programming set-up and output for Case 2a for the capital budgeting decision. One project is required.

Case 3: Select based on logical conditions. I will illustrate this case in the next section for a tactical scale-view.

Mixed Integer Programming

For a more complicated problem, consider a tactical problem for a firm that produces a product in a competitive industry. The *R&D* department developed four new products and proposed them to the CMO for inclusion in the current product line. The CMO must decide which of the four to produce and market. The Chief Sales Officer (CSO), however, informed her that the sales force can only manage at most two products. The manufacturing executive also informed the CMO that two of the products can be produced only if two others are produced. If the products are simply labeled "Product 1," "Product 2," "Product 3," and "Product 4," then assume that either Product 3 or Product 4 can be produced only if Product 1 or Product 2 is produced. This is a logical constraint. There are, then, two constraints on the product choice.

The CMO, however, also needs to know not only the one or two products but also the optimal amounts to have the manufacturing division produce. The amount is a continuous factor, not a binary one. The binary factor is an indicator of which product(s) to produce, while the continuous factor is the amount of production to order. The problem is a *Mixed Integer Programming Problem*: the binary integer for product selection and a continuous decision variable for the amount to produce.

Technical Overview

Technically, a mixed problem is just a generalization of the linear problem with continuous decision variables and the integer problem with discrete decision variables. You handle this problem the same way as the other two, except you have to include statements for both numeric and integer decision variables. Using OR-Tools makes this easy to do: just use the key words `NumVar` and `IntVar` as appropriate.

Python Use-Case

I show the set-up in Figure 5-20 for the new product problem along with the optimal solution. The optimal product to produce is Product 2, which should have 2,000 units. The objective function maximum is 120,000.

```
 1  ##
 2  ## Strategic mixed integer problem -- Strategic Capital Investment Decision
 3  ## Based on Hillier, 11.3-1, p. 525
 4  ##
 5  ## ===> Step 1: Specify the solver <===
 6  ##
 7  solver = pywraplp.Solver.CreateSolver( 'SCIP' )
 8  ##
 9  ## ===> Step 2: Specify the decision variables <===
10  ##
11  infinity = solver.infinity()  ## Sets upper bound
12  x1 = solver.NumVar( 0.0, infinity, 'x1' )
13  x2 = solver.NumVar( 0.0, infinity, 'x2' )
14  x3 = solver.NumVar( 0.0, infinity, 'x3' )
15  x4 = solver.NumVar( 0.0, infinity, 'x4' )
16  ##
17  y1 = solver.IntVar( 0.0, 1, 'y1' )
18  y2 = solver.IntVar( 0.0, 1, 'y2' )
19  y3 = solver.IntVar( 0.0, 1, 'y3' )
20  y4 = solver.IntVar( 0.0, 1, 'y4' )
21  ##
22  ## ===> Step 3: Specify the constraints <===
23  ##
24  solver.Add( 5*x1 + 3*x2 + 6*x3 + 4*x4 <= 6000 )
25  solver.Add( y1 + y2 + y3 + y4 <= 2 )
26  solver.Add( -y1 -y2 + y3 <= 0 )
27  solver.Add( -y1 -y2 + y4 <= 0 )
28  ##
29  ## ===> Step 4: Specify the objective function <===
30  ##
31  solver.Maximize( 70*x1 + 60*x2 + 90*x3 + 80*x4 - 50000*y1 - 40000*y2 - 70000*y3 -
                                             60000*y4 )
32  status = solver.Solve()
33  ##
34  ## ===> Step 5: Summarize the results <===
35  ##
36  print( f'Status: {solver.Solve()}' )
37  ##
38  print( solver.Objective().Value() )
39  print( x1.solution_value() )
40  print( x2.solution_value() )
41  print( x3.solution_value() )
42  print( x4.solution_value() )
43

    Status: 0
    120000.0
    0.0
    2000.0
    0.0
    0.0
```

Figure 5-20. An example of a mixed integer programming set-up and output for Case 3 for a capital budgeting decision.

Summary

I covered in this chapter the first of two non-stochastic methods for selecting from a decision menu: mathematical programming. The literature review of Chapter 2 revealed that this is the most used class of tools in Prescriptive Analytics. It is a complex set of methods for selecting values for decision variables to optimize an objective function when you have constraints. A classic example is in economics where production is maximized subject to constraints on the major inputs (capital and labor) and costs.

I discussed three categories of mathematical programming: linear, integer, and mixed programming. I provided examples of each for different cases and for the different scale-views. A powerful OR toolkit, OR-Tools, was introduced and its use was explained.

The main concepts, aside from extensive examples, from this chapter are:

- Mathematical programming and its genesis
- Feasible Region
- Objective function
- Constraints, including non-negativity constraints
- OR-Tools

CHAPTER 6

Decision Tree Analysis: Overview

I focused on selecting from a menu of options in the previous chapters. The menu results from the Predictive Analytics stage of the *Tripartite Analytics Paradigm* I described in Chapter 1.

I showed in Chapter 5 how you can select one option from the menu using mathematical programming. Although effective, and certainly the approach heavily used in Prescriptive Analytics as noted by Lepeniotia et al. (2020), it has two problems that overly simplify, and perhaps obscure, how decisions are really made. These are:

1. No time dimension for decisions
2. Fixed (i.e., non-stochastic) coefficients for the mathematical programming functions

In this chapter, I will introduce temporal decision making via a *decision tree* paradigm. Trees are useful for clarifying conditions and showing the logical components of the thought process leading to a decision. Specifically, I will describe and illustrate a general framework for decision analysis with different *states of the world* (SOWs) and associated prior probabilities playing key roles. I will focus on:

- Terminology
- The role of subjective probabilities in decision making
- The construction and structure of decision trees for decision making
- The use and value of decision trees in decision making

The leading questions for this chapter are:

1. What is a decision tree?
2. Are there different types of trees?
3. How does a decision tree reflect a time dimension?
4. What is the structure of a decision tree?
5. Does a decision tree reflect different SOWs?
6. What is the role of probabilities in a decision tree?
7. How are probabilities incorporated in a decision tree?

Extending the Menu into Time

The menu concept assumes that a single decision has to be made: pick one or two projects from the menu. My examples in Chapter 5 are consistent with this contention. Since there is only one decision, the implicit assumption is that it is made in only one period, which is now; the decision is once and for all, not to be changed or revisited.

Real-world decisions involve multiple periods in either one of two forms:

1. A single decision with one condition; and
2. Sequential decisions with changing conditions.

My mathematical programming discussion handled the first. For example, consider several projects with different initial investments and KPMs, say NPV. One is to be selected. Which one? The KPM is only one number that summarizes the total flow of returns from the projects. How that flow is developed is not important, at least for the mathematical programming approach. Time is not part of the equation, having been subsumed into the KPM calculations. This is especially true if an NPV is used because, by definition, a present value calculation includes a time factor that is collapsed into "now" (i.e., the present).

Sequential decisions are different. They explicitly take time into account because a project itself goes through stages. A decision to continue or not has to be made at each stage. The KPMs change depending on the SOW at key junctures in the project development. These may be considered at the Predictive Analytics stage before the menu is presented to the decision-maker. It would be better, however, to make them explicit so the decision-maker can better determine the optimal course of action to follow.

The fixed coefficients in a mathematical programming formulation are a second major problem. These are not estimated but specified. This means there is a range of possibilities. Most business people would interpret a range as just a minimum and maximum value with a most likely value somewhere in between. This is their view of a distribution. The most likely value does not necessarily have to be in the middle (i.e., the mean), but represents, instead, the mode. The distribution they envision could, thus, be skewed and have a triangular shape.

However, the range, the distribution, is specified, the values for the coefficients can only fluctuate in that range, which implies that the optimal solution also fluctuates. The optimization problem is then stochastic, not deterministic. And this implies probabilities.

Introduction to Decision Trees

I will introduce decision analysis in this chapter using decision trees for non-stochastic Prescriptive Analytics. Trees are popular because they have an intuitive appeal. You can easily see the progression of a project, a time perspective, under different conditions and their impact on the final KPM. More importantly, the decision tree paradigm incorporates the prior probability of one SOW versus another materializing at a point in time. This is important because you do not know at any time which SOW will materialize; you can only state the chance or probability of it happening. That probability can only be formed or specified in one way: a Bayesian way using the best Rich Information available *now* when the initial decision is made. Therefore, the Bayesian framework I introduced in Chapter 4 becomes important. But these probabilities do not make the tree stochastic. They merely reflect your inability to state with certainty what will happen next.

You may be questioning why I am including a discussion of decision analysis that relies on probabilities in the part of this book that deals with non-stochastic Prescriptive Analytics. After all, probabilities imply stochasticity. This is correct. However, I am reserving the notion of stochastic to a more complex set of Prescriptive Analytical problems involving simulations over multiple different situations or *scenarios*. Scenarios are the basis for the *Most Likely Views* I introduced in Chapter 1 and form the basis of the menus for decision-makers. Probabilities are critical for simulations, especially because they involve random draws from probability distributions. In simulations, different parameters, called *hyperparameters*, can be changed to reflect different conditions. The probabilities used in decision trees and this form of decision analysis reflect different SOWs, and not necessarily different hyperparameter values. Hence, I am focusing here on the probability of different SOWs, and not on hyperparameters per se.

Clarification of Decision Trees

I have to clarify the notion of a decision tree. There is a decision tree and then there is a decision tree. One is used in decision analysis per se, and the other is used in regression and classification analysis in statistics, econometrics, and machine learning. The latter arises when a data scientist wants to identify the best or optimal features and their levels, for explaining or classifying objects using a large historical data set. I will refer to this as a *Machine Learning Decision Tree* (MLDT) since they are mostly in the machine learning domain. See Paczkowski (2022a, Chapter 11) for an extensive treatment in Business Analytics.

 What is normally called a dependent variable in statistics and econometrics is called a *target* in machine learning. It is what you "aim" to explain. What are typically called independent variables in these two disciplines are referred to as *features* in machine learning. I use these terms interchangeably, so sometimes, for example, I will refer to a dependent variable and other times to a target.

The machine learning approach uses an algorithm to continually bifurcate each feature at a point the algorithm selects as optimal. It simultaneously explains or divides the target depending on whether you have a regression or classification problem, respectively. The bifurcation means that each feature variable is divided into two parts best explaining or accounting for the target.

A tree diagram summarizes the bifurcations with each part of a single bifurcation represented as a branch on the tree. The target is the root and the branches emanate from it. Each point on a branch is referred to as a *node* or *leaf*. Nodes are in the interior of the tree and leaves are at the end or final tip of each branch, so they are *terminal leaves*.

The path from a terminal leaf to the root is a series of *if-then* logical statements so the entire path from a terminal leaf to the root shows the conditions for explaining or accounting for the target. Obviously, there are several paths since a tree will have several branches due to the bifurcations. The minimum is two. The collection of *if-then* statements are decisions at each node. Hence, the tree is called a *decision tree*.

This form of decision tree is used in the Predictive Analytics portion of the *Tripartite Analytics Paradigm* rather than in the Prescriptive Analytics. It is one of many prediction tools. Although predictive, it can still be used for operational decisions. For example, consider a bank loan officer who must decide to accept a loan applicant. Basically, the loan applicant must be classified as loan-worthy or not. Clearly, a rule is needed.

For this example, I have a data set of 30,000 past loan applicants at a bank. The data include whether or not they defaulted on a loan payment plus some demographics.[1] I selected four demographic variables just for illustration. These are coded as:[2]

Gender
   1 = Male; 2 = Female

College
   1 = Some college; 0 = no college

Married
   1 = Married; 2 = Single; 3 = Other

Age
   Years

I show the Python code and the resulting tree in Figure 6-1. In this code snippet, I import the data into a pandas DataFrame and draw a random sample of size 50%. You can see the command for this random sampling in Line 8. Notice that I use an argument `random_state = 42`. This sets a random number seed to 42. I will discuss random number seeds in Chapter 7. For now, be aware that this allows the same random number to be selected each time this code is run; otherwise, a different result, including a different tree, will result.

---

1 Source: Yeh (2016). Last accessed August 7, 2023.

2 The college variable is a recoding of the original data set's education variable.

```
 1  ##
 2  ## Decision tree example
 3  ##
 4  ## Import data
 5  ##
 6  df_tree = pd.read_csv( "../data/Chapter6/subset of partition.csv" )
 7  cols = [ 'id', 'default', 'balance', 'gender', 'educ', 'college', 'married',
                                                                   'age' ]
 8  df_tree = df_tree.sample( frac = 0.50, random\_state = 42 )  ## Take a random
                                                           sample of 50%
 9  df_tree.columns = cols
10  df_tree.set_index( "id", inplace = True )
11  cols = [ 'default', 'gender', 'college', 'married', 'age' ]
12  df_tree = df_tree[ cols ]
13  ##
14  ## Check default distribution
15  ##
16  df_tree.default.value_counts( normalize = True )
17  Not Defaulted     0.781667
18  Defaulted         0.218333
19  Name: default, dtype: float64
20  ##
21  ## Fit the tree
22  ##
23  cols = [ 'gender', 'college', 'married', 'age' ]  ## Features to use
24  dtree = dtree.fit( df_tree[ cols ], df_tree[ 'default' ] )
25  tree.plot_tree( dtree, feature_names = cols, class_names = [ 'Defaulted', 'Not
                                 Defaulted' ], filled = True, impurity =
                                 False, proportion = True );
26
```

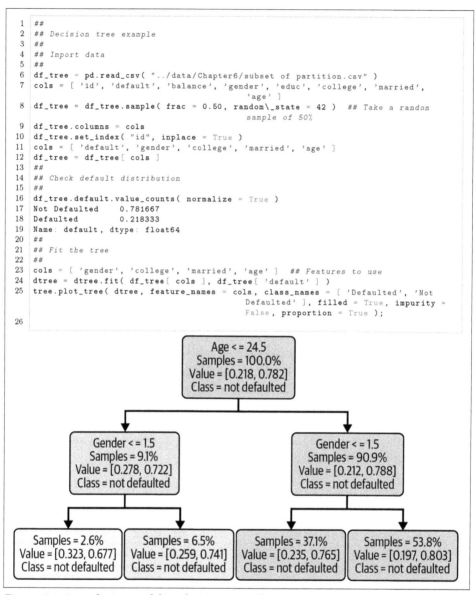

Figure 6-1. A predictive modeling decision tree. The tree was only grown to two levels below the root node for illustration purposes only. A much larger tree is possible.

Once the background set-up is done, the tree is then grown using the `plot_tree` method as in Line 18. This is a prediction tree. Beginning at a terminal leaf, say the one at the far-left last row, you have a prediction of a bank customer likely to default based on their history. I provide an annotated version of that terminal leaf in Figure 6-2 so you can see the parts.

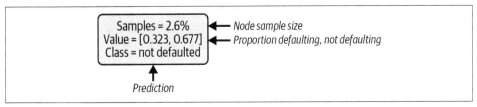

Figure 6-2. One of the terminal leaves from the tree in Figure 6-1.

I did a check in Lines 13 to 19 of the distribution of the target using the pandas `value_counts` method with the `normalize = True` argument. You can see that 78.2% of the sample did not default. This number appears on the third line of the root node. The predicted class, based on the largest percentage of the distribution, is "Not Defaulted."

The root indicates age is the most significant variable for categorizing the sample, and the dividing or bifurcating value for age is 24.5 years. For the sample, all applicants with an age less than or equal to 24.5 are sent to the left branch emanating from the root; all others are sent to the right. The proportion going to the left is 9.1% as can be verified using the `value_counts` method with the argument `normalize = True`.

At the left node on the second line of the tree, anyone with gender less than or equal to 1.5 is sent to the left branch beneath the node. What is $gender \leq 1.5$? Gender is coded as 1 and 2, with $male = 1$. Since $1 < 1.5$, clearly, all males are sent to the left.

The left-most node on the last row of the tree has all males aged less than 24.5 years old. This is 2.6% of the sample. Of these, 0.677 did not default. So a prediction is that all males less than 24.5 years old will not default.

This terminal node can be summarized as an *if-then* statement. For this example, the statement is:

```
if age <= 24.5 and gender = Male, then Not Default.
```

You can reach similar conclusions and have similar *if-then* statements for the other three terminal leaves. An operational manager could then use these statements to decide if a loan applicant should be extended credit. It is because of this decision that the tree is called a decision tree.

There are three important features of this tree you should note:

1. You can make a prediction (it is a prediction tool in the Predictive Analytics toolkit).

2. The classifier is trained on a large data set.

3. Probabilities are not associated with each bifurcation of a node, but result from the bifurcations.

The decision tree algorithm uses data to grow a tree "from scratch" without any preconceived notion about what it should look like. Once grown and, therefore, its structure is known, you can then make predictions using the *if-then* statements. You could, for example, write a Python script with these *if-then* statements to score a large database. Those predicted as credit-worthy could be mailed promotional material for a possible loan.

Finally, the only probabilities are the sample proportions at each node, but these are not known until the node is specified by the tree algorithm and are just characteristics of the sample at the node. They do not play a role in the branching leading to the node. So probabilities, say in the form of Bayesian probabilities, do not play a central role in these decision trees. Probabilities are an artifact.

Decision trees used in Prescriptive Analytics are different, although the name "decision tree" can create confusion. The decision trees I will discuss for Prescriptive Analytics: are based on a structure that is already known and are not based on data per se, although rich information extracted from data is definitely used for KPMs at the terminal nodes of the trees; and the probabilities, especially Bayesian probabilities, are used to weight the KPMs of the terminal nodes.

I will refer to these as *decision analysis decision trees* (DADT) and I will develop these ideas in the following section.

Background

Decision analysis and decision trees play a major role in OR. See, for example, Hillier and Lieberman (2010). What I will present is a combination of OR techniques and economic/financial analysis. The latter are included because all business decisions are economic/financial in nature.

Use of Trees in Decisions

Decision analysis decision trees (DADT) allow for a logical and visual analysis of possibilities for a complex decision, mainly at the tactical and strategic scale-view levels. Decisions at these levels have a long-range effect on the enterprise. Operational scale-view decisions are in real-time or very short time frames where random events can, and do, happen. Their effects, however, are quickly ameliorated by preventive actions. For tactical and strategic scale-view decisions, however, a multitude of unknown, random events could happen between the time of the decision and a future target date. The target date could be set, for example, as a one-year marketing objective or in a five-year business plan for the enterprise. It is incumbent upon the decision-makers at these levels to be prudent and allow for as many random events as they can imagine.

This implies that Prescriptive Analytics involves more than just deciding what should be done based on optimizing an objective function. Future SOWs must also be considered. This requires those involved in the development of the KPMs must not only predict their values from historical data using Business Analytic methods as developed in Paczkowski (2022a) and, especially, Paczkowski (2023), but also do so for different scenarios. One prediction is insufficient. I will return to this idea in Chapter 9.

A DADT reflects these SOWs and their impacts on the KPM such as an NPV. But it also reflects or incorporates probabilities of the SOW occurring. It is not true that a particular SOW will or will not occur based on a coin toss. Some are deemed more likely than others based on the best information available today. This is the Rich Information I discussed in Chapter 1. But that information is constantly updated during the predictive model development and the Prescriptive Analytics work to pick a project from a menu.

Formulating the required probabilities is subjective. They can be assigned by the decision-maker or the DAC. The latter is the preferred forum for developing them because the DAC's diverse opinions can be used. Regardless of how they are developed, Bayesian probabilities are the relevant ones, and the Bayesian methodology then enables you to update them as new rich information is obtained. I will illustrate their use in Chapter 10.

I illustrate a stylized decision tree in Figure 6-4 based on the set-up code in Figure 6-3. Notice the similarity in structure between this tree and the one in Figure 6-1. The structures are the same, and certainly, the names are the same. But their use and interpretation are vastly different.

```
 1  ##
 2  ## Specify: labels, target, edges, edge_hover labels, and terminal values for DADT
 3  ##
 4  labels = [ 'A', 'B', 'C', 'Q', 'D', 'E', 'G', 'H', 'I', 'J', 'K', 'L', 'M', 'N',
                'O', 'P' ]
 5  target = [ [0.0, 0.0], [0.5, 0.5], [-0.5, 0.5], [0.5, 2.0], [0.25, 1.0], [0.15,
             1.25], [0.35, 1.25], [0.05, 1.5], [0.25,
             1.5], [0.0, 2.0], [0.10, 2.0], [0.20,
             2.0], [0.30, 2.0], [-0.60, 2.0], [-0.5,
             2.0], [-0.40, 2.0] ]
 6  edges = [ (0, 0), (0, 1), (0, 2), (1, 3), (1, 4), (4, 5), (4, 6), (5, 7), (5, 8),
             (7, 9), (7, 10), (8, 11), (8, 12), (2,
             13), (2, 14), (2, 1 ) ]
 7  edge_hover = [ None, None, None, 'P = 0.30', 'P = 0.70', None, None, None, None,
                  None, None, None, None, None, None, None
                  ]
 8  terms = { 'N':670, 'O':-100, 'P':30, 'J':25, 'K':130, 'L':20, 'M':15, 'Q': 200 }
 9  ##
10  ## Create DataFrame
11  ##
12  data = { 'labels':labels, 'source':source, 'target':target, 'edges':edges,
                  'edge_hover':edge_hover }
13  df = pd.DataFrame( data )
14  dadt( df, title = 'Example DA Decision Tree', terms = terms, display_data = True,
                  show_edge_labels = True,
15          show_tick_labels = False )
16
```

Figure 6-3. The set-up for a decision analysis decision tree. The function for drawing the tree is shown in Line 14. The function itself is in the Appendix (Figure 6-15).

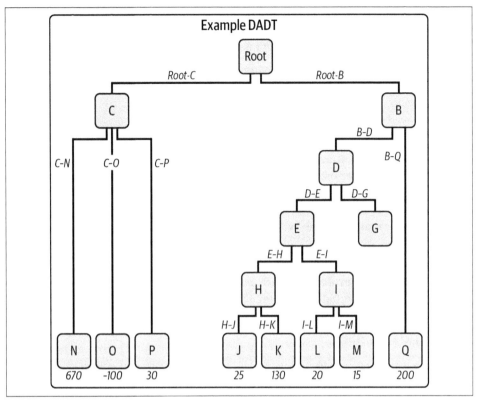

Figure 6-4. The data and the plot of a DADT. The set-up is in Figure 6-3.

Comparing the Two Decision Trees

In summary, the MLDT and DADT look similar, but there are subtleties that distinguish them:

1. An MLDT is derived from data and either categorizes or explains (in a least squares sense) a target variable. In both cases, an MLDT is really a member of the regression family of statistical methods. See Beck (2008) for a discussion of this point. Because of this membership, an MLDT finds structure in a data set that must be large enough to support growing a significantly large and meaningful tree. That structure is found using an algorithm. A DADT, on the other hand, does not rely on data to "grow" it and there is no algorithm behind it. Instead, it is specified to reflect a belief about how the world will evolve from or after a series of decisions.

2. Each node of an MLDT has characteristics of the underlying data set. These include, but are certainly not limited to, the sample size at the node, proportions of the levels of the target (for a classification problem), and predictions. For a

classification problem, the predictions are the proportions at that node, which are interpreted as estimated probabilities. A DADT does not have such information at each node. It just has the connection to the next lower node.

3. A node of an MLDT reflects only one type of information: the sample information at that node. A DADT, however, reflects either a decision or an SOW that may occur. The decision is based on the SOW that occurred and so it is a response. An MLDT does not have any responses to an event; the algorithm only knows the data.

4. An MLDT is not time-oriented. It is just a continuous grouping of data into smaller and smaller packs until a pre-specified sample size for a node is reached, at which point the tree is not grown any further. A DADT is time-oriented because the SOWs, which define some of the nodes, is a time concept. And then at that node defined by the SOW, a decision must be made.

5. In a DADT, each edge emanating from an SOW has a probability associated with it. It is a subjective probability about the likelihood or chance of the SOW occurring. These probabilities are assigned to that edge by the decision-maker, most likely in consultation with the DAC.

Python Use-Case

A use-case is the best way to understand a DADT. I will develop one in the following sections and then refer to it many times in the rest of this book.

Use-Case Background

A hotel chain wants a presence in a major mid-Atlantic metropolitan area. It could either build a new property in the downtown business district or at the local international airport. Both locations are highly desirable, but the choice depends on community developments. There is much discussion in the city council about upgrading the downtown area to make it more "citizen friendly" by widening sidewalk space for pedestrians, planting more trees, allowing sidewalk dining in the spring and summer months, and closing the main street to traffic for greater pedestrian access. There are intense debates between local merchants and consumer advocates. The budget is an issue since any renovation work will be expensive. At present, there are three proposals:

Modest Infrastructure Improvement
    Widen sidewalks and plant more trees

Major Infrastructure Overhaul
    The modest improvements plus repaving streets for pedestrian access and outdoor dining

No Development
    Keep status quo

Based on the intensity of the debates, the hotel management team specified subjective prior probabilities for each proposal which I show in Table 6-1. They were developed by the DAC and urban development consultants. These are priors, and so the distribution is a *prior distribution* as I introduced in Chapter 4.

Table 6-1. These are the prior distributions for three development scenarios by location.

	Location	
Proposal	Downtown	Airport
No development	0.15	0.20
Modest development	0.30	0.50
Major development	0.55	0.30

The airport development has the same problem, but it is more extensive because the airlines, concession merchants, restaurants, and vendors have a major political voice. They, however, oppose expansion because of noise pollution and perceived local road traffic congestion. I show the prior probability distribution, developed by the same hotel management team, for the airport in Table 6-1. The development proposals include:

Modest Modernization
    Replace terminal seating, add restaurants, and upgrade luggage carousels.

Major Development
    Add a new terminal and an inter-terminal computerized rail system, improve access roads, and modernize existing terminals.

No Development
    Keep status quo.

For each proposal, there are different scenarios for what will happen to hotel traffic, the primary concern of the hotel management. Hotel traffic includes overnight guests, conference room rentals, and restaurant patronage. For the downtown development, the traffic will likely be from local events, catering, and restaurant patronage. For the airport development, it would be from overnight guests and business meetings (with catering) in which people "fly in and fly out." Restaurant patronage is also expected to be impacted. For example, with a major development of the airport including a new terminal, traffic may increase significantly, while for a modest development there could be only a modest increase. No development, of course, means there will be no change in traffic. The traffic number for a "no change" scenario is just an average from the hotel's other airport properties. I show the prior distributions for downtown and the airport in Table 6-2. These were developed in a manner like the downtown priors.

Table 6-2. These are the prior distributions for hotel traffic (overnight guests and events) for the downtown and airport development proposals.

Proposal	Hotel traffic scenario	Downtown Prior	Downtown Earnings ($B)	Airport Prior	Airport Earnings ($B)
No development	Status quo	1.00	1.20	1.00	1.30
Modest development	Low	0.15	1.05	0.25	1.40
	Medium	0.60	1.10	0.65	1.50
	High	0.25	1.15	0.10	1.75
Major development	Low	0.20	1.10	0.15	1.60
	Medium	0.25	1.55	0.45	1.80
	High	0.55	1.95	0.40	2.00
Investment			$1.75 B		$1.50 B

Use-Case Detailed Data

The DST, working with the CFO and DAC, produced a summary table of the predicted revenue stream from each location for each traffic scenario. Hotels earn revenue from three sources:

Rooms
    Transient (i.e., overnight) guests, leisure/vacation travelers, and business guests

Events
    Conferences, weddings, banquets

Food and Beverages
    Restaurants, room service, event catering, and cocktail bars

Estimates of potential earnings from these three sources are in Table 6-2. In addition, the company's Property Management team estimated the cost of buying and developing each property and this is included in the summary table.

Finally, the DST, working with an outside economic forecasting consultant, developed prior probabilities for the hotel traffic. They used traffic designations for the next 10 years (the company's business planning horizon) as comparisons to their existing properties: low, moderate, or high. They also estimated the average discount factor (i.e., the cost of money in the capital markets) for this period based on a macroeconomic forecast of real GDP growth for the US economy. This factor is 5%.

The DST then developed predictive earnings models for each component using historical data from their other locations and data provided by the outside development consultants who formulated the priors. Other opinions on possible downtown and airport development paths were obtained from the DAC and outside consultants familiar with the development discussions. This allowed the team to include dummy variables reflecting key development options such as a new airport terminal, pedestrian walkways, and so forth. In terms of the *Tripartite Analytics Paradigm* in Figure 1-13, this is all the middle piece: Predictive Analytics.

The trained models were used to simulate different scenarios. These are the *Most Likely Views* I discussed in Chapter 1. The resulting revenue stream for each scenario is the predicted annual earnings in billions of dollars. These earnings are an annuity stream that has to be discounted back to today. An *annuity* is the payment or receipt of equal amounts per period for a specified number of periods. Common examples are consumer, auto, and mortgage loans. There are two types of annuities: *annuity due* with payments, or receipts, occurring at the beginning of each period, and *ordinary annuity* with payments or receipts at the end of each period. The present value of an annuity depends on the annuity amount, the discount factor, and the term of the annuity. The formula for calculating the present value of an ordinary annuity stream is

Equation 6-1.

$$PV_{ann} = \frac{Earnings}{r} \times \left[1 - \frac{1}{(1 + r)^t} \right]$$

where r is the discount factor (e.g., 5%) and t is the term (e.g., 10 years). The formula for an annuity due is similar but accounts for one less period since payments are at the beginning of each period. The ordinary annuity is used in most applications, and I will use it here. See Ross et al. (2006) for an explanation of annuities and this formula.

Annuity Streams

The discounting of the annuity stream is a very important step. A fundamental economic and financial principle is that a dollar earned in the future is not the same as a dollar earned today. But the decision is made today. So each component of the stream must be discounted.

As an example, consider an annuity of $1.20 billion per year for 10 years at a discount factor of 5%. I show a function in Figure 6-5 that implements Equation 6-1 for these numbers and the resulting present value. The present value is $9.26 billion.

```
 1  ##
 2  ## Annuity function
 3  ##
 4  def pv_annuity( amt, r, t ):
 5      x = ( amt/r )*(1 - 1/( 1 + r )**t)
 6      return( x )
 7  amount = 1.20  ## Earnings for Mc Development/Downtown
 8  disc = 0.05
 9  term = 10
10  pv = pv_annuity( amount, disc, term )
11  print( f'Present Value: ${pv:0.2f}' )
12

    Present Value: $9.26
```

Figure 6-5. A function for calculating the present value of an ordinary annuity and the result for the data in the text. The numbers are the values in Table 6-2 and Figure 6-6.

Try to use self-defined functions as much as possible. They will make your Python code more efficient and easier to read and interpret.

Role of the DADT

There are many possibilities to consider in any decision. This hotel decision is a simple one, but nonetheless, you could be overwhelmed by its possibilities. The best way to manage your perspective of the problem is to draw a decision tree such as the one I show in Figure 6-6. Such a tree is often used in textbooks for a purely pedagogical purpose, not a real-world application. Drawing a tree, even sketching one on an envelope, helps to clarify the problem's structure.

Always draw a decision tree to understand your problem's structure—but do not use it per se for the analysis.

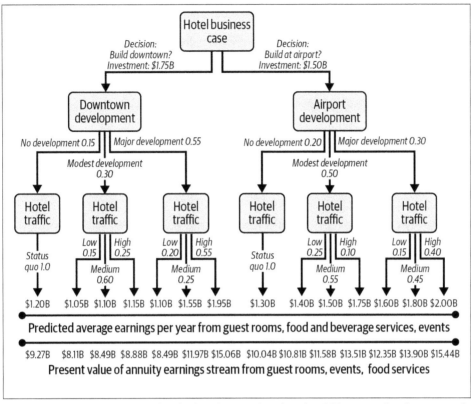

Figure 6-6. The decision tree for the hotel example. This should be viewed only as a guide to construct the DataFrame for analysis. The data in the tree correspond to the data in Tables 6-1 and 6-2. The tree succinctly summarizes both tables.

Note that the data in Tables 6-1 and 6-2 and Figure 6-6 are the same. Basically, the data in tables are the tree, but the representation in Figure 6-6 is easier to understand.

The structure of your decision tree is the basis for the data set you must construct. This is an initial DataFrame you can aggregate as needed to get answers for your problem. If the DataFrame is not properly constructed, then any aggregation will be either incorrect or too onerous to get. This is the DataFrame you want; the decision tree sketch reflects it. The DataFrame is the tree; they are one and the same. I will continue with this use-case to illustrate a simple DataFrame construction and subsequent aggregations.

DADT Analysis

Once the annual earnings annuity streams were discounted, the DST calculated the expected discounted earnings for each scenario's earning stream using the appropriate priors in Table 6-2. For each development possibility, whether downtown or at the airport, there are three possibilities that could materialize. Which one is purely due to chance, so the scenario is a random variable. Consequently, the present value of the earning stream annuity for a scenario is also a random variable. Each earnings random variable has a probability of it being realized as I show in Table 6-2. The weighted average of the three, where the weights are the priors, is the expected value of the discounted earnings annuity stream. Expected values are calculated by multiplying each random variable by its probability and then adding the products. For example, if the random variable X has probability p of occurring, and the random variable Y has probability $1 - p$, then the expected value is $p \times X + (1 - p) \times Y$.

Calculating expected values is another very important step. This reflects the different likelihoods of the discounted revenue streams.

The expected values are for the potential outcome for the downtown and airport cases. But these outcomes are also random variables. So the expected values were further aggregated using the prior distributions in Table 6-2. This gave the team two numbers to present to the decision-maker: the expected earnings for a downtown property, $1.75 billion, and the expected earnings for an airport property, $1.50 billion.

These calculations are easily handled with Python. I show the Python code in Figure 6-7 to create a DataFrame with all the data I just described. I first set the hyperparameters for the problem in Lines 6 and 7. There are two: the discount factor for the present value of the annuity stream and the planning horizon term which is also used for the present value calculations. These are hyperparameters because they are determined outside the overall decision tree framework.

```
 1   ##
 2   ## Hotel location decision: DataFrame construction
 3   ##
 4   ## Set hyperparameters
 5   ##
 6   disc = 0.05
 7   term = 10
 8   ##
 9   ## Define key measures
10   ##   NOTE: Use Numpy's repeat function for efficiency
11   ##
12   location = list( np.repeat( [ 'Downtown', 'Airport' ], [ 7, 7 ] ) )
13   ##
14   x = [ x + ' ' + 'DT Development' for x in [ 'No', 'Modest', 'Major' ] ] +\
15   [ x + ' ' + 'AIR Development' for x in [ 'No', 'Modest', 'Major' ] ]
16   develop = list( np.repeat( x, [ 1, 3, 3, 1, 3, 3 ] ) )
17   ##
18   lbls = ['Status Quo' ] + [ 'Low', 'Medium', 'High' ]*2
19   scenario = [ 'DT ' + str for str in lbls ] + [ 'AIR ' + str for str in lbls ]
20   scenario_prob = [ 1.0, 0.15, 0.60, 0.25, 0.20, 0.25, 0.55, 1.00, 0.25, 0.65,
                       0.10, 0.15, 0.45, 0.40 ]
21   scenario_earnings = [ 1.20, 1.05, 1.10, 1.15, 1.10, 1.55, 1.95, 1.30, 1.40, 1.50,
                            1.75, 1.60, 1.80, 2.00 ]
22   ##
23   ## Calculate present value of annuity stream and expected values
24   ##
25   pv = [ pv_annuity( x, disc, term ) for x in scenario_earnings ]
26   scenario_expected = [ pv[ i ] * scenario_prob[ i ] for i in range( len( pv ) ) ]
27   ##
28   ## Create DataFrame
29   ##
30   data = { 'location': location, 'develop': develop, 'scenario': scenario,
                           'scenario_prob': scenario_prob,
                           'Scenario_earnings': scenario_earnings,
                           'ann_pv': pv, 'scenario_expected':
                           scenario_expected }
31   df = pd.DataFrame( data )
32   df.set_index( [ 'location', 'develop' ], inplace = True )
33   fmt = { 'scenario_prob': '{:0.2f}', 'scenario_earnings': '${:.2f}', 'ann_pv':
                              '${:.2f}', 'scenario_expected':
                              '${:.2f}' }
34   df.style.format( fmt ).set_caption( 'Decision Tree Data' ).set_table_styles(
                              tbl_styles )
35
```

Figure 6-7. A code snippet showing how to create the data for the hotel example.

I then define the key measures in Lines 8 to 21. I use the NumPy function repeat in Line 12 to create a list of the two locations. This repeats each element of a list, the first argument to the function, a specified number of times which is contained in another list as the second argument to the function. For example, list(np.repeat(['a', 'b'], [2, 3])) yields the list ['a', 'a', 'b', 'b', 'b'].

I want a list with "Downtown" repeated seven times and "Airport" repeated seven times. You can see the reason for the sevens by looking at the terminal branches of the decision tree in Figure 6-6. The repeat function, however, returns a NumPy array which I coerce to a list using the Python list function. I use the same steps in Lines 14 to 16 to create a list of the development possibilities. I use two list comprehensions in Lines 14 and 15 to create the downtown (DT) and airport (AIR) development options and then concatenate them in Line 16 using the + operator.

 Use list comprehensions as much as possible. They are a great time saver and they will make your Python code easier to read.

I create a list of labels for the scenarios in Lines 18 and 19 by concatenating two lists, again using the + operator. The second list has the three levels, but, I repeat the list twice using the * operator. Then I use two list comprehensions in Line 19 to complete the scenario labels, but again I use the + operator to concatenate the lists.

I create two additional lists in Lines 20 and 21: one for the prior probabilities from Table 6-2 and the predicted earnings for each scenario. The present value of the earnings is calculated in Line 25 using Equation 6-1. The two hyperparameters are used here. The expected value of each present value is calculated with a list comprehension in Line 26.

Finally, I specify a dictionary in Line 30 which I use to create the DataFrame in Line 31. I display the DataFrame, with a nice format, in Line 34. I show the DataFrame in Figure 6-8.

				Decision Tree Data			
		scenario	scenario_prob	scenario_earnings	ann_pv	scenario_expected
location	develop					
	No DT Development	DT Status Quo	1.00	$1.20	$9.27	$9.27
	Modest DT Development	DT Low	0.15	$1.05	$8.11	$1.22
	Modest DT Development	DT Medium	0.60	$1.10	$8.49	$5.10
Downtown	Modest DT Development	DT High	0.25	$1.15	$8.88	$2.22
	Major DT Development	DT Low	0.20	$1.10	$8.49	$1.70
	Major DT Development	DT Medium	0.25	$1.55	$11.97	$2.99
	Major DT Development	DT High	0.55	$1.95	$15.06	$8.28
	No AIR Development	AIR Status Quo	1.00	$1.30	$10.04	$10.04
	Modest AIR Development	AIR Low	0.25	$1.40	$10.81	$2.70
	Modest AIR Development	AIR Medium	0.65	$1.50	$11.58	$7.53
Airport	Modest AIR Development	AIR High	0.10	$1.75	$13.51	$1.35
	Major AIR Development	AIR Low	0.15	$1.60	$12.35	$1.85
	Major AIR Development	AIR Medium	0.45	$1.80	$13.90	$6.25
	Major AIR Development	AIR High	0.40	$2.00	$15.44	$6.18

Figure 6-8. The DataFrame created using the code snippet in Figure 6-7.

I aggregate the expected earnings in the DataFrame by location and development type using the code in Figure 6-9. This makes use of the pandas groupby function in Line 6 which, as its name suggests, groups the earnings data by the location and develop variables.

```
1   ##
2   ## Hotel location decision: First data aggregation
3   ##
4   ## Aggregate expected earnings by location and development type
5   ##
6   df_activity = pd.DataFrame( { 'develop_earnings': df.groupby( [ 'location',
                                  'develop' ] )[ 'scenario_expected' ]
                                  .sum() } )
7   df_activity.reset_index( inplace = True )   ## Reset index
8   ##
9   ## Create dictionary to map development prior probabilities
10  ##
11  dt = { 'No AIR Development': 0.2, 'Modest AIR Development': 0.5, 'Major AIR
                                  Development': 0.3, 'No DT Development':
                                  0.15, 'Modest DT Development': 0.30,
                                  'Major DT Development': 0.55}
12  df_activity[ 'develop_prob' ] = df_activity[ 'develop' ].map( dt )
13  ##
14  ## Calculate expected earnings
15  ##
16  df_activity[ 'develop_expected' ] = df_activity.develop_earnings *
                                  df_activity.develop_prob
17  ##
18  ## Display with nice format
19  ##
20  fmt = { 'develop_earnings': '${:.2f}', 'develop_prob': '{:0.2f}',
                                  'develop_expected': '${:.2f}' }   ##
                                  display formats
21  tmp = df_activity.set_index( [ 'location', 'develop' ] )
22  tmp.style.format( fmt ).set_caption( 'Location and Development Aggregate Data'
                                  ).set_table_styles( tbl_styles )
23
```

Figure 6-9. A code snippet showing how to aggregate the hotel data in Figure 6-8.

Once grouped, the earnings data in each group are summed and returned as a new DataFrame. I define the development priors as a dictionary in Line 11 and then use the Python map function in Line 12 to map each prior to the appropriate development type in the grouped DataFrame. I finally calculate the expected values in Line 16 and display the final DataFrame. You can see what this looks like in Figure 6-10.

Location and Development Aggregate Data				
		develop_earnings	develop_prob	develop_expected
location	develop			
	Major AIR Development	$14.29	0.30	$4.29
Airport	Modest AIR Development	$11.58	0.50	$5.79
	No AIR Development	$10.04	0.20	$2.01
	Major DT Development	$12.97	0.55	$7.13
Downtown	Modest DT Development	$8.53	0.30	$2.56
	No DT Development	$9.27	0.15	$1.39

Figure 6-10. The DataFrame created using the code snippet in Figure 6-9.

I then do one final aggregation for the location using the DataFrame I just created. The same steps are used. The code is in Figure 6-11 and the result in Figure 6-12.

```
1   ##
2   ## Hotel location decision: Second data aggregation
3   ##
4   ## Aggregate by location
5   ##
6   df_location = df_activity.groupby( [ 'location' ] )[ [ 'develop_expected' ] ]
                                        .sum( )
7   df_location.rename( columns = {'develop_expected':'location_expected' }, inplace =
                                        True )
8   ##
9   ## Add investment outlay
10  ##
11  invest = { 'Airport': 1.50, 'Downtown': 1.75 }
12  df_location[ 'investment' ] = df_location.index.map( invest )
13  df_location[ 'net_earnings' ] = df_location.location_expected -
                                        df_location.investment
14  ##
15  ## Display with nice format
16  ##
17  df_location.index.name = None
18  fmt = { 'Airport': '${:.2f}', 'Downtown': '${:.2f}' }   ## display formats
19  df_location.T.style.set_caption( 'Expected Earnings by Location' ).format( fmt
                                        ).set_table_styles( tbl_styles )
20
```

Figure 6-11. A code snippet showing how to aggregate the hotel data in Figure 6-10. This is the final data for the hotel location decision.

Expected Earnings by Location		
	Airport	**Downtown**
location_expected	$12.08	$11.08
investment	$1.50	$1.75
net_earnings	$10.58	$9.33

Figure 6-12. The final DataFrame created using the code snippet in Figure 6-11. This is the final data for the hotel location decision. It is the menu presented to the decision-maker. The net earnings is the KPM, the menu option attribute.

Reaching a Decision Using a DADT

You do not reach a decision from the DADT itself, such as the one I show in Figure 6-6. The decision is reached from the data set you construct to reflect the tree. There is a data set for both the MLDT and the DADT, but the source of each is different. Regardless, the paradigm to keep in mind is that rich information is buried inside the data, and that information must be extracted. See Paczkowski (2022b) and Paczkowski (2023). Machine learning methods are used for the MLDT and aggregation methods are used for the DADT as I showed in Figure 6-9 and Figure 6-11.

 Remember, a DADT is based on constructed data.

For the hotel use-case, there is an expected value for each property. The decision-maker uses these to decide where to invest. The two properties constitute a menu, albeit a small one since it has only two options: downtown and airport. More properties, of course, would expand it. Regardless of the menu size, its options could be used in an integer programming set-up like the one I described in "Integer Programming" on page 162 to select the optimal property. In this use-case example with only two properties, the decision rule is simple: choose the property with the highest net earnings. This is the airport property.

This decision tree approach does not reflect any constraints. However, an integer programming approach requires constraints. These are the investment amounts bounded by how much can be invested. For this example, I set the upper bound at $2 billion. Also, since I want just one selection from the menu of two options, I set the sum of the decision variables to be less than or equal to 1. I show the integer programming approach set-up in Figure 6-13. The final solution is in Figure 6-14. Notice that the solution agrees with the one I mentioned: choose the airport.

```
1   ##
2   ## Strategic integer problem -- Hotel Location Investment Decision
3   ## Case: Select only one project
4   ##
5   ## ===> Step 1: Specify the solver <===
6   ##
7   solver = pywraplp.Solver.CreateSolver( 'SCIP' )
8   ##
9   ## ===> Step 2: Specify the decision variables <===
10  ##
11  x1 = solver.IntVar( 0.0, 1, 'x1' )  ## airport
12  x2 = solver.IntVar( 0.0, 1, 'x2' )  ## downtown
13  ##
14  ## ===> Step 3: Specify the constraints <===
15  ##
16  solver.Add( 1.50*x1 + 1.75*x2 <= 2.00 )
17  solver.Add( x1 + x2 <= 1 )
18  ##
19  ## ===> Step 4: Specify the objective function <===
20  ##
21  solver.Maximize( 12.08*x1 + 11.08*x2 )
22  status = solver.Solve()
23  ##
24  ## ===> Step 5: Summarize the results <===
25  ##
26  data = [
27              [ 12.08, 11.08 ],
28              [ 1.50, 1.75 ],
29              [ x1.solution_value(), x2.solution_value() ]
30  ]
31  sol_or = solver.Objective().Value()
32  cols = [ 'Airport', 'Downtown' ]
33  idx = [ 'Expected Earnings', 'Investment', 'Solution' ]
34  df = pd.DataFrame( data, columns = cols, index = idx )
35  display( df.style.set_caption( 'Hotel Integer Programming Solution'
                                      ).set_table_styles( tbl_styles ) )
36  print( f'Maximum NPV: ${sol_or:0.1f} Million' )
37
```

Figure 6-13. A code snippet showing how to set up the hotel location use-case as an integer programming problem.

```
          Hotel Integer Programming
                  Solution

                       Airport   Downtown

    Expected Earnings  12.080000  11.080000

          Investment    1.500000   1.750000

            Solution    1.000000   0.000000

    Maximum NPV: $12.1 Million
```

Figure 6-14. The integer programming solution based on the code in Figure 6-13.

Summary

I extended the non-stochastic methods to include Decision Trees. This was not mentioned in the literature review of Chapter 2, but it is important in the OR literature and toolkit for decision analysis. I distinguished between machine learning decision tree (MLDT) and a *Decision Analysis Decision Tree* (DADT): the former is used in machine learning to predict or classify features using large amounts of data; the latter is used in Prescriptive Analytics to visualize the possible paths and implications of decisions. The DADT is, as I showed, represented in a DataFrame which enables you to view your decision data in multiple ways. I also showed the connection between decisions using the DADT, Bayesian prior probabilities, and present value of an annuity stream. A hotel example was used which you should carefully study.

The main concepts from this chapter are:

1. The difference between an MLDT and DADT
2. The role and importance of priors
3. Calculating the present value of an annuity stream
4. How to reach a decision using a DADT

DADT Function

This is the function I used to create the decision analysis decision tree, Figure 6-4. I use the Python package Plotly, which must be installed on your computer.

```
 1  def dadt( df, terms = None, title = None, display_data = False, term_space = 30,
                                              show_edge_labels = False,
                                              show_tick_labels = False ):
 2      n = len( df )
 3      n_vertices = len( df )
 4      ##
 5      ## Create index, source, and edge labels
 6      ##
 7      df[ 'idx' ] = range( n )
 8      df[ 'source' ] = [ df.target[ df.edges[ i ][ 0 ] ] for i in df.idx ]
 9      x = [ df.labels[ df.edges[ i ][ 0 ] ].lower() + '-' + df.labels[ df.edges[ i ]
                                              [ 1 ] ].lower() for i in df.idx ]
10      x[ 0 ] = None
11      df[ 'edge_labels' ] = x
12      ##
13      ## Get root position
14      ##
15      Y = [ df.target[ k ][ 1 ] for k in range( n_vertices ) ]
16      root = 2 * max( Y )
17      ##
18      ## Get node positions
19      ##
20      position = { k: df.target[ k ] for k in range( n_vertices ) }
21      L = len( position )
22      Xn = [ position[ k ][ 0 ] for k in range( L ) ]
23      Yn = [ root - position[ k ][ 1 ] for k in range( L ) ]
24      ##
25      ## Get edges
26      ##
27      Xe = []
28      Ye = []
29      for edge in df.edges:
30          Xe += [ position[ edge[ 0 ] ][ 0 ], position[ edge[ 1 ] ][ 0 ], None ]
31          Ye += [ root - position[ edge[ 0 ] ][ 1 ], root - position[ edge[ 1 ] ][
                                              1 ], None ]
32      ##
33      ## Get edge label coordinates
34      ##
35      elabel_X = [ df.source[ i ][ 0 ] - ( df.source[ i ][ 0 ] - df.target[ i ][ 0 ]
                                              )/2 for i in range( n ) ]
36      elabel_Y = [ df.source[ i ][ 1 ] - ( df.source[ i ][ 1 ] - df.target[ i ][ 1 ]
                                              )/2 for i in range( n ) ]
37      df[ 'elabel_X' ] = elabel_X
38      df[ 'elabel_Y' ] = elabel_Y
39      cols = [ 'idx', 'labels', 'source', 'target', 'edges', 'edge_labels',
                                              'edge_hover', 'elabel_X', 'elabel_Y'
                                              ]
40      df = df[ cols ]
41      ##
42      ## Specify figure region
43      ##
44      layout = go.Layout( autosize = False, width = 800, height = 600 )
45      fig = go.Figure( layout = layout )
46      axis = { 'showline': True, 'zeroline': True, 'showgrid': True,
                                              'showticklabels': show_tick_labels }
```

Figure 6-15. The function to create a decision analysis decision tree. This uses Plotly for the plot. Code listing continued on next page.

```
47      ##
48      ## Draw tree
49      ##
50      fig.update_layout( title_text = title, title_x = 0.5, font_size = 18,
                                  showlegend = False, xaxis = axis,
                                  yaxis = axis, margin = { 'l': 40,
                                  'r': 40, 'b': 85, 't': 100 },
                                  hovermode = 'closest' )
51      fig.add_trace( go.Scatter( x = Xe, y = Ye, mode = 'lines', line = {
                                  'color':'rgb( 210, 210, 210 )',
                                  'width': 3 }, hoverinfo = 'none' ) )
52      fig.add_trace( go.Scatter( x = Xn, y = Yn, mode = 'markers+text', customdata =
                                  labels, marker = { 'symbol':
                                  'square-dot', 'size': 25, 'color':
                                  'red', 'line': { 'color': 'rgb( 50,
                                  50, 50 )', 'width': 1 } }, text =
                                  df.labels, opacity = 0.8 ) )
53      if show_edge_labels:
54          fig.add_scatter( x = df.elabel_X, y = [ root - df.elabel_Y[ i ] for i in
                                  range( n ) ], mode = 'text',
                                  text = df.edge_labels, hoverinfo
                                  = 'text', hovertext =
                                  df.edge_hover )
55      ##
56      if display_data:
57          display( df.head() )
58      ##
59      if terms != None:
60          for t in terms.items():
61              z = t[ 0 ]
62              fig.add_annotation(
63                  x = tuple( df.query( "labels == @z" ).target )[ 0 ][ 0 ],
64                  y = tuple( df.query( "labels == @z" ).target )[ 0 ][ 1 ],
65                  text = t[ 1 ],
66                  showarrow = False, yshift = -term_space
67              )
68      fig.show()
69
```

Figure 6-16. The function to create a decision analysis decision tree. This uses Plotly for the plot. Code listing continued from previous page.

PART IV

Stochastic Prescriptive Analytic Methods

In this fourth part, I will present methods for stochastic Prescriptive Analytics. The major one is simulations. This enables or aids the development of the decision-making menu. In typical expositions of selecting an optimal menu option, such as capital investment projects in OR and economics textbooks, the projects are just there, with no indication of where they came from. In addition, in those expositions, probabilities are assigned to different possible paths to an outcome, but, like the projects, there is no indication of where the probabilities came from; they are also just there. Yet these probabilities cannot be ignored because they are vital for expected value calculations.

In real-world problems, however, both the menu options and the probabilities must be developed. I acknowledge that, in some instances, a chief decision-maker, perhaps the CEO for strategic scale-views, may just state what they are without any discussion or consultation with others. I conjecture, however, that this is probably rare.

This fourth part is concerned with developing the two critical parts of a decision menu: the menu options and the probability distribution for the paths leading to the expected value calculations. This part is more extensive, with five chapters:

- Chapter 7, "Simulation Essentials"
- Chapter 8, "Simulation Examples"
- Chapter 9, "Developing Menu Options"
- Chapter 10, "Developing Menu Priors"
- Chapter 11, "One-Time Decisions"

Simulation Essentials

I will introduce simulations in this chapter as a powerful tool for Prescriptive Analytics. The inherent uncertainty in all decisions is the reason for simulations. As I argued in Chapter 1, all decisions made today are for a return tomorrow, whether "tomorrow" is literally tomorrow, next week, next month, next quarter, next year, or next decade; the return is in the future. The actual future period is immaterial regarding the uncertainty associated with the decision because it will be there regardless.

A major feature of a return is that you cannot say what it will be. It is due to shocks or disturbances with unknown or unknowable causes. Jurado et al. (2015, p. 1177) note that "uncertainty is typically defined as the conditional volatility of a disturbance that is unforecastable from the perspective of economic agents." In our context, the economic agents are the business decision-makers, but this situation holds for all decision-makers, whether they are in the business domain, the public policy domain, or just ordinary citizens deciding to buy a new house, invest in stocks, or accept a job offer.

A decision-maker, acting today, must factor uncertainty into the decision-making process. But uncertainty per se cannot be measured. There have been many attempts to develop proxies or indicators of uncertainty that can be measured and tracked over time. Jurado et al. (2015, p. 1178) note that these include:

- Volatility of stock market returns measured by the variance of returns;
- The cross-sectional variance of profits, stock returns, or productivity;
- The cross-sectional variance of survey-based forecasts; and
- Counts of "uncertainty-related" keywords in news publications.

They note, however, "[w]hile most ... measures have the advantage of being directly observable, their adequacy as proxies for uncertainty depends on how strongly they are correlated with this latent stochastic process." This correlation is unknown because the uncertainty process is unknown. That is what the latency refers to.

A sophisticated, quantitatively-based metric of uncertainty would have great value to all decision-makers, regardless of their domain. Jurado et al. (2015) is one such attempt. But this effort is in its early development, with a lot to be done before it can be of practical use, if it ever will be used.

Yet business decision-makers, unfortunately, do not have the luxury of waiting for this development. They must make decisions in real-time, make them constantly, and usually make them under pressure if not outright duress. This holds whether they are at the operational, tactical, or strategic scale-view levels. They need another approach to bound, at a minimum, the uncertainty. These bounds are best developed using simulations. This is my focus in this chapter.

The leading questions for this chapter are:

- What is a simulation?
- How important are simulations in our modern technology era?
- What is an advantage of doing a simulation?
- How is randomness introduced into a simulation?
- How are random numbers generated for a simulation?
- What are some example applications of simulations?

What Is a Simulation?

A simulation is the imitation of a process according to the Merriam-Webster Dictionary. In particular, it is "the imitative representation of the functioning of one system or process by means of the functioning of another." In our modern technology era, the other system is a computer program. These are now widely used in many areas, such as academic and commercial research, education, and training to mention a few.

Simulation use in research has increased over time. The *Google Books Ngram Viewer* allows you to search *Google Books* for a keyword or phrase in any books Google cataloged. See Google Books (2023). *Google Books* is a *corpus* the *Viewer* searches using advanced text analytics. An *ngram* is a series of n adjacent letters. See Paczkowski (2020) for the use of text analytics and the definition of *ngram*. I provide the time series graph from the *Viewer* for the word "simulation" for the period 1900 to 2019 (the last year provided by the *Viewer*) in Figure 7-1. You can see the growth of the word usage during the 20th century and the first quarter of the 21st century.

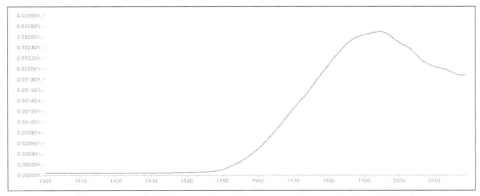

Figure 7-1. The time trend of the word simulation *in titles in the Google Books corpus.*

Simulations are important because of the complexity of modern problems. Of course, people in all prior periods (e.g., the 16th century) believed their problems were complex. So complexity is a relative term.

Complexity depends upon the size of the system you have (or had) to deal with. The more complex the system, the more complex the problems. For us in the 21st century, our systems are very complex involving many interacting and interdependent parts. In fact, the number of parts defines the complexity of a system and a system per se.

This is especially true in business. As a result, newer and more sophisticated tools are needed to not only understand complex business problems, but also to manage and solve them. This includes decision making for these complex business problems. See Paczkowski (2023) for a discussion of complexity, especially in a business context.

So how does a simulation help you deal with modern complex (business) problems and decisions? Simply stated, it is a way to imitate a system to understand how all its parts operate together. But the concept goes further. It also allows you to test different conditions that may be imposed on the system to determine likely outcomes from them as they evolve through time. This is important because it may be, and often is, impractical (i.e., too costly) to manipulate the system itself. A simulation is more cost-effective.

The Simulation Age

Figure 7-1 suggests we might be in a new age of analytical work. There is a belief that this is the case. Paczkowski (2023), based on work by Schweber and Wachters (2000), notes that there have been seven "ages" since the 16th century that have changed how we operate:

- Scientific
- Probabilistic
- Statistical
- Science-based technology
- Management science
- Computer science/engineering
- Simulation analytics

These are basically targeted at how we understand our world (and the cosmos), which is a scientific orientation; how we do business; and how we function in our daily lives. The last age, the one we are now in, is *The Age of Simulation Analytics*. This is a result of our use of simulations for all manner of tasks. This *Simulation Age* cannot be ignored, especially in business.

Types of Simulations

There are two types of simulations: non-stochastic and stochastic.

They differ by how you use random variations to test hypothetical situations. You impose these on a model of the system. For a non-stochastic simulation, there are no random variations; for a stochastic simulation, there are.

Both types require a model of the system since the purpose of a simulation is to do something to it without touching the real system. The model could be a physical one (e.g., a crash dummy for automobile crash simulations); a statistical/econometric/machine learning model trained on historical data; or a pure computer program with code that mimics the system (e.g., climate studies). In most, if not all, cases, computer technology is a key factor. For the business problems I am concerned about, ones that involve business decisions for operations, tactics, and strategies, the models are mostly of the statistical/econometric/machine learning ilk. The conditions are infinite but some possibilities are changing macroeconomic conditions leading to inflation, higher unemployment, and rising interest rates; changing consumer preferences; introducing new competitive price points or products; introducing new regulations or laws; confronting antitrust actions and lawsuits; and so on.

Non-stochastic

Non-stochastic simulations for business problems and decisions are basically "what-if" tests imposed on a model. A key decision-maker asks what would happen if a condition changed or a specific action or event occurred. This reflects the level of uncertainty for the decision-maker—"If this event happened, what would be the impact?"—who wants to have the level reduced by gaining some rich information. The DST makes the change in its model and reports the result. This is challenging if the event never occurred before so there is no historical record of it in training data. Nonetheless, the event could be simulated (i.e., tested) by changing some aspect of the trained model. The overall objective is to provide the decision-maker with rich information he or she did not have before.

As an example, a time series model could be trained on monthly historical sales data and used to forecast monthly sales for a five-year business plan. The CEO could ask what would happen to sales if another COVID shutdown occurred one year hence. This shutdown would be interpreted as a shock to the business and larger economic system, the shock being forced shutdowns, loss of productivity, and, of course, the loss of lives. In an econometric model, this shock is handled by defining a dummy variable for the COVID period in a time series DataFrame. A dummy usually allows only for the period when the shock occurred; a dynamic pattern is not included. In an *autoregressive integrated moving average* (ARIMA) time series model, however, a dynamic pattern for a class of variables can be included. The class of variables reflects an intervention of the shock on the underlying time series pattern. In either approach, a future shock could be accounted for using the dummies to address the CEO's question. See Wei (2006) for intervention analysis in ARIMA time series modeling.

Suppose there is no historical data. Is it impossible to train a model? After all: no data, no model. This problem can be handled by synthesizing data. I will discuss synthesizing in Chapter 9.

Stochastic

A stochastic simulation involves random shocks to a system, the shocks being random pulls from a probability distribution that specifies the probabilities of the shocks. They quantify the level of uncertainty about an event that could impact a decision. For example, for the hotel location decision in Chapter 6, you might have predicted the earnings per year for 10 years for each scenario outlined by the decision tree. Notice that the terminal leaves have one definite number. Which one will be realized will, of course, depend on the branch taken to the terminal points. But the number is fixed in this example. This implies that the present value of the annuity stream from that number is fixed.

Regardless of which branch you follow, you don't know the terminal numbers with certainty, let alone the numbers for each year of the planning period. They will follow a probability distribution reflecting this uncertainty. That distribution must be incorporated into the analysis.

This same reasoning applies to the mathematical programming problems I covered in Chapter 5. The values I used there were known with certainty, which is unrealistic. They were adequate for pedagogical purposes, but not real business decision problems.

The only way to handle this is to use draws from a probability distribution (i.e., randomly select from a distribution) and calculate the required data based on the draws. Then averages, or some other appropriate statistic, can be calculated for all the draws. For example, for the hotel problem, you could randomly take 1,000 draws from a normal distribution for each required number, calculate the present value and expected earnings for each draw, and then average the 1,000 results. The average will indicate what decision to make: airport or downtown. The advantage is that uncertainty is dealt with via the probability distributions. The disadvantage is that you must know how to do the simulation. I will discuss how to simulate this in the following sections and the next chapter.

Non-Stochastic Simulations: The Process

A non-stochastic simulation is often used with a *dynamic system* to help you better understand its operations. A dynamic system has a time dimension for the key variables' movements and developments. These can be represented by intricate mathematical equations: difference, differential, or simultaneous. Difference equations contain the difference in variables over time where time changes are finite. A differential equation is the same, but for infinitesimally small time changes. Simultaneous equations have variables determined by the whole set of equations while the values of other variables are determined independently of the set. Those determined within the set of equations are called *endogenous variables*; the others are *exogenous variables*. Exogenous variables can be specified either by assumptions that represent typical behavior or patterns; by management as targets for business planning such as a target ROI; or as a step in a what-if scenario analysis to determine what would happen if a key factor has a different setting. I will illustrate the last one in Chapter 9 where I will discuss what-if analysis.

Stochastic Simulations: The Process

Stochastic simulations consist of several integrated parts:

- A random number generator
- A model representing the system being studied
- KPMs to simulate

- A methodology to aggregate and statistically analyze the KPM data

Since a stochastic simulation involves random variations, those variations must be generated. They are created by random numbers. There is a wide literature on random number generation, some of which use computer algorithms, while others rely on natural phenomena. The latter consists of tracking and capturing, for example, atmospheric noise (see, for example, *https://www.random.org*) or using the digits of pi (see, for example, Tu and Fischbach [2005] and Paczkowski [2023]). The most common approach is algorithmic.

This, however, begs a question: "Are the resulting numbers truly random?" Algorithmically generated numbers can be tested for randomness (and have been), and they pass the tests. But they are still algorithmically, not naturally, generated, so they are referred to as *pseudo-random numbers* rather than pure or natural random numbers.

Pseudo-Random Number Generators: A Brief Introduction

Paczkowski (2023, Chapter 9) has an extensive discussion of algorithmic methods for generating random numbers. The two most used are the *linear congruential generator* (LCG) and the *Mersenne Twister*.

Linear congruential generator

The LCG uses a deterministic formula to generate pseudo-random numbers. These are then converted to numbers that lie in the closed interval $[0,1]$. All numbers in this interval are uniformly distributed. These are used, if needed, as input into a probability distribution formula to further generate a probability that follows that distribution. For instance, a uniformly distributed number in the interval $[0,1]$ could be interpreted as a probability and used to inversely solve the equation for a standardized normal probability density function. That solution is a Z-score. You did this in basic statistics when you first learned about the standard normal table. You first calculated the Z-score and then used the table to calculate a probability. After you mastered this, you reversed the direction by using a probability to enter the same table to determine a Z-score. So it is a procedure you already know, but it is now used for any distribution.

The formula for the LCG is

Equation 7-1.

$$X_{n+1} = (aX_n + c) \bmod m$$

where $0 < a < m$, $0 \leq c < m$ are constant integers. The term "mod" represents the *modulo operator* that returns the remainder of a division of two numbers. For example, $10 \bmod 6$ returns the remainder of 10 divided by 6, which is 4. In Python, this operator is the percent sign so my example is 10 % 6. I show this in Figure 7-2. For more on the modulo operation with some interesting viewpoints, see Cheng (2023).

```
1  ##
2  ## Example of 10 mod 6
3  ##
4  10 % 6
5

   4
```

Figure 7-2. The modulo operator in Python. The % is the modulo operator. I included the modulo operator in Table 3-1.

As noted in Paczkowski (2023, p. 235), Equation 7-1 "is a recursive formula meaning that it repeats itself based on a previous value generated by itself. The starting point, $0 < X_0 < c$, is the *seed*, usually the current computer clock time. The m is usually chosen to be very large. If w is the word size of a computer (such as 32 or 64 for 32 bits or 64 bits per word computers, respectively), then $m = 2^w$. That is, $m = 2^{32}$ or $m = 2^{64}$ for 32 bits or 64 bits per word computers, respectively." I show a simple Python script for Equation 7-1 in Figure 7-3.

I define a function in Line 6 that has five named arguments. The first is the random number seed that defaults to None; the other four correspond to the constants in Equation 7-1. The seed is important. It is the starting point for the recursive model in Equation 7-1. Without it, the model has no starting point, but it must start somewhere. The implementation in most software reverts to the computer system time as the seed if you do not provide one. So if you use seed = None, the current timestamp is used for the seed. See Lines 10 and 11 for this.

Line 15 has the basic equation, Equation 7-1, which is recursively executed in a list comprehension. The number of elements added to the list is the number of pseudo-random values you want to generate. In each iteration, the equation is evaluated, added to the list, and a new seed is set to this number. The seed is then always updated. If this is not done, the same pseudo-random number will be generated, so the final list will be filled with the same numbers.

This list comprehension makes use of a feature in Python 3.8 and later: an assignment expression to retain the last value in the comprehension iteration. Basically, an assignment expression "names the result of an expression…allowing [the] descriptive name to be used in place of a longer expression, and permitting [its] reuse." This is the expression seed :=. See Python Enhancement Proposals (2023).

```
1   ##
2   ## Linear Congruential Generator
3   ##
4   ## Define a LCG function; num = number of random values to generate
5   ##
6   def lcg( seed = None, m = 2**32, a = 1103515245, c = 12345, num = 10 ):
7       ##
8       ## Initialize the seed state
9       ##
10      if seed == None:
11          seed = pd.Timestamp.now().value
12      ##
13      ## Generator; use assignment expression
14      ##
15      X = [seed := ( a * seed + c ) % m for x in range( num ) ]
16      ##
17      ## Calculate uniform random numbers
18      ##
19      uniform = [ ran/m for ran in X ]
20      ##
21      ## Return results
22      ##
23      return X, uniform
24  ran, uniform = lcg( seed = 42, num = 10 )
25  data = { 'random':ran, 'uniform':uniform }
26  df = pd.DataFrame( data )
27  df.head().style.set_caption( "Linear Congruential Method" ).set_table_styles(
                                 tbl_styles ).\
28      format( {'random':"{:,.0f}", 'uniform':"{:0.4f}" } ).hide( axis = 'index' )
29
```

	Linear Congruential Method	
random	**uniform**
3,397,979,675	0.7912
3,263,785,912	0.7599
3,148,160,401	0.7330
3,816,158,454	0.8885
3,055,579,383	0.7114

Figure 7-3. A script showing how to implement a linear congruential generator. Based on Paczkowski (2023, p. 237).

The pseudo-random numbers are quite large as you can see in the output in Figure 7-3. To be useful, they are scaled to lie in the interval $[0,1]$ by dividing by m which was set as an argument to the function. I do this in Line 19 using another list comprehension. See Paczkowski (2023, Chapter 9) for an explanation of this scaling. The scaled pseudo-random numbers are returned as I show in Figure 7-3.

This algorithm is efficient and widely used. But it has a drawback, which usually is of little practical significance, but it is a limitation nonetheless. Depending on the size of the m-factor in the function, the series of pseudo-random numbers generated repeats every m times. This is called the *period*. For example, using $seed = 42$, $a = 1$, $c = 4$, $m = 6$, and $num = 12$, the function generates the random sequence [4,2,0,4,2,0,4,2,0,4,2,0]. The repetition is clear, but clearly unacceptable; it negates the whole concept of randomness. This is why m is so large in Figure 7-3: it avoids repetitions (i.e., it has a long period) for almost all real-world problems.

Mersenne Twister generator

Another algorithm sets the period so large you will never (for all practical purposes) see repeats. This algorithm is based on the *Mersenne Prime Numbers* and is called the *Mersenne Twister*. A *Mersenne Prime Number* has the form $2^n - 1$ for an integer n. There are only 51 known Mersenne primes. See Wikipedia (2023i). The period for the *Mersenne Twister* is $2^{19937} - 1$, which is very large. Unfortunately, the mathematics behind this approach is complicated, but, nonetheless, many sophisticated statistical packages use it. The Python random package uses this generator. See Paczkowski (2023, Chapter 9). Also see Wikipedia (2024f).

Generating random numbers in Python

You certainly do not have to worry about the actual mechanism used in Python (or any software) for generating random numbers. There are several built-in functions in two key Python packages that generate them for you. In all instances, you just tell your selected function the required number of random numbers you need. Each package's random number generator creates an integer which is then transformed to a uniformly distributed value as I illustrated previously. The two Python packages are random and NumPy.

random. The random package generates random floating point numbers in the interval [0,1), which is called a half-open interval because it does not include the upper bound (1.0), using the function random. A random integer in the interval [`min`, `max`], where you specify the minimum and maximum values, is generated using another function, `randint`. I illustrate both in Figure 7-4. I set the seed at 42 in Line 7 and call the two random functions in Line 11. The random float is a uniformly distributed value. Notice I specified the interval for the random integer as [1,10]. The returned integer is 1.

 You could specify the mean and standard deviation (labeled "sigma"); do not use the variance which is just the square of the standard deviation. The defaults are $mean = 0.0$ and $sigma = 1.0$ for the standard normal.

```
1   ##
2   ## Generate random numbers using the random package
3   ##
4   ## Set the seed for reproducibility
5   ##
6   seed = 42
7   random.seed( seed )
8   ##
9   ## Print a random float and integer
10  ##
11  print( f'Random float: {random.random( )}\nRandom integer: {random.randint( 1, 10
                                              )}' )
12
```

Random float: 0.6394267984578837
Random integer: 1

Figure 7-4. How to generate a random float number and a random integer using the random package. I set the seed to 42 for reproducibility.

The random package has many other functions to randomly sample from a list (used for random sampling in survey and opinion polling studies) and randomly shuffle a list, as well as randomly draw from a wide variety of probability distributions. The (Gaussian) normal distribution is the most used distribution next to the uniform distribution. In fact, a draw from the normal is based on the uniformly distributed float random number. See Paczkowski (2023) for a discussion of how this works. If you need a (Gaussian) normal random number, you would use the gauss function, which I illustrate in Figure 7-5.

```
1   ##
2   ## Gaussian Normal
3   ##
4   ## Set the seed for reproducibility
5   ##
6   seed = 42
7   random.seed( seed )
8   ##
9   ## Print the standard normal random number
10  ##
11  print( f'Standard Normal: {random.gauss( mu = 0.0, sigma = 1.0 )}' )
12  ##
13  ## Print the normal random number for a mean = 1 and variance = 4
14  ##
15  print( f'Normal: {random.gauss( mu = 1.0, sigma = math.sqrt( 4 ) )}' )
16
```

Standard Normal: -0.14409032957792836
Normal: 0.6541927993369614

Figure 7-5. How to generate Gaussian normal random numbers. I set the seed to 42 for reproducibility.

I once more set the random seed to 42 in Line 7 and printed the standard normal in Line 11. Notice that I explicitly specified the mean and standard deviation. Starting in

Python version 3.11, "mu" and "sigma" have the default values 0 and 1, respectively. I repeated the print statement in Line 15 by specifying a mean of 1.0 and a variance of 4. Since this function requires a standard deviation, I used the math package's square root function to calculate the standard deviation. If I mistakenly used 4, this implies a variance of 16, which is not what I want.

The random package generates and returns a single value, but you may want a list of values. You could create it using a list comprehension. I show a code snippet for this in Figure 7-6. I set the random seed in Line 4, which is outside the list comprehension. If you did not set the random seed, the list would change each time you ran the script. The list comprehension itself is in Line 5.

```
1  ##
2  ## Generate a list of random integers with a list comprehension
3  ##
4  random.seed( 42 )
5  [ random.randint( 1, 10 ) for i in range( 7 ) ]
6

   [2, 1, 5, 4, 4, 3, 2]
```

Figure 7-6. How to use a list comprehension to generate a list of random integers. I set the random seed to 42 outside the list comprehension.

NumPy. An easier way to generate a list of random numbers, however, is to use the NumPy random number functions. NumPy returns an array, which is a generalization of a vector or matrix, depending on its dimensions. A 1-dimensional array can be converted to a list by using the list function in Python. For example, the expression list(np.array([0.058, 0.866])) takes the array of two elements created using NumPy's np.array function and converts it to a list. The result is [0.058, 0.866]. I show an example using the NumPy random functions in Figure 7-7. Notice the returned values are automatically in a list format.

```
 1  ##
 2  ## Generate random numbers using the Numpy package
 3  ##
 4  ## Set the seed for reproducibility
 5  ##
 6  seed = 42
 7  np.random.seed( seed )
 8  ##
 9  ## Print a random float and integer
10  ##
11  print( f'Random float: {np.random.random( size = 2 )}\nRandom integer:
                                {np.random.randint( 1, 10, size = 2 )}' )

12
```

Random float: [0.37454012 0.95071431]
Random integer: [8 5]

Figure 7-7. How to generate a random float number and a random integer using NumPy's random package. I set the seed to 42 for reproducibility.

You can calculate an array or list of Gaussian normal variates using NumPy in a manner like the random package. The difference (there must be one!) is that the function is named `normal`, the mean is called "loc," and the standard deviation is called "scale." The defaults are `loc = 0` and `scale = 1`. There is also a `size` argument since NumPy works with arrays, which have a size. The default for the `normal` function is `size = None` which itself defaults to `size = 1`. I show how to use the NumPy Gaussian normal in Figure 7-8.

```
 1  ##
 2  ## Gaussian Normal
 3  ##
 4  ## Set the seed for reproducibility
 5  ##
 6  seed = 42
 7  np.random.seed( seed )
 8  ##
 9  ## Print the standard normal random number
10  ##
11  print( f'N(0, 1): {np.random.normal( loc = 0.0, scale = 1.0, size = 3 )}' )
12  ##
13  ## Print the normal random number for a mean = 1 and variance = 4
14  ##
15  print( f'N(0, 4): {np.random.normal( loc = 1.0, scale = math.sqrt( 4 ), size = 3
                                )}' )

16
```

Standard Normal: [0.49671415 -0.1382643 0.64768854]
Normal: [4.04605971 0.53169325 0.53172609]

Figure 7-8. How to generate Gaussian normal random numbers using the NumPy package. The seed is set at 42 for reproducibility. Notice that the function is named normal, the mean is called "loc," and the standard deviation is called "scale."

Be aware of the different parameter names for random and NumPy for the Gaussian normal distribution. See Table 7-1 for parameter specifications.

Table 7-1. A summary of the parameters for random and NumPy's normal distribution functions.

	random	NumPy
Function name	gauss	normal
Mean	mu = 0	loc = 0
Standard deviation	sigma = 1	scale = 1
Size	–	size = None

Notes: random returns one value, while NumPy returns an array with one element even if it defaults to None. Values in this table are defaults.

The `size` can be specified in a complex fashion allowing for a multi-dimensional array. This is the generalization of a matrix I mentioned earlier. For example, you could specify `size = ( 2, 3, 4 )` which designates two 3×4 arrays. The 3×4 arrays are matrices. I show an example in Figure 7-9.

```
1  ##
2  ## Complex size for a normal sample using Numpy
3  ##
4  np.random.seed ( 42 )
5  np.random.normal( size = ( 2, 3, 4 ) )
6

   array([[[ 0.49671415, -0.1382643 , 0.64768854, 1.52302986], [-0.23415337, -0.23413696, 1.57921282,
   0.76743473], [-0.46947439, 0.54256004, -0.46341769, -0.46572975]],

   [[ 0.24196227, -1.91328024, -1.72491783, -0.56228753], [-1.01283112, 0.31424733, -0.90802408, -
   1.4123037 ], [ 1.46564877, -0.2257763 , 0.0675282 , -1.42474819]]]])
```

Figure 7-9. How to generate Gaussian normal random numbers for a complex array.

Just as the random package has many other functions, so does the NumPy package. See Paczkowski (2023) for more examples.

Simulation Models: Overview

Defining a simulation model is the hardest part of developing a simulator. A *simulator* is the program that produces the simulation. A model has to be constructed that represents, to the extent possible, the structure of the system to be simulated. Since the number of possible systems is infinite, the number of possible simulators is also infinite. Nonetheless, one must be specified and created to solve a decision problem under uncertainty.

The best way for you to specify a simulator is to gather insight into the structure of the system. This can come from your experience working in your business and similar domains. It can also come from consultation with key business stakeholders: SMEs, KOLs, the DAC, and the *C-level* team itself.

The simulator, of course, depends on the scale-view of the decision-maker. Insight at the operational level could, as examples, come from:

- Short-term predictive models of daily sales, inventory, and supplies from supply-chain partners
- Queueing models of hourly or daily customer order placements and concomitant staffing requirements

For a tactical view, they could include:

- Short-term sales projections for different price points or advertising and promotional initiatives
- Potential take rates from new product choice models for different price points and product attributes

See Paczkowski (2018) for choice models. And, finally, for a strategic view they could include:

- Near- and long-term forecasts of real GDP and interest rates
- New technological developments such as improved self-checkout kiosks for retail stores

KPMs to Measure

Just as there is an infinite number of models, there is also an infinite number of KPMs. The most reasonable ones, of course, are those applicable to the relevant scale-view. For an operational scale-view, it may be the mean time to process daily orders. For a tactical scale-view, it may be the projected sales of a new product, expected market share for a new product, or the improvement in the *gross rating points* (GRP) for an advertising campaign. For a strategic scale-view, it may be the rate of return on investments (ROI), the rate of return on assets (ROA), or the earnings per share (EPS) in the stock market.

Aggregation Methods

Like the KPMs, the aggregation methods used in a simulation are many. The most typical, of course, are the sum and average, but which one you use depends on the quantities simulated.

The Need for Stochastic Simulations

I covered several methods for selecting from a decision menu in Part III. They all have a flaw, regardless of which one you use. They implicitly assume the key factors defining the problem are non-stochastic. For instance, consider the advertising reach problem of Chapter 5. This has assumptions, which I show in Table 5-5, about the reach, cost of reaching, the number of person-hours to design the reach campaign, and the number of person-hours to make a sale in the six marketing channels (TV, Trade magazine, Newspaper, Radio, Popular magazine, and a Promotional campaign). In this formulation of the problem, I assume you know these quantities perfectly, with no uncertainty as reflected in a variance, for each of them. In other words, their variance is zero. This is highly unrealistic.

This example, and others like it, are deterministic or non-stochastic. To be more realistic, the data should contain an element of indeterminacy reflecting our lack of perfect knowledge. A stochastic approach is required.

The Extent of Uncertainty

Uncertainty extends beyond not knowing the values for decision variables such as those for the reach example. Unknown events, such as supply-chain disruptions which cannot be (perfectly?) predicted, can disrupt previously made plans and decisions. These are obviously external to the business and so are outside the control of the firm's decision-makers. See Ehrenstein et al. (2019) for insightful comments on these types of disruptions. But, not only are they external to the firm, there is no way to determine when they will occur, their magnitude, or the extent of their effects. I summarize this by saying there are random or *stochastic* events that just happen (after all, that is what random means!), but they are important and cannot be ignored.

I strongly recommend a stochastic simulation approach for most, if not all, business problems.

There are two forms of randomness. The first is a small shock that, in the end, is inconsequential; it is just a nuance. Some examples are:

- A temporary power outage in an office complex, perhaps because an electrical transformer blew out, delaying operations for a few minutes

- Bad weather causing airline flight delays resulting in canceled hotel room bookings for a day

---

- A sudden supply-chain disruption for several days, perhaps caused by a temporary work stoppage by a supplier's workforce, halting raw material deliveries
- More customers than usual arrive at a bank mid-morning when a full teller staff is unavailable, resulting in a long queue of (probably upset) customers

These may be normal operational scale-view issues easily dealt with. The second form of random shock has a major disruptive impact. Some examples are:

- The oil embargoes in 1973 and 1979
- The 2008 financial crisis
- The world-wide COVID-19 shutdowns that began in 2020
- The Israel-Hamas conflict of October 2023

These are all negative, having deleterious effects. Shocks, however, could also be positive. Some examples are:

- An unexpected interest rate cut by the Federal Reserve
- An increase in real GDP above expectations
- An unexpected positive buy-recommendation from a major financial adviser
- A key materials supplier announcing an across-the-board price cut

None of these, both positive and negative, can be predicted (or are predictable). Even the government shutdowns are not completely predictable because of last-minute political negotiations and "deals," yet they have major effects. I will discuss ways to handle these in Chapter 9.

Randomness and the Degree of Uncertainty

Aside from random shocks, randomness also imposes or affects the degree of uncertainty in decision making. Recall from my discussion in Chapter 1 that all decisions are made under a cloud of uncertainty because we have finite knowledge and understanding of what will happen in the future due to decisions made today. This is compounded by the additional uncertainty from the predicted values used in optimization procedures such as mathematical programming. I will illustrate this in the next chapter.

Summary

This is the third of three primers on core material. In this chapter, I covered the essential background for simulations in preparation for the discussions in this part on stochastic methods for Prescriptive Analytics. I covered pseudo-random number generation and the use of the numbers to further generate probability distributions. I also outlined the need for simulations and a process for doing a simulation.

The main concepts from this chapter are:

- Simulation
- Natural random numbers
- Pseudo-random numbers
- Two random number generators: Linear Congruential and Mersenne Twister
- How to generate pseudo-random numbers in Python

CHAPTER 8

Simulation Examples

I provide five extensive examples of stochastic simulations in this chapter by building on and extending the material in Chapter 7. I will gradually make the examples more complicated, beginning with a simple coin toss problem and progressing to the hotel investment decision tree problem. More examples and explanations are in Paczkowski (2023).

The leading questions for this chapter are:

- How do you specify a simulation?
- How do you analyze a simulation's results?

Example 1: Coin Toss

I discussed a simple coin toss experiment in Chapter 4 to introduce frequency-based probabilities. I simply noted that most people are familiar with the basic probability concept from tossing a coin. The assertion is that the probability of a heads-up on a toss of a fair coin is 0.50. I demonstrated where this number comes from in Chapter 4. But this does not mean it is correct in the real world. I also noted that probabilities are interpreted in terms of infinite series giving them a "long-run" interpretation. Of course, we cannot do something (e.g., flipping a coin) an infinite number of times. The question is then: "Can we devise an experiment to determine if, in the long-run (however defined), on the average, the probability is indeed 0.50?" You can do this with a simulation.

I provide a script in Figure 8-1 for simulating a coin toss. I first set some simulation parameters in Lines 4 to 11. A random seed is set at 42 followed by the number of coin tosses in an experiment. This gives me the flexibility to use as many tosses as I want. I set this to one toss for this example. The experiment will be done or iterated 10,000 times, so there will be 10,000 tosses. Next, I want the coin to be fair, so I specify weights for the heads and tails, each at 0.5. Finally, I create an empty DataFrame to hold the toss results.

```
1   ##
2   ## Set simulation parameters
3   ##
4   random.seed( 42 )           ## seed
5   n = 1                            ## tosses or trials in an experiment
6   iter = 10000                     ## iterations or experiments
7   weights = [ 0.5, 0.5 ]     ## weights for coins: equal for unbiased
8   df = pd.DataFrame()
9   ##
10  iteration = [ i for i in range( iter ) ]
11  tosses = iteration * n
12  heads = [ sum( random.choices( [ 0, 1 ], weights = weights, k = n ) ) for i in
                                          range( iter )]
13  s = 0
14  cumsum = [ ( s := s + i ) for i in heads ]
15  prop = [ 0 if i == 0 else cumsum[ i ]/tosses[ i ] for i in range( iter ) ]
16  data = { 'iteration':iteration, 'heads':heads, 'cumsum':cumsum, 'tosses':tosses,
                                          'prop':prop }
17  df = pd.DataFrame( data )
18  df.tail( )
19
```

Figure 8-1. The script for simulating a coin toss.

I do the experiment in Line 12 using a list comprehension. This first uses the random package's choice function to randomly select one of two values in a list: 0 for tails and 1 for heads. The selection is based on weights which are in the weight variable I previously defined. The argument $k = n$ specifies that n selections will be made in one iteration of the experiment. Since $n = 1$, only one value is randomly selected from the list. Once this is done, the selected values are summed.

I then accumulate the results in Line 14, calculate the proportion of heads in Line 15, then populate the DataFrame and display the tail of the DataFrame. I want to see the tail to confirm the last cumulative sum, which should be 0.50 (or close). I show this tail in Figure 8-2. You can see that the proportion is about 0.50 as predicted. The number will get closer to 0.50 the more iterations are done.

	iteration	heads	cumsum	tosses	prop
9995	9995	1	5008	9995	0.501051
9996	9996	1	5009	9996	0.501100
9997	9997	1	5010	9997	0.501150
9998	9998	0	5010	9998	0.501100
9999	9999	0	5010	9999	0.501050 ←

Figure 8-2. The result of the simulation using the script in Figure 8-1.

Example 2: Die Toss

Another basic, but instructive, example of a simulator is a die toss. In this example, the die is assumed to be fair, which means one side is no more likely to be face-up than any other side. The implication is that each side has the same probability of being face-up: $\frac{1}{6}$. But what is the *expected value*?

An expected value of a random variable is a weighted average of the values of the random variable. In the case of a single die, the random variable is the outcome of a toss: the outcome could be any value in the set {1,2,3,4,5,6}. The weights for the averaging are the probabilities of seeing a particular value. For a die toss, the probabilities are $\frac{1}{6}$, as I just noted. The averaging is written differently depending on whether the random variable is discrete or continuous, but the interpretation is the same in either case.

From "Binomial distribution" on page 130, you know that if the random variable, X, is discrete, then

Equation 8-1.

$$E(X) = \sum_{-\infty}^{+\infty} x_i \times p(x)$$

where $p(x) = Pr(X = x)$ is the probability that $X = x$. This is a *probability mass function (pmf)* with $0 \leq p(x) \leq 1$ and $\sum_{-\infty}^{+\infty} p(x) = 1$. For a die toss, the summation indexes are $i = 1$ to $i = 6$. I show a script in Figure 8-3 for creating a simple bar chart of the *pmf* for a die toss and the resulting chart in Figure 8-4. You can see that the bars (i.e., the masses) are all at the same height.

```
1   ##
2   ## Probability mass function for die toss
3   ##
4   p = [ 1/6 for i in range( 1, 7 ) ]
5   data = { 'toss': range( 1, 7 ), 'prob': p }
6   df = pd.DataFrame( data )
7   df.set_index( 'toss', inplace = True )
8   df.plot( y = 'prob', kind = 'bar', legend = False, ylabel = 'Probability Mass',
9           xlabel = 'PIP on the Face of a Die',
10          title = 'Probability Mass for Die Toss', ylim = (0, .25 ), rot = 0 );
11
```

Figure 8-3. The script to produce a graph of the probability mass function for a single die toss. See Figure 8-4.

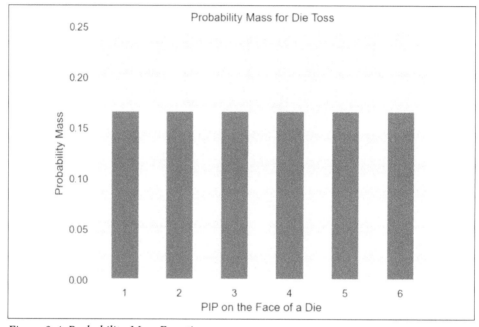

Figure 8-4. Probability Mass Function

For a continuous random variable, the summation in Equation 8-1 is replaced by an integral, and the *pmf* is replaced by the *probability density function* (*pdf*) for that random variable. Regardless, the interpretation is the same.

For the die toss, the expected value is calculated as:

$$E(X) = 1 \times \frac{1}{6} + 2 \times \frac{1}{6} + 3 \times \frac{1}{6} + 4 \times \frac{1}{6} + 5 \times \frac{1}{6} + 6 \times \frac{1}{6}$$

$$= \frac{1}{6} \times (1 + 2 + 3 + 4 + 5 + 6)$$

$$= \frac{1}{6} \times 21$$

$$= 3.5.$$

 There is an elementary number theory result that is useful for summing the first n integers. The sum is $\frac{[n \times (n+1)]}{2}$. For $n = 6$, $\frac{[n \times (n+1)]}{2} = \frac{[6 \times 7]}{2} = 21$.

An additional important expected value is the variance around the $E(X)$. This is calculated as:

$$V(X) = \sum_{-\infty}^{+\infty} [x_i - E(X)]^2 \times p(x).$$

For the die toss, the variance is 2.917.

The result that the expected value of a die toss is 3.5 and the variance is 2.917 could be viewed as just theoretical results that do not hold "in practice." Do they really hold if you toss the die many times? You can answer this question by simulating tossing the die many times. This is a *simulation experiment*. I show the simulation code for it in Figure 8-5.

A simulation set-up consists of the:

- Specification of the object to simulate
- Number of trials in an experiment
- Number of iterations (i.e., experiments) in the simulation
- Random number seed for reproducibility

The parameters for this simulation are set in Lines 6 to 9:

Object
Number of sides on a fair die: Line 6

Trials
Number of tosses (i.e., the trials) in an iteration: Line 7

Iterations
Number of iterations: Line 8

Seed
Random number seed for reproducibility: Line 9

I create an empty DataFrame in Line 13 to hold the simulation results. The main simulation code is in Lines 14 to 17. This consists of a for loop, Line 14, to iterate iter times; a list comprehension, Line 15, to randomly select integers for the sides of the die for each of the tosses; a dictionary in Line 16 with the iteration number, the mean, and the variance (with $n - 1$ degrees-of-freedom) of the list from Line 15; and finally filling the DataFrame in Line 17 using the dictionary.

The remaining lines in Figure 8-5 print some results and graph the Kernel Density Estimation (KDE) of the means and variances. The KDE is a smoothed version of a histogram that better shows the underlying pattern of a distribution without the clutter of the histogram bars. You can see from the two graphs that the distributions are centered on the theoretical values which are indicated by the dashed lines. These values are 3.5 for the expected value and 2.917 for the variance.

Use a KDE plot to highlight a distribution.

There is another point to note about the simulation. The distribution of the expected values and variances should be normally distributed based on the *Central Limit Theorem*. If you examine the distributions in Figure 8-5, you will notice that they appear to be normal. I included a normality test in the script to check this. The Null Hypothesis is that the data are normally distributed. The *p*-value is 0.843, so the Null Hypothesis is not rejected.

An alternative formulation of the list comprehension in Line 15 of Figure 8-5 uses the random package's *choice* function. This function randomly selects an object (integers in this case) from a list. I show how to use this function in Figure 8-6.

```
1   ##
2   ## Die roll Simulation
3   ##
4   ## Set simulation parameters
5   ##
6   sides = 6                  ## Objects
7   tosses = 1000              ## Trials
8   iter = 1000                ## Iterations
9   random.seed( 42 )  ## Seed
10  ##
11  ## Do simulation
12  ##
13  df = pd.DataFrame()
14  for i in range( iter ):
15      x = [ random.randint( 1, 6 ) for x in range( tosses ) ]  ## simulation list
                                                                     comprehension
16      data = { 'iteration':'iter.' + str( i ), 'means': np.average( x ),
                                                  'variances': np.var( x, ddof = 1 ) }
17      df = df.append( data, ignore_index = True)
18  df.set_index( 'iteration', inplace = True )
19  ##
20  ## Calculate means and plot KDE
21  ##
22  fig, ( ax1, ax2 ) = plt.subplots( nrows = 1, ncols = 2, figsize = ( 10, 3 ) )
23  df.plot( y = 'means', kind = 'kde', ax = ax1, legend = False, title = 'KDE
                                            Distribution of Means' )
24  df.plot( y = 'variances', kind = 'kde', ax = ax2, legend = False, title = 'KDE
                                            Distribution of Variances' )
25  ##
26  ## Calculate expected and simulated value
27  ##
28  e_dice = ( sides*( sides + 1 )/2 )/sides    ## Use formula [n*(n + 1)]/2
29  se_dice = df.means.mean()
30  print( f'Expected Value: {e_dice:0.3f}' )
31  print( f'Simulated Expected Value: {se_dice:0.3f}' )
32  ax1.axvline( x = se_dice, color = 'k', linestyle = 'dashed' )
33  ##
34  ## Calculate expected and simulated variance
35  ##
36  v_dice = sum( [ ( ( i - e_dice )**2)/6 for i in range( 1, sides + 1 ) ] )
37  sv_dice = df.variances.mean()
38  print( f'Variance: {v_dice:0.3f}' )
39  print( f'Simulated Variance: {sv_dice:0.3f}' )
40  ax2.axvline( x = sv_dice, color = 'k', linestyle = 'dashed' );
41
```

```
Expected Value: 3.500
Simulated Expected Value: 3.501
Variance: 2.917
Simulated Variance: 2.918
```

Figure 8-5. How to simulate a toss of a single die.

```
1   ##
2   ## Alternative list comprehension with random.choice
3   ##
4   random.seed( 42 )
5   [ random.choice( range( 1, 7 ) ) for x in range( 25 ) ]
6

    [6, 1, 1, 6, 3, 2, 2, 2, 6, 1, 6, 6, 5, 1, 5, 4, 1, 1, 1, 2, 2, 5, 5, 1, 5]
```

Figure 8-6. An alternative to the list comprehension in Line 14 of Figure 8-5. Notice that the first range is set for 1 to 7, but the 7 is not included.

You can get a better perspective on the development of the mean for the die toss by graphing the mean as it evolves from one iteration to the next. Remember, for this example, there are 1,000 tosses per iteration and 1,000 iterations as indicated in Figure 8-5, Lines 7 and 8, respectively. The DataFrame has the mean for each iteration. In Figure 8-7, I show the calculation of the cumulative mean, which shows its evolution. These are added to the DataFrame and then graphed. See Figure 8-7. This is called a *trace* or *trace graph* because it traces the evolution of the simulation through the iterations.

I use a list comprehension in Line 4 to add the iteration number to the DataFrame. Then I calculate the cumulative mean using the cumsum() method for a DataFrame and the iteration number in Line 5. Finally, I retrieve the last cumulative mean for display purposes in Line 9. Observe that this value agrees with the simulated expected value in Figure 8-5.

The mean starts high (at least at iteration 2), but eventually settles down around iteration 400 to a long-term mean of about 3.5, which is the expected value. The iteration period up to 400 is called a *burn-in* period in which the simulator "gets its bearings" on the expected value. This is typical. Because of this burn-in period, many analysts omit these values when analyzing simulation results. See Paczkowski (2023) for more discussion about the burn-in period. After period 400 (for this example), the means settle to a *steady-state equilibrium* which is the expected value. You want this steady-state.

```
 1  ##
 2  ## Calculate cumulative mean
 3  ##
 4  df[ 'n' ] = [ x for x in range( 1, len( df ) + 1 ) ]
 5  df[ 'cumMean' ] = df.means.cumsum()/df.n
 6  ##
 7  ## Graph the cumulative mean
 8  ##
 9  cumMean = df.cumMean.tail( 1 )[ 0 ]
10  print( f'Last Cumulative Mean: {cumMean:0.03f}' )
11  df.plot( y = 'cumMean', x = 'n', legend = False, title = 'Cumulative Mean',
                                     xlabel = 'Iteration', ylabel =
                                     'Iteration Mean' );
12
```

Last Cumulative Mean: 3.501

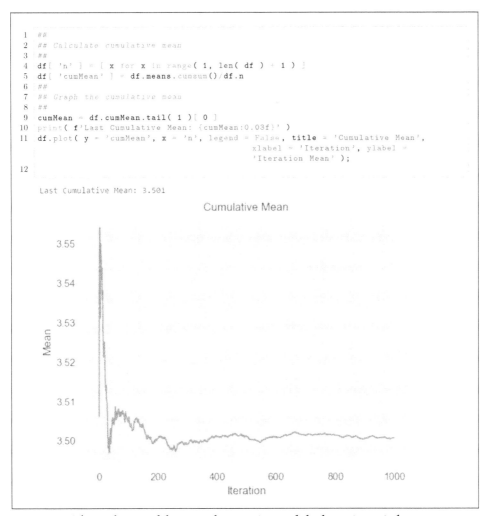

Figure 8-7. The evolution of the mean by iteration and the burn-in period.

Example 3: Regression Analysis

Consider the hotel capital investment problem I introduced in Chapter 6 for this example. The decision menu has two options: build downtown or at the airport. The decision was based on the present value of the revenue annuity stream under different situations or *scenarios*. I will examine scenarios further in Chapter 9. For now, I want to look into the revenue that led to the annuity streams.

Hotel revenue is generated by three sources:

- Room occupancy
- Food and Beverage Sales
- Catering large events (e.g., conferences, weddings)

I will focus on the beverage sales.

Assume the hotel chain as five years (60 months) of monthly beverage sales for all its properties. They know that sales vary directly with the number of occupied rooms. There will, of course, be additional variation depending on the property location: downtown properties generally have lower sales because patrons can easily eat and drink at local restaurants and taverns, while those at airport properties generally stay on the premises for meals and drinks.

Using this data, the DST calculates the average monthly sales (in dollars) per occupied room for both locations and assembles them into a single DataFrame of 120 records: 60 for each location. An indicator variable is included to identify the locations.

I show a script in Figure 8-8 that generates this data for this use-case. I first set the parameters for the generator in Lines 6 to 12. The data are then generated in Lines 16 to 30. The `if` statement on Line 20 is for the Downtown; the `else` statement on Line 24 is for the Airport. The two differ by the historical occupancy rates and the intercept for the population regression line. Notice that I use the NumPy `triangular` random number generator in Lines 21 and 25 because I want bounds on the occupancy rates. I create the location dummy variable in Line 28: 60 observations of each property location. Finally, I collect the data into a DataFrame and plot them using seaborn.

```
 1   ##
 2   ## Generate artificial data for hotel beverage sales example
 3   ##
 4   ## Specify parameters
 5   ##
 6   seed = 42
 7   mu = 0       ## Disturbance mean
 8   sig2 = 2     ## Disturbance variance
 9   sde = math.sqrt( sig2 )
10   B0 = 75      ## Population intercept
11   B1 = 25      ## Population slope for occupy
12   n = 120      ## Fixed number of observations for the regressions
13   ##
14   ## Create data
15   ##
16   np.random.seed( seed )
17   occupy = []
18   sales = []
19   for i in range( n )
20       if i <= n/2   ## Downtown
21           x = np.random.triangular( 0.55, 0.85, 0.95, size = None )
22           occupy.append( x )
23           sales.append( B0 + B1 * x + np.random.normal( mu, sde, size = None ) )
24       else:
25           x = np.random.triangular( 0.60, 0.90, 0.98, size = None )
26           occupy.append( x )   ## Airport
27           sales.append( ( B0 + 5 ) + B1 * x + np.random.normal( mu, sde, size =
                                            None ) )
28   location = [ 'Downtown' ]*60 + [ 'Airport' ]*60
29   data = { 'Location':location, 'sales':sales, 'occupy':occupy }
30   df = pd.DataFrame( data )
31   ##
32   ## Plot the data
33   ##
34   ax = sns.scatterplot( y = 'sales', x = 'occupy', data = df, hue = 'Location',
                                            style = 'Location' )
35   ax.set( title = 'Monthly Average Food & Beverage Sales ($POR)\nvs\nMonthly
                                            Occupancy Rate', xlabel = 'Occupancy
                                            Rate', ylabel = 'Monthly Average Food &
                                            Beverage Sales ($POR)')
36   plt.show()
37
```

Figure 8-8. The script to generate artificial data for the hotel food & beverage sales per occupied room (POR).

Table 8-1. These are the occupancy distributions for the two locations based on historical data. The Airport distribution is higher because of air travel traffic.

	Location	
	Downtown	Airport
Sample Size (n)	60	60
Minimum	0.55	0.60
Mode	0.85	0.90
Maximum	0.95	0.98

Let me digress a moment on the triangular random number generator. I want positive numbers in the interval [0, 1], but I want them more specifically bounded to match average historical occupancy rates in Table 8-1. The triangular distribution allows for a draw from a distribution with a minimum, maximum, and mode. See "Example 4: Mathematical Programming" on page 246 for more information.

I show a scatter plot of this data in Figure 8-9. Notice how the Airport data are generally higher and right-shifted compared to the downtown data. This reflects more airport patrons who tend to stay at the airport, perhaps for meetings, before they fly to another destination.

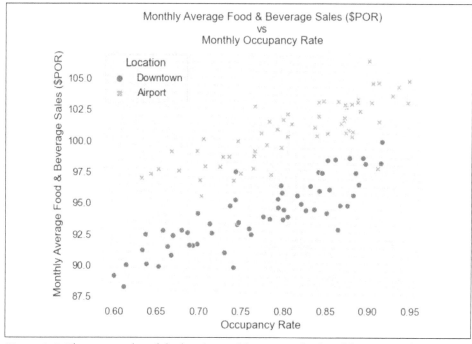

Figure 8-9. The scatter plot of the hotel monthly average food and beverage sales versus the occupancy rate. The script in Figure 8-8 generated the data.

I estimated a regression model using this data and the script in Figure 8-10. The model is

Equation 8-2.

$$sales_i = \beta_0 + \beta_1 \times occupy_i + \beta_2 \times location_i + \epsilon_i$$

```
1   ##
2   ## Specify the regression model and estimate parameters in four steps
3   ##
4   formula = 'sales ~ occupy + C( location )'    ## ===> Step 1 <===
5   mod = smf.ols( formula, data = df )           ## ===> Step 2 <===
6   reg01 = mod.fit()                             ## ===> Step 3 <===
7   display( reg01.summary() )                    ## ===> Step 4 <===
8
```

Figure 8-10. The script to regress food and beverage sales on the monthly occupancy rate with a dummy variable for the hotel locations.

where $\epsilon \sim \mathcal{N}(0,\sigma^2)$ is the disturbance term and $i = 1,2,...,120$. The *location* variable is a dummy variable defined as

$$location = \begin{cases} 1 & \text{if Downtown} \\ 0 & \text{othewise.} \end{cases}$$

The Airport is interpreted as the base. The parameter β_2 shifts the intercept, β_0, based on the location. So for the Downtown location, the intercept is $\beta_0 + \beta_2$, and for the Airport it is just β_0.

The regression estimation is specified in four steps:

Step 1

Define a model formula using *patsy* notation. This is an efficient sub-language for specifying statistical models. It is minimalistic, requiring just the dependent and independent variable(s). In this case, I also include a term, C(location), which is a function to create a dummy variable from the categorical variable, location. See Paczkowski (2022a) for comments about this function.

Step 2

Instantiate the model. This indicates the estimation routine (ols in this case), the model, and the data. Estimations are not done at this stage; it is just a set-up for estimation.

Step 3

Estimate or *fit* the model using the instantiated version. The results are stored in the variable reg01. I use "reg" for regressions and number them sequentially, hence the "01."

Step 4

Display the results by passing reg01 to a summary method. The display is conventional.

I show the final estimation results in Figure 8-11. First notice $R^2 = 0.87$ for both the unadjusted and adjusted versions. This indicates a good fit to the data: approximately 87% of the variation in sales is accounted for by the occupancy rate and the dummy variable for the location.[1] The parameters are all highly significant as is the F-Statistic, which compares this model to a constant-only model (i.e., $sales_i = \beta_0 + \epsilon_i$). The F-Test Null Hypothesis is that the constant-only model is better. This is clearly rejected.

---

1 Recognize, of course, that this must be a good fit because the data are artificial!

```
                        OLS Regression Results
        Dep. Variable:              sales        R-squared:        0.875

               Model:                OLS    Adj. R-squared:        0.873

              Method:      Least Squares        F-statistic:        410.8

                Date:    Mon, 30 Oct 2023  Prob (F-statistic):    1.25e-53

                Time:          15:17:35     Log-Likelihood:      -215.74

    No. Observations:                120                AIC:        437.5

        Df Residuals:                117                BIC:        445.8

            Df Model:                  2

     Covariance Type:          nonrobust


                              coef   std err         t   P>|t|   [0.025   0.975]

              Intercept    80.9834     1.294    62.567   0.000   78.420   83.547

 C(location)[T.Downtown]   -5.5472     0.277   -19.991   0.000   -6.097   -4.998

                 occupy    24.2660     1.575    15.403   0.000   21.146   27.386


         Omnibus:     6.019    Durbin-Watson:      1.954

   Prob(Omnibus):     0.049   Jarque-Bera (JB):    6.752

            Skew:    -0.313          Prob(JB):    0.0342

        Kurtosis:     3.979          Cond. No.     20.8
```

Figure 8-11. The regression output for the hotel average monthly food & beverage sales regressed on the occupancy rate. The script in Figure 8-8 generated the data and the script in Figure 8-10 estimated the model.

Finally, notice that the location dummy variable's estimated coefficient is −5.5. But for which location? The variable name is cryptic: C(location)[T.Downtown]. It is in three parts. The first is the C(location) which identifies the categorical variable: location in this example. This is important because you could have several categorical variables. The second part is the T which indicates how the dummy variable is defined. There are several definitions, but the most common uses 0/1 values with 0 for the base level. The base is the first level in alphanumeric order, which is Airport in this case. The "T" stands for "treatment," another name for dummy. Another method that you could use is sum which uses −1/+1 for the dummy. The "sum" indicates *effects coding* in which the dummy sums to zero over all observations. See Paczkowski (2018) for an extensive discussion of dummy and effects coding of categorical variables. For this example, the location that is the base (and codes as 0) is "Airport." So the coefficient is −5.5 when the location is Downtown; the whole term is $-5.5 \times 1 = -5.5$. For the airport, the coefficient is ignored since $-5.5 \times 0 = 0$. What is the effect of this? The effect is to shift the intercept. In this case, the line is shifted downward for the downtown properties.

A fundamental result in regression theory is that the estimated parameters are normally distributed with the mean equal to the true population parameter and the variance equal to the variance of the disturbance term adjusted by the sum of squares and cross-products of the independent variables. The question is: "Is this correct?" This can be answered using a simulation that repeats the regression many times, each time storing the estimated parameters and then examining their distribution. Of course, just repeating the regression will yield the same results because nothing has changed. To create a change, a whole new DataFrame must be generated for each simulation iteration. A different random number seed is used for each iteration to ensure that the DataFrames will all differ. I do this in Line 24 of Figure 8-12 where the iteration number is used for the seed.

A regression is run for each new DataFrame, and the estimated parameters are saved to lists. I show the script to implement this simulation in Figure 8-12 and the output in Figure 8-14. Notice that the three distributions, one for each parameter in Equation 8-2, is normally distributed with a mean at the population parameter I used when I generated the artificial data.

```
1   ##
2   ## Regression Monte Carlo Simulation
3   ##
4   ## Parameters from original data generator
5   ##
6   mu = 0      ## Disturbance mean
7   sig2 = 2    ## Disturbance variance
8   sde = math.sqrt( sig2 )
9   B0 = 75     ## Population intercept
10  B1 = 25     ## Population slope
11  n = 120     ## Fixed number of observations for the regressions
12  ##
13  ## Simulation
14  ##
15  ## Create empty estimate lists.  Note that the order matches the regression output
16  ##
17  b0 = []     ## Empty list for B0 estimates
18  b1 = []     ## Empty list for B1 estimates; location dummy
19  b2 = []     ## Empty list for B2 estimates; occupy variable
20  location = [ 'Downtown' ]*60 + [ 'Airport' ]*60
21  ##
22  iter = 10000   ## Number of simulation runs
23  for i in range( iter ):
24      np.random.seed( i )
25      occupy = []
26      sales = []
27      for i in range( n ):
28          if i <= n/2:   ## Downtown
29              x = np.random.triangular( 0.55, 0.85, 0.95, size = None )
30              occupy.append( x )
31              sales.append( B0 + B1 * x + np.random.normal( mu, sde, size = None ) )
32          else:
33              x = np.random.triangular( 0.60, 0.90, 0.98, size = None )
34              occupy.append( x )   ## Airport
35              sales.append( ( B0 - 5 ) + B1 * x + np.random.normal( mu, sde, size =
                                             None ) )
36
37      data = { 'Location':location, 'sales':sales, 'occupy':occupy }
38      tmp = pd.DataFrame( data )
39      mod = smf.ols( formula, data = tmp )
40      b0.append( mod.fit().params[ 0 ] )
41      b1.append( mod.fit().params[ 1 ] )
42      b2.append( mod.fit().params[ 2 ] )
43  data = { 'iteration': range( iter ), 'b0':b0, 'b1':b1, 'b2':b2 }
44  boot = pd.DataFrame( data )
45  fig, ( ax0, ax1, ax2 ) = plt.subplots( nrows = 1, ncols = 3, figsize = ( 10, 3 ) )
46  boot.plot( y = 'b0', kind = 'kde', ax = ax0, legend = False, title = r'KDE
                              Distribution of $\beta_0$' )
47  ax0.axvline( B0 + 5, color = "red", linestyle = "dashed" )
48  boot.plot( y = 'b1', kind = 'kde', ax = ax1, legend = False, title = r'KDE
                              Distribution of $\beta_1$' )
49  ax1.axvline( -5, color = "red", linestyle = "dashed" )
50  boot.plot( y = 'b2', kind = 'kde', ax = ax2, legend = False, title = r'KDE
                              Distribution of $\beta_2$' )
51  ax2.axvline( B1, color = "red", linestyle = "dashed" )
52  ##
53  b0_test = scipy.stats.normaltest( boot.b0 )
54  b1_test = scipy.stats.normaltest( boot.b1 )
55  b2_test = scipy.stats.normaltest( boot.b2 )
```

Figure 8-12. The script for the hotel food and beverage simulation. The output is in Figure 8-14. Code listing continued on next page.

```
56  print( 'Normality Tests:' )
57  print(  f'\tb0 (Intercept) Normality Test\t\tb1 (Location) Normality Test' )
58  print(  f'\t\tTest Statistic: {b0_test.statistic:0.3f}\t\tTest Statistic:
                                    {b1_test.statistic:0.3f}' )
59  print( f'\t\tp-Value: {b0_test.pvalue:0.4f}\t\t\tp-Value: {b1_test.pvalue:0.4f}' )
60  ##
61  print(  f'\tb2 (Occupy) Normality Test' )
62  print( f'\t\tTest Statistic: {b2_test.statistic:0.3f}' )
63  print( f'\t\tp-Value: {b2_test.pvalue:0.4f}' )
64
```

Figure 8-13. The script for the hotel food and beverage simulation. The output is in Figure 8-14. Code listing continued from previous page.

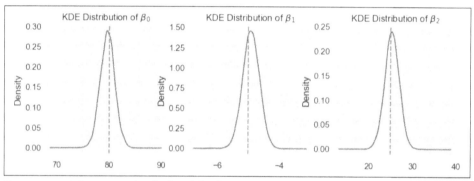

Figure 8-14. The output for the hotel food and beverage simulation. The script to produce this is in Figure 8-12.

Example 4: Mathematical Programming

I introduced mathematical programming for choosing from a menu in Chapter 5. This is a family of methods that includes linear programming, integer programming, and mixed programming. These are all popular for the Prescriptive Analytics phase of a business decision; the method used is dependent on the problem. For example, I used an integer programming approach for the marketing reach problem in "Tactical scale-view" on page 165.

These are all deterministic methods with fixed coefficients for the objective function and constraints. This poses a problem in providing Rich Information to decision-makers because random shocks will cause these coefficients to differ from those originally planned for the programming optimizations. This is the uncertainty. Decision-makers will not be given the correct rich information; in fact, they will be given incomplete information, which is more insidious than poor information, and which is correct, but just not enough or insightful.

Consider using stochastic coefficients in your mathematical optimizations to reflect uncertainty.

You can use simulation methods to introduce randomness into a mathematical programming set-up. For example, you could iterate through a set-up a large number of times, each time randomly selecting values for the coefficients from probability distributions, solving the mathematical programming problem, and saving the solutions in a DataFrame for later analysis.

There are two decisions you must make to implement this strategy. You must identify:

- The values to randomly select
- The probability distributions to use

The first decision depends on what you believe is random. The possibilities are:

- The objective function coefficients
- The constraint function coefficients
- The bounds on the constraints
- A combination of the above, including all three

Allowing randomness for the coefficients' constraints and/or bounds may be justified if, for example, there are known historical patterns you want to include. However, the constraint coefficients and bounds may be set by current technology, capacity, contracts, and so on. So they may not be as amendable to random variation, at least in the short run, as you may hope or believe. This will especially hold for the constraint coefficients if technology is involved.

The objective function, however, is different. In many, but not all, real-world applications, it is a profit or cost function. Consider a profit function. The decision variables are quantities, and the coefficients are prices. In a deterministic problem, the coefficients are fixed, expected market prices. This is, however, unrealistic. Prices randomly fluctuate depending on market forces: competition, consumer taste changes, technology, and macroeconomic changes (e.g., a recession). These are the most likely candidates for random variation in a simulation.

You could randomize combinations of the objective function coefficients, the constraint coefficients, and the bounds. These are $2^n - 1$ possibilities without regard to what is randomized of n coefficients. For objective function coefficients only: is it all of them, 1 of them, etc.? If $n = 3$, there are $2^3 - 1 = 7$ possibilities. A problem with this approach is the computational burden. Simulations will take longer to run, and increased run-time may delay getting results, thus impacting decisions; in short, this is costly. The magnitude of this cost depends on the problem's complexity. The more complex it is, the more simulation runs you need, affecting costs. More importantly, changing several coefficients at once will not allow you to determine which change had the most significant impact on the optimal solution. You would use experimental design concepts as outlined in Paczkowski (2023) to avoid this, but this also increases costs in terms of time and skill-set requirements to create the experimental design.

My recommended strategy is to randomize the objective function coefficients.

You also have to select a probability distribution. There are, of course, many possibilities, although the most used are the normal, log-normal, and triangular distributions. The normal distribution is an obvious first choice because it is the most familiar to data analysts. But this does not make it the best one because it is possible to select negative values. These will not make sense if, for example, the objective function coefficients are prices. The log-normal distribution avoids this because it always returns a positive number. This follows from the use of the natural log. If $Y \sim \mathcal{N}(\mu, \sigma^2)$ and $X = e^{\mu + \sigma \times Z}$ where Z is the standardized normal, then $\ln(X) = \mu + \sigma \times Z$, so $\ln(X)$ is normally distributed; that is, $\ln(X) \sim \mathcal{N}(\mu, \sigma^2)$ and $\ln(X) > 0 \ \forall X > 0$.

The standardized normal random variate is $Z = \frac{(Y - \mu)}{\sigma}$, so $Y = \mu + \sigma \times Z \sim \mathcal{N}(\mu, \sigma^2)$.

I show a script for plotting the log-normal distribution in Figure 8-15 and the resulting graph in Figure 8-16. I define a function to plot the log-normal distribution in Lines 4 to 8 of Figure 8-15. The lognorm function from from scipy.stats import lognorm is called in Lines 5 and 6. The method ppf is the *percent point function*. The log-normal pdf method is called in Line 8 and plotted. Random draws from this distribution using the scale factors 1.0, 0.5, and 0.25 are in Lines 10 to 11. For each loop, the distribution is added to a graph which is Figure 8-15.

```
1   ##
2   ## Log-Normal Distribution
3   ##
4   def lnorm( s, num = 1000 ):          ## s is shape parameter
5       min = lognorm.ppf( 0.01, s )   ## 1th percentile
6       max = lognorm.ppf( 0.99, s )   ## 99th percentile
7       x = np.linspace( min, max, num )
8       plt.plot(x, lognorm.pdf( x, s ), lw = 1, label = 'Scale ' + str( s ) )
9   ##
10  for item in [ 1, 0.5, 0.25 ]:
11      lnorm( item )
12  plt.xlim( [ 0, 3 ] )
13  plt.ylim( [ 0, 1.75 ] )
14  ##
15  plt.title( 'Log-Normal Density Function' )
16  plt.ylabel( 'Density' )
17  plt.xlabel( 'Random Variable' )
18  plt.legend( )
19  plt.show()
20
```

Figure 8-15. A script to plot the log-normal distribution. The graph is in Figure 8-16.

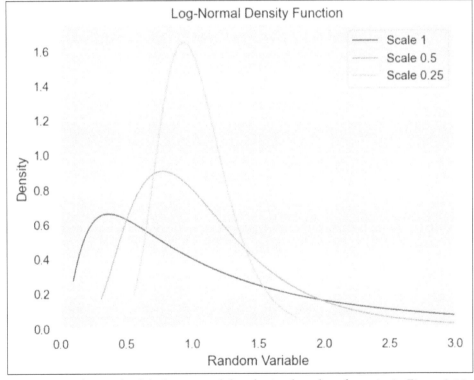

Figure 8-16. The graph of the log-normal distribution based on the script in Figure 8-15.

A problem with the log-normal distribution's parameters is the information requirement. You need to know the mean and standard deviation (i.e., scale) values, but these are for the associated normal distribution, not the (natural) logged version. So if $Y \sim \mathcal{N}(\mu, \sigma^2)$ and X is the log-normal version, the mean, μ, and variance, σ^2, are for Y. Specifying them may require more information than you have, and certainly more than any decision-maker (e.g., CEO) has.

Most business decision-makers, including the DAC can state worst-case, best-case, and most likely-case values because these are concepts they readily understand and think about daily; a scale for a normal distribution is foreign to them. The triangular distribution is a better choice. It requires just the low, high, and mode (most likely) values. If a is the low value, b the high value, and c the mode, then $a \leq c \leq b$.

 Use the triangular distribution because it is based on the intuitive concepts of low, medium, and high.

I show a script in Figure 8-17 to generate a triangular distribution. I use the random package's triangular function with parameters low, mode, and high in that order. I show the graph in Figure 8-18. Notice that the shape is triangular, hence the name. This is the distribution I will use in the following examples.

```
1  ##
2  ## Triangular Distribution
3  ##
4  data = { 'y': [ random.triangular( 1.5, 2.5, 2.0 ) for i in range( 10000 ) ] }
5  df = pd.DataFrame( data )
6  df.plot( kind = 'kde', ylabel = 'Density', xlabel = 'Random Variable', legend =
                          False, title = 'Triangular Distribution'
                          );
7
```

Figure 8-17. A script to plot the triangular distribution. The graph is in Figure 8-18.

 I used a triangular distribution in "Example 2: Die Toss" on page 231, but it was from NumPy's random package. The order of its parameters is low, high, and mode in that order. Here, it is low, mode, and high in that order. Watch the ordering!

I used a list comprehension in Line 4 to create the values for the triangular distribution. The 10,000 values are generated by calls to the random package's triangular function. The minimum is 1.5, the maximum is 2.5, and the mode is 2.0.

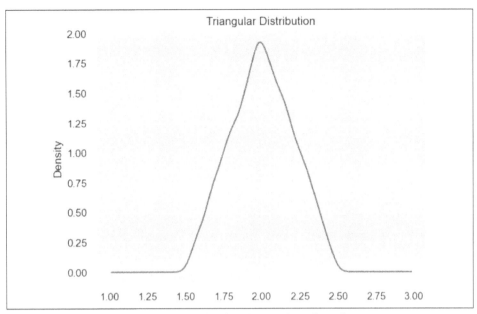

Figure 8-18. The graph of the triangular distribution based on the script in Figure 8-17. Notice the lower and upper bounds and the mode.

The best set-up for a simulation involves a function definition for the calculations for each iteration, and a separate script for managing the simulation. "Managing" means specifying the solver for the mathematical programming function, the key parameters for the solver and problem, running the simulation, and reporting the results. This is a modularization of the simulation components.

I show an example simulation function in Figure 8-19 and the simulation script in Figure 8-20 for the mixed integer problem of "Integer Programming" on page 162. I define the function with the key parameters in Line 1 and then get the number of objective function coefficients in Line 6. I use list comprehensions in Lines 10 and 11 to create labels for the decision variables and the integer bounds (0, 1) for use in the solver, respectively. The constraints are specified in Lines 15 to 21 and added to the solver. Notice that the bounds are set in Lines 20 and 21. Then in Lines 25 to 29, I set the objective function, specify that the function is to be maximized (Line 28), and solve the maximization problem. Finally, in Lines 33 to 35, I create a DataFrame for the main summary data, retrieve the optimization solution, and return these to the calling script.

```
1    def lp_func( solver = None, coefs = None, invests = None, max_invest = None ):
2        ##
3        ## Strategic integer problem -- Strategic Capital Investment Decision
4        ## Case 2a: Select only one project
5        ##
6        n = len( coefs )
7        ##
8        ## Specify the decision variables
9        ##
10       x_lbls = [ 'x' + str( i ) for i in range( 1, n + 1 ) ]
11       xs = [ solver.IntVar( 0, 1, item ) for item in x_lbls ]
12       ##
13       ## Specify the constraints
14       ##
15       invest = 0
16       summ = 0
17       for i in range( n ):
18           invest += invests[ i ]*xs[ i ]
19           summ += xs[ i ]
20       solver.Add( invest <= max_invest )
21       solver.Add( summ <= 1 )
22       ##
23       ## Specify the objective function and solve
24       ##
25       objective = 0
26       for i in range( n ):
27           objective += xs[ i ]*coefs[ i ]
28       solver.Maximize( objective )
29       status = solver.Solve()
30       ##
31       ## Return the results
32       ##
33       data = [ coefs, invests, [ xs[ i ].solution_value() for i in range( n ) ] ]
34       sol = solver.Objective().Value()
35       return( data, sol )
36
```

Figure 8-19. The function used to simulate a mathematical programming problem. See Figure 8-20.

For the script in Figure 8-20, I specify the solver, SCIP, in Line 4. I then specify the parameters and labels for the output in Lines 8 to 11. The number of iterations is set in Line 9 as 1,000. The heart of the simulation is in Lines 15 to 29. The for loop iterates iter times, each time generating objective function coefficients in Line 17 using the triangular distribution. The constraint coefficients are set in Line 19. Line 20 calls the simulation function. The remaining lines process the returned data. Finally, Lines 33 to 40 report the results.

```
1  ##
2  ## ===> Step 1: Specify the solver <===
3  ##
4  solver = pywraplp.Solver.CreateSolver( 'SCIP' )
5  ##
6  ## ===> Step 2: Specify the key parameters <===
7  ##
8  max_invest = 25
9  iter = 1000
10 cols = [ 'Project ' + str( i ) for i in range( 1, 6 ) ]
11 idx = [ 'NPV', 'Investment', 'Solution' ]
12 ##
13 ## ===> Step 3: Do the simulation iter times <===
14 ##
15 for i in range( iter ):
16     random.seed( i )
17     coefs = [ random.triangular( 1.5, 2.5, 2.0 ), random.triangular( 2.1, 3.4,
                                      2.8 ), random.triangular( 2.1, 2.9,
                                      2.6 ), random.triangular( 1.4, 2.0,
                                      1.8 ), random.triangular( 2.0, 2.8,
                                      2.4 ) ]
18     ##coefs = [ 2, 2.8, 2.6, 1.8, 2.4 ]
19     invests = [ 8, 14, 12, 6, 10 ]
20     data, sol = lp_func( solver = solver, coefs = coefs, invests = invests,
                            max_invest = max_invest )
21     tmp = pd.DataFrame( data, columns = cols )
22     tmp[ 'idx' ] = idx
23     tmp[ 'iteration' ] = i
24     if i == 0:
25         lst = [ sol ]
26         df = tmp.copy()
27     else:
28         lst.append( sol )
29         df = pd.concat( [ df, tmp ] )
30 ##
31 ## ===> Step 4: Report results <===
32 ##
33 display( pd.DataFrame( { 'y': lst } ).plot( y = 'y', kind = 'kde', legend = False,
                                     xlabel = 'Optimal Solution Values',
                                     title = 'Distribution of Optimal
                                     Solutions' ) )
34 ##
35 tmp = df.query( "idx == 'Solution'" )[ cols ]
36 data = { 'Projects': list( tmp.columns[ tmp.to_numpy().argmax( axis = 1 ) ] ) }
37 freq = pd.DataFrame( data ).value_counts( normalize = True )
38 freq = freq.rename_axis( 'Projects' ).reset_index( name = 'freq' )
39 freq.reset_index( inplace = True )
40 freq.plot( x = 'Projects', y = 'freq', kind = 'barh', legend = False, xlabel =
                                     'Normalized Frequency', title = 'Project
                                     Distribution' );
41
```

Figure 8-20. The script for the simulation of the mathematical programming problem in "Integer Programming" on page 162. It uses the function defined in Figure 8-19.

I show the distribution of the optimal solutions in Figure 8-21. This is based on the 1,000 iterations used in the simulation. Notice that it appears to be normal, with a mean of about 2.75. The selected projects are summarized as a bar chart in Figure 8-22. There are two points to note about this chart. First, Project 4 is not shown. This is because it was never selected in all the iterations. Line 38 selects projects with the maximum value in each row; Project 4 is never one of these. Second, notice that Project 2 is the consensus winner, which agrees with the non-stochastic conclusion in "Integer Programming" on page 162.

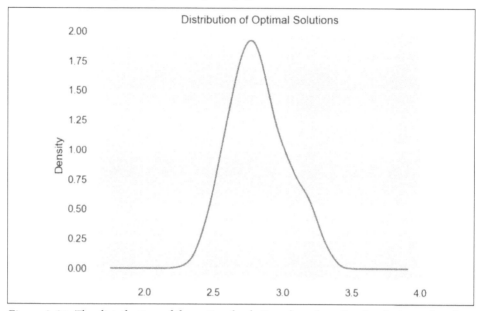

Figure 8-21. The distribution of the optimal solutions based on the simulation using the script in Figure 8-20.

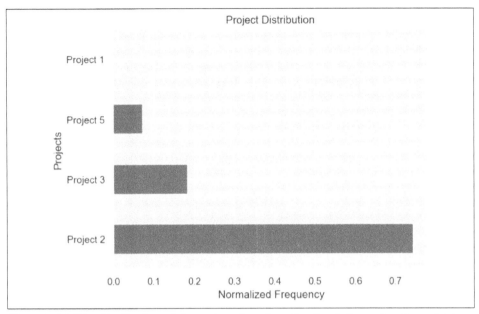

Figure 8-22. The distribution of the projects based on the simulation using the script in Figure 8-20.

Finally, I show the script for the trace for the simulation in Figure 8-23. The trace itself is in Figure 8-24. The steady-state is reached at approximately 2.82 at 200 iterations, so convergence is very fast for this problem. This may not be the case for large business applications.

```
1  ##
2  ## Script for trace chart
3  ##
4  ## Create the DataFrame of the trace data
5  ##
6  data = { 'solution':lst }
7  df_sol = pd.DataFrame( data )
8  df_sol[ 'iteration' ] = range( 1, len( df_sol ) + 1 )
9  df_sol[ 'cumulativeMean' ] = df_sol.solution.cumsum()/df_sol.iteration
10 ##
11 ## Plot the trace
12 ##
13 df_sol.plot( x = 'iteration', y = 'cumulativeMean', legend = False, xlabel =
                                 'Iteration', ylabel = 'Mean Solution
                                 Value', title = 'Simulation Trace' );
14
```

Figure 8-23. The script for the trace diagram to simulate a mathematical programming problem. See Figure 8-24 for the trace diagram produced by this script.

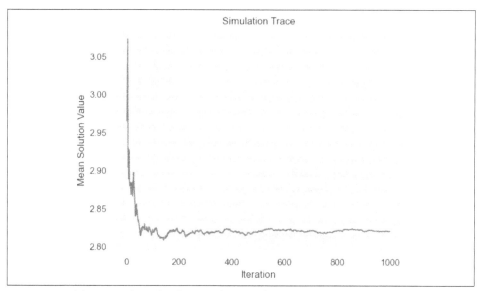

Figure 8-24. The trace chart for the simulation. The chart is based on the script in Figure 8-23.

Example 5: Decision Tree

This is a more complicated example involving a series of functions to do the hotel simulation for one scenario. I list these and their parameters in Table 8-2. I provide a flowchart in Figure 8-25 showing their connections to help you make sense of them and their role in a simulation. Figure 8-26 contains the main function, df_func, to create a DataFrame for the simulation.

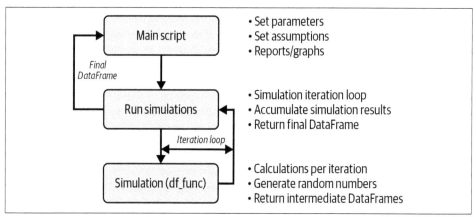

Figure 8-25. An outline of the basic process for a simulation.

Table 8-2. These are the main functions for the simulation of the hotel problem.

Function	Purpose/returns	Parameter	Values
df_func	Creates main DataFrame with calculations	assumps	Values for main assumptions as a dictionary with lists
		idx	List of labels for DataFrame index
		years	Number of years for *NPV* calculations
		disc	Discount factor as decimal (e.g., 0.05 for 5%)
		seed	Random number seed; default = 42
		iter	Number of simulation iterations as whole number > 0; default = 1
		display_df	Display DataFrame; for checking purposes only; can be large; default = False
	Returns: DataFrame of idx by years values		
npv_plot	Displays *KDE* plot of *NPV* values by iterations	data	DataFrame, preferably the one returned by df_func
		disc	Discount factor as decimal (e.g., 0.05 for 5%)
	Returns: Graph		
npv_trace	Displays trace of *NPV* values by iterations	data	DataFrame, preferably the one returned by df_func
	Returns: Graph		
run	Runs simulation	assumps	Values for main assumptions as dictionary with lists
		idx	List of labels for DataFrame index
		years	Number of years for *NPV* calculations
		disc	Discount factor as decimal (e.g., 0.05 for 5%)
		seed	Random number seed; default = 42
		iter	Number of simulation iterations as whole number > 0; default = 1
		display_df	Display DataFrame; for checking purposes only; can be large; default = False
	Returns: DataFrame of idx by years values		

```
1   ##
2   ## Define DataFrame creation function
3   ##
4   def df_func( assumps = None, idx = None, years = None, disc = None, seed = 42,
                                 iter = 1, display_df = False ):
5       ##
6       ## Set parameters
7       ##
8       random.seed( seed )
9       idx = idx
10      cols = [ 'Year_' + str( i ) for i in range( years + 1 ) ]
11      lines = len( idx )
12      construction = random.triangular( assumps.get( 'construct' )[ 0 ],
                                          assumps.get( 'construct' )[ 1 ],
                                          assumps.get( 'construct' )[ 2 ] )
13      ##
14      ## Create DataFrame
15      ##
16      tmp = pd.DataFrame( np.zeros( ( lines, years + 1 ) ), index = idx, columns =
                                      cols )
17      tmp.loc[ 'Construction', 'Year_0' ] = construction
18      ##
19      ## Populate DataFrame
20      ##
21      for i in range( 1, years + 1 ):
22          yr = 'Year_' + str( i )
23          tmp.loc[ 'Rooms', yr ] = random.triangular( assumps.get( 'rooms' )[ 0 ],
                                                        assumps.get( 'rooms' )[ 1 ],
                                                        assumps.get( 'rooms' )[ 2 ] )
24          tmp.loc[ 'Food', yr ] = random.triangular( assumps.get( 'food' )[ 0 ],
                                                       assumps.get( 'food' )[ 1 ],
                                                       assumps.get( 'food' )[ 2 ] )
25          tmp.loc[ 'Meetings', yr ] = random.triangular( assumps.get( 'meet' )[ 0 ]
                                                         , assumps.get( 'meet' )[ 1 ],
                                                           assumps.get( 'meet' )[ 2 ] )
26          ##
27          ## Calculate revenue and present value
28          ##
29          for j in range( lines - 3 ):
30              tmp.loc[ 'Revenue', yr ] = tmp.loc[ 'Revenue', yr ] + tmp.iloc[ j, i
                                                   ]
31              tmp.loc[ 'PV', yr ] = tmp.loc[ 'Revenue', yr ]/( (1 + disc )**i )
32      if display_df == True:
33          display( tmp.style.format( '${:,.2f}' ) )
34          print( f"Present Value of Revenue Stream: ${tmp.loc[ 'PV',
                                                   ].sum():,.2f}\n\
35  Net Present Value of Revenue Stream: ${tmp.loc[ 'PV', ].sum() -
                                          construction:,.2f}" )
36      ##
37      ## Create simulation summary DataFrame
38      ##
39      pv = tmp.loc[ 'PV', ].sum()
40      data = { 'Iteration':iter, 'PV':pv , 'Initial_Cost':construction }
41      df = pd.DataFrame( data, index = [ iter ] )
42      ##
43      ## Calculate NPV
44      ##
45      df[ 'NPV' ] = df.PV - df.Initial_Cost
46      return( df)
47
```

Figure 8-26. The main function to create a DataFrame for the hotel simulation decision.

The main function definition begins in Line 4 in Figure 8-26 with the def command followed by the function name: df_func. Lines 5 to 11 have the parameters to create the DataFrame. The cols list comprehension creates the column labels and the idx variable is the row index labels. Line 12 is where I randomly select the construction investment from a triangular distribution. A DataFrame is created to hold the data in Line 16. The cells are populated with zeros using the NumPy zeros function.

 NumPy's zeros function is useful for creating an array filled with zeros. There is a comparable function called ones for an array filled with ones.

In Line 17, I insert the construction amount, from Line 12, into the base year of the DataFrame. The entire DataFrame is populated in Lines 21 to 31. The triangular distribution randomly selects the revenue amounts: rooms, food, and meetings. I complete the DataFrame in Lines 29 to 31 by adding the total revenue and the Present Value of each yearly total revenue. The total Present Value is calculated in Line 39 using the pandas sum method. The remaining lines are self-evident.

The DataFrame returned by df_func is the main DataFrame used in subsequent functions to display the results. I show a sample returned DataFrame in Figure 8-27.

	Year_0	Year_1	Year_2	Year_3	Year_4	Year_5
Rooms	$0.00	$10,856,738.78	$10,375,464.22	$10,044,952.54	$11,295,592.15	$10,851,671.96
Food	$0.00	$8,467,171.77	$8,406,413.66	$8,691,883.01	$8,809,080.76	$9,321,326.95
Meetings	$0.00	$4,055,899.24	$3,986,274.89	$4,008,749.63	$4,051,822.33	$4,057,440.20
Revenue	$0.00	$23,379,809.79	$22,768,152.77	$22,745,585.19	$24,156,495.24	$24,230,439.11
Construction	$26,590,355.86	$0.00	$0.00	$0.00	$0.00	$0.00
PV	$0.00	$21,254,372.54	$18,816,655.18	$17,089,094.80	$16,499,211.28	$15,045,196.31

Figure 8-27. A sample of a DataFrame returned by the df_func function.

Once the main function is defined, you can then use two functions to plot the simulation results. The first one, Figure 8-28, plots the NPV distribution using the Kernel Density Estimation (KDE) plot in pandas rather than a histogram. In this case, I prefer the KDE to highlight the distribution's shape without the underlying bars' clutter. For reference, I also drew a vertical line at the simulated mean NPV. The second function, which I show in Figure 8-29, creates the trace of the simulation.

```
1  def npv_plot( data = None, disc = None ):
2      ##
3      ## Create a string variable of the mean NPV
4      ##
5      mean = str( f'${data.NPV.mean():,.2f}' )
6      ##
7      ## Plot the KDE of the NPV
8      ##
9      ax = data.plot( y = 'NPV', kind = 'kde', title = 'NPV Distribution\nMean NPV
                                     = ' + mean + '\nDiscount Rate: ' +
                                     str( round( disc*100, 1 ) ) + '%',
                                     legend = False, xlabel = 'NPV ($)' )
10     ax.axvline( x = data.NPV.mean(), color = 'k', linestyle = 'dashed' );
11
```

Figure 8-28. The function to plot the simulated NPV values. A KDE smoothed histogram is used.

For Figure 8-28, I create a string variable in Line 5 which I will later use in the graph title. The NPV distribution is plotted in Lines 9 and 10 using the DataFrame plot method. Notice that the plot kind is kde. The mean variable from Line 5 is used in the title. I enhanced the graph in Line 11 by drawing a vertical line at the mean NPV value. The pandas *mean* method calculates the mean.

```
1  def npv_trace( data = None ):
2      ##
3      ## Trace Diagram
4      ##
5      ## Calculate cumulative mean
6      ##
7      data[ 'iteration' ] = [ x for x in range( 1, len( data ) + 1 ) ]
8      data[ 'cumMean' ] = data.NPV.cumsum()/data.iteration
9      display( data.tail().style.format( '${:,.2f}' ) )
10     ##
11     ## Graph the cumulative mean
12     ##
13     cumMean = data.cumMean.tail( 1 ).values[ 0 ]
14     ##
15     print( f'Last Cumulative Mean: ${cumMean:,.2f}' )
16     data.plot( y = 'cumMean', x = 'iteration', legend = False, title = 'NPV Trace
                                     Diagram', xlabel = 'Iteration',
                                     ylabel = 'Iteration Mean ($)' );
17
```

Figure 8-29. The function to plot the trace of the NPV simulation.

For Figure 8-29, I used a list comprehension in Line 7 to create the iteration numbers ranging from 1 to the length of the DataFrame. This list adds a new variable, "iteration," to the DataFrame. The DataFrame's cumsum method is used to cumulatively calculate the sum of the NPV values. These are divided by the iteration numbers from Line 7 to get the cumulative mean NPV. The means are added to the DataFrame as the new variable cumMean.

A `run` function runs the whole simulation. I show this function in Figure 8-30. The main part of this function is the `for` loop for the simulation. It loops `iter` times. The function `df_func` from Figure 8-26 is called for each iteration. The returned values from this call are temporarily saved in a DataFrame named `tmp`. On the first iteration, `tmp` is copied to a new name of `df`. This is in Line 16. For each subsequent iteration, "tmp" is concatenated to `df`. At the end of the iterations, the DataFrame `df` index is set to the iteration number. The script in Figure 8-31 is where you define the key assumptions for the simulation:

- The ranges (minimum, maximum) and most likely values for a hotel's revenue components: rooms, food and beverages, and meeting/conference rooms. The values are in millions of dollars in my example. For example, the most likely value for room revenue is $10,200,000.

- The discount rate for the present value calculations. I assume 5%.

- The number of iterations in the simulation. I assume 1,000 iterations.

- The number of years ahead for the discounting. I assume 10 years. This will be the number of columns in a summary DataFrame.

- The random number seed for reproducibility.

```
1   def run( assumps = None, idx = None, years = None, disc = None, seed = None, iter
                                = None, display_df = True ):
2       ##
3       ## Hotel Construction Simulation
4       ##
5       ## Do iter iterations
6       ##
7       print( f'Simulation with {iter} iterations for {years} years at
                                {disc*100:.1f}% discount rate' )
8       for i in range( iter ):
9           ##
10          ## Create temporary DataFrame based on df_func
11          ## Set the seed to the for-loop index to randomly generate on each
                                iteration
12          ##
13          if i == 0:
14              tmp = df_func( assumps = assumps, idx = idx, years = years, seed = i,
                                disc = disc, iter = i,
                                display_df = display_df )
15              df = tmp.copy()
16          else:
17              tmp = df_func( assumps = assumps, idx = idx, years = years, disc =
                                disc, seed = i, iter = i )
18              df = pd.concat( [ df, tmp ] )
19      df.set_index( 'Iteration', inplace = True )
20      df.tail().style.format( '${:,.2f}' )
21      return( df )
22
```

Figure 8-30. A function that runs the simulation.

```
1   ##
2   ## Simulation main script
3   ##
4   ## Set prediction assumptions
5   ##
6   assumps = { 'rooms':[ 9000000 , 12000000 , 10200000 ],
7               'food':[ 10000000 , 13000000 , 1180000 ],
8               'meet':[ 4150000 , 3970000 , 3960000 ],
9               'construct':[ 13000000 , 32000000 , 22100000 ]
10            }
11  ##
12  ## Set DataFrame index labels
13  ##
14  idx = [ 'Rooms', 'Food', 'Meetings', 'Revenue', 'Construction', 'PV' ]
15  ##
16  ## Print assumptions
17  ##
18  print( f'Assumptions:' )
19  for keys, values in assumps.items():
20      print( f'\t{keys}: {values}' )
21  ##
22  ## Run simulation, plot results
23  ##
24  disc = 0.05
25  ##disc = random.triangular( 0.03, 0.10, 0.05 ) ## Or randomly pick a discount
                                                  rate within a range
26  iter = 1000
27  seed = 42
28  years = 10
29  df = run( assumps = assumps, idx = idx, years = years, seed = seed, iter = iter,
                                    disc = disc, display_df = False )
30  print( f'NPV: ${df.NPV.mean():,.2f}' )
31  npv_plot( df, disc = disc )
32  npv_trace( df )
33
```

Figure 8-31. The main script for the simulation. All the parameters are defined here and are passed to the run function.

In this script, I use a dictionary to define the key values for the rooms, food (which includes beverages), and meeting revenues. The construction cost is also included. The values for each are in a list in the order: minimum, maximum, most likely or mode. These lists will be passed to the triangular distribution generating function in the df_func function shown in Figure 8-26. The rest of the script is obvious.

The simulation was run for 1,000 iterations. I show the output in Figures 8-32, 8-33, and 8-34. Notice that the trace settles at the steady-state at approximately 600 iterations. After that point, there is little variation in the average NPV. The KDE distribution graph suggests normality for the NPV. The vertical dashed line is drawn at the last cumulative mean, which is shown in the summary in Figure 8-32.

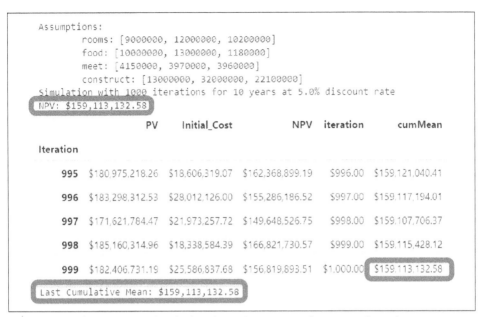

```
Assumptions:
    rooms: [9000000, 12000000, 10200000]
    food: [10000000, 13000000, 1180000]
    meet: [4150000, 3970000, 3960000]
    construct: [13000000, 32000000, 22100000]
Simulation with 1000 iterations for 10 years at 5.0% discount rate
NPV: $159,113,132.58

                    PV         Initial_Cost         NPV      iteration        cumMean

Iteration

    995  $180,975,218.26  $18,606,319.07  $162,368,899.19   $996.00   $159,121,040.41

    996  $183,298,312.53  $28,012,126.00  $155,286,186.52   $997.00   $159,117,194.01

    997  $171,621,784.47  $21,973,257.72  $149,648,526.75   $998.00   $159,107,706.37

    998  $185,160,314.96  $18,338,584.39  $166,821,730.57   $999.00   $159,115,428.12

    999  $182,406,731.19  $25,586,837.68  $156,819,893.51  $1,000.00  $159,113,132.58

Last Cumulative Mean: $159,113,132.58
```

Figure 8-32. The summary for the hotel simulation. It is the output from the main script.

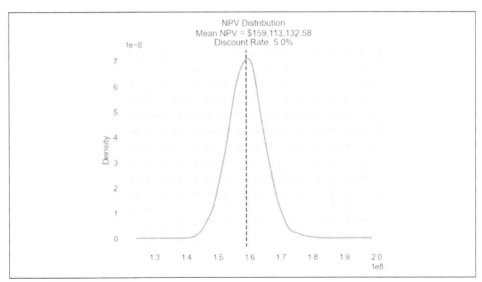

Figure 8-33. The KDE distribution graph for the hotel simulation. It is the output from the main script. The vertical dashed line is drawn at the total cumulative mean. The "1e-8" on the Y-axis indicates that the tick labels should be multiplied by that factor. Similarly for the X-axis.

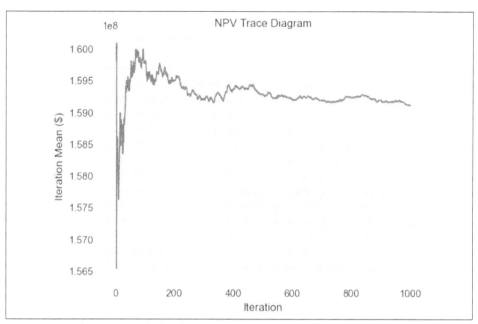

Figure 8-34. The trace graph for the hotel simulation. It is the output from the main script. The "1e8" on the Y-axis indicates that the tick labels should be multiplied by that factor.

You may believe from this example that the whole problem rests on this one simulation. Unfortunately, this is only the beginning. You need to run it with a different set of assumptions for each of the possibilities for the hotel at the downtown and airport locations. If you refer back to Figure 6-6, you will see that there are 14 terminal nodes on the decision tree. Each one is based on a different set of assumptions. So you need 14 simulations. The flow chart in Figure 8-25 is for one. I show an enhanced flow chart in Figure 8-35. In addition, you need to incorporate the (subjective, Bayesian) probability distributions. The basic process is the same regardless of the number of nodes on the decision tree.

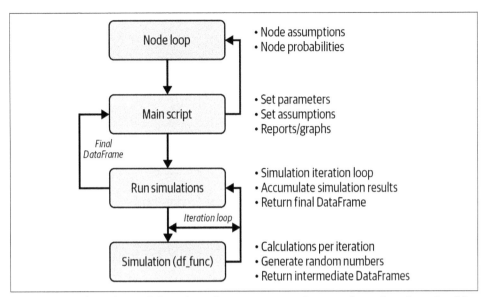

Figure 8-35. The enhanced flow chart that incorporates looping through each node of the hotel decision tree. The looping is controlled by the topmost block of the flow chart.

Summary

This chapter is packed with simulation examples from basic coin and die tosses to regression analysis, mathematical programming, and decision trees. This is a steady progression in simulation complexity. The main advice is to carefully study the examples.

CHAPTER 9

Developing Menu Options

I showed you in previous chapters how you can help decision-makers make the best choice from a menu of choice possibilities. This was all predicated on knowing the menu. The menu, however, must be developed somehow and by someone. This simple observation leads to an important question I will address in this chapter: "Where does the menu come from?"

You, as the data scientist, along with the DAC, have a major input into menu development. The decision-makers themselves, however, also contribute to creating it through the questions they ask you and the DAC. This broadens their scope and responsibilities, making them the deciders and, simultaneously, the creators of the very menu they must decide on. The questions are *what-if questions* reflecting their curiosity about possible, unforeseen events and their impacts.

In this chapter, I will address the following leading questions:

- What is the difference between what-if and scenario analyses?
- How can menu items be generated using what-if questions and scenarios?
- How do you do what-if analyses using a basic and an advanced, more complicated predictive model?
- How do you generate a synthetic data set for scenario analysis?

I will first introduce in this chapter *What-if Analysis* for non-stochastic Prescriptive Analytics. This allows you to develop a menu with each option as a different what-if case. A stochastic approach, however, can be used to generate synthetic data for more complicated scenario-type what-if analyses for which real data do not exist. In this situation, the what-if questions are indistinguishable from scenarios. I will discuss this in "Stochastic Use-Case: Synthetic Data" on page 292. See Paczkowski (2023) for a discussion of scenarios.

The Nature of What-If Questions

A question can be simple or complex. More importantly, it could take one of two forms. The first reflects a curiosity about what would happen if something under the decision-maker's control is changed, that something being an existing part of the business for which data exists and predictive models can be constructed. This is where you play a major role. You know the company's data and how to work with them. Plus, you know how to build predictive models, so you can answer the question. In so doing, you provide a menu item. The question is of the form "What if…?" and so is a *what-if question*. It can be asked at any of the three scale-view levels.

Sometimes the menu items just present themselves as reflections of normal business activities. Remember that a business is a complex system with many interrelated and interconnected subsystems. These could be sub-business units (SBU) with their own budgets and planning operations. They are frequently headed by an SBU president (or corporate executive vice-president) who reports to the CEO and who has his own high-ranking management team. The SBU president is free to manage and direct his SBU as he sees fit. After all, this is why he has a presidential rank.

Yet, despite some degree of autonomy, the SBU president and his high-level team are still constrained. They can only proceed with large capital investments with the CEO's approval and allocation of corporate funds to support the investments. Once they are allocated, the SBU's own budget team then begins to manage them. For the CEO to approve the investment, she must consider it along with those from other SBUs; they all compete for limited corporate funding.

It is in this context of an SBU corporate structure that the CEO is presented with a menu of projects. Of course, the SBU president is also presented with a menu in the normal course of its operations and he also must make an investment decision (i.e., choose from a menu), one of which may be the one to present to the CEO. You can ask: "Where does his menu come from?" Unfortunately, this would set up an infinite loop of such questions because every decision-maker at all the scale-view levels in every SBU will have a menu. To avoid this, I will stick to the menu given to the CEO by her SBU presidents.

The second form also entails a curiosity, but about events that are major shifts in the business, technology, environment, laws and regulations, and so forth. These are external changes with potentially significant positive or negative impacts on the business. They are beyond management's control, yet must be responded to if and when they occur. You can view them as SOWs that may materialize at some time in the future.

These second-form questions are presented as stories that could become reality. They are of the form "I wonder what would happen if…?" or "Suppose…?" and so on. They are *scenario questions*. Scenario questions have the same sense as what-if questions, but are more intricate and complicated since they involve the whole business as a dynamic complex system, affecting processes and personnel. Consequently, they are at the strategic scale-view level. This does not mean they are restricted to this level; there is certainly no law that says they cannot be asked at the operational or tactical scale-view levels. However, their broad scope biases them to the strategic level. Also, there is a broader involvement across the enterprise in addressing them to ensure that KPMs are accurately reflected.

Answering scenario questions is problematic because of the scarcity or, in the extreme, the complete lack of data. Data are unavailable because, by the very nature of a scenario, that SOW has not occurred; there can be no data for something that has not happened. This implies that predictive models are unavailable since they rely on data.

You could, nonetheless, analyze scenarios by creating *synthetic data*. I will address synthetic data generation in "Stochastic Use-Case: Synthetic Data" on page 292. But first, I will dive deeper into menu generating questions.

Menu Generating Questions: A Deep Dive

As I noted, a decision menu does not magically appear in front of a decision-maker, regardless of their scale-view. It must be developed, which includes developing the KPM details for each menu option. The details are relatively easy to create. Financial specialists, for example, are well trained in estimating ROIs and NPVs. And marketing personnel are very good at estimating potential market size and demand.

Notice that I said "relatively easy." The menu options themselves define the calculations that are the challenge.

A major source for the menu options is the decision-makers themselves. It is their questions in the form of what-if questions, although the term "what-if" is too broad to be useful. People tend to confuse them with scenarios. They are frequently used interchangeably because both give the sense of a currently non-existent case or situation that may exist in the future. They are, nonetheless, different. I need to distinguish between them so you can use the correct tools to develop the right menu options.

Some examples of questions decision-makers could ask, without any concern about a what-if/scenario distinction, are:

- What would happen if we increased our product's price 5%?
- What would happen to sales if we used an in-store promotional display?
- What would happen to our stock price if we had another labor strike?
- What would happen if the Antitrust Division of the Department of Justice (DOJ) filed a lawsuit to break up the company and it succeeded?

- What would happen to our product's sales if a competitor introduced a technologically revolutionary new product that immediately obsoletes our flagship product?
- What would happen to our shareholder value, credit rating, customer loyalty, and legal exposure if we have a data breach of what we believe is a very secure system and our customers' financial records are revealed on the internet?

These are perfectly legitimate questions. The answers to each could lead to several options, which are courses of action, hence, a menu.

If you examine those questions, you may think they are of the same ilk: they ask about the impact of an event on an aspect of the business. There is a subtle difference, however, that you as a data scientist, who might be asked to contribute to answering them, should immediately notice. The first three imply historical data availability to build a predictive model. Historical sales and promotion data, for instance, in company databases will address the first two. The strike in the third question can be reflected in a predictive model by dummy or indicator variables. So past impacts are known. Answering these three questions is then simply a matter of using that data. They are examples of historically-based what-if questions.

The pricing what-if question has a specific number (5%) so a specific answer is expected (e.g., sales would decline 2%). The price point itself is not drawn from a probability distribution to determine a range of prices with different likelihoods. The proposed price increase is 5%, and that is it. It is non-stochastic. A Monte Carlo simulation is not implied for this what-if analysis. Such questions are common in businesses.

The strike question, however, may be stochastic. How long will it last? The historical data will only show what happened for a strike of a fixed length that *did* occur. The same length of time may not, and probably will not, repeat. It could be shorter or longer. If shorter, it could be just disruptive; if longer, it could be devastating. The length of time and the impact are random variables. A Monte Carlo simulation may be needed.

The last three examples do not suggest any historical data. The DOJ does not repeatedly try to break up a company, although there are exceptions. So there is probably no historical data for this company regarding a break-up. Any new technological advance is, well, new without a history. And finally, if the computer system was believed to be secure, that immediately implies no historical data on breaches and certainly no shareholder, credit, or loyalty impacts due to a breach. These are examples of scenarios: specific, descriptive, yet hypothetical situations about conditions that could, not will, affect the business with no historical precedents. They are stories.

Notice that I said "could, not will." They are hypothetical situations. Hypotheticals are not guaranteed; there is a chance they will and a chance they will not happen. Some people downplay hypotheticals, claiming they only deal with practical matters and not fantasies. But these people misunderstand the purpose of a hypothetical: they are a long-run planning tool to develop action plans so that, if they did come to fruition, management is prepared. Otherwise, it might be too late to respond.

The Long Run

I use the compound term "long run" the way economists do: a planning horizon in which anything can change; there are no restrictions. So in the long run, you can do anything and be prepared for anything.

A scenario is futuristic; it is another world. Analyzing that alternative world is as complex as analyzing the current real one. The lack of data to generate the alternative to match the scenario story is the reason. The DOJ files a lawsuit; a data breach damages shareholder value. If these situations never happened, then there is no data you can use to examine what would happen if they did occur in the future. A what-if question could also be difficult to answer, but in many instances, the Predictive Analytics model can be used with "tweaks."

My three scenario examples are contingency-type questions appropriate for advanced planning for worse-case situations. But what-if questions, such as my first three, could also be asked to define variations for a single project. For example, the hotel construction example I used in Chapter 6 had two cases: build at the airport or downtown. Somewhere in the planning stage, someone (e.g., the CEO) asked about location, perhaps because of the adage: "There are three things that matter in property: location, location, location." The what-if question was simply: "What if we built here or there?"

Any what-if question, whether for contingency or planning purposes, usually contains multiple components that imply not one, but several possible answers. These are menu options no different than the project menu options I used as examples in prior chapters.

The Structure of What-If Questions

What-if questions usually involve discrete settings of key business parameters such as price (a common one), delivery time, and the use of a particular promotional device, to mention a few of an almost infinite number of possibilities.

To be more practical, however, they are usually expressed as three cases:

- Best (Optimistic) Case
- Most Likely Case
- Worst (Pessimistic) Case

The Most Likely Case is the one usually advocated and supported by the management team, the one in most agreement with, say, market conditions, regulations, and prior research, to mention a few. The Best and Worst Cases are bounding extremes. The Best Case is what the team would be ecstatic to get, but they know it is outside their reach; it is a stretch case. The Worst Case is the one they want to avoid, and almost dread happening, but they must prepare for it nonetheless. All other possibilities lie between these two. This is manageable for decision-makers to think about.

Many managers are reluctant to specify extreme, almost unrealistic, Best and Worst Cases, preferring instead to specify "mild" ones likely to happen. They will frequently say something like: "It's impossible for price to go any lower in the market. It's never happened before." I always tell my clients that your competitors will go to that low price point the day after they utter the statement. See Paczkowski (2018, p. 74) for comments about this.

You can give a probability distribution interpretation to these three cases. The distribution is the triangular distribution I used in Chapter 8. The Worst Case is the minimum value, the Best Case is the maximum, and the Most Likely Case is the mode. I illustrate this correspondence in Figure 9-1. The case likelihoods on the vertical axis are posterior probabilities for the case occurring. I will use this distribution when I discuss synthetic data generation.

 I previously referred to *Most Likely Views* as MLs, such as $ML_1, ML_2, \ldots$. These are meaningless general labels since everything is "Most Likely." The three cases I mention here are meaningful, specific cases that bound possibilities. They are a subset of *Most Likely Views*. In addition, the distribution for the *Most Likely Views* is uniform since they are all most likely. For these three cases, they define a triangular distribution.

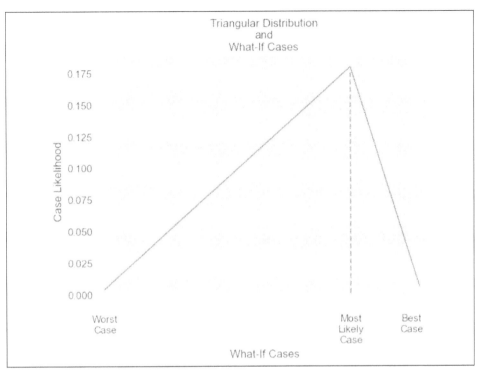

Figure 9-1. The relationship between the triangular distribution and the three what-if cases. The Case Likelihoods are the posterior probabilities for the three cases.

What-If Analysis Versus Sensitivity Analysis

What-if analysis differs from *sensitivity analysis*. To understand the difference, it is best to consider a simple econometric model used to predict a business metric, say sales (i.e., the amount sold) to law firms of online subscriptions of legal rulings and precedents with detailed analyses and commentary.

To keep the model simple, I will assume, following economic theory, that sales are inversely related to the price of the product. The price is per search; I will ignore any subscription price. So the higher the price per search, the lower the sales (i.e., the number of searches). This much any marketing or pricing manager would agree is reasonable and acceptable. But suppose sales are also dependent on the size of the law firm where size is strictly a function of the number of lawyers in the firm. The cut-off is five: small firms are less than five; otherwise, they are large firms.

I hypothesize large firms have a larger volume of complex legal issues and, therefore, a larger need for legal research. Smaller ones have smaller, less demanding issues (e.g., a standard real estate transaction, an estate plan, a contested traffic violation) and, therefore, a smaller research need. Large law firms are, therefore, more price inelastic:

they can more easily pass onto their clients the cost of a search for legal precedents and rulings because more is at stake; smaller firms are, therefore, more elastic.

A basic sales model is then:

$$Sales_i = e^{\beta_0} \times P_i^{\beta_1 + \beta_2 \times Size_i} \times e^{\epsilon_i}$$

where $Size_i$ is a size dummy variable for firm $i, i = 1, 2, \ldots, n$, defined as:

$$Size_i = \begin{cases} 0 & \text{if small firm } (< 5 \text{ lawyers}) \\ 1 & \text{if large firm } (\geq 5 \text{ lawyers}). \end{cases}$$

In linearized form, the model is:

Equation 9-1.

$$\ln(Sales_i) = \beta_0 + (\beta_1 + \beta_2 \times Size_i) \times \ln(P_i) + \epsilon_i.$$

Notice the interaction between the price and the firm size. For a small firm, $Size = 0$ so the price elasticity is just β_1. For a large firm, $Size = 1$ so the elasticity is $\beta_1 + \beta_2$. These elasticities (along with β_0) are estimated by OLS.

Now, to distinguish between sensitivity and what-if analysis. Sensitivity analysis addresses the question: "What happens if the parameters vary slightly from the estimated values?" For this problem, this is tantamount to asking what happens to the estimated price elasticity for both small and large law firms. This is answered by simply changing the elasticity estimates by small amounts. This can be addressed using the Monte Carlo simulation I described in Chapter 7.

Usually, elasticities per se are not the issue, although they are certainly important, but rather their implications for the KPMs such as revenue, contribution, and contribution margin. Contribution is the difference between revenue and the cost-of-goods-sold (COGS), while margin is the contribution as a percent of revenue. A simple spreadsheet simulator could be written to do the calculations to check the effects.

 See Paczkowski (2016, Chapter 2) for a detailed discussion of the importance of price elasticities.

What-if analysis requires determining the effect on the KPMs for different settings of the factors, holding the estimated parameters fixed. For the model Equation 9-1, this means a question such as: "What happens to our KPMs if we raise the search price 5% for only large law firms?" So the law firm dummy is set to 1, and the price is increased 5%. You could, of course, try different price points, say three: low, medium, and high. This implies three tests for large firms. But you could do the same for the small ones (set the dummy to 0) so you have nine possibilities (i.e., nine answers). This means the decision menu has nine items; a decision-maker must decide which of the nine is the best to select. You can see the nine items in Figure 9-2. For this cube representation, the nine menu items are clearly visible on the floor of the cube. I only show two KPMs (revenue and margin), but certainly others are possible.

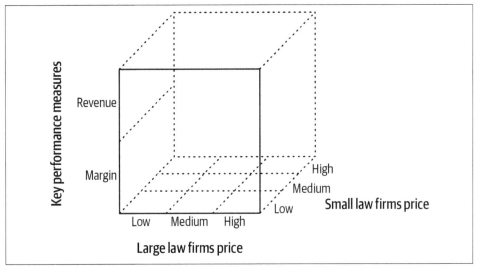

Figure 9-2. An illustration of a pricing cube for the law firm example. You can see the nine combinations of prices on the cube's floor.

There are nine because for each of the three cases for the small firms, there are three for the large ones: $3 \times 3 = 3^2 = 9$. However, you could change the large firms' price without changing the small firms' price. If the changes are then None/Low/Medium/High for each, then you have $4^2 = 16$. But there is no change for either. So the menu size could actually be $2^4 - 1 = 15$ rather than 9.

You will see a more extensive example in "Pricing What-If Analysis: Advanced" on page 280, also for a simple problem, but one nonetheless resulting in a very large (much larger than nine items) menu.

Non-Stochastic Use-Cases

I will present two use-cases of what-if analysis using Python. The first is a simple product pricing and contribution analysis. It has three factors that can be changed to accommodate pricing questions. Although simple, it will still highlight how you can address what-if questions.

The second use-case is more complex. It is also a pricing application, but one involving multiple factors that can interact in complicated ways. This application is probably more realistic.

Pricing What-If Analysis: Basic

I will first describe the pricing problem, then the predictive model, and finally the what-if application.

The pricing problem

A new online news organization plans to offer an online subscription-based service for stock market news coverage of high-tech companies. The service will contain continuous feeds on stock prices, a special high-tech stock index constructed by professors of financial economics at a leading northeastern university, and running commentary by them and select Wall Street analysts. Early market research indicates the number of potential subscribers (an *addressable market*) is 10 million investment professionals and people interested in monitoring and investing in the high-tech sector. This implies two price elasticities, much like the law firm example. But I will ignore this for simplicity.

The KPMs the management targets are the:

- Number of subscribers
- Subscription revenue
- Total subscriber acquisition cost
- Dollar contribution ($= Revenue - Cost$)
- Contribution margin ($= \frac{Contribution}{Revenue}$)

The acquisition cost is the cost per subscriber to get a person to subscribe and become a customer. The marketing team estimates this is $1.50. The contribution is commonly known as profit or *net earnings*. The word "contribution" indicates the amount from one product, product line, or even SBU, that helps cover the fixed costs of the business. Each piece of the business earning revenue contributes to the whole enterprise.

Contribution is calculated as the revenue less cost, in this case the acquisition cost, and in other cases the cost of goods sold (COGS). It is, thus, a dollar figure. It is quite often expressed as a percent of total revenue, in which case it is called *contribution margin*, or just *margin*. This is easier to interpret: for each dollar earned from sales, the margin is the percent that covers fixed costs. Expressing contribution in percentage terms makes it easier to compare products, product lines, and various company divisions (e.g., SBUs).

Predictive model estimation

An outside consultant was commissioned to estimate a price elasticity for different price points and build a simple pricing simulator so that marketing personnel can test different price points (i.e., the what-if analysis). The simulator is non-stochastic.

The consultant conducted a survey of potential subscribers in which each respondent was asked about their subscription intent at a stated price point. If they said yes, they would subscribe (a "Yes" response), then another price point was stated, and the subscription question was repeated. This was continued until they responded no, they would not subscribe (a "No" response). The data, therefore, consists of a series of price points and *Yes/No* pairs. The consultant estimated a *logit regression model* for the probability of subscribing as a function of the prices. The probability is sometimes called the *take rate*. If $Z = \beta_0 + \beta_1 \times P$, where P is a price point, then the subscription take rate is

Equation 9-2.

$$take = \frac{e^Z}{1 + e^Z}$$

where β_0 and β_1 are parameters to estimate and $0 < take < 1$. See Paczkowski (2018, Chapter 7) for this data collection approach, called the *Gabor-Granger Pricing Model*, and discussions of the logit regression model.

The estimation of the two parameters in Equation 9-2 is unimportant. Paczkowski (2018) provides ample information about their estimation. For this example, it is sufficient to know that the estimates are $\widehat{\beta_0} = 3.65529739$ and $\widehat{\beta_1} = -0.559989$.

What-if analyses

I show a script in Figure 9-3 to calculate Equation 9-2 and the KPMs. This is called using the script in Figure 9-4. The results are in Figure 9-5.

```
1  formatter = { 'takeRate': '{:0.2f}', 'marketSize': '{:,.0f}', 'price':
                                         format_dollar, 'subscribers': '{:,.0f}',
                                         'acqCostPerSub': format_dollar,
                                         'revPerSub': format_dollar, 'totalRev':
                                         format_dollar_no, 'totalAcqCost':
                                         format_dollar_no, 'contribution':
                                         format_dollar_no, 'margin': format_pct }
2  def calc( df, scenario = None ):
3      ##
4      ## Set model parameters
5      ##
6      coefs = [ 3.65529739, -0.559989 ]  ## order: beta0, beta1
7      price = df.loc[ scenario ].price
8      mkt = df.loc[ scenario ].addMkt
9      ##
10     ## Calculate the take rate
11     ##
12     num = math.exp( coefs[ 0 ] + coefs[ 1 ] * price )
13     takeRate = num / (1 + num)
14     ##
15     ## KPM calculations
16     ##
17     subscribers = takeRate * mkt
18     revPerSub = takeRate * price
19     acqCostPerSub = df.loc[ scenario ].costPerSub
20     totalRev = revPerSub * subscribers
21     totalAcqCost = acqCostPerSub * subscribers
22     contribution = totalRev - acqCost
23     margin = ( contribution / totalRev )
24     data = { 'marketSize': mkt, 'price': price, 'acqCostPerSub': acqCostPerSub,
                                   'takeRate': takeRate, 'subscribers':
                                   subscribers, 'revPerSub': revPerSub,
                                   'totalRev': totalRev,
                                   'totalAcqCost': totalAcqCost,
                                   'contribution': contribution,
                                   'margin': margin }
25     results = pd.DataFrame( data, index = [ scenario ] )
26     return( results )
27
```

Figure 9-3. The script for the calculations for the pricing study. I defined a function to make what-if analysis more compact. Formatting statements to make the results easier to read and interpret are also included.

Line 1 in Figure 9-3 is just formatting statements for the results display. I use a dictionary for these. The main calculation function definition is in Line 2. The parameters are the DataFrame for the calculations and the scenario for the calculations. Line 7 is the estimated parameters for the logit model in Equation 9-2 and the logit model calculations are in Lines 12 and 13. These follow Equation 9-2.

Three what-if cases are used in this example. I show these in Table 9-1. The first two hold the size of the addressable market at 10,000,000 potential subscribers but there is a higher price point in the second case. The first case is the Most Likely Case and the second is the Best Case. Management really believes they will be unable to get its higher price point. In the third case, a Worst Case, the price point is held constant, but the addressable market is only half what the team previously assumed: 5,000,000 potential subscribers. In all three, the acquisition cost per subscriber is held constant. These scenario assumptions are inputs in the script in Figure 9-4.

Table 9-1. The three what-if scenarios for the subscription service example.

	Addressable market	Cost per subscriber	Price point
Scenario 1 (most likely)	10,000,000	$1.50	$5.95
Scenario 2 (best)	10,000,000	$1.50	$6.95
Scenario 3 (worst)	5,000,000	$1.50	$6.95

```
1   ##
2   ## Define scenarios DataFrame
3   ##
4   data = { 'Scenario 1': {'addMkt': 10000000, 'costPerSub': 1.50, 'price': 5.95 },
                            'Scenario 2': {'addMkt': 10000000,
                            'costPerSub': 1.50, 'price': 6.95 },
                            'Scenario 3': {'addMkt': 5000000,
                            'costPerSub': 1.50, 'price': 6.95 } }
5   df = pd.DataFrame( data ).T
6   display( df.style.set_caption( 'Scenarios' ).set_table_styles( tbl_styles
                                ).format( { 'addMkt':'{:,.0f}',
                                'costPerSub'.format_dollar,
                                'price':format_dollar } ) )

7   ##
8   ## Run what-if, get results, and display with formats
9   ##
10  df_scenarios = pd.DataFrame()  ## dummy DataFrame
11  scenarios = [ 'Scenario 1', 'Scenario 2', 'Scenario 3' ]
12  for scenario in scenarios:
13      tmp = calc( df, scenario = scenario )
14      df_scenarios = pd.concat( [ df_scenarios, tmp ] )
15  display( df_scenarios.style.format( formatter ).set_caption( 'Pricing What-If
                                Results' ).\
16          set_table_styles( tbl_styles ).bar( subset = [ 'takeRate',
                                'contribution', 'margin' ],
                                color = 'red' ) )

17
```

Figure 9-4. The main calling script for the pricing study.

The script for Figure 9-4 contains the scenarios Table 9-1 in Line 4. A dictionary collects each one. The labels "Scenario X" are the keys with a nested dictionary for the values. A DataFrame is created in Line 5 using the dictionary, but then transposed for a better display. Lines 10 and 11 are the set-up for looping through the scenarios. The results are concatenated in Line 14 into one grand DataFrame which I initially defined in Line 10 as an empty DataFrame.

You can see from Figure 9-5 that Scenario 1 is best based on the contribution margin. The take rate for this scenario is also the highest. If you interpret the take rate as the market share, then this scenario's price point results in a 58% market share.

Scenarios	addMkt	costPerSub	price
Scenario 1	10,000,000	$1.50	$5.95
Scenario 2	10,000,000	$1.50	$6.95
Scenario 3	5,000,000	$1.50	$6.95

Pricing What-If Results

	marketSize	price	acqCostPerSub	takeRate	subscribers	revPerSub	totalRev	totalAcqCost	contribution	margin
Scenario 1	10,000,000	$5.95	$1.50	0.58	5,801,436	$3.45	$20,025,711	$8,702,154	$20,025,710	100.0%
Scenario 2	10,000,000	$6.95	$1.50	0.44	4,411,179	$3.07	$13,523,661	$6,616,769	$13,523,659	100.0%
Scenario 3	5,000,000	$6.95	$1.50	0.44	2,205,590	$3.07	$6,761,830	$3,308,385	$6,761,829	100.0%

Figure 9-5. The pricing analysis results using the script in Figure 9-3.

Pricing What-If Analysis: Advanced

This is an advanced version of a what-if analysis for another pricing problem. This example is more complicated because there are far more possible scenarios. This implies that the decision menu is more extensive.

The pricing problem

A large grocery chain sells beverages to a diverse clientele in highly competitive regional markets. Its customers are segmented into low-, medium-, and high-income groups. There are many brands on its store shelves for each type of beverage these customers can buy, such as water, fruit juices, and alcohol. The competition for any brand and type is intense, to say the least.

The product manager of one brand wants to improve sales, so he encourages the grocery chain's management to aggressively market its brand using promotional fliers and in-store displays. The focus is on pricing.

Any analysis of this company's pricing strategy must distinguish between its product price (known as *own-price*) and its competitors' prices (known as *cross-prices*). The price elasticity of any of the beverages in this market, regardless of the seller, is highly elastic. This means that a 1% increase in the own-price (the price of the product we are considering) will result in a more than 1% decrease in its sales. Consequentially, own-revenue will decline. See Paczkowski (2018, Chapter 2) for a detailed analysis of pricing, price elasticities, and the effect of price changes on revenue when the price elasticity is considered.

Elasticities Defined

Elasticities are very commonly used in economic and econometric research. A price elasticity is a measure of the percentage change in quantity or unit sales for a 1% change in the price. See Paczkowski (2018, Chapter 2) for a full discussion of price elasticities.

Predictive model estimation

Let us look at an example. The beverage company hired an outside consultant to estimate its own-price elasticity using data on sales and prices of its beverage and a competitor's beverage. The data were provided by the grocery store chain. For legal reasons, the competitor was not identified. The data were aggregated to months with a flag for whether a promotional flier or in-store display was used in that month. In addition, the data were segmented by the three income groups (low, medium, and high) based on the store's shopper ID cards. The owners of the cards were, of course, not identified.

The consultant estimated the model

$$sales = e^{\beta_0} \times P_{own}^{\beta_1} \times P_{cross}^{\beta_2} \times$$
$$e^{\beta_3 \times flier + \beta_4 \times display + \beta_5 \times medIncome + \beta_6 \times highIncome} \times e^{\epsilon}$$

where $sales$ is the historical sales, P_{own} and P_{cross} are the own- and cross-prices, respectively, and the remaining factors are dummy variables for the flier, display, and income levels. Notice that only two dummies are defined for income even though there are three income levels. The low-income-level dummy was omitted to avoid multicollinearity, although its parameter's value can be retrieved from the constant term (i.e., β_0). The last factor, e^{ϵ}, is the random disturbance term.

??? is a non-linear model typically used for demand and pricing studies because it can be linearized by taking the natural log of both sides. When you do this, the model becomes:

Equation 9-3.
$$\ln(sales) = \beta_0 + \beta_1 \times \ln(P_{own}) + \beta_2 \times \ln(P_{cross}) + \beta_3 \times flier + \beta_4 \times display + \beta_5 \times medIncome + \beta_6 \times highIncome + \epsilon.$$

The parameters are easily estimated using OLS. This ease of estimation is unimportant, but the fact that the parameters, especially β_1 and β_2, are directly price elasticities is important. The own-price elasticity, β_1, can be used to calculate a revenue elasticity as $1 + \beta_1$. This is important to know because revenue is a KPM for most businesses. See Paczkowski (2018) for an extensive discussion of models like Equations ??? and Equation 9-3, the revenue elasticity, and elasticities in general.

 If η_Q^P is the own-price elasticity and η_{TR}^P is the total revenue elasticity, then $\eta_{TR}^P = 1 + \eta_Q^P$. See Paczkowski (2018, Chapter 2).

I show the estimated parameters in Table 9-2. Using the mean own- and cross-prices, setting the flier and display to 0 (no fliers and no displays), and assuming a low-income store area, the predicted sales on a log scale are:

$$\overline{\ln\,(sales)} = 5.8077 + (-4.6216) \times \ln\,(1.75) + 1.5418 \times \ln\,(1.85)$$
$$= 4.1699$$

where the own-price is \$1.75 and the cross-price is \$1.85.

On the non-log scale, sales are $e^{4.1699} = 64.7090$, or 64,709 units in the low-income area. The sales data are in thousands, so the predicted value must be multiplied by 1,000.

Table 9-2. The parameter estimates. Notice that the prices are on the natural log scale.

Variable	Estimate
Constant	5.807648
Log own-price	−4.621638
Log cross-price	1.541772
Flier dummy	0.262971
Display dummy	0.087485
Income dummy: medium	1.525915
Income dummy: high	1.373745

It is important to note that the model, ???, allows for several different what-if situations based on different settings for the two price variables and the dummy variables. Recall that the whole purpose of Prescriptive Analytics is to help a decision-maker choose from a menu. ??? provides an extensive menu. With the flier, display, and two income dummies alone, there are $2^4 = 16$ possible menu options. For each of these, several price points can be examined. For example, it is not unreasonable to test three (low, medium, and high) for both the own- and cross-prices. This means that the number of menu options is now $2^4 \times 3^2 = 144$. Some of these can be quickly eliminated, perhaps because a revenue target is not met or the what-if itself is unrealistic. Nonetheless, the list will be very large. Prescriptive Analytics methods are definitely needed!

The description I just presented really focuses on a single KPM: revenue. Unfortunately, businesses typically have more than one. For example, the obvious one is *contribution*. The implication of adding this KPM to our performance measures is that the COGS must be specified. This is usually done, from a what-if point of view, by proposing several values for the COGS. Just the way you could have three cases for the price points, so you could have three cases for the COGS: low, medium, and high. The medium case might be the current value of the COGS.

If there are now three cases for COGS, the number of menu options increases by a factor of three. Without the COGS, you had $2^4 \times 3^2 = 144$. Now you have $2^4 \times 3^3 = 432$ menu options. And this is only if you assume low, medium, and high values for the two prices and the COGS.

Regardless of the number of what-if levels, the need for a Prescriptive Analytical function is obvious. The menu is too large so it must be dealt with in a more analytical manner.

What-if analyses

I show the functions necessary for this more advanced what-if analysis in Figure 9-6. Line 4 in is a formatting specification I use to display results in Figure 9-7. Line 5 is the sales calculation function. The estimated demand function coefficients are in Line 9. Lines 11 to 13 do the calculations using the math package's exp function. The KPM calculations function is in Line 15.

```
1   ##
2   ## Some basic functions and an output formatter
3   ##
4   formatter = { 'OP': format_dollar, 'CP': format_dollar, 'cost': format_dollar,
                  'flyer': '{:,.0f}', 'display':
                  '{:,.0f}', 'incomeMed': '{:,.0f}',
                  'incomeHigh': '{:,.0f}' }
5   def sales( OP, CP, dumFlyer, dumDisplay, dumIncomeMed, dumIncomeHigh ):
6       ##
7       ## Coefficients
8       ##
9       coefs = [ 5.807648, -4.621638, 0.262971, 0.087485, 1.541772, 1.525915,
                  1.373745 ]
10      ##
11      x = math.exp( coefs[ 0 ] ) * OP ** coefs[ 1 ] * math.exp( coefs[ 2 ] *
                  dumFlyer ) * math.exp( coefs[ 3 ] * \
12              dumDisplay ) * CP ** coefs[ 4 ] * math.exp( coefs[ 5 ] * dumIncomeMed
                  ) * math.exp( coefs[ 6 ] *\
13              dumIncomeHigh )
14      return( x )
15  def kpm( OP, sales, cost ):
16      rev = OP * sales                    ## revenue
17      totalCost = cost * sales            ## total cost
18      contribute = rev - totalCost        ## contribution = revenue - cost
19      margin = (contribute/rev)           ## contribution margin
20      return( rev, totalCost, contribute, margin )
```

Figure 9-6. Two basic functions for the what-if analysis. An output formatter definition is included.

Figure 9-7 is the main calculation function. It calculates the base case scenario sales and corresponding KPMs. Line 1 is the calculation function definition. The argument, data, is a DataFrame of the what-if assumptions: a base case and a scenario in my example. It then collects these and returns a DataFrame.

```
1   def calc( data, display_summary = True, display_assumptions = True ):
2       ##
3       df = pd.DataFrame( data ).T
4       ##
5       x_b = df.loc[ 'base' ]
6       baseSales = sales( x_b.OP, x_b.CP, x_b.flyer, x_b.display, x_b.incomeMed,
                                x_b.incomeHigh )
7       baseRev, baseTotalCost, baseContribute, baseMargin = kpm( x_b.OP, baseSales,
                                x_b.cost )
8       ##
9       x_s = df.loc[ 'scenario' ]
10      scenarioSales = sales( x_s.OP, x_s.CP, x_s.flyer, x_s.display, x_s.incomeMed,
                                x_s.incomeHigh )
11      scenarioRev, scenarioTotalCost, scenarioContribute, scenarioMargin = kpm(
                                x_s.OP, scenarioSales, x_s.cost )
12      ##
13      ## Create DataFrame
14      ##
15      idx = [
16          [ 'Unit Price', 'Unit Price', 'Unit Sales', 'Average Cost', 'KPM', 'KPM',
                                'KPM', 'KPM', 'KPM',
17            'Dummy Setting', 'Dummy Setting', 'Dummy Setting', 'Dummy Setting' ],
18          [ 'Own ($)', 'Competitor ($)', 'Own ($)', 'Average COGS ($)', 'Revenue
                                ($)', 'Average COGS ($)',
19            'Total COGS ($)', 'Contribution ($)', 'Contribution Margin (%)',
                                'Flyer', 'Display', 'Medium
                                Income', 'High Income' ]
20      ]
21      base = [ x_b.OP, x_b.CP, baseSales, x_b.cost, baseRev, x_b.cost,
                                baseTotalCost, baseContribute,
                                baseMargin*100, x_b.flyer,
                                x_b.display, x_b.incomeMed,
                                x_b.incomeHigh ]
22      scenario = [ x_s.OP, x_s.CP, scenarioSales, x_s.cost, scenarioRev, x_s.cost,
                                scenarioTotalCost,
                                scenarioContribute,
                                scenarioMargin*100, x_s.flyer,
                                x_s.display, x_s.incomeMed,
                                x_s.incomeHigh ]
23      pct = [ ( ( scenario[ i ]/base[ i ] ) - 1 ) * 100 if i <= 7 else scenario[ i ]
                                - base[ i ] if i == 8
24              else None for i in range( len( base ) ) ]
25      df_data = { 'Base Amounts': base, 'Scenario Amounts': scenario, 'Pct Chg from
                                Base': pct }
26      df_summary = pd.DataFrame( df_data, index = idx )
27      if display_assumptions == True:
28          display( df.style.format( formatter ).set_caption( 'Beverage What-If
                                Assumptions' ).set_table_styles(
                                tbl_styles ) )
29      if display_summary == True:
30          display( df_summary.style.set_caption( 'Results Summary'
                                ).set_table_styles( tbl_styles )
                                )
31      return( df_summary )
32
```

Figure 9-7. The main calculation function. All what-if scenarios are based on this function.

```
1   def kpm_summary( data ):
2       keys = [ ( 'KPM', 'Revenue ($)' ), ( 'KPM', 'Total COGS ($)' ), ( 'KPM',
                                          'Contribution ($)'), ( 'KPM',
                                          'Contribution Margin (%)' ) ]
3       display( tmp.loc[ keys, : ].style.bar( subset = [ 'Pct Chg from Base' ]
                                          ).set_caption( 'KPM Summary' ).\
4                set_table_styles( tbl_styles ) )
5   def demand_plot( data ):
6       pltPrice = np.round( np.arange( 1, 5, 0.1 ), 2 )
7       pltBaseSales = sales( pltPrice, data[ 'base' ][ 'CP' ], data[ 'base' ][
                                          'flyer' ], data[ 'base' ][ 'display'
                                          ], data[ 'base' ][ 'incomeMed' ],
                                          data[ 'base' ][ 'incomeHigh' ] )
8       pltScenarioSales = sales( pltPrice, data[ 'scenario' ][ 'CP' ], data[
                                          'scenario' ][ 'flyer' ], data[
                                          'scenario' ][ 'display' ], data[
                                          'scenario' ][ 'incomeMed' ], data[
                                          'scenario' ][ 'incomeHigh' ] )
9       ##
10      df_data = { 'price':pltPrice, 'baseSales':pltBaseSales,
                                          'scenarioSales':pltScenarioSales }
11      df = pd.DataFrame( df_data )
12      ax = df.plot( y = [ 'baseSales', 'scenarioSales' ], x = 'price', legend =
                                          False, color = [ 'blue', 'red' ],\
13                    xlabel = 'Beverage per Unit Price ($)', \
14                    ylabel = 'Beverage Sales (Units)', ylim = ( 0, 1000 ),
                                                              title =
                                                              'Beverage
                                                              Demand Curve' )
15      ##
16      ax.legend( [ "Base", "Scenario" ] )
17      ##
18      x = sales( data[ 'base' ][ 'OP' ], data[ 'base' ][ 'CP' ], data[ 'base' ][
                                          'flyer' ], data[ 'base' ][ 'display'
                                          ], data[ 'base' ][ 'incomeMed' ],
                                          data[ 'base' ][ 'incomeHigh' ] )
19      ax.plot( data[ 'base' ][ 'OP' ], x, marker = "o", markersize = 10,
                                          markerfacecolor = "blue" )
20      ax.text( data[ 'base' ][ 'OP' ] + 0.075, x + 0.05, 'Price: $' + str( data[
                                          'base' ][ 'OP' ] ),
                                          horizontalalignment = 'left', color =
                                          'blue' )
21      ##
22      x = sales( data[ 'scenario' ][ 'OP' ], data[ 'scenario' ][ 'CP' ], data[
                                          'scenario' ][ 'flyer' ], data[
                                          'scenario' ][ 'display' ], data[
                                          'scenario' ][ 'incomeMed' ], data[
                                          'scenario' ][ 'incomeHigh' ] )
23      ax.plot( data[ 'scenario' ][ 'OP' ], x, marker = "o", markersize = 10,
                                          markerfacecolor = "red" )
24      ax.text( data[ 'scenario' ][ 'OP' ] + 0.075, x + 0.01, 'Price: $' + str(
                                          data[ 'scenario' ][ 'OP' ] ),
                                          horizontalalignment = 'left', color =
                                          'red' ) ;
25
```

Figure 9-8. Two summary functions to display the results and to plot the demand curve
for the base case and the what-if scenario.

Line 5 in Figure 9-7 locates the base scenario in the input data and Line 6 calculates the base case sales using the `sales` function from Figure 9-6. Then in Line 7, I calculate the KPMs using the `kpm` function in Figure 9-6. These calculations are repeated in Lines 9 to 11 for the what-if scenario.

Figure 9-8 has functions to display the output from the calculations.

Figure 9-9 is the main calling function for the what-if scenario. This is where you specify your assumptions and then call the other functions for the calculations and output display. You do not have to display any results at this point. You could, if you want, just assemble the results into one large DataFrame for a collective analysis of several scenarios. I only illustrate the one what-if scenario.

Line 6 in Figure 9-9 defines the settings for the what-if analysis in a dictionary. "OP" is the own-price; "CP" is the cross- or competitor price; "cost" is the per unit cost (i.e., COGS); the remaining variables are the dummies. This is used for the main calculations. The KPM summary function is called in Line 14 and the demand function plotting function is called in Line 18.

```
1  ##
2  ## Beverage Scenario Analysis: Main Call
3  ##
4  ## Set case assumptions
5  ##
6  data_assumptions = { 'base': { 'OP': 1.75, 'CP':1.85, 'cost': 1.25, 'flyer': 0,
                                   'display': 0, 'incomeMed': 0,
                                   'incomeHigh': 0 }, 'scenario': { 'OP':
                                   2.00, 'CP': 1.85, 'cost': 1.25, 'flyer':
                                   1, 'display': 0, 'incomeMed': 0,
                                   'incomeHigh': 1 } }
7  ##
8  ## Calculations
9  ##
10 tmp = calc( data_assumptions )
11 ##
12 ## KPM Summary
13 ##
14 kpm_summary( tmp )
15 ##
16 ## Plot Demand Curve
17 ##
18 demand_plot( data_assumptions )
19
```

Figure 9-9. The main set-up for the what-if scenario analysis. You specify the base case and scenario here and then call the relevant functions to do the calculations and display results.

The main calling script in Figure 9-9 returns three pieces of output, although you can select what you want to display; I included display options in the scripts. I show some output in Figures 9-10 to 9-12 using the base display settings.

Beverage What-If Assumptions

	OP	CP	cost	flyer	display	incomeMed	incomeHigh
base	$1.75	$1.85	$1.25	0	0	0	0
scenario	$2.00	$1.85	$1.25	1	0	0	1

Results Summary

		Base Amounts	Scenario Amounts	Pct Chg from Base
Unit Price	Own ($)	1.750000	2.000000	14.285714
	Competitor ($)	1.850000	1.850000	0.000000
Unit Sales	Own ($)	64.701372	179.354563	177.203648
Average Cost	Average COGS ($)	1.250000	1.250000	0.000000
	Revenue ($)	113.227400	358.709125	216.804169
	Average COGS ($)	1.250000	1.250000	0.000000
KPM	Total COGS ($)	80.876715	224.193203	177.203648
	Contribution ($)	32.350686	134.515922	315.805472
	Contribution Margin (%)	28.571429	37.500000	8.928571
	Flyer	0.000000	1.000000	nan
	Display	0.000000	0.000000	nan
Dummy Setting	Medium Income	0.000000	0.000000	nan
	High Income	0.000000	1.000000	nan

Figure 9-10. A summary of the scenario output.

KPM Summary

		Base Amounts	Scenario Amounts	Pct Chg from Base
	Revenue ($)	113.227400	358.709125	216.804169
KPM	Total COGS ($)	80.876715	224.193203	177.203648
	Contribution ($)	32.350686	134.515922	315.805472
	Contribution Margin (%)	28.571429	37.500000	8.928571

Figure 9-11. A summary of the scenario KPM output.

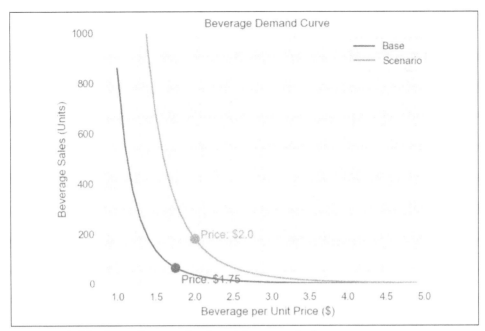

Figure 9-12. The demand curves for the pricing scenario for two cases.

In some instances, you may have to run all possible scenarios so that you can present the best cases, and perhaps the worst cases, to the decision-makers. The worst cases might be presented just to minimize the chance that someone would insist on one that is not a good option. You can easily create a script to generate a *what-if cube* (i.e., a DataFrame) that has all the cases (Figure 9-13). I refer to the arrangement as a cube because it is a convenient way to display the possible arrangements. We cannot see more than 3-dimensions, so the cube is the largest dimensional figure possible.

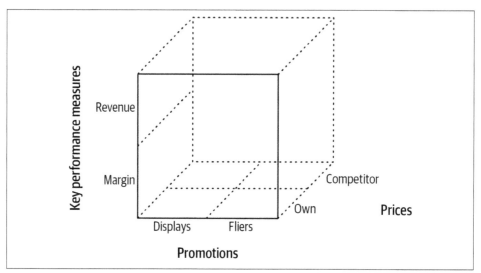

Figure 9-13. A stylized version of a what-if cube that summarizes an arrangement of what-if inputs and outputs. The outputs are the KPMs.

The script to generate the cube is shown in Figure 9-14.

```
 1  ##
 2  ## Assumptions
 3  ##
 4  OP = [ 1.75, 1.85, 1.95 ]
 5  CP = [ 1.85, 1.95, 2.05 ]
 6  cost = [ 1.25, 1.35, 1.45 ]
 7  ##
 8  ## Some display settings
 9  ##
10  idx = [ 'Own Price ($)', 'Competitor Price ($)', 'Unit COGS ($)', 'Sales
                                  (Units)', 'Revenue ($)', 'Total COGS
                                  ($)', 'Contribution ($)', 'Contribution
                                  Margin (%)', 'Flyer', 'Display',
                                  'Income: Low', 'Income: Medium',
                                  'Income: High' ]
11  formats = [ format_dollar ] * 3 + [ '{:,.0f}' ] + [ format_dollar ] * 3 + [
                                  format_pct ] + [ '{:,.0f}' ] * 5
12  formatter = { k:v for ( k, v ) in zip( idx, formats ) }
13  ##
14  ## Populate What-If Cube
15  ##
16  cube = pd.DataFrame()
17  scen = 0
18  for op in range( len( OP ) ):
19      for cp in range( len( CP ) ):
20          for cst in range( len( cost ) ):
21              for fly in [ 0, 1 ]:
22                  for disp in [ 0, 1 ]:
23                      for incMed in [ 0, 1 ]:
24                          for incHigh in [ 0, 1 ]:
25                              scen += 1
26                              Sales = sales( OP[ op ], CP[ cp ], fly, disp, incMed,
                                                                  incHigh )
27                              Rev, TotalCost, Contribute, Margin = kpm( OP[ op ],
                                                                  Sales, cost[
                                                                  cst ] )
28                              if incMed + incHigh == 0:
29                                  incLow = 1
30                              else:
31                                  incLow = 0
32                              data = { 'Case ' + str( scen ): [ OP[ op ], CP[ cp ],
                                                                  cost[ cst ],
                                                                  Sales, Rev,
                                                                  TotalCost,
                                                                  Contribute,
                                                                  Margin, fly,
                                                                  disp,
                                                                  incLow,
                                                                  incMed,
                                                                  incHigh ] }
33                              tmp = pd.DataFrame( data, index = idx ).T
34                              cube = pd.concat( [ cube, tmp ] )
35  display( cube.head().style.format( formatter ).set_caption( 'All Possible What-If
                                  Cases' ).set_table_styles( tbl_styles ) )
36
```

Figure 9-14. A script to generate a Dataframe (i.e., cube) with all possible what-if cases.

I show the results of the script in Figure 9-15.

	Own Price ($)	Competitor Price ($)	Unit COGS ($)	Sales (Units)	Revenue ($)	Total COGS ($)	Contribution ($)	Contribution Margin (%)	Flyer	Display	Income: Low	Income: Medium	Income: High
					All Possible What-If Cases								
Case 1	$1.75	$1.85	$1.25	65	$113.23	$80.88	$32.35	28.6%	0	0	1	0	0
Case 2	$1.75	$1.85	$1.25	256	$447.26	$319.47	$127.79	28.6%	0	0	0	0	1
Case 3	$1.75	$1.85	$1.25	298	$520.77	$371.98	$148.79	28.6%	0	0	0	1	0
Case 4	$1.75	$1.85	$1.25	1.175	$2.057.11	$1.469.37	$587.75	28.6%	0	0	0	1	1
Case 5	$1.75	$1.85	$1.25	71	$123.58	$88.27	$35.31	28.6%	0	1	1	0	0

Figure 9-15. The first five records of the what-if cube of all possible cases.

You can select the n-largest cases in the what-if cube using the pandas `nlargest` method. To use this method, you need to specify n, the number of cases to return, and the variable to search on. In my example in Figure 9-16, I set $n = 2$ for the two cases with the largest contribution.

```
1  ##
2  ## Find two largest cases by contribution
3  ##
4  cube.nlargest( 2, columns = 'Contribution ($)' ).style.format( formatter )
5
```

	Own Price ($)	Competitor Price ($)	Unit COGS ($)	Sales (Units)	Revenue ($)	Total COGS ($)	Contribution ($)	Contribution Margin (%)	Flyer	Display	Income: Low	Income: Medium	Income: High
Case 112	$1.75	$2.05	$1.25	1.955	$3.421.33	$2.443.80	$977.52	28.6%	1	1	0	1	1
Case 256	$1.85	$2.05	$1.25	1.512	$2.797.63	$1.890.29	$907.34	32.4%	1	1	0	1	1

Figure 9-16. A script to extract the two what-if cases with the largest dollar contribution.

Stochastic Use-Case: Synthetic Data

There is an obvious problem with the non-stochastic what-if analysis methods I showed earlier. Although changing a factor, or simultaneously changing a set of them, to see the effects on the KPMs is often done for business decisions at all scale-view levels, that does not mean this is the best or the correct way to develop a decision menu. As I noted earlier in this chapter, there may be insufficient historical data, or no data at all, that contain instances of the events in a decision-maker's question. In this situation, a stochastic simulation can be used to generate the data which I refer to as *synthetic data*. I will use the phrases "synthetic data" and "simulated data" interchangeably.

I will describe how to generate synthetic data and produce an extensive example in the next section.

Specifying the Process to Simulate

Constructing a synthetic data generator is more complex than the analytical methods I showed. The first step is to design or specify the *process* (aka system dynamics) behind the what-if question. The reason for knowing the process is that the what-if question itself, which almost mandates that simulated data be used, is usually at a system level. And systems are composed of processes.

Defining a system is not easy. Forrester (1968) provides a definition that is probably the simplest, yet the most used. Variations exist, of course, but the gist is the same. According to Forrester (1968, p. 1), a system "is a grouping of parts that operate together for a common purpose." The parts, in many instances, are themselves systems, appropriately called *subsystems*. And, in fact, these subsystems also have subsystems. You should see that any system can become quite complex. Hence, they are referred to as *complex systems*.

It is best to view the whole collection of parts as a master system composed of subsystems as parts. The canonical example of a master system is an automobile with subsystems such as an on-board computer, electrical, safety, fuel, and so forth. All work together for a common purpose: to provide safe and comfortable transportation.

The dynamics I referred to earlier are the real-time operation of the complex system. This movement through time involves flows of information, documents, parts, people, and financial assets through the system. For example, in a large business, one department could be responsible for producing all the forecasts used in strategic planning. These are delivered (i.e., handed off) to the decision-making team, corporate planner, manufacturing, sales, and other key internal stakeholders. However, these organizations would, in turn, provide input (i.e., feedback) to the forecasting department regarding actual outcomes (e.g., actual sales) for use in the next round of forecast development. They could also provide criticisms of the forecast. For example, that it places an unrealistic, unachievable sales-quota burden on the sales force. The dynamics I mentioned are the hand-offs and feedback loops around the entire system. These loops constitute the processes of the system

It should be clear that constructing an overview of the processes of a complex system is not trivial. All the flows must be identified and mapped from one part of the system to another. This holds for the entire system as well as any of its subsystems.

Example of a System's Process Flow

Consider the introduction of a new technology product. Most people would interpret this as the introduction of a modification of an existing product. This is not correct. There are two types of new products:

- New-to-the-world (NTW)
- Not-new-to-the-world (NNTW)

NTW products are revolutionary as noted by Paczkowski (2020, p. 172). They "have never been seen before in any form and people have no inkling they are about to be introduced to the market. In fact, these products create new markets." The telephone, electric light, Ford Model T, and the Apple iPad are classic examples. NNTW products, on the other hand, are variations of an existing product. They could be new to the business as product line extensions or enhancements to an existing product, but not the market.

Regardless of its type, the new product must be marketed and sold. Prior to its introduction, a sales forecast is needed for the business case development. This must show the sales volume for each period (e.g., each month) post-launch to determine if the product will be viable in the market. The sales will grow over time from the launch date, with each succeeding period showing (hopefully!) an expansion of sales due to advertising and word-of-mouth (WOM) recommendations. This information is diffused throughout the market over time, and as it does so more people become aware of it and will opt to buy it.

The marketing effort will attract and incent two types of people to buy the new product as the information about it diffuses throughout the market over time. The first consists of *early adopters*, also called *innovators*, of almost anything new. They love having the latest gadgets, the newest fashions, the most up-to-date items whatever they may be. Why? One reason is they just love anything new, even though it has not been tested for market acceptance. After all, when it comes to any product, new or otherwise, the market is the supreme judge of the product's success or failure. For a new product, the market has not yet judged it. This means there is some risk associated with the new product—it may fail or not meet forecasted expectations. In this sense, these people are comparable to risk lovers in financial theory: people who invest in the riskiest assets simply because of the risk.

The second type consists of people who wait to see if the new product is accepted by the market. They prefer to let the early adopters take the risk and wait for an update. They believe the market will judge a product (as it will), so they will wait for that judgment. These are *imitators*.

In this example, the complex system is the market and the subsystems are the diffusion mechanisms. The total market adoption is the sum of innovators and imitators. Or:

$$Adopters = Innovators + Imitators.$$

Let me consider an NTW product that has no counterpart or analog in the present market. Since it is new, data are unavailable for a forecasting model. The only way one can be developed is to construct synthetic data by simulating the buying process over time as information about the product is diffused throughout the market. This data can then be applied to a diffusion model to predict the number of customers at any point in time. The projected sales are the basis for the KPMs for the new product. The KPMs could be sales volume, ROI in research and development of the new product, and the increase in shareholder value (i.e., the stock price) because of the product.

There are three questions:

- What are the what-if questions?
- What is the diffusion model?
- How is the synthetic data generated?

The what-if questions

An infinite number of what-if questions can be asked of the synthetic data just as there is an infinite number for normal data. Two possibilities are:

- What is the mean ROI one-year post-launch if the price is $3.00?
- What is the mean total sales for the third-year post-launch if the price is $4.00?

A diffusion model

The classic diffusion model is the *Bass Model* developed by Frank Bass in 1969. See Bass (1969). It is based on a differential equation relating three factors:

- A coefficient of innovation, p. This is a probability of adoption by innovators. Studies have found $0.01 < p < 0.03$ with mode $p = 0.03$.
- A coefficient of imitation, q. This is a probability of adoption by imitators. Studies have found $0.3 < q < 0.5$ with mode $q = 0.38$.
- The market size, or what I call the addressable market, M.

See Wikipedia (2024b) for the bounds on these two parameters. These determine the shape of new product adoption curves. Both curves have the number of new adopters/buyers on the vertical axis and the time after launch on the horizontal axis. Both are right-skewed, approaching zero new adopters as time passes after launch.

The curve for innovators looks like a "lazy S-shaped" curve. The bulk of innovators are close to the time of launch and then steadily decline after that; the newness wears off. The curve for imitators is also right skewed, with the bulk of them buying later (they are, after all, followers, so they wait to buy) but then declining over time. So this curve first rises as these people gradually enter the market, tops out after the product has been available for some time, and then falls to zero new adopters as more time passes after launch. Both curves approach zero growth as time passes and the product is no longer "new" to the market.

The curves could also be drawn with the cumulative percent market penetration on the vertical axis. For this version, they appear to be like cumulative probability curves. In fact, they are just that. The speed of the curve approaching 1.0 (100% cumulative penetration) is determined by p and q. The smaller these are, the longer the curves take to reach 1.0; the greater they are, the sooner they approach 1.0.

The model is not difficult to derive but does require advanced mathematics. The final form is:

$$F(t) = \frac{1 - e^{-(p+q) \times t}}{1 + \frac{p}{q} \times e^{-(p+q) \times t}}$$

where $F(t)$ is the cumulative proportion of the addressable market (i.e., the market potential for sales, M_t). This is the vertical axis on the cumulative proportion of potential sales chart with respect to time.

Marketing mix factors are not included in this version of the Bass Model. The mix is important for adoption. For example, if price, one component of the mix, is too high, the product may never be adopted regardless of how innovative it is.

This omission is remedied by incorporating an additional factor for the mix. If $Z(t)$ is this factor, and focusing only on price, then:

$$F(t) = \frac{1 - e^{-(p+q) \times t}}{1 + \frac{p}{q} \times e^{-(p+q) \times t}} \times Z(t)$$

where $Z(t) = 1 + \alpha \times \left(\frac{P_t - P_{t-1}}{P_{t-1}} \right)$, P is the price at time t and $t-1$, and α is a "coefficient capturing the percentage increase in diffusion speed resulting from a 1% decrease in price." See Balakrishnan (2023).

I implemented this function in `bassCalc` in Figure 9-17. I also provide a plotting function that produced Figures 9-18 and 9-19. Notice how the cumulative sales proportion asymptotically approaches 1.0 like a cumulative probability distribution. For the comparative sales, notice that the innovator sales drop to zero as you should expect: the innovators are no longer interested since the product is no longer "new"; they just move on to the next new product.

```
 1  def bass_model( t ):
 2      expon = math.exp( ( p + q )*t )
 3      num = p * ( expon - 1 )
 4      denom = p * expon + q
 5      return num/denom
 6  def expon( t ):
 7      return( math.exp( -( p + q ) * t ) )
 8  def bassCalc( ):
 9      F = [ bass_model( t ) for t in range( months ) ]
10      sales = [ M * ( math.pow( pq, 2 )/p ) * expon( t ) / math.pow( 1 + (q/p) *
                                     expon( t ), 2 ) for t in range(
                                     months ) ]
11      innov = [ M * p * ( 1 - F[ t ] ) for t in range( months ) ]
12      adopt = [ M * q * ( 1 - F[ t ] ) * F[ t ] for t in range( months ) ]
13      data = { 'month': range( months ), 'market': [ M ] * months, 'p':[ p ] *
                                     months, 'q':[ q ] * months,
14                  'months':[ months ] * months, 'cumDiffusion':F, 'sales':sales,
                                                  'innov':innov, 'adopt':adopt
                                                  }
15      df = pd.DataFrame( data )
16      df[ 'totalSales' ] = df.innov + df.adopt
17      df[ 'missedSales' ] = df.market - df.sales
18      return( df )
19  def bassPlot( df ):
20      display( df.head() )
21      display( df.plot( x = 'month', y = 'cumDiffusion', legend = False, xlabel =
                                     'Time in Months Since Launch', \
22          ylabel = 'Cumulative Proportion of Potential Sales',\
23          title = 'Cumulative Proportion of Potential Sales\nof the New Product in
                                     the Market\n' +
24                  str( months ) + ' Months Since Launch' ) )
25      ax = df.plot( x = 'month', y = 'innov', title = 'Sales Patterns\n' + str(
                                     months ) + ' Months Since Launch',
26          xlabel = 'Time in Months Since Launch', ylabel = 'Sales (Units)', style =
                                                  'b.-.' )
27      df.plot( x = 'month', y = 'adopt', ax = ax, style = 'r--' )
28      df.plot( x = 'month', y = 'sales', xlabel = 'Time in Months Since Launch', ax
                                     = ax, color = 'k', linewidth = 2 )
29      ax.legend( [ 'Innovator Sales', 'Adopter Sales', 'Total Sales' ] );
30  ##
31  M = 100000
32  p = 0.01
33  q = 0.30
34  months = 36
35  ##
36  df = bassCalc()
37  bassPlot( df );
38
```

Figure 9-17. The main function, plus a plotting function for the Bass Diffusion Model.

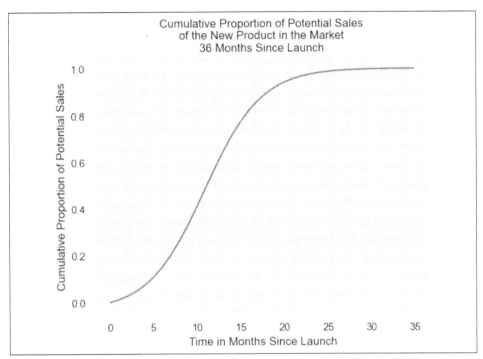

Figure 9-18. The cumulative proportion of potential sales for 36 months post-launch.

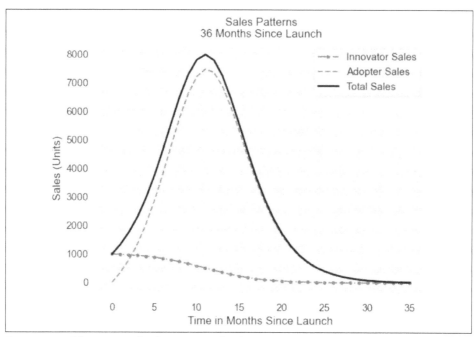

Figure 9-19. The potential sales patterns for the two groups of buyers for 36 months post-launch.

The marketing mix is included via the addressable market potential parameter, M_t. This is exogenous, meaning it is determined by conditions in the market outside the control or influence of the business; the market potential is whatever it is. Boehner and Gold (2012), however, disagree with this. They recommend specifying M to be a function of the marketing mix. The addressable potential market is then endogenous. This makes the complex system even more complex because the firm's pricing policy (inversely) impacts the market size which, in turn, impacts the KPMs.

Endogenizing the market size makes sense because the marketing mix does influence who will enter the market and at least shop for, or seek information on, the new product. This does not mean they will buy it; it only means they would consider it. The Bass Model then predicts how many of these people will buy. A good example of an influencing marketing mix factor is advertising: more advertising makes more people aware of the new product. Part of the advertising will, of course, be the price. For some, the price point may be too high so they would not even enter the market.

Boehner and Gold (2012) incorporate an addressable potential market factor via a Cobb-Douglas function:

Equation 9-4.

$$M = \lambda \times P^{-\alpha} \times A^{\beta}$$

where λ is a constant scaling factor, P is the price point, α is the price elasticity, A is the advertising factor (e.g., gross rating points) or the amount spent on advertising, and β is the advertising elasticity.

The Cobb-Douglas Function in Economics

The Cobb-Douglas function is very popular in economics with a wide array of applications, such as in Economic Growth Theory and the Theory of the Firm. See Henderson and Quandt (1971) for the Cobb-Douglas Production Function in economics.

The general form for the Cobb-Douglas function in economic theory is $Q = A \times K^{\alpha} \times L^{\beta}$, where Q is output, K is the amount of capital, L is the amount of labor, and A is total factor productivity.

Boehner and Gold (2012, p. 86) provide ranges for the two elasticity terms in Equation 9-4, which I show in Table 9-3. They cite some previous research to support these ranges. These are the ones I use.

Table 9-3. The marketing mix elasticities reported in Boehner and Gold (2012, p. 86).

Elasticity	Low	Medium	High
Price (a)	0.35	1.00	3.00
Advertising (β)	0.25	0.50	0.75

The elasticities determine the shape of the addressable potential market curve. See Figure 9-21 and my script that generates it in Figure 9-20. In that script, I define a marketing mix function in Lines 8 and 9 that implements Equation 9-4. In this case, I set $\lambda = M$. Then I create two lists in Lines 15 and 16 using this marketing mix function and the data in Table 9-3. These are used to create a DataFrame. The remainder of the script produces Figure 9-21.

Notice the negative exponential shape of the curves in Figure 9-21. It is common for econometric market studies (e.g., demand studies) to use an exponential curve rather than a linear one.

```
 1  ##
 2  ## Set market parameter
 3  ##
 4  M = 100000
 5  ##
 6  ## Define a marketing mix function
 7  ##
 8  def mix( M, alpha, beta, price, Ad ):
 9      x = M * price**( -alpha ) * Ad**( beta )
10      return( x )
11  ##
12  ## Calculate potential
13  ##
14  prices = np.linspace( 0.50, 3.00, 100 )
15  potential35 = [ mix( M, 0.35, 0.25, price, 1.00 ) for price in prices ]
16  potential75 = [ mix( M, 0.75, 0.25, price, 1.00 ) for price in prices ]
17  data = { 'price':prices, 'potential35':potential35, 'potential75':potential75 }
18  df = pd.DataFrame( data )
19  df.set_index( 'price', inplace = True )
20  ##
21  ## Plot potential curve
22  ##
23  ax = df.plot( title = 'Addressable Market Potential vs. Price', style = [
                                    'b','r--'],
24          ylabel = 'Addressable Market Potential Size', xlabel = 'Price Points'
25          )
26  ax.legend( [ r'$\alpha = 0.35$', r'$\alpha = 0.75$' ] );
27  ticks = ax.get_xticks()
28  new_xlabels = [ f'${tick:,.2f}' for tick in ticks ]
29  ax.set_xticklabels( new_xlabels )
30  ##
31  ticks = ax.get_yticks()
32  new_xlabels = [ f'{tick:,.0f}' for tick in ticks ]
33  ax.set_yticklabels( new_xlabels );
34
```

Figure 9-20. A script that creates the addressable potential market curves in Figure 9-21. It used Equation 9-4.

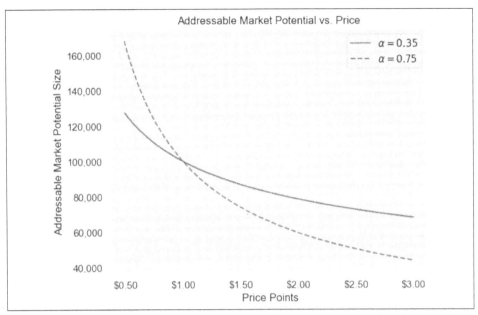

Figure 9-21. The curves generated by the script in Figure 9-20. Notice that the curve for $\alpha = 0.35$ is "flatter" as it should be since it is more inelastic.

Generating synthetic data

Synthetic data are simulated using the same methods I discussed and illustrated Chapters 7 and 8. The difference, however, is that these simulation techniques were used in Monte Carlo experiments to check distributions. In this case, they are used to develop data for statistical, econometric, and machine learning methods. For an example application, see Biller (2022). The following Python code and development are based on the synthetic data generation procedure outlined by Biller (2022). The difference is that she used an SAS environment.

I define several functions to generate the data:

`priceFunc`
> Calculates a price point for each month of an initial marketing campaign (a 36-month campaign is planned); see Figure 9-22.

`calc`
> Does the main calculations; see Figure 9-23.

`parms`
> Creates a dictionary for the parameters; see Figure 9-24.

`run`
> Runs the generator by calling the previous functions; see Figure 9-25.

The synthetic price function is the most conceptually complicated function. It reflects a life cycle pricing strategy developed by the marketing department. Since this is an NTW product, the initial price point is at their discretion. They did, however, conduct market research studies, including focus groups, to select a plausible range of prices. These studies, along with the R&D department's input, indicate that competitors will quickly enter the market. This increased competition will force them to reduce the price point to meet that competition. This life cycle pricing strategy, therefore, has two parts:

1. An introductory price
2. A planned price decrease to meet anticipated competitive entry

They formulated this pricing strategy for a 36-month planning horizon.

The marketing department anticipates the introductory price point could be $3.00, $4.00, $4.50, or $5.00. The $3.00 is the base. Which is used will not be known until approved by the CEO. They, therefore, must have each price in the synthesized data. They have suspicions regarding the CEO's likely choice, so they assign prior probabilities of 0.35, 0.25, 0.20, and 0.20, to each price point, respectively, to reflect their suspicions. Notice that the priors sum to 1.0. The price function allows for the synthetic data to include any one of these four price points based on the associated prior probability.

The marketing department assumes the price will have to be reduced due to increased competition after the product is introduced. Changes will occur at 12- and 24-months post-introduction. The anticipated price reductions are $0.00 (i.e., no change), $1.00, $0.75, $0.50, or $0.25 with prior probabilities of 0.35, 0.25, 0.15, 0.10, and 0.15, respectively. These priors sum to 1.0.

I show the first three functions separately in Figures 9-22 to 9-24. These are used in one main simulation function which I show in Figure 9-25.

The first function is the price function in Figure 9-22. This randomly selects the initial price point using the NumPy *choice* function and then creates two adjustments, each selection based on the appropriate prior probability. A net price equal to the initial price reduced by the two adjustments is then calculated. The function returns a list that contains a net price point for each of the 36 months of the planning horizon. The composition of the list will vary by simulation iteration so there will be a distribution of price points, the distribution being a function of the prior probabilities.

```
1   def priceFunc( base = None, deltas = None, adjusts = None, months = None, seed =
                                                   None ):
2       np.random.seed( seed = seed )
3       delta = np.random.choice( deltas, 1, p = [ 0.35, 0.25, 0.20, 0.20 ] )[ 0 ]
4       adjust1 = np.random.choice( adjusts, 1, p = [ 0.35, 0.25, 0.15, 0.10, 0.15 ]
                                                   )[ 0 ]
5       adjust2 = np.random.choice( adjusts, 1, p = [ 0.35, 0.25, 0.15, 0.10, 0.15 ]
                                                   )[ 0 ]
6       tups = [ ( 0, 0 ), ( 1, 0 ), ( 1, 1 ) ]
7       ##
8       tup = []
9       for i in range( 3 ):
10          tup = tup + list( itertools.repeat( tups[ i ], 12 ) )
11      ##
12      return( [ base + delta - tup[ i ][ 0 ] * adjust1 - tup[ i ][ 1 ] for i in
                                                   range( months ) ] )
13
```

Figure 9-22. A function that generates price data for the synthetic data.

The second function in Figure 9-23 creates the synthetic data and calculates the KPMs. It uses the marketing mix function in Line 6 and the Bass model function in Line 12. A DataFrame holds all the data, including the KPMs, which are calculated in Lines 21 to 26.

```
 1  def calc( iteration = None, prices = None, alpha = None, beta = None, Ad = None,
                                                    invest = None,
 2          M = None, p = None, q = None, cost = None, months = None ):
 3      ##
 4      ## Calculate potential
 5      ##
 6      potential = [ mix( M, alpha, beta, price, Ad ) for price in prices ]
 7      data = { 'price':prices, 'potential':potential }
 8      tmp = pd.DataFrame( data )
 9      ##
10      ## Calculate sales
11      ##
12      df = bassCalc( p, q, months, M )
13      df[ 'iteration' ] = [ iteration ] * months
14      cols = [ 'iteration', 'month', 'months', 'market', 'p', 'q', 'cumDiffusion',
                                            'sales', 'innov', 'adopt',
                                            'totalSales',
15              'missedSales' ]
16      df = df[ cols ]
17      df = pd.concat( [ df, tmp ], axis = 1 )
18      ##
19      ## Add financial factors
20      ##
21      df[ 'revenue' ] = df.sales * df.price
22      df[ 'marginalCost' ] = [ cost ] * months
23      df[ 'totalCost' ] = [ df.sales[ i ] * cost for i in range( months ) ]
24      df[ 'earnings' ] = df.revenue - df.totalCost
25      df[ 'margin' ] = ( df.earnings/df.revenue ) * 100
26      df[ 'roi' ] = ( df.earnings/invest ) * 100
27      ##
28      return( df )
29
```

Figure 9-23. The function that does the calculations to generate the synthetic data. Notice that it calls the bassCalc *function in Figure 9-17.*

The third function in Figure 9-24 creates the parameters for the Bass Model (i.e., α, β, M, p, q) using the triangular distribution function in the random package.

```
 1  def parms( months = None, cost = cost, ad = None, invest = None ):
 2      data = { 'alpha': random.triangular( 0.35, 3.00, 1.00 ), 'beta':
                                            random.triangular( 0.25, 0.75, 0.50
                                            ),
 3          'Ad': ad, 'invest': invest, 'M': random.triangular( 75000, 125000, 100000
                                            ),
 4          'p': random.triangular( 0.005, 0.015, 0.01 ), 'q': random.triangular(
                                            0.20, 0.40, 0.30 ), 'cost': cost,
 5          'months': months }
 6      return( data )
 7
```

Figure 9-24. The parameters for the Bass Model implementation. I used a dictionary, which is returned by the function, for convenience.

Finally, the main simulation function in Figure 9-25 uses a for loop in Lines 18 to 25 to create the data. The loop is controlled by the number of iterations which I set to 5,000 in Line 13. A DataFrame is populated in each iteration. Each one creates 36 months of data which are put into a temporary DataFrame. Each row is a month. The temporary DataFrame is then concatenated with a master DataFrame at the end of a loop. Since there are 5,000 iterations and each produces 36 months of data, the final DataFrame will have 180,000 (= 5,000 × 36) rows of synthesized data.

```
1  ##
2  ## Run sim
3  ##
4  ## Set parameters
5  ##
6  cost = 1.50
7  ad = 1
8  invest = 5000
9  months = 36
10 basePrice = 3
11 deltas = [ 0, 1, 1.50, 2.0 ]
12 adjusts = [ 0, 1.0, 0.75, 0.50, 0.25 ]
13 iterations = 5000
14 ##
15 ## Generate the synthetic data
16 ##
17 df = pd.DataFrame()
18 for iteration in range( iterations ):
19     random.seed( iteration )
20     vals = parms( months = months, cost = cost, ad = ad, invest = invest )
21     prices   = priceFunc( base = basePrice, deltas = deltas, adjusts = adjusts,
                                    months = months, seed = iteration )
22     tmp = calc( iteration = iteration, prices = prices, alpha = vals[ 'alpha' ],
                                    beta = vals[ 'beta' ], Ad = vals[
                                    'Ad' ],
23                invest = vals[ 'invest' ], M = vals[ 'M' ], p = vals[ 'p' ], q =
                                    vals[ 'q' ],
24                cost = vals[ 'cost' ], months = vals[ 'months' ] )
25     df = pd.concat( [ df, tmp ] )
26 df.reset_index( drop = True, inplace = True )
27 display( df.shape )
28
```

Figure 9-25. The main run function to generate the synthetic data for the Bass Model.

What-if analysis with the synthetic data

You can begin answering the what-if questions once your synthetic data are generated. You should first, of course, examine your data. You have several options:

- Display the simple descriptive statistics using the pandas `describe()` function.
- Examine distributions using value counts, boxplots, and histograms
- Look for patterns using scatter plots.

The descriptive statistics could be displayed using *df*.`describe()`.*T* where df is the name of your DataFrame and T is the transpose function. I find they are easier to read when the display is transposed. This is a personal preference.

The boxplots and histograms can be created using the seaborn data visualization package. This provides a convenient wrapper for creating boxplots by a grouping variable. For example, you could examine the distribution of monthly ROI using the code I show in Figure 9-26. The result is in Figure 9-27. Notice the pattern over time. The decline in years 2 and 3 reflects an assumed increase in competition.

```
1   ##
2   ## Boxplot of ROI by months
3   ##
4   ax = sns.boxplot( data = df, y = 'roi', x = 'month' )
5   ax.set( xlabel = 'Months', ylabel = 'ROI', title = 'ROI Distributions by Months' )
6   ax.tick_params( axis = 'x', labelrotation = 90 );
7
```

Figure 9-26. The distribution of the ROI by months for the synthetic data. See Figure 9-27.

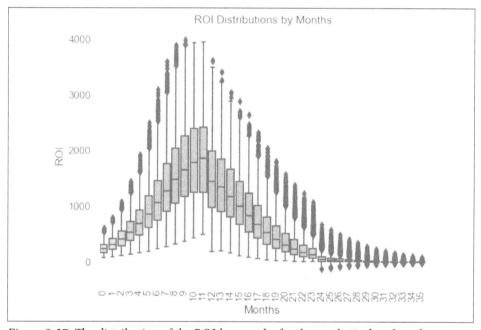

Figure 9-27. The distribution of the ROI by months for the synthetic data based on Figure 9-26.

You can check the initial price point distribution to see if it matches the prior distribution used in the price function. I show how to do this in Figure 9-28. The two distributions match (aside from random variation).

```
1  ##
2  ## Check price point for first month
3  ##
4  x = df.query( "month == 1" ).price.value_counts( normalize = True )
5  df_price = x.to_frame().reset_index().sort_values( by = 'price' )
6  df_price[ 'prior' ] = [ 0.35, 0.25, 0.20, 0.20 ]
7  df_price.set_index( 'price', inplace = True )
8  df_price
9
```

	proportion	prior
price		
3.0	0.3678	0.35
4.0	0.2420	0.25
4.5	0.1894	0.20
5.0	0.2008	0.20

Figure 9-28. The distribution of the initial synthetic price point and the prior distribution for those points. Notice that the synthesized proportions approximately match the priors.

You can also do queries using the what-if questions as guides. For example, the two questions in "The what-if questions" on page 295 can be answered by querying the DataFrame and using an appropriate summary command.

One query could be df.query("price == 3.00 and month == 12").roi.mean() for question 1 and df.query("price == 4.00 and month >= 24").sales.sum() for question 2.

Finally, you can extend the analysis beyond the what-if questions using machine learning methods. This is beyond the scope of this book. See Paczkowski (2023) and Paczkowski (2022a) for these methods.

Summary

A major concept I introduced for Prescriptive Analytics is the menu of decision options. There are several examples of menus in the chapters before this one. This chapter is the first of two on the development of a decision menu.

The main concepts from this chapter are:

- The nature of a what-if question
- How to develop what-if cases and analyze them
- The nature of a scenario
- How to generate synthetic data for scenario analysis

CHAPTER 10

Developing Menu Priors

I will introduce several methods for developing the prior probabilities for Prescriptive Analytics in this second of two *Menu Development* chapters. These are used in the expected value calculations for each menu option. The expected values finalize the information decision-makers need to complete their assessments of each menu option to make a rational choice.

In this chapter, I will address these two leading questions:

1. How are beliefs incorporated in probabilities?
2. How are subjective probability weights developed?

Background

I asked an important question in the previous chapter: "Where does the menu come from?" It comes from questions decision-makers ask, regardless of their scale-view. For example, in the context of a strategic scale-view, these could originate as part of a five-year business planning process.

Although my question is of paramount importance—after all, there can be no decision without decision options (i.e., a menu)—another factor is also significantly important. If you study the use-cases, especially the airport-downtown hotel development example, you will notice probability distributions associated with the menu options. I had displayed these in Table 6-1. These distributions played an important role in the analysis of that use-case.

You should immediately ask: "What is the basis for the probabilities?" I just assumed the hotel management team, in conjunction with the DAC and urban development consultants, specified subjective probabilities for each site. But there must be more to their development, especially because they are so important. This is the question I will address in this chapter.

Digression on Beliefs and Priors

I introduced Bayes' Theorem in Chapter 4 not only for estimating a subjective probability but also for expressing beliefs about an event based on knowledge (i.e., information) about that event. If you recall my rain example, you have a belief that it will rain tomorrow—you do not know with certainty if it will or will not. Your belief today is binary regardless of the weather tomorrow. For the stock market, as another example, it will rise, fall, or stay the same tomorrow; you do not know with certainty which will materialize, but one of them will. Your belief today is trinary regardless of the market tomorrow.

The probability you assign to your belief is your prior. Its magnitude measures your belief, a measure called your *credence*. Credence and prior probability are the same concept. See Lin (2023), Earman (2018), Reed (2022), Eagle (2021), and Hajek (2019).

You use your knowledge of a situation, such as the current environment, to form the prior, your credence, and then you update it with the likelihood as you learn more. The updating process is given by *Bayes Theorem* in Equation 4-6.

As a refresher, $Pr(A)$ is the prior probability for event A, $Pr(I \mid A)$ is the likelihood of the information or knowledge you have given or conditioned on the event A occurring, and $Pr(I)$ is the marginal probability for information over all possible events where A is one of them. The term on the left-hand side, $Pr(A \mid I)$, is the posterior probability of A given your information or knowledge.

A probability distribution reflects our beliefs of all possible outcomes. For my example in Figure 4-8, the distribution for gender is a uniform distribution: it is the same probability for males and females. This may reflect the market for this new product concept, but barring any initial knowledge of the market, which would be the case for a new product, a uniform distribution may be reasonable: 50% of the potential customers will be male. Such a prior is uninformative and reflects vague, weak, or sparse information. This is Poor Information. See Zellner (1971, pp. 41-53) for this description of an uninformed prior. The posterior reflects a more informed belief.

My first focus is on a probability distribution, the credence associated with the menu options developed by the methods in Chapter 9. These are elicited from key stakeholders comprising the DAC: the C-level team, SMEs, and KOLs. I will describe how you can do this in "Eliciting Probability Distributions of Beliefs" on page 314. Once you have the probabilities, you can update them using Bayesian methods to give the posterior probabilities. These *posteriors* are used in, say, the decision tree approach to decision making.

Developing Probability Weights

I argued that decisions are made under the duress of uncertainty. What compounds this situation is the menu of options (aka projects) from which the decision-maker must select. The decision is aided by each menu option's attributes, but also by the probabilities you assign to the options. For example, in the decision tree approach, there are probabilities assigned to each branch. These indicate which path down the tree is most likely to occur or what conditions are most likely to happen to affect the decision.

As an example, consider the hotel development example in Figure 6-6. Notice that the sets of three branches (ignoring the two Status Quo branches) below the downtown and airport decision points each have probabilities attached to them. Each set of probabilities forms a probability distribution for that tree segment. The probabilities sum to 1.0 (which you can verify by inspection), as should all probabilities in a distribution. These are used as weights to calculate the expected values of earnings as I discussed in Chapter 6.

These are posterior distributions reflecting consensus subjective views of what might happen at each stage of the decision tree. For example, for the downtown set of branches, the posterior distribution consists of the probabilities [0.15, 0.30, 0.55] for the possible paths [No Development, Modest Development, Major Development], respectively. Just as a sanity check, you can see that these sum to 1.0.

Since the type of development has not occurred yet, it cannot be replicated even if and when it occurs. These probabilities are clearly subjective. But whose subjectivity? There are, after all, several players involved in the development of the decision tree per se, and in the decision process itself. Most likely they reflect a consensus view. The question is then: "How is the consensus probability distribution determined?"

I recommend a three-step process for developing probability weights:

1. Elicit probability distributions from key DAC members and relevant stakeholders for the scenarios under consideration.

2. Create a DataFrame of these elicited distributions, one distribution per stakeholder.

3. Determine a single, aggregate summary distribution.

Notice I referred to "key and relevant" stakeholders. Not all enterprise stakeholders must be questioned regarding their beliefs about a future event. For example, referring to the hotel development example, the probability input of a line manager with an operational scale-view is irrelevant for a capital investment decision regarding new properties.

Staying with the hotel property development example, the key and relevant stake-holders are the members of the DAC:

- *C-level team*
- SMEs
- KOLs

Regarding the scenarios, these are the possible branches of the decision tree. I will provide an example of these later. I will cover elicitation methods in the next section. I will then follow this with two ways to aggregate the elicited distributions into a single distribution, such as the [0.15, 0.30, 0.55] for the decision tree in Figure 6-6.

Eliciting Probability Distributions of Beliefs

In most textbook examples, and I certainly did it here, the priors are just stated as part of the problem. This is fine for textbook examples, but where do they come from in real-world problems? They could simply be stated by a decision-maker with the understanding that they are to be used without question. This is, of course, impractical, unrealistic, and (internally) politically dangerous since people will try to undermine a project when their opinions are ignored. Instead, the priors should be elicited from all DAC members for a business decision.

Eliciting priors means following a procedure or methodology to get someone to reveal their preference, opinion, or assessment of something. The "something" could be a new product, an upcoming event (e.g., an election), and medical treatments to mention a few.

The elicitation should not be for every business decision. That is impractical since some are just too small or inconsequential for the full operation of the enterprise to warrant an elaborate procedure. The time and cost of eliciting priors must be considered. The cost at the operational scale-view level, for example, would be very high considering the many small, but nonetheless important, routinely made decisions. The operational manager must use his best judgment based on experience with similar operational problems and decisions. I contend that this is not the case at the tactical and strategic scale-view levels where decisions are more unique and impactful, require more evidence and time to consider, and usually have more personnel of different and diverse skill and knowledge levels to draw on. So my focus is on elicitation methods for major enterprise decisions at these two levels.

There are three classes of elicitation methods:

- Experimental design-based
- Direct question-based

- Activity-based

I will address these in the following sections.

Elicitation Method 1: Experimental Design-Based

Elicitation methods are commonly used in market research studies, mostly through surveys, to obtain information and insight into consumers' preferences for products and services, especially new ones. They are quantitative so the results are quantitative. These methods include, but are certainly not limited to:

- Conjoint analysis
- Discrete choice analysis
- MaxDiff analysis

 MaxDiff is short for Maximum Difference.

Each method requires survey respondents to make trade-off choices for prototype products. These are fictitious products resulting from an *experimental design*. A probability is estimated for each product based on the choice decisions. See Paczkowski (2018) for an extensive discussion of experimental designs for these methods.

Conjoint and discrete choice involve identifying attributes for a concept, say a new product that, obviously, does not exist in the market. The attributes are under consideration. The question is: "What is the best set of attributes for the new product?" where "best set" defines a product, hence the prototype. You must elicit consumers' preferences for the attributes to answer this question.

Attributes are features such as price point, product size, shape, weight, and so forth. Each one has a set of levels which makes them discrete. Weight, for example, could be extra light, light, and heavy. The price points could be cheap, market average, and premium. The levels for all the attributes can be combined using experimental design methods to create the prototype products. For example, suppose a beverage company produces coffee pods for an instant coffee maker. This is a highly competitive market with many other coffee pods available. The company developed a new pod concept it wants to sell. Manufacturing capacity restricts production to just one type of pod. The company's Food Science Team specifies three attributes: flavor, strength, and brewing time, each at three levels. The marketing team, meanwhile, developed three price points they believe are realistic for their competitive market. I summarize these and their levels in Table 10-1. The four attributes can be combined to produce $3^4 = 81$ possible combinations, each one being a product. But the company can only produce one! Which is the best product to offer in the market?

Table 10-1. An example of four attributes for a coffee product. Each attribute has three levels.

Attribute	Level
Flavor	French vanilla decaffeinated, hazelnut creme, pumpkin spice
Strength	Lite, medium, strong
Brewing time	1 minute, 2 minutes, 5 minutes
Price per pod	$1.10, $1.25, $1.50

A conjoint analysis

The DST wants to conduct a conjoint study in which consumers are asked to evaluate each pod product and then state their purchase likelihood. The team realizes it cannot test all 81 potential products with each consumer because no one would tolerate evaluating that many. An experimental design is used to narrow the 81 possibilities to a manageable number. See Paczkowski (2018) for a discussion about experimental designs for this situation.

The 81 combinations is called a *full factorial design*. Typically, a fraction of the full design is used. For this problem, a one-ninth fraction, resulting in nine prototypes, is doable. Experimental design procedures determine the arrangement of the attribute levels for that fraction.

The prototypes are important because, if you are considering new products, they do not yet exist, but you will want to present the product concept to consumers for them to judge. Judging a product is tantamount to revealing a preference for it, given the levels of its attributes.

In a conjoint study, only one prototype is shown to a survey respondent at a time. In this case, they see a menu with only one option, so it is a singleton menu. Several prototypes are shown (i.e., they see several singleton menus), the number determined by the experimental design. For my example, this is nine products, so nine singleton menus are shown.

For each of the nine a consumer sees, he/she is asked to rate their likelihood of purchasing that version of the product. A 10-point likelihood-to-purchase scale is typically used. Sometimes the scale is described as chances out of a base of 100, so they are asked what are the chances they will buy the product. For example: 0 to 10 chances out of 100, 11 to 20 chances out of 100, ..., and 91 to 100 chances out of 100. Each chances-group is called a *bin* or *box*. The first box is usually interpreted as indicating the consumer would not buy the product under any circumstance, while the last is interpreted to mean they will definitely buy it.

The reported chance choices are recoded to a binary value: 0 and 1. The 1 indicates they will buy it; 0 indicates otherwise. The value 1 is assigned to the prototype the consumer evaluated if they selected any of the last three boxes; 0 otherwise. A logit model is then estimated using these 0/1 values and the predicted value from the estimation is interpreted as the probability of a randomly selected consumer buying the prototype for a set of attributes and their levels. These probabilities are the credences I mentioned in "Digression on Beliefs and Priors" on page 312.

The statistical model is a *logit* model. See Paczkowski (2018) for this model.

Discrete choice analysis

Discrete choice is like conjoint except several prototypes are shown at once. Some of these, incidentally, could be competitors' products if the DST or a Competitive Assessment Group has that information. Consumers are asked to choose one of the products (or none of them) as opposed to rating each one on a likelihood-to-purchase scale. In this sense, they are presented with a menu of multiple-choice options no different than what I am considering in this book, although there is one slight difference. This slight difference is the use of experimental design features to create the prototype products based on the attributes and their levels. Our decision menus are not created this way; they are just stated or developed as I described in Chapter 9. Nonetheless, a statistical model, slightly different from the conjoint model but in the same family of models, is estimated, and the predicted values are again interpreted as probabilities. These are also estimates of credences.

The statistical model is a *multinomial logit* model, a generalization of the logit model I mentioned earlier.

See Paczkowski (2016), Paczkowski (2018), and Paczkowski (2022b) for a detailed discussion of these two methods. Also, see Paczkowski (2020) for the use of conjoint and discrete choice analysis for new product development. Also Train (2009) and Louviere et al. (2000) provide detailed, technical discussions of these models.

MaxDiff analysis

MaxDiff is in the same family as conjoint and discrete choice (they are all choice-based preference elicitation methods), but this one differs from the other two. MaxDiff only has product descriptions, and consumers are asked which one in a set (determined, again, by experimental design principles) they prefer the most and which one they prefer the least. The menus, in this case, are descriptions of several products, but the choice is two from the menu, unlike conjoint and discrete choices where only one option is selected. For conjoint, it is one by default since the menu is a singleton. This is also comparable to the integer programming approach in Chapter 5 for selecting two projects. Probabilities, or credences, are estimated just as for the other two methods.

Methods' problem

These methods have a problem with our menu probabilities issue. They are usually used with large samples. The more complex and numerous the attributes, the larger the required sample. A rule of thumb in market research is that the

> sample needs to be at least 300 to be credible, and 1,000 if it is an "important" study. The choice of 300 is not quite as arbitrary as it seems. Its origin is polling research, where a sample size of 300 means that the margin of error (half the confidence interval) is less than or equal to 5.6%, which, for many real-world problems, sounds like a sufficiently small number. In a conjoint study the goal is usually to predict preference shares, which makes this rule of thumb applicable for choice modeling.[1]

This sample size issue is worsened if estimates for population subsets are needed. A fixed sample must be divided among the subsets resulting in a smaller sample for each one. Your options, in this case, are to reduce the number of subsets or increase the overall sample size. The first is problem-dependent and may be impractical in a decision-making context. The second may not be viable because of costs. Your project budget must always be considered.

For our menu problem, a large sample would be a luxury which you generally do not have. The DAC, for example, may number only in the low teens, if that much.[2] Very large enterprises, such as AT&T, have large *C-level* teams and certainly many internal SMEand external KOLs so they can have large DAC support. However, not all members of the *C-level* team, for instance, are relevant for a DAC at any instance, which means that the DAC will be smaller than you might expect. For instance, a hotel company may, and probably does, have a Chief Security Officer (CSO). This person, however, would not be relevant for a strategic scale-view problem regarding where to build or develop new properties. The CSO would also be irrelevant for a pricing decision at a tactical scale-view level. The same holds for SMEs and KOLs: many of them may be irrelevant to a particular problem. In addition, any of these people could be so busy that they may be unable to allocate sufficient time for a study.

---

1 "What Sample Sizes Do You Need for Conjoint Analysis?" (*https://www.qresearchsoftware.com/what-sample-sizes-do-you-need-for-conjoint-analysis*) by Tim Bock. Last accessed January 29, 2024.

2 Based on my personal experience.

Another method is needed that allows for small sample sizes and time constraints. I will address this next.

 As an example of the number of potential internal executives an enterprise may have for a DAC, consider AT&T. It has scores of executives. Zippia, a career management company, claims AT&T has 79 people in a leadership position.[3]

Elicitation Method 2: Direct Questioning

A distinguishing feature of what I described in the previous section is that the priors are estimated from survey data. The surveys per se do not provide them. Another approach, which is still survey-based, is to ask respondents for their priors. This could be done in one of two ways:

- Ask them to directly state their prior
- Ask them to reveal their prior on a Likert Scale

The first is the direct elicitation of subjective probabilities of future events. Delavande et al. (2011, p. 152) note that this is now more commonly done regarding future events in developed and developing countries. Dominitz and Manski (1997), for instance, used the direct elicitation method to determine people's believed prospects of future employment. Delavande et al. (2011, p. 152) cite other examples.

Although effective, these methods, nonetheless, have problems. For example, it is not uncommon to need estimates of means, variances, and so forth, but the self-reported subjective probabilities are not those values. This means an extra step, such as fitting distribution functions to the data, must be used. This requires imposing assumptions about an underlying distribution of the data.

There is also the issue of whether those providing the subjective distributions really understand the concept of probability. This seems to be an especially important concern when teenagers are surveyed, yet they do seem to understand the concept better than expected. See de Bruin and Fischhoff (2017) for an interesting collaborative study of economists and psychologists on this issue. To circumvent or minimize the chance of this problem, some survey writers use wording such as "percent chance," give elaborate instructions or use visual aids such as allocating beans, stones, chips, and so forth. The latter is commonly used in studies in developing countries. See Delavande et al. (2011) for examples. For the elaborate instructions, de Bruin and Fischhoff (2017, p. 3299) cite the instructions from the U.S. Bureau of Labor Statistics "National Longitudinal Surveys:"

---

3 See *https://www.zippia.com/at-t-careers-1041/executives/*, last accessed January 30, 2024.

Instructions for the Expectation Module of NLSY97

Each of the next set of questions will ask you for your best guess at the chance that something will happen in the future. You can think of the PERCENT CHANCE that some event will occur as the number of CHANCES OUT OF 100 that the event will take place.

If you think that something is impossible, consider it as having a 0% chance. If you think the event is possible but unlikely, you might say there is a 3% chance or a 15% chance. If you think the chance is pretty even, you can say there is a 46% chance or perhaps a 52% chance. If you think the event is likely, but not certain, you might say there is a 78% chance or a 94% chance. If you think it is certain to happen, give it a 100% chance. Just to make sure that you are comfortable with the scale, I'd like you to do a few practice questions, and explain your answer to me.

What do you think is the percent chance that you will get the flu sometime in the next year?

What do you think is the percent chance that you will eat pizza sometime in the next year?

There is a problem with the direct elicitation of subjective probabilities: respondents could, and many do, cite a 50-50 chance as their answer. This could be due to ambivalence, truly not knowing, or not caring enough to answer the question. Your problem is handling such a response, especially if you have many of them. Ignoring this will, of course, jeopardize any statistical analysis. See Fischhoff and de Bruin (1999) and de Bruin et al. (2002) for discussions.

A related problem is a tendency to assign all the probability weight to one option, resulting in a degenerate distribution. This means a probability of 1.0 is assigned to one option and a zero to all others. It is the zero values that are a problem for some calculations.

Another approach uses a Likert Scale in a survey. This is popular in market research studies, despite a controversy about its interpretation. A typical scale is five points (or five "boxes"), such as "Very Unlikely," 'Somewhat Unlikely," "Neither Unlikely nor Likely," "Somewhat Likely," and "Very Likely." The scale is easy to include in a questionnaire, and respondents can easily select the box that matches their subjective prior probability.

There are problems with this scale for eliciting subjective probabilities. One involves how the respondents interpret it, which leads to interpersonal comparison difficulties. For example, some people may interpret "Very Likely" as implying the event will definitely happen (i.e., 100% probability), while others may place a lower rating on the phrase (e.g., say 80% chance). The implications of the two interpretations are vast, but you have no way to know about the differences. See Delavande et al. (2011, p. 152).

Elicitation Method 3: Activities

The method I will review uses a chip assignment approach. A survey respondent is given a fixed number of chips and is asked to allocate them to bins representing the options. The allocations are normalized by dividing each option's bin allocation by the total number of chips. One hundred chips is, of course, the most logical. The normalized allocations are the probabilities or credences. See Iacovone et al. (2023) for the development of this elicitation approach for scenario analysis.

This uses the same "chances" concept as the conjoint approach, but this is the extent of their similarities. Conjoint, as well as discrete choice and MaxDiff, heavily rely on experimental design concepts. This is not an issue for a chips approach. The major difference is that products are replaced by menu projects or scenario options. For example, for the hotel problem in Chapter 6, the scenarios presented to DAC members could be:

Scenario 1

What are the chances the local metropolitan planning board proposes no development?

Scenario 2

What are the chances the local metropolitan planning board proposes a modest development?

Scenario 3

What are the chances the local metropolitan planning board proposes a major development?

These questions could be easily programmed so that each respondent will see the questions on a screen on their computer's monitor. They could then simply move chips around or type in numbers. The underlying software would keep track of the assignments to ensure all chips are assigned. It could also check that they are not all assigned to one option to avoid a degenerate distribution and avoid a 50-50 allocation. Each respondent would be shown a series of such questions, and their responses recorded, for however many menu option components are involved. In my previous example, there are three.

This is the approach I advocate. There are many ways to analyze the data. The simplest is to just aggregate the responses in each chances box and calculate the proportion "voting" for each box. A second one is to do a *compositional data analysis* which I will briefly describe in the next section. A third is to *bootstrap* a distribution. I will describe aggregation in the next section and bootstrapping in the one following that section.

Analyzing Elicited Probability Distributions

You have three options for analyzing the elicited probabilities:

- Average all responses by scenarios
- Do compositional data analysis
- Bootstrap the distributions

The first, simple averaging, will only tell you the average probability for each level of the distribution—for the sample. This qualifier is important because the sample does not tell you about the population of key and relevant DAC members. This means the risk associated with a decision cannot be assessed. I will review this in "Elicitation Analysis 1: Averaging" on page 322.

The second approach, compositional data analysis (CoDA), is based on the structure of the data. This structure is a summation of allocated chips or their normalized version. In the normalized version, the sum is 1.0. There is a complex set of methods for analyzing compositional data that go beyond the scope of this book. I will, however, review it in "Elicitation Analysis 2: CoDA" on page 323.

The third method, bootstrapping, addresses the distribution problem using your sample of elicited probabilities. This involves resampling the sample to approximate the population distribution. You can then extract, say, a 95% confidence interval to assess that risk. I will describe the bootstrap in "Elicitation Analysis 3: Bootstrapping" on page 324.

Elicitation Analysis 1: Averaging

I will assume you have the elicited probabilities in a DataFrame. Each row should be a stakeholder with a categorical variable identifying that stakeholder. You can move this variable to the row index position if you want to better identify the rows, but it is not necessary.

The columns following the stakeholder column should be the elicited probabilities, one column for each level of the distribution. For example, for the three downtown development levels for the hotel problem, [No Development, Modest Development, Major Development], there would be three columns, one for each type of development.

Once the DataFrame is specified and populated with the sample data, you can use a simple pandas `groupby` method followed by a `describe` method to calculate the aggregate distributions. I will show an example in "Python Use-Case" on page 326.

This averaging is an example of developing poor information. The DataFrame has a lot more structure and content (i.e., information) left buried inside that could be used for decisions.

Elicitation Analysis 2: CoDA

Compositional data analysis (CoDA) is based on the structure of the data as I noted previously. This structure is a summation of allocated units or their normalized versions. Which one you use is irrelevant. In fact, for the unnormalized data, the total number of units allocated (e.g., chips in our case) is also unimportant. You could use any number such as 20 or 100. In both the count and normalized count cases, the summations are the same constant. In the case of allocating chips, the sum is the number of chips DAC members are given to allocate into bins where the bins are scenarios. Each person has the same number. In the normalized version, the allocated chips are interpreted as a probability, and the sum of these probabilities is 1.0 for each person.

CoDA Definition

CoDA is in the multivariate data analysis area of statistical analysis. A multivariate collection x_1, x_2, ...,x_J of nonnegative values such that $\sum_{j=1}^{J} x_j = 1$ is called a *composition*. The 1 is a unit-sum constraint for the normalized version. The components of the composition are called the composition parts. These lie in a simplex which I introduced in Chapter 5. For a three-part composition, the simplex is a triangle; for four parts, it is a tetrahedron. The parts themselves lie within the simplex.

The chip assignment asks DAC members to express their belief about each possible future SOW for some aspect of a project. The SOWs are scenarios of what might happen. These scenarios should be mutually exclusive and completely exhaustive; that is, they should cover all possibilities for that aspect of the project. The allocations express their beliefs about the likelihood of each one occurring. This means, of course, the probabilities do the same since they are just the normalized allocations. Since the future SOW is composed of these scenarios, the probabilities likewise compose the total belief. Compositional Data Analysis is a set of methods for analyzing this type of data.

Compositional data occur very often in real-world applications, in business and otherwise. Some examples are:

- Chemical composition of materials such as soil for agriculture
- Sediment composition of water beds in oceanography
- Household budget allocations in economics

- Portfolio composition in finance
- Ceramic composition of pottery in archeology
- Shape composition (e.g., head, trunk, leg) in biology
- Time allocations in work-productivity studies in business

See Aitchison (2005) for more examples. Also see Greenacre (2021), Greenacre (2018), Pawlowsky-Glahn and Buccianti (2011), and van den Boogaart and Tolosana-Delgado (2013) for the technicalities of compositional data analysis.

My focus is the normalized allocations which are probabilities about perceived future SOWs for the scenarios. The allocations compose the sum and these compositions, not just a summary of them as with a mean, can be used to assess the strength of agreement among DAC members. There is a complex set of methods for analyzing compositional data that go beyond the scope of this book. However, there is one aspect, a data visualization, that is helpful for showing or revealing patterns in the allocations just the way a scatter plot reveals patterns; the difference, however, is that each axis of the compositional plot is constrained to 1.0. You can, of course, overlay the mean of the probabilities to see deviations from the mean.

Elicitation Analysis 3: Bootstrapping

Bootstrapping is a well-accepted statistical procedure to obtain a probability distribution for a key statistical quantity, such as a mean or any complicated statistic, using just the sample at hand.[4] The sample you have, say of size n, is resampled with replacement a large number of times. The sample size of each resampling equals that of the original sample. On each resample of size n, the needed statistic is calculated and saved. At the end of the resampling, the total collection of calculated statistics is a distribution you can then use to calculate population values and confidence intervals.

There are two versions of bootstrapping. The first is what I call "basic," "classical," or "frequency" bootstrapping following the original method. This is simple for you to program—just a few lines of code are needed. There are, of course, well-written functions in most statistical packages that implement these steps so you do not have to do any programming per se.

To implement the classical bootstrap, first assume you have a random sample of size n from a population, and this data are in a DataFrame. You want to estimate a population parameter, such as the mean, using the sample mean. You can use the following pseudo-code to implement a bootstrap estimation:

---

4 I was once asked by a client to determine confidence intervals for a complicated "home-grown" statistic which made no statistical sense. The client had used it for years and believed it was great. The only way I could develop confidence intervals was by bootstrapping.

1. Sample n observations, with replacement, from the DataFrame of n observations.
2. Calculate the desired statistic (e.g., the sample mean) and store it in another DataFrame.
3. Repeat Steps 1 and 2 many times (e.g., 10,000 times).
4. Calculate the aggregate statistic when the iterations are completed.

For example, if you want an estimate of the population mean, you can average the bootstrapped sample means, which will be your population mean.

This procedure relies on simple arithmetic averaging. In the classical bootstrap, resampling is tantamount to drawing from a *multinomial distribution*. The distribution is the proportion of the population in each discrete category of the population. These proportions are the probabilities. Sampling with replacement leaves these probabilities unchanged in succeeding independent draws. These probabilities are used as weights to calculate a weighted average of the bootstrapped sample.

A multinomial distribution is a generalization of a binomial distribution from "Binomial distribution" on page 130.

From an interpretation perspective, notice that for each resample draw, the chances of a data point being selected is $\frac{1}{n}$ where n is the original sample size. This selection chance can be interpreted as a prior probability. These are discrete. The resulting selected values can be interpreted as a posterior distribution. This gives the classical bootstrap a (loose) interpretation of a Bayesian bootstrap. This is the second bootstrap version. There is an actual formal Bayesian bootstrap that uses a continuous prior, but this is more complex. You can use this Bayesian approach, but the results will be like the classical results; the differences are frequently small and inconsequential. Since the classical bootstrap is simpler to implement, it is the recommended method. See Hastie et al. (2008, p. 272) who state:

> The bootstrap distribution represents an (approximate) nonparametric, noninformative posterior distribution for our parameter. But this bootstrap distribution is obtained painlessly—without having to formally specify a prior and without having to sample from the posterior distribution. Hence we might think of the bootstrap distribution as a "poor man's" Bayes posterior. By perturbing the data, the bootstrap approximates the Bayesian effect of perturbing the parameters, and is typically much simpler to carry out.

The bootstrap procedure can be applied to our elicited probabilities and the result will be an estimate of the unknown population mean probability.

Python Use-Case

To illustrate the elicitation procedure, suppose you need the probability distribution for the three downtown development branches of the decision tree in Figure 6-6. The DAC for this strategic scale-view project consists of 36 people: 20 SMEs, 10 KOL's, and 6 *C-level* representatives. Each DAC member is requested to allocate 20 chips to the three-branch scenarios using an online system.

It is important to note that what I show next is for just one part of the hotel decision tree. It has to be repeated for each relevant part of the tree, but this should not be too onerous if the right computer program is designed and used for the chip allocations.

I show the Python script in Figure 10-1 that generates synthetic data for these 36 people. I define the number of chips to allocate (i.e., 20) in Line 6 and the number of DAC members, by their groups, in Line 7. A dummy DataFrame is defined in Line 8. This will be populated with the synthetic data. I define two key functions in Lines 12 and 16. The first creates random weights for the choice selection which is in the second function (see Line 21). These are normalized to sum to 1.0 so they have the interpretation of probabilities. The second function uses these weights, as you can see in Line 21, to randomly choose (using the NumPy function choice) how to assign the 20 chips to the three bins. This is done so that the sum of the assigned chips is 20 for each person. Both functions are then used in Lines 29 to 33 to do the actual chip assignment for the three groups of DAC members.

The resulting data are in Figure 10-2. Notice that the DataFrame has three columns labeled "bin" for the number of assigned chips. These three sum to 20 for each row. The three columns labeled "scenario" are the respective "bin" columns divided by 20 so that they sum to 1.0 for each person. These are the elicited probability estimates.

```
1   ##
2   ## Generate synthetic data for chip assignment
3   ##
4   ## Set parameters
5   ##
6   n_chips = 20
7   dac = { 'SME':20, 'KOL':10, 'C_Level':6 }
8   df = pd.DataFrame( columns = [ 'dac', 'bin1', 'bin2', 'bin3' ] )
9   ##
10  ## Define key functions
11  ##
12  def wghts( ):
13      x = np.random.randint( 0, 100, 3 )
14      x = list( x/sum( x ) )
15      return( x )
16  def chip( n = None, who = None, seed = None ):
17      counts = { 'bin1' : 0, 'bin2' : 0, 'bin3' : 0 }
18      keys = [ k for k in counts.keys() ]
19      np.random.seed( seed )
20      for _ in range(n):
21          counts[ np.random.choice( keys, p = wghts() ) ] += 1
22      chips = [ x for x in counts.values() ]
23      chips.insert( 0, who )
24      return( chips )
25  ##
26  ## Do chip assignments
27  ##
28  who = [ k for k in dac.keys() ]
29  for j in range( len( who ) ):
30      for i in range( dac[ who[ j ] ] ):
31          seed = i
32          chips = chip( n = n_chips, who = who[ j ], seed = seed )
33          df.loc[ len( df ) ] = chips
34  for i in range( 1, 4 ):
35      df[ 'scenario' + str( i ) ] = df[ 'bin' + str( i ) ]/n_chips
36  cols = [ 'scenario' + str( x ) for x in range( 1, 4 ) ]
37  display( df.head() )
38
```

Figure 10-1. How to generate synthetic data for the chip allocation elicitation example. Some output is shown in Figure 10-2. The assignment code is based on a Stack Overflow example (https://stackoverflow.com/questions/62590429/distribute-number-randomly-into-bins).

	dac	bin1	bin2	bin3	scenario1	scenario2	scenario3
0	SME	4	6	10	0.20	0.30	0.50
1	SME	9	8	3	0.45	0.40	0.15
2	SME	5	9	6	0.25	0.45	0.30
3	SME	11	5	4	0.55	0.25	0.20
4	SME	9	7	4	0.45	0.35	0.20

Figure 10-2. The head of a DataFrame that has the synthetic elicitation data generated by the script in Figure 10-1. The full DataFrame has 36 rows, one row for each DAC member.

Elicitation Example Analysis 1: Averaging

You can analyze the data in Figure 10-2 in many ways using the tools of statistics, econometrics, and machine learning. See Paczkowski (2023) for discussions of some of these. The simplest, and perhaps most intuitive, is calculating descriptive statistics for each DAC group and the total DAC. You can then use these to plot 95% confidence intervals by the groups to get a perspective on how the DAC members view the proposed menu options.

I show how this can be done by first summarizing the data using the script in Figure 10-3. This uses the pandas `describe` method with the `percentiles` argument in Line 9 to get the endpoints of a 95% confidence interval (0.025 and 0.975, which have a difference of 0.95) and the median. The script summarizes the data for each member group in Lines 16 to 20 and then all the groups together in Lines 9 to 14. I then calculate the summary statistics for each group using a combination of the pandas `groupby` and `describe` methods in Line 24. I show the final DataFrame of summarized data in Figure 10-4.

```
1   ##
2   ## Summarize the elicited data by all DAC members
3   ##
4   cols_what = [ 'dac', 'scenario1', 'scenario2', 'scenario3' ]
5   cols_stats = [ 'count', 'mean', '2.5%', '50%', '97.5%' ]
6   ##
7   ## Calculate descriptive stats
8   ##
9   df_all = pd.DataFrame( df[ cols_what ].describe( percentiles = [ 0.025, 0.50,
                                            0.975 ] ) ).T
10  df_all = df_all[ cols_stats ]  ## Subset needed descriptive columns
11  df_all.reset_index( inplace = True )  ## Reset index
12  df_all.rename( columns = {'index':'scenarios'}, inplace = True )  ## Rename column
13  df_all[ 'dac' ] = [ 'All' ]*3  ## Add new column
14  df_all.set_index( [ 'dac', 'scenarios' ], inplace = True )  ## Set new index
15  ##
16  ## Summarize DAC members individually
17  ##
18  tmp = df[ cols_what ].set_index( 'dac' ).stack()  ## Use Stack method
19  tmp = pd.DataFrame( tmp, columns = [ 'prior' ] ).reset_index()
20  tmp.rename( columns = {'level_1':'scenarios'}, inplace = True )
21  ##
22  ## Calculate descriptive stats by DAC groups
23  ##
24  tmp = tmp.groupby( by = [ 'dac', 'scenarios' ] ).describe( percentiles = [ 0.025,
                                            0.50, 0.975 ] )
25  tmp.columns = tmp.columns.droplevel()
26  tmp = tmp[ cols_stats ]
27  ##
28  ## Concatenate All and Group descriptive stats
29  ##
30  df_sum = pd.concat( [ df_all, tmp ] )
31  df_sum
32
```

Figure 10-3. A script showing how to summarize the data in Figure 10-2. All DAC members and then the individual group members are summarized and put into a DataFrame. The result is in Figure 10-4.

dac	scenarios	count	mean	2.5%	50%	97.5%
All	scenario1	36.0	0.372222	0.15000	0.375	0.60000
	scenario2	36.0	0.331944	0.10000	0.325	0.65000
	scenario3	36.0	0.295833	0.14375	0.300	0.50000
C_Level	scenario1	6.0	0.416667	0.20625	0.450	0.59375
	scenario2	6.0	0.308333	0.11875	0.325	0.44375
	scenario3	6.0	0.275000	0.15625	0.250	0.47500
KOL	scenario1	10.0	0.385000	0.16125	0.425	0.58875
	scenario2	10.0	0.330000	0.13375	0.300	0.60500
	scenario3	10.0	0.285000	0.16125	0.300	0.46625
SME	scenario1	20.0	0.352500	0.17375	0.350	0.57625
	scenario2	20.0	0.340000	0.14750	0.350	0.57875
	scenario3	20.0	0.307500	0.12375	0.300	0.50000

Figure 10-4. The DataFrame of the summarized synthetic elicitation data generated by the script in Figure 10-3.

Once you have the summarized data, you can plot 95% confidence intervals as I show in Figures 10-5 and 10-6. Notice that the intervals overlap, suggesting agreement among the members.

```
1   ##
2   ## Script for CI
3   ##
4   what = 'scenario1'
5   df_ci = df_sum.query( "scenarios == @what" )
6   fig, ax = plt.subplots()
7   for lower, upper, mean, median, y in zip( df_ci[ '2.5%' ] , df_ci[ '97.5%'],
                                               df_ci[ 'mean' ], df_ci[ '50%' ], range(
                                               len( df_ci ) ) ):
8       ax.plot( ( lower, upper ), ( y, y ), 'ro-', color = 'blue' )
9       ax.plot( mean, y, 'o', color = 'red' )
10      ax.plot( median, y, '*', color = 'black' )
11  ax.set_yticks( range( len( df_ci ) ), list( df_ci.index.get_level_values( 0 ) ) )
12  ax.set_xlabel( 'Sample Probabilities\nMean: Red Dot; Median: Black Asterisk' )
13  ax.set_ylabel( 'DAC Group' )
14  ax.set_title( 'Sample Probability Confidence Intervals\nby DAC
                                     Membership\nScenario:' + what[ -1 ] );
15
```

Figure 10-5. A script showing how to produce a confidence interval graph as I show in Figure 10-6. Based on a Stack Overflow example (https://stackoverflow.com/questions/59747313/how-can-i-plot-a-confidence-interval-in-python).

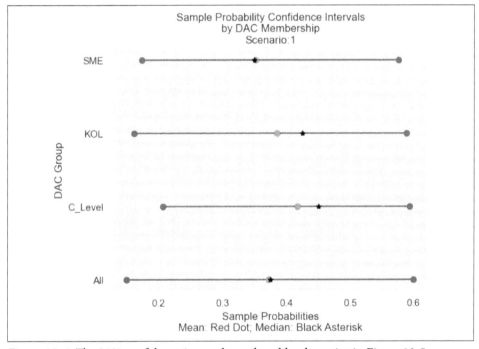

Figure 10-6. The 95% confidence intervals produced by the script in Figure 10-5.

```
 1  ##
 2  ## Create boxplots of elicited priors
 3  ##
 4  ## First, create DataFrame of stacked data
 5  ##
 6  cols_what = [ 'dac', 'scenario1', 'scenario2', 'scenario3' ]
 7  tmp = df[ cols_what ].set_index( 'dac' ).stack()
 8  tmp = pd.DataFrame( tmp, columns = [ 'prior' ] ).reset_index()
 9  tmp.rename( columns = {'level_1':'scenarios'}, inplace = True )
10  display( tmp.head() )
11  ##
12  ## Next, use Seaborn for boxplots
13  ##
14  ax = sns.boxplot( x = 'dac', y = 'prior', hue = 'scenarios', data = tmp )
15  ax.legend( bbox_to_anchor = (1.25, 1), loc = 'upper right', borderaxespad = 0 )
16  ax.set_title( 'Elicited Prior Probabilities\nby Scenarios within DAC Groups' )
17  ax.set_xlabel( 'DAC Group' )
18  ax.set_ylabel( 'Elicited Prior Probability' );
19
```

	dac	scenarios	prior
0	SME	scenario1	0.20
1	SME	scenario2	0.30
2	SME	scenario3	0.50
3	SME	scenario1	0.45
4	SME	scenario2	0.40

Figure 10-7. A script showing how to create boxplots for the elicited probabilities by DAC members and scenarios. Some of the rearranged data are shown here. The boxplots are in Figure 10-8.

I also created boxplots by the DAC groups for the three scenarios which I show in Figure 10-8 using the script in using the script in Figure 10-7. They also indicate agreement among the DAC adviser groups. These two pieces of agreement information are important to know because they add credibility to the elicited priors. A large difference in the distributions implies a large disagreement among the members, which could jeopardize a decision. The chief decision-maker (e.g., the CEO) would have less confidence in any menu because of a large disagreement. Strong agreement, however, would instill confidence and strengthen any decision. Agreement is superior to disagreement.

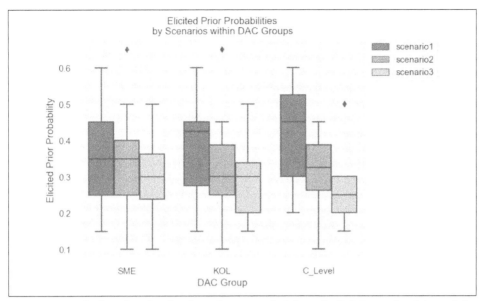

Figure 10-8. The boxplots for the elicited prior probabilities by DAC membership and the three hotel scenarios. The script is in Figure 10-7.

 The script uses the Plotly graphics package, which you have to install on your computer if you do not already have it. Use `pip install plotly` or `conda install -c plotly` if not. There is an "express" version that you import using `import plotly.express as px`.

Plotly Documentation

According to the Plotly documentation (*https://plotly.com/python/px-arguments*): "Plotly Express is the easy-to-use, high-level interface to Plotly, which operates on a variety of types of data and produces easy-to-style figures."

Finally, I created a variation on the boxplot display for scenarios rather than DAC members. A small tweak to the code in Figure 10-7 produced Figure 10-9. The interpretation is obvious.

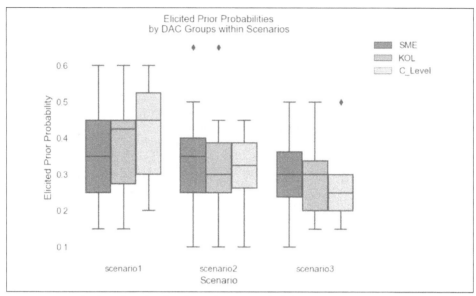

Figure 10-9. The boxplots for the elicited prior probabilities by scenarios for the DAC members. The script is the same as the one in Figure 10-7, but with a slight tweak.

Although these data visualizations are suggestive and convey the same message, they are still subject to interpretation. A formal statistical test would forestall any interpretation issues. Your normal first inclination to check for difference among the groups may be to do pair-wise t-tests for the difference in group means. Since there are three DAC groups, this implies three tests.

The count of three tests is based on the number of combinations of 3 groups taken 2 at a time (i.e., pairs). From Chapter 4, this is $\frac{3!}{(2! \times 1!)} = 3$.

There is a problem with this approach: it does not allow for the effect of multiple comparisons. Your Null Hypothesis is $H_0: \mu_{C-level} = \mu_{SME} = \mu_{KOL}$. This is equivalent to three separate hypotheses:

$H_{01}: \mu_{C-level} = \mu_{SME}$

$H_{02}: \mu_{C-level} = \mu_{KOL}$

$H_{03}: \mu_{SME} = \mu_{KOL}$.

As noted by Paczkowski (2016, p. 159): "A little reflection will show that this must be true: if all the means are equal, then all pairs of means must be equal." Since there are three pairs, there are three separate Null Hypotheses as I just listed. These three mean-differences lead to an *experiment-wise error rate* as opposed to a *comparison-wise error rate* which is the $\alpha = 0.05$ that you are used to using for a single t-test of a difference in means.

The general formula for the experiment-wise error rate is

$$Pr(Falsely\ Rejecting\ H_0) = 1 - (1 - \alpha)^k$$

where k is the number of tests. For our problem, $k = 3$, so the probability of falsely rejecting H_0 is 0.1426 for $\alpha = 0.05$. You may specify a comparison-wise error rate of $\alpha = 0.05$ as you would do for any hypothesis test (remember, your inclination is to do three separate t-tests), but the true error rate is almost three times that α level.

The entire topic of multiple comparison tests is complicated and well beyond the scope of what I can cover here. Regardless how complicated it is, you still need to do better than strict pair-wise t-tests. An appropriate test is Tukey's HSD Test, which allows for the inflated error rate. HSD stands for "Honestly Significant Difference." See Paczkowski (2016) for some discussions.

I show how to implement Tukey's test in Figure 10-10. This is for the first of the three scenarios. The results shown in the figure are for six permutations of the DAC groups. You still do pair-wise comparisons. Obviously, there are three combinations since two permutations are identical. There are sign reversals on the statistics so the comparison of, say, group 0 and group 1 (i.e., 0 − 1) is the same as the comparison of group 1 and group 0 (i.e., 1 − 0). The signs on the confidence intervals are also reversed. Only the p-values, as probabilities, are unchanged as you should expect. The p-values are adjusted for the multiple comparisons. Notice that they are all above 0.05 indicating agreement among the DAC members, which is consistent with the data visualizations. I do not show the test for the other two scenarios, but the results are the same. The DAC members are in full agreement. Therefore, they allocated the same number of chips to each scenario since if they are the same for two of them, then they must be the same for the third.

Doing a Tukey's HSD Test moves you past the Poor Information of simple averaging to somewhat Richer Information because you now know more about the relationships among the groups.

```
 1   ##
 2   ## Tukey HSD Test for DAC members for scenario 1
 3   ##
 4   ## Create groups
 5   ##
 6   temp = tmp.query( "scenarios == 'scenario1'" )
 7   grp = temp.groupby( by = 'dac' )
 8   ##
 9   C_Level = grp.get_group( 'C_Level' )
10   SME = grp.get_group( 'SME' )
11   KOL = grp.get_group( 'KOL' )
12   ##
13   ## Set-up test
14   ##
15   tukey = tukey_hsd( C_Level.prior, SME.prior, KOL.prior )
16   print( tukey )
17


    Tukey's HSD Pairwise Group Comparisons (95.0% Confidence Interval)
    Comparison  Statistic  p-value  Lower CI  Upper CI
      (0 - 1)     0.064     0.563    -0.089     0.217
      (0 - 2)     0.032     0.891    -0.138     0.201
      (1 - 0)    -0.064     0.563    -0.217     0.089
      (1 - 2)    -0.033     0.806    -0.160     0.095
      (2 - 0)    -0.032     0.891    -0.201     0.138
      (2 - 1)     0.033     0.806    -0.095     0.160
```

Figure 10-10. A script showing how to do the Tukey HSD Test to compare the mean elicited probabilities by DAC members for Scenario 1.

Elicitation Example Analysis 2: CoDA

There is a three-part composition with scenarios as the parts for the hotel problem. The values for the parts are the probabilities with the unit constraint. Doing a full compositional analysis of this multivariate data is beyond the scope of what I can do in this book. Greenacre (2021) is a very good source for an introduction to the analysis of this data.

Although the analysis methods are more advanced, a chief form of analysis is data visualization. Recall from "Elicitation Analysis 2: CoDA" on page 323 that for a three-part composition, the multivariate data can be displayed in a simplex, which is a triangle in two dimensions. The triangle is usually drawn as an equilateral triangle with each side being the scale for one of the parts. The scale on each side ranges from 0 to 1 for normalized data. Most data visualization software will automatically normalize your data if you do not use pre-normalized data.

The graph is called a *ternary plot*. "Ternary" means composed of three parts or using three as a base according to the Oxford Languages Dictionary.

I show an example of a ternary plot in Figure 10-11. This one is empty because it is the structure I want to display. For insight into how this structure is created, see Wikipedia (2024j). Notice that the scales run from 0 to 1 on each axis. The crisscrossed lines in the interior are guidelines to help you read or identify the probabilities on the axes for any interior point. These are unnecessary, as I will explain.

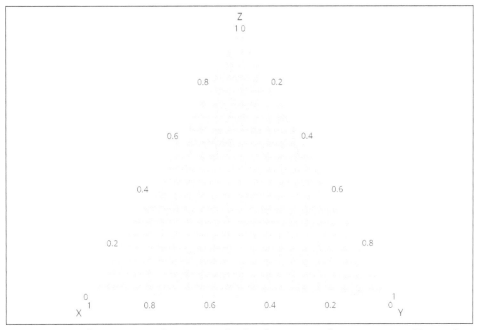

Figure 10-11. The structure of a ternary plot for three parts of a composition. Notice the scales on the axes.

I show a script to produce a ternary plot and the resulting plot in Figure 10-12 and Figure 10-13, respectively. Notice the cluster of points just below the center of the triangle. Also, notice that there are fewer data points shown than there are rows in the original DataFrame (which is 36). The reason is that several rows have duplicate allocations, so the plotting points are on top of each other.

You can subset the data in two ways to see individual groups. The first is to use the pandas `query` method. For instance, to see just the SMEs, you would use `tmp = df.query( "dac == 'SME'" )` and then use `tmp` in place of `df` in the script, Figure 10-12. The second way, which is what I recommend, is to click on the legend keys for the group(s) you do *not* want to see. For example, to see just the SMEs, click on the `KOL` and `C_Level` keys. This will remove those two and leave just the SME data points. This is more interactive.

```
1  ##
2  ## Ternary plot of hotel scenarios elicited probabilities
3  ##    The DataFrame df has the raw bin allocations
4  ##
5  fig = px.scatter_ternary( df, a = "scenario1", b = "scenario2", c = "scenario3",
                             width = 600, height = 600, labels = {
                             'scenario1': 'Scenario 1', 'scenario2':
                             'Scenario 2', 'scenario3': 'Scenario 3'
                             }, color = 'dac', title = 'Ternary Plot
                             of Scenario Elicited Probabilities' )
6  fig.show()
7
```

Figure 10-12. The script to produce the ternary plot for the hotel example's scenarios. The plot is in Figure 10-13.

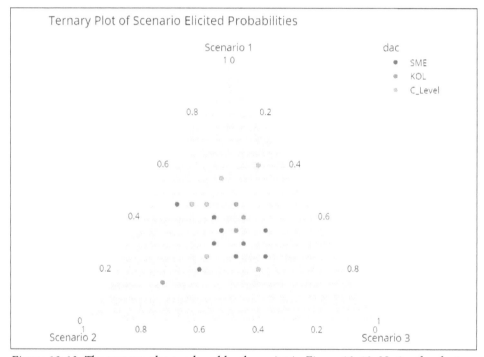

Figure 10-13. The ternary plot produced by the script in Figure 10-12. Notice the cluster of points slightly below the center.

I previously said that you do not have to read the probabilities from the graph using the guidelines. You can see what they are merely by placing your cursor over a data point. A box will appear that will tell you the plotting coordinates for all three axes as well as the group the point belongs to. In most instances, the actual probabilities are of little value. What is important is the pattern among the points. Do they cluster together or are they spread out? Are they evenly distributed in the triangle's space?

You do not have to use the ternary graph. An alternative is a simple stacked bar chart with each bar representing a respondent. The length of each bar is either the number of chips allocated or the normalized allocations (i.e., the elicited probabilities). The latter is recommended. I show a script and the resulting stacked bar chart in Figure 10-14 and Figure 10-15, respectively.

```
1   ##
2   ## Alternative display: stacked bar chart
3   ##
4   cols = [ 'scenario' + str( x ) for x in range( 1, 4 ) ]
5   lbl = [ 'Scenario ' + str( x ) for x in range( 1, 4 ) ]
6   colors = { 'scenario1': 'black', 'scenario2': 'red', 'scenario3': 'blue' }
7   ax = df[ cols ].plot.barh( stacked = True, color = colors, title = 'Elicited
                                        Probabilities\nStacked Bar Chart',
                                        xlabel = 'Elicited Probabilities' )
8   ax.tick_params( labelleft = False )   ## remove y-axis labels
9   ax.legend( lbl, bbox_to_anchor = ( 1.0, 1.0 ), fontsize = 'small' );
10
```

Figure 10-14. The script for an alternative display of the elicited probabilities. Each bar is a respondent. See Figure 10-15 for the result.

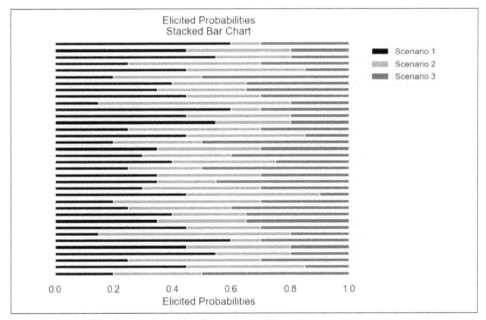

Figure 10-15. The plot produced by the script in Figure 10-14.

Elicitation Example Analysis 3: Bootstrapping

The problem with Analysis 1: Averaging is that you are using a sample from a population. You may believe the DAC members are the population because there is no one else who could be a member. This is not correct since the SMEand KOLs are just part of a larger group of experts. This is especially true for the KOLs who are usually outside the company and come from many wide and diverse areas. For example, they could come from academia, consulting firms, and publication enterprises (e.g., trade magazines, thought-leading authors, and the blogosphere) to mention a few. The SMEs could likewise come from these same sources as well as internal people. And the *C-level team* is often quite vast, especially in large, multinational enterprises, so that the available pool of talent is likewise large.

The bootstrap method I outlined is a way to handle this issue. I show a script in Figure 10-16 to implement it. It uses a function named bootstrap which is available in the SciPy stats package. You need to import this as I show in Line 4. The data I used are from the DataFrame of synthetic data I created earlier. This is all the DAC members for the three groups. I did 9,999 iterations, which is the function's default. You can change this using the argument n_resamples = *iter* where iter is the number you want. This default should be sufficient.

```
 1  ##
 2  ## Bootstrap probability distribution
 3  ##
 4  from scipy.stats import bootstrap
 5  what = 'scenario1'
 6  ##
 7  data = ( df[ what ], )   # samples must be in a sequence
 8  boot = bootstrap( data, np.mean, random_state = 42 )
 9  mean = np.mean( boot.bootstrap_distribution )
10  ##
11  ## Plot the bootstrap distribution
12  ##
13  fig, ax = plt.subplots()
14  ax.hist( boot.bootstrap_distribution, bins = 25 )
15  ax.set_title( 'Bootstrapped Probability Distribution\n All DAC
                    Members\nScenario:' + what[ -1 ] )
16  ax.set_xlabel( 'Bootstrapped Probabilities\nVertical Line is Bootstrapped Mean of
                    Probabilities\nFor Scenario ' + what[ -1
                    ] )
17  ax.set_ylabel( 'Bootstrapped Frequency' )
18  ax.axvline( x = mean, color = 'red', linewidth = 3 )
19  plt.show()
20
```

Figure 10-16. A script showing how to implement a bootstrap. I show the resulting distribution in Figure 10-17. Based on a bootstrap script (https://docs.scipy.org/doc/scipy/reference/generated/scipy.stats.bootstrap.html).

For this script, I extracted only the Scenario 1 data which is the first of the three I listed in "Elicitation Method 3: Activities" on page 321. You would do a similar bootstrapping for the other two.

Once the bootstrap is completed, I then calculate the mean from the results using the NumPy `mean` function to highlight the mean of the distribution. You can see this in Line 9.

You can see from Figure 10-17 that the distribution is normal.

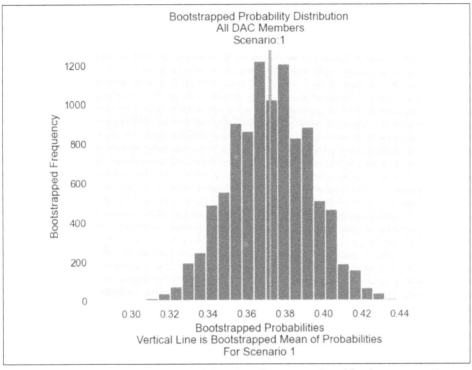

Figure 10-17. The bootstrapped probability distribution produced by the script in Figure 10-16.

Bootstrapping one scenario is not enough; you need to do all of them. I repeated the bootstrapping for the remaining two scenarios and placed all the data into one DataFrame. I then created boxplots of the posterior probability values by the three hotel scenarios. The script for this is in Figure 10-18. I grouped the data by scenario in Line 4 using the pandas `groupby` method and then created the boxplots by appending the `boxplot` method to the groups. The `subplots = False` argument forces the boxplots to be in one graph panel. You could also use the seaborn boxplot function. The result is in Figure 10-19. You can see that the boxes do not overlap, suggesting three different mean values for the posterior probability. This suggests that, although the DAC members agree on a scenario, they also agree that the three scenarios are different; there are different beliefs about them.

```
1  ##
2  ## Boxplot of posterior probabilities
3  ##
4  grp = df_boot.groupby( by = 'scenario' )
5  ax = grp.boxplot( subplots = False )
6  ax.set_xticks( range( 1, 4 ), [ 'Scenario ' + str( i ) for i in range( 1, 4 ) ] )
7  ax.set_ylabel( 'Bootstrapped Probabilities' )
8  ax.set_title( 'Bootstrapped Posterior Probability Distributions\nby Scenarios' );
9
```

Figure 10-18. A script showing how to create boxplots for the bootstrapped posterior probabilities by scenarios. The boxplots are in Figure 10-19.

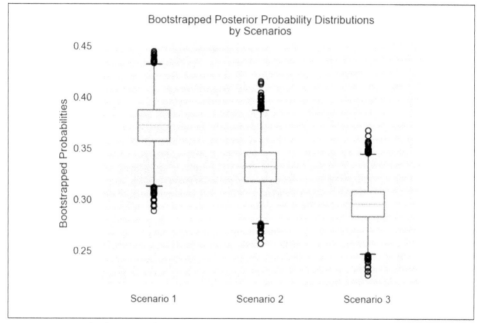

Figure 10-19. The boxplots for the bootstrapped posterior probabilities by the three hotel scenarios. The script is in Figure 10-18.

You can statistically check the mean posterior probability for each scenario is different by using the Tukey HSD test of means.

Summary

This is the second of two chapters on developing decision menus. This one was focused on prior probabilities and their development as weights in the expected value calculations. The priors are part of the Bayesian approach to probabilities and reflect beliefs of something happening. I described several elicitation methods for identifying priors.

The main concepts from this chapter are:

- Beliefs
- The role of SMEs, KOLs, and the DAC in developing priors
- Three elicitation methods
- Methods for analyzing the results of the elicitation methods

CHAPTER 11

One-Time Decisions

A bold but subtle assumption for Prescriptive Analytics is concerned with the frequency of decisions. This has two parts. First, decision-makers make only one decision, and, second, they make it now, today. The process for developing the decision menu has been underway in stages for some time before it reaches the desk of the decision-maker. That process involves a series of decisions. Think of these as *stage-decisions*. This is unimportant for when the "final" decision is made—it is still made now—and it is made only once. There is a no follow-up decision. But there are follow-up decisions, which is why "final" is in quotes. Decisions are always revisited, reviewed, and changed so that nothing is really final. The stage-decisions never stop.

I will address two leading questions in this chapter:

- When is a decision made?
- What is the frequency of decision making?

The second question is very complex. Therefore, I will only highlight some of its features.

Evidence of the Problem

You may wonder why I view frequency as a subtle assumption. I never mentioned in prior chapters that decisions are made today, however you define today, and that they are neither repeated nor revised. I just developed methods, such as mathematical programming, where there is a menu of projects from which the decision-maker chooses. If you examine the example in "Mixed Integer Programming" on page 178 for new-product selection, you will see that the decision-maker is only asked to choose, but is not asked or told when to choose. From an analytical perspective, it is only reasonable the decision is made when the menu is presented. Also, and this is important, there is no follow-up decision. It is final.

You could argue this is inconsequential for Prescriptive Analytics because its concern is the methods to guide the decision-maker in what should be done; a real-world application just involves tailoring them to that application's requirements. If a requirement is multiple decisions, especially in sequence, then you merely repeat the methods. This is then a computer software effort; no additional framework is needed. So you might say the real issue is repeatability, which has nothing to do with understanding Prescriptive Analytics.

This is naive.

In real-world business problems, and, in fact, all problems where decisions are made, whether in business, public policy, or everyday life, they are made sequentially. There are steps, stages, or hurdles to overcome with before a final decision is made, if, in fact, there is a final one. A decision at each stage is a build-up to a final one which is a cumulative decision. Those stage-decisions are just as important to consider and make as the final one. In some situations, the stages never end, which further complicates matters. This is the case at the operational scale-view level more than at the tactical and, especially, the strategic levels. In this situation, there is no final decision, per se, but ongoing ones of the same ilk.

Stages represent the acquisition of new rich information which could alter a previous decision. This new information is not about events built into, say, a decision tree. Those are specified when the menu is constructed with the tree as part of the data. They are already accounted for at the root of the decision tree. Whether the events occur or not is immaterial. They are discounted to the present when the decision is made. The discount factors are the posterior probabilities assigned to the future possible events.

As an example, consider the hotel decision tree in Chapter 6. The strategic planner, with input from the DAC, determined three possible airport development scenarios and assigned each a prior probability. The three possibilities are completely exhaustive and mutually exclusive. The probabilities, therefore, sum to 1.0. The expected value for the three scenarios is $\sum_{i=1}^{3}(p_i \times R_i)$, where p_i is the posterior probability of scenario i and R_i is its KPM. If the second scenario (i.e., moderate development) is realized, its effect on the decision is of no consequence since it was already factored into the decision via the expected value. This is the discounting. The same holds for the first and third scenarios. So no matter which one is realized at some future date, its effect is already included in the decision.

Discounting Uses

This is the same discounting mechanism used to describe the stock market. Any future event (e.g., the unemployment rate announcement), if it is fully realized, will have no effect on stock prices. The event is said to be already fully discounted in stock prices. This is the basis for the *Efficient Markets Hypothesis*. See Wikipedia (2024e) for an explanation of this important economic and financial hypothesis.

This probabilistic interpretation of discounting is for the occurrence of an event. The value of the KPM may be further discounted to today by the typical financial present value discounting method. And, in fact, this is reflected in the tree as an NPV. For any of the development scenarios, the NPV is $\frac{1}{(1 + r)^n} \times \Sigma_{i\,=\,1}^{3} \left(p_i \times R_i \right)$ where n is the number of discounting periods. The summation term is the expected value in period n. If you assume this is a constant period amount (i.e., an annuity), then you must use the annuity discounting formula, Equation 6-1.

Information is difficult to define, philosophically and pragmatically. See, for example, Floridi (2019), Floridi (2008), and Floridi (2010). The collection of articles in Sommaruga (2009) is especially relevant. I simply refer to information as a *surprise*; something completely unexpected. So the new information I am referring to is a surprise, something not already built into the menu structure—or something so fluid and dynamic that accounting for it and all its possibilities is daunting at best and impossible at worst.

This new information is not available during menu construction simply because surprises cannot be anticipated; an anticipated surprise is, after all, not a surprise. Once it does become available, the menu must be changed, which implies revising any decisions already made. This, in fact, happens quite often when business cases are created. I will discuss business cases in the next section.

The implication of these stage-decisions is that they are not one-time events, but sequential events. Most real-world decisions are *sequential decisions*. I will elaborate on all of this in the next section.

Sequential Decisions: Introduction

Consider once more the new-product problem in "Mixed Integer Programming" on page 178. My focus was the selection from a menu, and nothing more. The menu was developed and a mathematical programming method was applied. In a real-world application, however, the products comprising the menu pass through several proof-of-concept stages collectively called the *business case process* (BCP). This is a pre-final decision sequence of steps that set the stage for the final one. There are now two sets of decisions:

- Pre-final
- Final

The final decision is made using the tools from the previous parts of this book. However, there is more to the story. But remember, "final" does not literally mean final.

Once the final decision is made, the circumstances leading to it could change unexpectedly. This is the surprise or information.

There are two possibilities. First, the environment changes which is outside the decision-maker's control. For example, a pandemic forces work-site closures. Second, the decision made today has an effect tomorrow, but the effect is unknown at the time of the decision. In both cases, decisions are revisited which establishes another sequence of decisions.

The implication is that the methods for Prescriptive Analytics become more extensive and complicated. For example, the standard mathematical programming methods of Chapter 5 assume only a one-time decision. These are not applicable to sequential decisions. It is the sequence of business case and post-business case decisions that I will discuss next.

Sequential Decisions 1: The Business Case

A business case is a *pipeline* all new product concepts must (at least theoretically) pass through from concept identification to concept development to market and financial testing. A business case analysis is done for each new product with the results summarized in the final menu.

 The business case pipeline is a metaphor for a series of stages in which concepts flow in for evaluation and then flow out either through termination or by being added to the menu. I show a stylized pipeline for new product development in Figure 11-1.

As I noted in Paczkowski (2020, p. 8), a business case is an ongoing check of the market and financial viability of the new product concept. "It is a gate-keeping function that allows a new product to enter the pipeline and to pass from one stage to the next or be terminated." The actual process varies from business to business. Some are formal; others are not. Some involve numerous large organizations; others, only a few which may be small. But all (major) business enterprises have such a process.

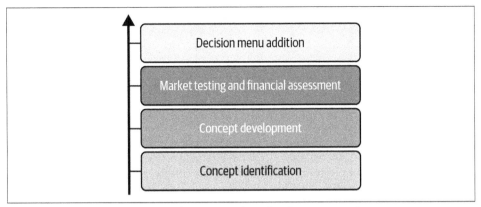

Figure 11-1. A stylized version of a new product development pipeline.

I outline a stereotypical business case process in Figure 11-2. It has two stages of assessment:

Stage I
    Preliminary Assessment

Stage II
    Detail Assessment.

More steps are certainly possible. The number is business-defined. Two suffice for my purpose.

Stages I and II are drill-downs of the third piece of Figure 11-1. I assume the concept has been sufficiently identified and developed for serious consideration for funding and resource allocation.

In my rendition, the two stages seem identical since they have similar structures:

- Financial and market assessments
- Input from the DAC
- Hurdle tests (to be explained)

But they differ by their focus and intent.

A concept or project is introduced for funding and resource allocation (i.e., non-funding allocation such as R&D personnel) in Stage I. Funds are a scarce resource in any enterprise (no business has infinite funds), so they must be optimally allocated across several proposals. Similarly for non-funding resource allocations. Data are compiled for a preliminary view of the concept. At this stage, it has little substance. It is more an idea than anything else, but one that warrants serious consideration. Hence, it enters the pipeline.

In the pipeline of Figure 11-2, a new concept, *Concept #1*, is introduced for consideration. It may come from a wide range of sources. An example is product reviews analyzed using text analytical methods. Reviews often contain suggestions for enhancements as well as new products, so they are a rich source to mine. For sources for new product development ideas, especially using text analytics, see Paczkowski (2020, Chapter 2).

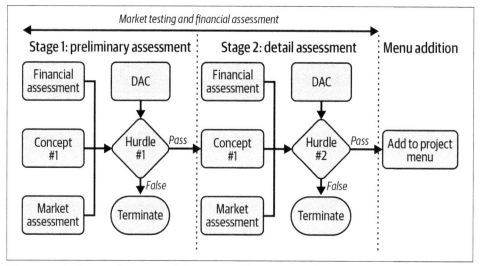

Figure 11-2. A typical sequential decision-making process for a new product business case. The collection of three Stages is a project pipeline. It is a drill-down of the third part of Figure 11-1.

Whatever the source, the introduction into the pipeline includes a full concept description and at least two assessments: financial and market. These are preliminary, with scant detail, since the concept is, well, just a concept. It must meet some hurdle requirements, primarily the KPMs. The DAC has input into these, including an evaluation of the concept. If it passes the hurdles, it then proceeds to Stage II; otherwise, it is terminated.

If the concept enters Stage II, more detailed financial and market assessments are developed. For the market assessment, for example, decision trees, as I described at the beginning of Chapter 6, or conjoint/discrete choice/MaxDiff choice studies, as I described in Chapter 10, may be developed. Further hurdle requirements, which are more detailed and stringent KPMs, must be passed. If the concept passes them, it is added to the decision menu presented to the decision-maker; otherwise, it is terminated.

The projects added to the menu have information associated with them. This is information, data, from Stage II. No new information is added. If there is new information after a project is added but before the decision is made, then it may influence the decision about the project, perhaps taking it off the menu. The complexion of the menu may be changed. The way the methods in the prior chapters were presented, the menu given to the decision-maker is fixed and final. The decision-maker just chooses from it.

All concepts will go through this BCP and all that pass are added to the project menu for the decision-maker's consideration. The full process for n concepts is illustrated in Figure 11-3, Panel (a). Notice how this one differs from what I described in Chapter 9. That process just added projects to the menu. I show this in Figure 11-3, Panel (b). The difference is subtle.

In the scheme I show in Figure 11-3, Panel (a), the decisions are sequential—and this is before the menu decision itself. If there are n projects and each one passes two hurdles, then there are $2^n + 1$ decisions: n decisions, each at two hurdles, and one final menu decision.

In Figure 11-3, Panel (b), there are just n projects, but no business case process. Adding a project to the menu must still be decided, so there are $n + 1$ decisions. Clearly, the business case process is more decision-intensive. This means more resources are involved, and, thus, higher costs.

Once the menu is constructed using either the process in Figure 11-3, Panel (a) or (b), the Prescriptive Analytics methods I described earlier are used as I stated several times. But this may be unrealistic since more sequential decisions may have to be made, as I will briefly explain in the next section.

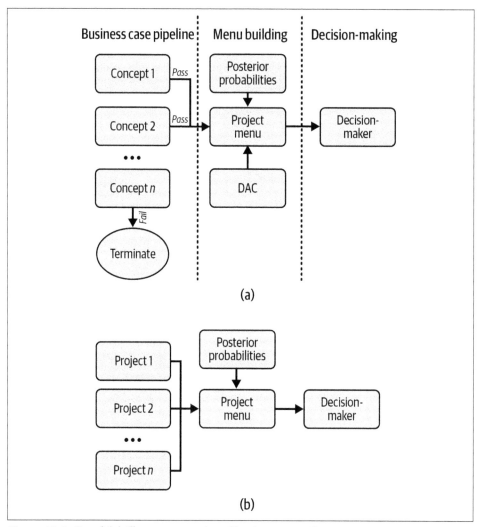

Figure 11-3. Panel (a) illustrates a series of business cases for non-terminate concepts. The result is the project menu for the decision-maker. Panel (b) illustrates a series of projects without consideration of business cases.

Sequential Decisions 2: Post-Business Case

The sequential nature of decisions at the business case level in Figure 11-2 ended at the menu level. One decision remained, and that was made only once. This is the "final" decision. But post-menu decisions are possible so the sequential nature of decision making continues.

There are many real-world projects that are continually reviewed. These decisions are ubiquitous. A few examples are:

- Freight transportation
- Manufacturing and supply chain management
- Energy systems
- Healthcare systems

See Powell (2022, p. 5). For each of these, the driving force is the acquisition of new rich information (as surprises), and new information always develops. This information, however, is about SOW conditions not factored into a business case or any prior decision. This new information is acquired in time, so this time dimension is an additional complication.

 The information I am referring to is rich information. Poor information is insufficient for incenting a major new decision.

The paradigm for decision making incorporating new information in time is a series of two-tuples:

Equation 11-1.

$$(information, decision)_0, (information, decision)_1, (information, decision)_2, \ldots$$

whereas in a non-sequential framework, it is just a single two-tuple:

Equation 11-2.

$$(information, decision)_0.$$

See Powell (2022, p. 11), although he does not use the two-tuple notation. I use tuples to indicate that the information and the decision are a pair that cannot be separated. The pair is an *ordered pair*.

> In mathematics, a tuple is a finite sequence or *ordered list* of numbers or, more generally, mathematical objects, which are called the elements of the tuple. An n-tuple is a tuple of n elements, where n is a non-negative integer. There is only one 0-tuple, called the empty tuple. A 1-tuple and a 2-tuple are commonly called a singleton and an *ordered pair*, respectively. (See Wikipedia [2024k, emphasis added] on tuples.)

In my notation, the subscripts are time periods. The naught (0) represents today, the time when the initial decision is made. This is the decision from the menu, post-business case. The 1, 2, and so on are future time periods after the menu selection is made. So the two-tuples are a time series. However, the time periods for the two-tuples are not uniform since the new information, the surprises, can occur at any time. I illustrate this in Figure 11-4. Seven time periods are shown, so seven two-tuples are possible. No information develops in periods 2, 4, 5, and 7. The amount varies in periods 1, 3, and 6 since not all information is the same amount (however, information is measured). So the two-tuples are

$$(information, decision)_1, (information, decision)_3, (information, decision)_6.$$

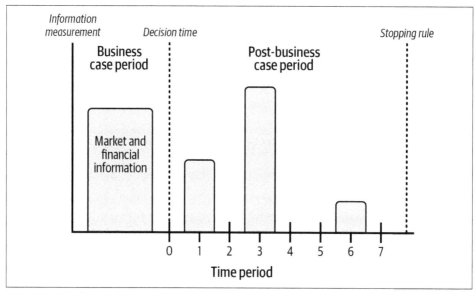

Figure 11-4. The random arrival of information.

In the first two-tuple of Equation 11-1, the information is from the business case as part of the menu properties. The decision in that two-tuple is the menu choice. The succeeding two-tuples are due to the new unexpected information. The project, even though it was selected, is still open for continuous review. This is not without a cost, however.

In Equation 11-2, there is just the one two-tuple. This naive case assumes nothing more will ever happen; all that needs to be known and considered is already in the information component of the business case. There is one associated decision and no others. This is an implicit assumption of the prior chapters.

The mathematics now becomes complicated because of the stochasticity of the new information. Information does not appear on a regularly timed basis. The world does not work that way. In the business case framework, it did because organizations set timelines (i.e., schedules) for internal information hand-offs, and even these may have some random variation resulting in delays. These delays cascade throughout the organization, but they can be planned for and monitored; external information cannot.

The decision component in Equation 11-2 was handled using the, say, mathematical programming framework of Chapter 5. The perspective and the analytical method are relatively simple. Most analysts are trained in them which explains, in part, their popularity. This is why mathematical programming is so dominant in the literature reviewed by Lepeniotia et al. (2020). See Chapter 2 and especially Figure 2-1. The other part of the explanation is the narrow perspective of a decision made just once. The one-time case is easier to conceptualize and handle. However, the information collection and processing costs, plus the organizational structure needed for sequential decisions, are much higher and onerous, especially if you factor in the length of time this information must be collected. So it is not surprising that Lepeniotia et al. (2020) found the mathematical programming methods to be so widely used for Prescriptive Analytics.

Closely examine Equation 11-1. Notice it has a major problem: the number of two-tuples continues *ad infinitum*. You cannot say what the decision-maker should do about a process that does not converge, that continues to infinity. It is not practical, especially for a pragmatic and normative topic (i.e., Prescriptive Analytics). This infinity problem is handled by specifying a *stopping rule* for when to stop collecting new information. As noted by Diederich (2001, p. 13918), this is also called an *optimal strategy* or *optimal policy*. I indicated a stopping rule point in Figure 11-4.

Information collection is costly. Resources must be expended for not only collecting information but also processing it, which means storing it in an electronic form (e.g., a database), interpreting it for its meaning and significance/importance, and transmitting it to the decision-maker. Overall costs will increase the further out in time information is collected and the two-tuples are increased. At some point, the costs will outweigh the returns on the project which makes the project non-viable.

A stopping rule determines when information collection ceases and a final decision is made. That decision could be to continue the project, but without any more information collection, or terminate it altogether regardless of how far into it you are. And if the newly acquired information is highly negative for the project, a stopping rule could kick in automatically forcing its termination. For instance, for the hotel construction, a highly negative and unexpected economic five-year projection for, say, airport passenger flights would be sufficient to terminate the project.

For Equation 11-2, the stopping rule is to cease data collection and information processing at the end of the BCP. This is a special case of a stopping rule, one automatically built into the process itself. Otherwise, for Equation 11-1, the stopping rule can become very elaborate. This elaborateness depends on several factors, such as:

- Number of decision criteria
- Knowledge of the sampling distribution for the information (i.e., single or multiple distributions; known or unknown)
- Number of information sources
- Number of interrelated decisions

See Diederich (2001) for comments about these. The last two are especially interesting because the prescriptive methods I presented in the previous chapters deal with only one decision that is implicitly independent of any others, and there is only one source of information. This latter factor is not relevant for the BCP because financial and market information (most likely with multiple supporting sources) is the foundation for the business case Stages I and II. Refer to Figure 11-2. However, once the business case is completed and the project is started, but always open for review per Equation 11-1, the number of information sources may become unlimited.

Sequential Analysis: Advanced Framework

This is an advanced view of a modeling framework for sequential decisions based on Equation 11-1, but with a modification: the inclusion of a random variable in the two-tuples to account for uncertainty. When a decision is made at time t, the result will not be known until some future time. This is well established from normal experience, but it is also a main theme of this book. The random variable can reflect any news, information, shock, or just a disturbance at time t that has significance for future decisions. Three-tuples replace the two-tuples to express each decision. The extra element is the random variable. The modified framework is:

$$(information, decision)_0, (information, decision, random)_1,$$
$$(information, decision, random)_2,....$$

There is no random variable in period 0 because this is when the first decision is made.

For notation for a better exposition, let

S_t

State of the world or the system, dependent on the decision-maker's scale-view

---

X_t

Decision variable or action variable

ϵ_t

Random variable for news, information, and so forth

The random variable, ϵ_t, is very important because it is responsible for the main issue with the sequential decisions: unknown variations in the system. It is a draw from a probability distribution:

$$\epsilon_t \sim Pr(\Delta \mid S_t, X_t).$$

where Δ represents the distribution's parameters.

For instance, an inventory management problem at the operational scale-view level of a production manager is a traditional example of sequential decisions. See Hillier and Lieberman (2010, Chapter 18). The current amount of inventory is the current state of the system, S_t. The unknown demand at time t is the random variable, ϵ_t. As a random variable, demand, when it arrives, must be satisfied, which could deplete the inventory. It must be replenished. The restocking amount is the decision variable, X_t. When the inventory is restocked, the state of the system is changed by a transition from a previous state. A *transition function* expresses this move: $S_{t+1} = S_t + X_t - \epsilon_t$. More generally, $S_{t+1} = S(S_t, X_t, \epsilon_t)$.

All actions have a cost. The cost function for these sequential decisions is written as

$$C_T(S_T) + \sum_{t=0}^{T-1} C_t(S_t, X_t, \epsilon_t)$$

where T is the end of a reasonable time into the future for the sequential decisions. This is determined by the stopping rule. Notice the cost in the last period, T. It is just a function of the state in that period because there is no transition to the next period (because there is none!).

There is one final component to consider, one that makes this sequential decision framework more complicated and distinguishes it from the prior methods. In, say, the mathematical programming framework (whether continuous, integer, or mixed), you searched over a set of decision variables that represented projects. The set is the menu. If you let X_t be the set, then $x_t \in X_t$ is the decision variable or project from that set. The goal of the search is the optimal project from the menu, $x_t \in X_t$. Once selected, the enterprise, regardless of the scale-view, would enact or follow that project. You can interpret it as a *policy*, a "course or principle of action"[1] enacted to achieve a goal. The goal, of course, is the maximum KPM (e.g., maximum profit).

In sequential decision making, a policy has a different interpretation because of the different SOWs that can be realized. Before, there was no detailed discussion of states, but now they are explicitly considered because they are the reason for the sequential decisions: different SOWs can be realized either by environmental factors or by a prior decision.

Instead of a single decision variable, x_t, there is a *function* that returns the optimal decision (e.g., a project) given the SOW. This function is dependent on hyperparameters, say θ, as well as the SOW. This *policy function* is $X^{\pi}(S_t \mid \theta)$ using the notation of Powell (2022, p. 5). The superscript π is said to "carry the information" about the function. For example, the function may be a linear model with hyperparameters θ. This policy function is now tied to statistics, econometrics, and machine learning methods.

Since ϵ_t is a random variable, the entire cost function is a random variable. The best way to deal with this is by determining the expected value of the cost function expressed as

Equation 11-3.

$$V(x_0) = E\left[C_T(S_T) + \sum_{t=0}^{T} C_t(S_t, X^{\pi}(S_t \mid \theta), \epsilon_t)\right].$$

This is a *value function*, hence the V notation. The search is over this function for the best policy to optimize the returns.

The question is: *How is this search implemented?* The task is to find a policy that minimizes Equation 11-3. This is stated as:

$$Min_{\pi} E\left[C_T(S_T) + \sum_{t=0}^{T} C_t(S_t, X^{\pi}(S_t \mid \theta), \epsilon_t)\right].$$

If Equation 11-3 is written in terms of profits, then the objective is to find the policy that maximizes the function. If it is in terms of costs, then find the policy that minimizes the function. The procedure is the same for a maximization and minimization problem since $max_x[f(x)] = min_x[-f(x)]$. See Herlau (2024, Chapter 4).

---

1 Source: Oxford Languages Dictionary.

There are many ways to optimize the value function. The most common are a *dynamic programming algorithm* and simulations. The first is based on an *optimality principle* due to Richard Bellman. See Bellman (1957) and Dreyfus (2002). Also see Wikipedia (2024c). This is a complicated algorithm that is well beyond the scope of this book. See Herlau (2024) for some intuitive development along with technicalities. Also see Powell (2022) and Powell (2024) and Wikipedia (2024d) for detailed treatments of the algorithm.

Markov Decision Problem

The inventory management problem at the operational scale-view level is an example of a *Markov Decision Problem* (MDP). Inventories are run down or depleted on a random basis during normal operations because of random customer demand. The operational manager must replenish the inventory by placing an order with the supply chain, but this order has a risk. The manager could order too much, which is costly, or too little, which is also costly. The costs reflect the unknown states of the inventory when the materials arrive: they could be too much or too little. If too much, then the surplus must be stored somewhere, perhaps in a temporary facility, or allowed to perish. If it is too little, then a new order must be placed, which reproduces the original inventory problem.

This simple, but enhanced, description of an inventory management problem has several key concepts:

Initial state of a system
    Initial inventory level which is the state

Transition to a future state
    Inventory restocking or further depletion

Probability of transition to a new state
    Unexpected customer demand

Reward (or penalty)
    Cost of too much or too little inventory

The transition from one state to the next is governed by the random event of customer demand. So it is the transition probabilities that matter.

More generally, the collection of all possible states is called the *state space*, the transitions are compiled in a *transition matrix*, and their associated probabilities are in a *transition probability matrix*. The reward or penalty is a *reward function* or *value function*.

These four elements define an MDP, summarized as a four-tuple: $M(S,A,T,R)$ with:

- S: Set of all possible states, including the initial one
- A: Set of actions
- T: Matrix of transition probabilities
- R: Reward function

This is based on a *Markov Process*, sometimes referred to as a *memoryless process*. This process develops over time as you move from one state to another, but the movements only depend on the current state, not any states before that one. All earlier states are irrelevant, hence the memoryless designation.

The implication is that a prediction of the probability of a future event depends only on the current state of the system. Of course, that state changes from period to period, but, nonetheless, earlier ones are irrelevant.

A classic example of a Markov Process is a random walk which is a series of transitions. These are $+1$ and -1 along a number line. The initial state is an arbitrary number on the line and subsequent states are other numbers on the line. The transition probabilities are assumed to be the same for the two states: 0.50. So the transitions from the current state are to the next one $(+1)$ with probability 0.50, or to the previous one (-1) with probability 0.50. Any earlier state is irrelevant for that transition (i.e., the next walk).

More formally, the Markov Process probabilities are defined as

$$Pr(S_{t+1} = s \mid S_0 = s_0, S_1 = s_1,...,S_t = s_t) = Pr(S_{t+1} = s \mid S_t = s_t)$$

where the subscripts designate successive time periods from the initial state, 0, to the current state, t.

For a decision problem, such as the inventory problem, there are not only the transitions and their probabilities but also the rewards for a correct decision and penalties for an incorrect one. For inventories, these are satisfied/dissatisfied customers, profits/losses, excess inventory carrying costs (including insurance and inventory policing or monitoring costs), and so on. To solve this MDP, you must specify all these elements; that is, all the elements in the four-tuple. For large systems, the storage and computational burdens are onerous to say the least, even with modern computer, data management, and software technologies. See, for example, Das et al. (1999) and Zhang et al. (2023).

An efficient way to handle the problem is needed. I touch on this in the next section.

Simulations and Reinforcement Learning

Simulations and *simulation-based reinforcement learning (RL)* have been proposed as alternatives to MPD methods to avoid or overcome their high computational costs. RL, it is argued, avoids the need to calculate probability transition and rewards matrices. In addition, the large state spaces can be more easily handled, further reducing computational expenses. See Das et al. (1999, p. 561).

 As stressed by Kaelbling et al. (1996, p. 238), reinforcement, as used here, resembles the psychology concept but yet is independent of it. It is best to avoid thinking of the phrase "reinforcement learning" in a psychological sense.

In RL, a decision-maker approaches an optimal decision through trial and error. The trials and errors are results of interactions with a random, dynamic environment that constantly presents new situations or new states by sending a signal to the decision-maker. The decision-maker must make an action choice for each new state, but the action changes the state and the change is sent back to the decision-maker via a *reinforcement signal*. There is a reward or penalty for the action which the system sends back to the decision-maker. I illustrate this process in Figure 11-5.[2] For more discussion about reinforcement learning, see Sutton and Barto (2018), Li (2023), Vamvoudakis et al. (2021) and Wikipedia (2024h).

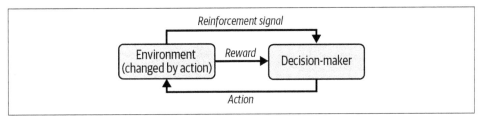

Figure 11-5. The general reinforcement learning process.

---

2 Based on a diagram at AWS Amazon (2024).

The AWS website describes it as

> a machine learning (ML) technique that trains software to make decisions to achieve the most optimal results. It mimics the trial-and-error learning process that humans use to achieve their goals. Software actions that work towards your goal are reinforced, while actions that detract from the goal are ignored.

This makes a computer the decision-maker. See AWS Amazon (2024).

The aim is to find the actions, called *behaviors*, that perform well (i.e., give the optimal reward) in response to the random states. Kaelbling et al. (1996) summarize two methods for doing this:

- Search the entire space of all possible actions (i.e., behaviors); and
- Use statistical methods to estimate a utility function based on the actions.

Searching the entire space of all possible behaviors is just as onerous as the method I outlined in the previous section. Simulation per se, or in conjunction with the RL framework, has been proposed, but this is also complicated and costly to run. Simulations are not cheap. They require computational resources and expertise to design them and analyze results. But, nonetheless, there is a growing interest in their applications to handle sequential decision-making problems. See Zhang et al. (2023).

Automating Sequential Decision Making

Data, and the information hidden inside that data, are more voluminous in our modern, technology-driven and dependent world than, say, 50 years ago. Managing and controlling that *volume* is a huge issue for all major enterprises. More importantly, regarding this volume, is how to extract rich information from it to describe the current business environment, make predictions about likely outcomes from decisions made now and sequentially through time, and design recommendation systems to guide decision-makers at all scale-view levels. There is extensive literature on data analytic methods for extracting rich information. See, for example, Paczkowski (2022a) and Paczkowski (2023) for discussions of these methods.

The volume of data is one issue. Another is just as important and cannot be overlooked: the speed or *velocity* of the acquisition of data. A third characteristic is the *variety* of data that are now routinely collected: numeric, text, scanner, audio, and video data. All three—volume, velocity, and variety—directly impact decision making, especially the velocity. In fact, they are used to define *Big Data*. There is a big literature on Big Data just as there is one on methods for dealing with it. See Paczkowski (2022a) for comments on Big Data.

Decision-makers at all scale-view levels must keep up with the information extracted from this data, and to an extent they must do it in, or almost in, real time. They need assistance that takes them beyond the methods I described in this book.

The assistance is in the form of an automated set of tools that can process the huge amount of rapidly arriving data to distill trends, patterns, problems, and opportunities in the enterprise and its markets and then make recommendations for decisions. There has been interest in developing and implementing systems to do just this for a very long time, but with varying success. The more recent focus on *Artificial Intelligence* (AI) systems may change this, especially for sequential decision analytics.

The future development and application of AI, however, may result in systems that go beyond assisting decision-makers to becoming the decision-makers. In other words, AI could replace human decision-makers. But this is another story.

Summary

In this chapter, I focused on time for decision making and its importance for Prescriptive Analytics. Time was not explicitly considered in the previous chapters, but this cannot be ignored because time is a critical component of all three parts of the *Tripartite Analytics Paradigm*.

The main concepts from this chapter are:

- The sequential nature of decisions
- The business case process (BCP)
- A framework for analyzing sequential decisions

Glossary

These are abbreviations I used in this book:

aka
Also known as

ARIMA
Autoregressive integrated moving average

BCP
Business Case Process

BOD
Board of Directors

CAGR
Compound annual growth rate

CEO
Chief Executive Officer

CF
Cash flow

CFO
Chief Financial Officer or Chief Financial Organization

CLO
Chief Legal Officer

CMO
Chief Marketing Officer or Chief Marketing Organization

COGS
Cost of goods sold

COO
Chief Operating Officer (President)

CPO
Chief Pricing Officer or Chief Pricing Organization

CRM
Customer Relationship Management

CRO
Chief Research Officer

CSO
Chief Security Officer or Chief Sales Officer

DAC
Decision Advisory Council

DADT
Decision Analysis Decision Tree

DOJ
Department of Justice

DST
Data science team

E(X)
Expected value of X

EDA
Exploratory data analysis

EPS
Earnings per share

GDP
Gross Domestic Product

GRP
Gross rating points

I&R
Implications and ramifications

ICO
Initial cash outlay

IDE
Integrated development environment

KDE
Kernel Density Estimation

KOL
Key opinion leader

KPM
Key performance measure

LCG
Linear congruential generator

MDP
Markov Decision Problem or Markov Decision Process

ML
Machine learning

ML_n
Most Likely View n

MLDT
Machine Learning Decision Tree

NNTW
Not-new-to-the-world

NPV
Net present value

NTW
New-to-the-world

OLS
Ordinary Least Squares

OR
Operations research

POR
Per occupied room

Pr()
Probability

R&D
Research & development

RL
Reinforcement learning

ROA
Return on assets

ROE
Return on equity

ROI
Return on investment

SBU
Strategic business unit

SME
Subject matter expert

SOW
State of the world

V(X)
Variance of X

WOM
Word-of-mouth

Bibliography

Aitchison, J. (2005). "A Concise Guide to Compositional Data Analysis." In Proceedings of CoDaWork05. Available at *https://imae.udg.edu/Activitats/CoDa Work05/A_concise_guide_to_compositional_data_analysis.pdf*.

Alpaydin, E. (2014). *Introduction to Machine Learning*. 3rd ed. *Adaptive Computation and Machine Learning* series. MIT Press.

Anaconda (2023). "Ortools-Python." Available at: *https://anaconda.org/conda-forge/ortools-python*. Last accessed: July 24, 2023.

Anaconda (2024). "Understanding conda and pip." Available at: *https://www.ana conda.com/blog/understanding-conda-and-pip*. Last accessed: May 3, 2024.

Avriel, M. (2003). *Nonlinear Programming: Analysis and Methods*. Dover.

AWS Amazon (2024). "Tuple." Available at: *https://aws.amazon.com/what-is/reinforcement-learning/*. Last accessed: March 22, 2024.

Balakrishnan, P. S. (2023). "The Bass Model: Marketing Engineering Technical Note." Available at: *http://faculty.washington.edu/sundar/NPM/BASS-Forecasting%20Model/Bass%20Model%20Technical%20Note.pdf*. Last accessed: December 21, 2023.

Baltagi, B. H. (1995). *Econometric Analysis of Panel Data*. John Wiley & Sons.

Bass, F. (1969). "A New Product Growth for Model Consumer Durables." *Management Science* 15 (5), 215–227.

Baumol, W. J. (1965). *Economic Theory and Operations Analysis*. 2nd ed. *Prentice-Hall Behavioral Sciences in Business*. Prentice-Hall.

Bazaraa, M. S. and C. Shetty (1979). *Nonlinear Programming: Theory and Algorithms*. John Wiley & Sons.

Beck, R. A. (2008). *Statistical Learning from a Regression Perspective*. Springer Series in Statistics. Springer.

Bellman, R. E. (1957). *Dynamic Programming*. 6th printing, 1972 ed. Princeton University Press.

Biller, B. (2022, December). "Accelerating What-If Analysis with Machine Learning." *https://blogs.sas.com/content/subconsciousmus ings/2022/12/14/accelerating-what-if-analysis-with-machine-learning/.*

Bodie, Z., A. Kane, and A. J. Marcus (2022). *Essentials of Investments.* 12th ed. Finance, Insurance, and Real Estate. McGraw Hill.

Boehner, R. and S. Gold (2012). "Modeling the Impact of Marketing Mix on the Diffusion of Innovation in the Generalized Bass Model of Firm Demand." *Developments in Business Simulation and Experiential Learning* 39, 75–91.

Bolusani, S., M. Besancon, K. Bestuzheva, A. Chmiela, J. Dionsio, T. Donkiewicz, J. van Doornmalen, L. Eifler, M. Ghannam, A. Gleixner, C. Graczyk, K. Halbig, I. Hedtke, A. Hoen, C. Hojny, R. van der Hulst, D. Kamp, T. Koch, K. Kofler, J. Lentz, J. Manns, G. Mexi, E. Muhmer, M. E. Pfetsch, F. Schlosser, F. Serrano, Y. Shinano, M. Turner, S. Vigerske, D. Weninger, and L. Xu (2024, February). "The SCIP Optimization Suite 9.0." ZIB-Report 24-02-29. Zuse Institute Berlin.

Bradley, S. P., A. C. Hax, and T. L. Magnanti (1977). *Applied Mathematical Programming.* Addison-Wesley. See *http://web.mit.edu/15.053/www/AMP.htm.*

Brigham, E. F. and M. C. Ehrhardt (2002). *Financial Management: Theory and Practice.* Thomson Learning.

Cheng, E. (2023). *The Joy of Abstraction: An Exploration of Math, Category Theory, and Life.* Cambridge University Press.

Chongchitnan, S. (2023). *Exploring University Mathematics with Python.* Springer.

Clayton, A. (2021). *Bernoulli's Fallacy: Statistical Illogic and the Crisis of Modern Science.* Columbia University Press.

Conway, J. H. and R. K. Guy (1996). *The Book of Numbers.* Springer.

Cote, C. (2021, November). "What Is Descriptive Analytics? 5 Examples." Available at: *https://online.hbs.edu/blog/post/descriptive-analytics.* Last accessed: April 11, 2023.

Dantzig, G. B. (1951). "Maximization of a Linear Function of Variables Subject to Linear Inequalities." In *Activity Analysis of Production and Allocation*, edited by T. C. Koopmans. Wiley & Chapman-Hall.

Das, T. K., A. Gosavi, S. Mahadevan, and N. Marchalleck (1999). "Solving Semi-Markov Decision Problems Using Average Reward Reinforcement Learning." *Management Science* 45 (4), 560–74.

Data Camp (2023). "Association Rule Mining in Python: Tutorial." Available at: *https://www.datacamp.com/tutorial/association-rule-mining-python.* Last accessed: May 21, 2023.

de Bruin, W. B., P. S. Fischbeck, N. A. Stiber, and B. Fischhoff (2002). "What Number Is 'Fifty Fifty'?: Redistributing Excessive 50% Responses in Elicited Probabilities." *Risk Analysis* 22 (4): 713–23.

de Bruin, W. B. and B. Fischhoff (2017, March). "Eliciting Probabilistic Expectations: Collaborations Between Psychologists and Economists." Proceedings of the National Academy of Sciences 114 (13): 3297–304.

Deisenroth, M. P., A. A. Faisl, and C. S. Ong (2020). *Mathematics for Machine Learning*. Cambridge University Press.

Delavande, A., X. Gine, and D. McKenzie (2011). "Measuring Subjective Expectations in Developing Countries: A Critical Review and New Evidence." *Journal of Development Economics* 94, 151–63.

Diederich, A. (2001). "Sequential Decision Making." In *International Encyclopedia of the Social & Behavioral Sciences*, edited by N. J. Smelser and P. B. Baltes. Elsevier.

Dominitz, J. and C. Manski (1997). "Using Expectations Data to Study Subjective Income Expectations." *Journal of the American Statistical Association* 92 (439), 855–67.

Dreyfus, S. (2002, January). "Richard Bellman on the Birth of Dynamic Programming." *Operations Research* 50 (1), 48–51.

Eagle, A. (2021). "Chance Versus Randomness." In *The Stanford Encyclopedia of Philosophy*. Spring 2021 ed. Edited by E. N. Zalta. *https://plato.stanford.edu/entries/chance-randomness/*.

Earman, J. (2018, 06). "The Relation Between Credence and Chance: Lewis' 'Principal Principle' Is a Theorem of Quantum Probability Theory." Unpublished. Available at *http://philsci-archive.pitt.edu/14822/1/Credence%20and%20Chance%206.26.18.pdf*.

Egan, A. and M. G. Titelbaum (2022). "Self-Locating Beliefs." In *The Stanford Encyclopedia of Philosophy*. Winter 2022 ed. Edited by E. N. Zalta and U. Nodelman. *https://plato.stanford.edu/entries/self-locating-beliefs*.

Ehrenstein, M., C.-H. Wang, and G. Guillen-Gosalbez (2019, June). "Planning of Supply Chains Threatened by Extreme Events: Novel Heuristic and Application to Industry Case Studies." In *Proceedings of the 29th European Symposium on Computer Aided Process Engineering*, edited by A. A. Kiss, E. Zondervan, R. Lakerveld, and L. Ozkan. Elsevier.

Feller, W. (1950). *An Introduction to Probability Theory and Its Applications*. Vol. 1. John Wiley & Sons.

Feller, W. (1971). *An Introduction to Probability Theory and Its Applications*. Vol. 2. John Wiley & Sons.

Ferguson, C. (1972). *Microeconomic Theory*. 3rd ed. Richard D. Irwin.

Fischhoff, B. and W. B. de Bruin (1999, May). "Fifty-Fifty = 50%?" *Journal of Behavioral Decision Making* 12 (2), 149–163.

Floridi, L. (2008). "Trends in the Philosophy of Information." In *Philosophy of Information*. Vol. 8 of *Handbook of the Philosophy of Science*, edited by Pieter Adriaans and Johan Van Benthem. Elsevier.

Floridi, L. (2010). *Information: A Very Short Introduction*. Oxford University Press.

Floridi, L. (2019). "Semantic Conceptions of Information." In *The Stanford Encyclopedia of Philosophy*. Spring 2022 ed. Edited by E. N. Zalta. *https://plato.stanford.edu/entries/information-semantic/*.

Forrester, J. W. (1968). *Principles of Systems*. Wright-Allen Press.

Gelman, A. (2006). "Prior Distributions for Variance Parameters in Hierarchical Models." *Bayesian Analysis* 1 (3), 515–33.

Gelman, A., J. Carlin, H. Stern, D. Dunson, A. Vehtari, and D. Rubin (2013). *Bayesian Data Analysis*. 3rd ed. Chapman and Hall/CRC.

Google Books (2023). Google Books Ngram Viewer. Available at: *https://books.google.com/ngrams/graph?content=simulation&year_start=1900&year_end=2019&corpus=en-2019&smoothing=4*. Last accessed: September 4, 2023. See the Viewer documentation at https://books.google.com/ngrams/info.

Gould, J. P. and E. P. Lazear (1989). *Microeconomic Theory*. 6th ed. Irwin.

Greenacre, M. (2018). *Compositional Data Analysis in Practice*. Chapman and Hall/CRC.

Greenacre, M. (2021). "Compositional Data Analysis." *Annual Review of Statistics and Its Application* 8 (1), 271–99.

Hadley, G. (1970). *Nonlinear and Dynamic Programming*. Addison-Wesley.

Hadley, G. F. (1962). *Linear Programming*. Addison-Wesley.

Hajek, A. (2019). "Interpretations of Probability." In *The vpedia of Philosophy*. Fall 2019 ed. Edited by E. N. Zalta. *https://plato.stanford.edu/entries/probability-interpret/*.

Hall, J. (2023). "Highs: High-Performance Open-Source Software For Linear Optimization." Available at: *https://co-at-work.zib.de/slides/Montag_21.9/HiGHS%20slides%20%281%29.pdf*. Last accessed: June 30, 2023.

Hand, D., H. Mannila, and P. Smyth (2001). *Principles of Data Mining*. MIT Press.

Hartley, H. O. (1977). "Solution of Statistical Distribution Problems by Monte Carlo Methods." In *Statistical Methods for Digital Computers*. Vol. 3 of *Mathematical Methods for Digital Computers*. John Wiley & Sons.

Hastie, T., R. Tibshirani, and J. Friedman (2008). *The Elements of Statistical Learning: Data Mining, Inference, and Prediction*. 2nd ed. Springer.

Henderson, J. M. and R. E. Quandt (1971). *Microeconomic Theory: A Mathematical Approach*. 2nd ed. McGraw-Hill.

Herlau, T. (2024, March). "Sequential Decision-Making: Lecture Notes 02465." Technical University of Denmark. Version 1.3.1. Lecture notes available at *https://02465material.pages.compute.dtu.dk/02465public/index.html*.

Hillier, F. S. and G. J. Lieberman (2010). *Introduction to Operations Research*. 9th ed. McGraw-Hill.

Hsiao, C. (1986). *Analysis of Panel Data*. Cambridge University Press.

Hunt, J. (2019). *Advanced Guide to Python 3 Programming*. Springer.

Hunt, J. (2020). *A Beginners Guide to Python3 Programming*. Springer. Corrected publication.

Iacovone, L., D. McKenzie, and R. Meager (2023, January). "Bayesian Impact Evaluation with Informative Priors: An Application to a Colombian Management and Export Improvement Program." World Bank. Development Economics Development Research Group.

Jurado, K., S. C. Ludvigson, and S. Ng (2015, March). "Measuring Uncertainty." *The American Economic Review* 105 (3), 1177–216.

Kaelbling, L. P., M. L. Littman, and A. W. Moore (1996). "Reinforcement Learning: A Survey." *Journal of Artificial Intelligence Research* 4, 237–85.

Kenett, R. S., G. Perruca, and S. Salini (2012). "Modern Analysis of Customer Surveys: With Applications Using R." In *Bayesian Networks Applied to Customer Surveys*. John Wiley & Sons.

Keynes, J. M. (1921). *A Treatise on Probability*. Macmillan.

Knight, F. H. (1921). *Risk, Uncertainty, and Profit*. Houghton Mifflin.

Lennox, J. (2019). "Darwinism." In *The Stanford Encyclopedia of Philosophy*. Fall 2019 ed. Edited by E. N. Zalta. *https://plato.stanford.edu/entries/darwinism/*.

Lepeniotia, K., A. Bousdekisa, D. Apostoloua, and G. Mentzasa (2020). "Prescriptive Analytics: Literature Review and Research Challenges." *International Journal of Information Management* 50, 57–70.

Li, S. E. (2023). *Reinforcement Learning for Sequential Decision and Optimal Control*. Springer.

Liebhafsky, H. (1968). *The Nature of Price Theory*. Rev. ed. *The Dorsey Series in Economics*. Dorsey Press.

Lin, H. (2023). "Bayesian Epistemology." In *The Stanford Encyclopedia of Philosophy*. Winter 2023 ed. Edited by E. N. Zalta and U. Nodelman. *https://plato.stanford.edu/entries/epistemology-bayesian/*.

Louviere, J. J., D. A. Hensher, and J. D. Swait (2000). *Stated Choice Methods: Analysis and Applications*. Cambridge University Press.

McCarthy, E. J. and W. D. Perreault (1987). *Basic Marketing: A Managerial Approach*. 9th ed. Irwin.

McFarland, A. (2024). "9 Best AI Translation Software & Tools." Available at: *https://www.unite.ai/best-ai-translation-software-tools/*. Last accessed: May 2, 2024.

McGrayne, S. B. (2012). *The Theory That Would Not Die: How Bayes' Rule Cracked the Enigma Code, Hunted Down Russian Submarines, and Emerged Triumphant from Two Centuries of Controversy*. Yale University Press.

McKinney, W. (2018). *Python for Data Analysis: Data Wrangling with Pandas, Numpy, and ipython*. 2nd ed. O'Reilly.

Mosteller, F. and J. W. Tukey (1977). *Data Analysis and Regression: A Second Course in Statistics*. Addison-Wesley.

Muller, A. C. and S. Guido (2017). *Introduction to Machine Learning*. O'Reilly.

Paczkowski, W. R. (2016). *Market Data Analysis Using JMP*. SAS Press.

Paczkowski, W. R. (2018). *Pricing Analytics: Models and Advanced Quantitative Techniques for Product Pricing*. Routledge.

Paczkowski, W. R. (2020). *Deep Data Analytics for New Product Development*. Routledge.

Paczkowski, W. R. (2022a). *Business Analytics: Data Science for Business Problems*. Springer.

Paczkowski, W. R. (2022b). *Modern Survey Analysis: Using Python for Deeper Insights*. Springer.

Paczkowski, W. R. (2023). *Predictive and Simulation Analytics: Deeper Insights for Better Business Decisions*. Springer.

Pawlowsky-Glahn, V. and A. Buccianti (2011). *Compositional Data Analysis: Theory and Applications*. John Wiley & Sons.

Peters, T. (2023). "The Zen of Python." Available at: *https://peps.python.org/ pep-0020/ #the-zen-of-python*. Last accessed: April 17, 2023.

Pink, T. (2004). *Free Will: A Very Short Introduction*. Oxford University Press.

Pinker, S. (2021). *Rationality: What It Is, Why It Seems Scarce, Why It Matters*. Viking Press.

Powell, W. B. (2022). *Reinforcement Learning and Stochastic Optimization: A Unified Framework for Sequential Decisions*. John Wiley & Sons.

Powell, W. B. (2024). *Sequential Decision Analytics and Modeling: Modeling Exercises with Python*. Available at *https://tinyurl.com/sequentialdecisionanalytics*.

pypi (2023). "Ortools." Available at: *https://pypi.org/project/ortools/*. Last accessed: July 24, 2023.

Python Enhancement Proposals (2023). "PEP 572—Assignment Expressions." Available at: *https://peps.python.org/pep-0572/*. Last accessed: September 11, 2023.

Raschka, S. and V. Mirjalili (2017). *Python Machine Learning: Machine Learning and Deep Learning with Python, scikit-learn, and TensorFlow*. 2nd ed. Packt Publishing.

Reed, B. (2022). "Certainty." *The Stanford Encyclopedia of Philosophy*. Spring 2022 ed. Edited by E. N. Zalta. *https://plato.stanford.edu/entries/certainty/*.

Ross, S. A., R. W. Westerfield, and B. D. Jordan (2006). *Fundamentals of Corporate Finance*. 7th ed. Finance, Insurance and Real Estate. McGraw-Hill/Irwin.

Ross, S. M. (2014). *Introduction to Probability Models*. 11th ed. Academic Press.

Rossi, P. E., G. M. Allenby, and R. McCulloch (2005). *Bayesian Statistics and Marketing*. John Wiley & Sons.

Schweber, S. and M. Wachters (2000). "Complex Systems, Modelling and Simulation. "*Studies in History and Philosophy of Science Part B: Studies in History and Philosophy of Modern Physics* 31 (4), 583–609.

Sedgewick, R., K. Wayne, and R. Dondero (2016). *Introduction to Python Programming: An Interdisciplinary Approach*. Pearson.

Sloan, P. (2019). "Evolutionary Thought Before Darwin." In *The Stanford Encyclopedia of Philosophy*. Winter 2019 ed. Edited by E. N. Zalta. *https://plato.stanford.edu/entries/evolution-before-darwin/*.

Sommaruga, G. (2009). *Formal Theories of Information: From Shannon to Semantic Information Theory and General Concepts of Information*. Springer.

Stackoverflow (2024). "What's the Difference Between PyPy and PyPI." Available at: *https://stackoverflow.com/questions/47117884/whats-the-difference-between-pypy-and-pypi*. Last accessed: May 3, 2024.

Sun, H., Y. Yang, J. Yu, Z. Zhang, Z. Xia, J. Zhu, and H. Zhang (2022). "Artificial Intelligence of Manufacturing Robotics Health Monitoring System by Semantic Modeling." *Micromachines* 13 (300), 1–12.

Sutton, R. S. and A. G. Barto (2018). *Reinforcement Learning: An Introduction*. MIT Press.

Train, K. (2009). *Discrete Choice Methods with Simulation*. 2nd ed. Cambridge University Press.

Triola, M. F. (2022). *Elementary Statistics*. 14th ed. Pearson Education.

Tu, S.-J. and E. Fischbach (2005). "A Study on the Randomness of the Digits of Pi." *International Journal of Modern Physics C* 16 (02), 281–94.

Tukey, J. W. (1977). *Exploratory Data Analysis*. Pearson.

United States Department of Justice (2023). Freedom of Information Act statute. Available at: *https://www.foia.gov/foia-statute.html*. Last accessed: May 23, 2023.

Vamvoudakis, K. G., Y. Wan, F. L. Lewis, and D. Cansever (2021). *Handbook of Reinforcement Learning and Control*. Springer.

van den Boogaart, K. and R. Tolosana-Delgado (2013). *Analyzing Compositional Data with R*. Springer.

VanderPlas, J. (2017). *Python Data Science Handbook: Essential Tools for Working with Data*. O'Reilly Media.

Wei, W. W. (2006). *Time Series Analysis: Univariate and Multivariate Methods*. 2nd ed. Pearson.

Weiss, N. A. (2005). *Introductory Statistics*. 7th ed. Pearson Education.

Wikipedia (2023a). "Bayesian Statistics." Available at: *https://en.wikipedia.org/wiki/Bayesian_statistics#cite_note-4*. Last accessed: April 10, 2023.

Wikipedia (2023b). "Camel Case." Available at: *https://en.wikipedia.org/wiki/Camel_case*. Last accessed: April 18, 2023.

Wikipedia (2023c). "Dashboards (Business)." Available at: *https://en.wikipedia.org/wiki/Dashboard_(business)*. Last accessed: April 10, 2023.

Wikipedia (2023d). "Evolutionary Computation." Available at: *https://en.wikipedia.org/wiki/Evolutionary_computation*. Last accessed: May 21, 2023.

Wikipedia (2023e). "Exploratory Data Analysis." Available at: *https://en.wikipe dia.org/wiki/Exploratory_data_analysis*. Last accessed: April 10, 2023.

Wikipedia (2023f). "HiGHS Optimization Solver." Available at: *https://en.wikipe dia.org/wiki/HiGHS_optimization_solver*. Last accessed: June 30, 2023.

Wikipedia (2023g). "Interior Point/Method." Available at: *https://en.wikipe dia.org/wiki/Interior-point_method*. Last accessed: June 30, 2023.

Wikipedia (2023h). "Linear Programming." Available at: *https://en.wikipe dia.org/wiki/Linear_programming*. Last accessed: May 15, 2023.

Wikipedia (2023i). "Mersenne Primes." Available at: *https://en.wikipedia.org/wiki/ Mersenne_prime*. Last accessed: October 23, 2023.

Wikipedia (2023j). "Reach (Advertising)." Available at: *https://en.wikipe dia.org/wiki/Reach_(advertising)*. Last accessed: June 23, 2023.

Wikipedia (2023k). "Revised Simplex." Available at: *https://en.wikipedia.org/wiki/ Revised_simplex_method*. Last accessed: June 29, 2023.

Wikipedia (2023l). "SAS." Available at: *https://en.wikipedia.org/wiki/SAS_(soft ware)*. Last accessed: April 10, 2023.

Wikipedia (2023m). "Stochastic." Available at: *https://en.wikipedia.org/wiki/Sto chastic*. Last accessed: April 25, 2023.

Wikipedia (2024a). "5-Cell." Available at: *https://en.wikipedia.org/wiki/5-cell*. Last accessed: January 12, 2024.

Wikipedia (2024b). "Bass Diffusion Model." Available at: *https://en.wikipe dia.org/wiki/Bass_diffusion_model#cite_note-Bass1969-2*. Last accessed: May 14, 2024.

Wikipedia (2024c). "Bellman Equation." Available at: *https://en.wikipe dia.org/wiki/Bellman_equation*. Last accessed: March 14, 2024.

Wikipedia (2024d). "Dynamic Programming." Available at: *https://en.wikipe dia.org/wiki/Dynamic_programming*. Last accessed: March 14, 2024.

Wikipedia (2024e). "Efficient Markets Hypothesis." Available at: *https://en.wikipe dia.org/wiki/Efficient-market_hypothesis*. Last accessed: March 7, 2024.

Wikipedia (2024f). "Mersenne Twister." Available at: *https://en.wikipe dia.org/wiki/Mersenne_Twister*. Last accessed: May 30, 2024.

Wikipedia (2024g). "Number." Available at: *https://en.wikipedia.org/wiki/Num ber#Classification*. Last accessed: May 28, 2024.

Wikipedia (2024h). "Reinforecement Learning." Available at: *https://en.wikipe dia.org/wiki/Reinforcement_learning/*. Last accessed: March 22, 2024.

Wikipedia (2024i). "Simplex." Available at: *https://en.wikipedia.org/wiki/Simplex*. Last accessed: January 12, 2024.

Wikipedia (2024j). "Ternary Plot." Available at: *https://en.wikipedia.org/wiki/Ter nary_plot*. Last accessed: May 14, 2024.

Wikipedia (2024k). "Tuple." Available at: *https://en.wikipedia.org/wiki/Tuple*. Last accessed: March 7, 2024.

Winston, W. L. (2004). *Operations Research: Applications and Algorithms*. 4th ed. Brooks/Cole.

Witten, I. H., E. Frank, and M. A. Hall (2011). *Data Mining: Practical Machine Learning Tools and Techniques*. 3rd ed. Elsevier.

Wolfram Mathworld (2024). "Proper Subset." Available at: *https://mathworld.wolfram.com/ProperSubset.html*. Last accessed: June 11, 2024.

Wooldridge, J. M. (2002). *Econometric Analysis of Cross Section and Panel Data*. MIT Press.

Yeh, I.-C. (2016). Default of Credit Card Clients. UCI Machine Learning Repository. *https://doi.org/10.24432/C55S3H*.

Zdanowicz, C. (2015, June). "Designing Choice: Hick's Law." Available at: *https://medium.com/@craigzdanowicz/designing-choice-hick-s-law-138e581f2120*. Last accessed: June 13, 2023.

Zellner, A. (1971). *An Introduction to Bayesian Inference in Econometrics*. John Wiley & Sons.

Zhang, Z., D. Wang, H. Yang, and S. Si (2023). "A Review of Sequential Decision Making via Simulation." Preprint, arXiv, December 7, 2023. *https://doi.org/10.48550/arXiv.2312.04090*.

Index

A

abbreviations in this book, 365
abs operator, 70
academics, methods developed by, 42
Action Directives, 19
Action Processors, 19
actions (behaviors), 362
activities (elicitation method), 321
addition operator (+), 69
addressable market, 276, 295
  cumulative proportion of, 296
addressable market potential parameter, 300
addressable potential market curve, 301
Age of Simulation Analytics, 214
Age of Simulations, 51
aggregation methods in simulations, 225
AI (artificial intelligence)
  aiding in decision making, 38
  evolutionary computation, 50
  machine learning and data mining methods, 47
  sequential decision analytics and, 363
  translators, 67
aleatoric uncertainty, 29
aliases for package names, 102
  np for NumPy, 91
Anaconda
  updating Python packages with Anaconda Navigator, 101
  using to manage Python package installation, 100
analytics
  evolution of, 7
  flow of, 37

how Descriptive and Predictive Analytics fit together, 13
  workflow for Descriptive, Predictive, and Prescriptive Analytics, 14
and (logical), 118
annuities, 195
  discounting of annuity streams, 195
  formula for annuity due, 195
  formula to calculate present value of ordinary annuity, 195
  present value for earning stream for hotel development scenarios, 198
  present value of revenue stream under different scenarios, 238
annuity due, 195
append method, 76
arguments, 70
  named, in Python user-defined functions, 84
  parameters versus, 85
  positional, in Python user-defined functions, 83
ARIMA times series models, 152, 215
arithmetic operators (Python), 69, 78
arrangements, unique, number of, 117
array function, 91
arrays, 91
  operations on, 92
  returned by NumPy, converting to lists, 222
artificial intelligence (see AI)
as keyword (Python), 102
assignment problems, 51, 158
  balanced, 158
  unbalanced, 160

Association Rules, 51
attributes, 91
  for a concept, 315
  example, for a coffee product, 316
autoregressive integrated moving average (see
  ARIMA time series models)
averaging (elicitation analysis), 322
  about, 322
  Python use-case for, 328-336

B

balanced problems, 158
Bass Model, 295, 305
Bayes' Theorem, 31, 126, 312
  derivation of, 126
  Python implementation of, 127
Bayesian bootstrap, 325
Bayesian probability, 31, 57, 183, 189
  in decision trees for predictive analysis, 188
Bayesian statistics, 10
BCP (Business Case Process), 22, 347
  stopping information collection at end of,
    356
behaviors, 362
beliefs (gut-feel, intuition, suspicion), 31
  eliciting probability distributions of beliefs,
    314-321
  and priors, 312
  subjective probabilities and, 111
bell-shaped distribution, 132
Best Case, 272
  in pricing what-if analysis, basic, 278
Big Data, 11, 362
bin, 316
binary integer programming problems, 164
binomial distribution, 130
binomial probability mass function (pmf), 131
blocks of code (Python), 66
bootstrap function (SciPy stats), 340
bootstrapping a distribution, 321, 322, 324
  Python use-case for, 339-342
box, 316
boxplots, 308
  of bootstrapped probabilities, 341
branches (decision tree), 56, 184
built-in functions, 71
burn-in period, 236
business analytics, 14
business case, 22, 348

defined, 348
  new product, sequential decision-making
    process for, 351
  post-business case sequential decisions, 352
  series of business cases for non-terminate
    concepts, 351
  stages of assessment, 349
Business Case Process (see BCP)
business constraints, 36
business decision makers
  information required from data, 12
business goals, 36
business intelligence, 14
business research, 5

C

C-level team, 5, 314
  data scientist interviewing to find out how
    they use data to make decisions, 117
  information needs of managers, 13
  interest in KPMs and dashboards, 16
  large, 318
  strategic scale-view, 58
camel case names, 72
capital budgeting, 172
  process combining predictive and Prescrip-
    tive Analytics, 173
capital budgeting decision
  case, select a specific number, 175
  case, select as many as needed, 174
  case, select based on logical conditions, 177
  case, select only one, 176
  mixed integer programming for selecting
    based on logical conditions, 178
capital investments, 268
capital markets, 173
case-sensitivity in Python, 72
cash flow (CF), 173
casting, 70
categorical variables, 244
Central Limit Theorem, 234
CEO (Chief Executive Officer), 5
  approval of capital investments, 268
  decision on which capital project to choose,
    27
  interest in KPMs and dashboards, 16
  Most Likely predictions, 35
  strategic scale-view, 58
  wide-scale view, 33

comparison of MLDT and DADT, 191
introduction to, 183
probabilities assigned to each branch, 313
simulation of hotel problem for one location, 256-265
  enhanced flow chart looping through each node, 264
  KDE plot of simulated NPV values, 259
  main functions for the simulation, 256
  main script defining parameters and passing them to run function, 261
  run function for simulation, 261
  sample of DataFrame returned by df_func, 259
decision types, 59
decision variables, 49
  specifying in linear programming bakery problem, 156
decision-makers
  analysis of decision menu by, 24
  menu-generating questions from, 269
  source for menu options, 269
decision-making framework, 4
  enhanced recommendations with Prescriptive Analytics as focal point, 34
decisions
  predicting outcome of, 18
  sequential decisions with changing conditions, 182
  single decision with one condition, 182
  use of trees in, 188
def command, 83, 259
default values for named arguments in Python user-defined functions, 84
dependent variables, 184
describe function (pandas), 307
Descriptive Analytics, 9, 14, 15
  in analytics flow, 37
  and decision making, 38
  providing business decision makers with rich information, 12, 12
descriptive statistics, 8, 307
deterministic events, 108
df_func, 256, 259
  sample of DataFrame returned by, 259
dict, 77
  (see also dictionaries)
dictionaries (Python), 77

collections interpreted as, enclosing in curly brackets ({}), 77
creating, accessing, and slicing elements of, 77
in die toss simulation, 234
settings for what-if analysis, 287
using to create DataFrames, 94
die toss simulation example, 231-238
difference equations, 216
differential equations, 216
diffusion model, 295
direct questioning elicitation method, 319 ·
discount factor (annuities), 195
discounting, uses of, 347
discrete choice analysis, 315
  example of, 317
division operator (/), 69
division quotient operator (//), 69
divmod operator, 70
  two-tuple returned by, 73
dot notation (.), 102
dot product, 128
drill-down interactivity (dashboards), 16
DST (data science team), 3, 8
  analysis of decision menu by, 24
  predictions for revenue and costs generated by, 173
dual-simplex method, 148
dummy assignees or tasks, 158
  dummy task, 160
dummy variables, 215, 244
DuPont Analysis, 6
dynamic programming algorithm, 359

E

early adopters, 294
earnings per share (EPS), 225
econometrics, 7, 19
  mapping of Python packages to, 96
economics
  Cobb-Douglas function, 301
  production function, 145
effects coding, 244
Efficient Markets Hypothesis, 347
elasticities
  defined, 281
  marketing mix, 301
  own-price and revenue elasticity, 282
elif (else if) statements (Python), 86

mode, 183
modules (Python), 65
modulo (remainder) operator (%), 69, 217
Monte Carlo simulation, 51, 58, 274
Most Likely Case, 272
    in pricing what-if analysis, basic, 278
Most Likely Views, 20, 27, 34
    Best Case, Most Likely Case and Worst Case
        as subset of, 272
    scenarios for hotel development in DADT
        use-case, 195
    for tactical and strategic scale-views, 162
multidimensional decisions, 59
multinomial distribution, 325
multinomial logit model, 317
mutually exclusive or disjointed events, 118

N

n-factorial or n-bang, 115
named arguments
    in Python user-defined functions, 84
naming conventions (Python), 72
NaN (not a number), 84
natural numbers, 163
natural projects, 22
negative of natural numbers (integers), 163
net earnings, 276
net present value (see NPV)
new product adoption curves, 296
new product development pipeline, 348
new-to-the-world (NTW) products, 294
    constructing synthetic data for forecasting
        model, 295
    introductory price, 304
ngrams, 212
nlargest method (pandas), 292
nodes (decision tree), 56, 184
Noise, 57
non-stochastic events, 108
non-stochastic methods
    defined, 57
    examples based on scale-views, 58
non-stochastic operational scale-view prob-
    lems, 141
non-stochastic simulations, 215
    process of, 216
None data type, 84, 218
normal distribution, 132, 221
    in die toss simulation, 234

normal function (NumPy), 223
normalized crosstab, 121
not-new-to-the-world (NNTW) products, 294
NPV (net present value), 6, 172, 173
    decision rule for capital investment projects,
        173
    plotting in decision tree simulation exam-
        ple, 259
    potential projects selected by, 21
    predicted NPV and investment costs for
        strategic projects (example), 27
    simulated values, function plotting trace of,
        260
NTW (see new-to-the-world products)
Null Hypothesis, 234
    F-Test Null Hypothesis, 242
numbers specifying restrictions in integer pro-
    gramming, 163
NumPy package, 91
    choice function, 305
    np alias for, 103
    random number functions in, 222
    triangular random number generator, 238
    zeros function, 259
NumVar method, 156

O

objective functions, 49
    decision variables that optimize, 139
    KPM as in mathematical programming, 140
    linear and non-linear, 140
    in linear programming, 144
    randomizing coefficients of, 247
    specifying for linear programming bakery
        problem, 157
offsets, 73
OLS (ordinary least squares), 8, 58, 242
    price elasticity estimates, 274
one-time decisions, 345-363
    evidence of a problem, 345-347
only one problems, 164
operating systems, Python on, 65
operational managers
    information needs, 13
    inventory management problem, 45
operational scale-views, 6, 58, 141
    Descriptive Analytics at, 16
    example decision menu for, 26
    KPMs to measure in simulations, 225

nature of, 268
structure of, 271
for synthetic data, 295
what-if tests on models, 215
while loops, 66
word size of a computer (32 or 64 bits), 218
word-of-mouth (WOM) recommendations, 294
Worst Case, 272
in pricing what-if analysis, basic, 278

Y

Yes/No pairs, 277

Z

Zen of Python, 65
zero (0), integer, 163
zero-based indexes in Python, 73
zeros function (NumPy), 259

About the Author

Walter R. Paczkowski earned his PhD in economics at Texas A&M University. He has worked at AT&T's Analytical Support Center, Market Analysis and Forecasting Division, and Business Research Division. He was also a member of the technical staff at AT&T Bell Labs before founding Data Analytics Corp., a statistical consulting and data modeling company, in 2001. Dr. Paczkowski is a part-time lecturer in the Department of Economics and the Department of Statistics at Rutgers University. He has published six books in what he refers to as his Analytics Series. His latest are *Business Analytics: Data Science for Business Problems* (Springer 2021), *Modern Survey Analysis: Using Python for Deeper Insights* (Springer 2022), and *Predictive and Simulation Analytics: Deeper Insights for Better Business Decisions* (Springer 2023).

Colophon

The animal on the cover of *Hands-On Prescriptive Analytics* is a common wall gecko (*Tarentola mauritanica*), also known as a moorish gecko, crocodile gecko, or European common gecko. It is native to the Mediterranean region, with a range stretching from Egypt to Western Sahara in the south and from Spain to Greece in the north. It is light grayish-brown with darker spots or stripes, and its back, legs, and tail are covered with spines called tubercles. Adults can reach up to 8 inches long.

Common wall geckos are so named because they are often found sunning themselves on walls in urban areas. Like many geckos, they have special toe pads that enable them to climb onto smooth vertical surfaces, and they are capable of losing their tails to escape predators and then regrowing them. Common wall geckos are often kept as pets, which has occasionally led to them being introduced in areas outside their normal range.

Due to its wide distribution, it is considered a species of least concern. Many of the animals on O'Reilly covers are endangered; all of them are important to the world.

The cover illustration is by Karen Montgomery, based on an antique line engraving from Lydekker's *Royal Natural History*. The cover fonts are Gilroy Semibold and Guardian Sans. The text font is Adobe Minion Pro; the heading font is Adobe Myriad Condensed; and the code font is Dalton Maag's Ubuntu Mono.

www.ingramcontent.com/pod-product-compliance
Lightning Source LLC
Jackson TN
JSHW052003131224
75386JS00036B/1178